Advances in Information Security

Volume 72

Series editor
Sushil Jajodia, George Mason University, Fairfax, VA, USA

More information about this series at http://www.springer.com/series/5576

Mauro Conti • Gaurav Somani • Radha Poovendran
Editors

Versatile Cybersecurity

 Springer

Editors
Mauro Conti
Department of Mathematics
University of Padua
Padua, Italy

Gaurav Somani
Department of Computer Science
and Engineering
Central University of Rajasthan
Ajmer, India

Radha Poovendran (iD)
Department of Electrical Engineering
University of Washington
Seattle, WA, USA

ISSN 1568-2633
Advances in Information Security
ISBN 978-3-319-97642-6   ISBN 978-3-319-97643-3   (eBook)
https://doi.org/10.1007/978-3-319-97643-3

Library of Congress Control Number: 2018959413

This Springer imprint is published by the registered company Springer Nature Switzerland AG
The registered company address is: Gewerbestrasse 11, 6330 Cham, Switzerland

Preface

Cybersecurity is one of the important areas in the computer science domain which also plays a major role in the life of almost every individual, enterprise, society, and country. After the IT revolution, an unprecedented growth has been seen in the number of cyber-attacks and their impact in terms of financial damages and data losses. A steady growth is also visible in the newer forms of attacks with sophistication, stealth, scale, persistence, and intelligent penetration. Cyber-attacks also necessitate continuous and unified efforts on designing defensive mechanisms to combat the range of evolving attacks and minimizing the damages incurred by various attacks. Cybersecurity as a discipline is also able to attract a good number of young minds opting to study and divulge into this area. There is a range of online and printed resources available to study various research topics, relevant contributions, and open problems related to cybersecurity.

A large number of advanced security books focus on either cryptography or system security which covers both information and network security. However, there is hardly any text available for advanced students and research scholars in security research to systematically study how the major attacks are studied, modeled, planned, launched, and combated by the community. The *Versatile Cybersecurity* book aims to fill this gap by providing focused content related to specific attacks or attack families. These dedicated discussions in the form of individual chapters cover the application or area-specific aspects while discussing about the placement of defense solutions to combat the attacks. This book has eight high-quality chapters from established security research groups worldwide which address important attacks from theoretical (modeling) as well as practical aspects.

We anticipate that this edited book can serve as a good resource to security researchers and students as each chapter brings comprehensive and structured information about an attack or an attack family. The authors in these chapters present crisp detailing on the state of the art with quality illustration of defense mechanisms and open research problems. This book covers various important attack families such as insider threats, semantics social engineering attacks, distributed denial of service attacks, botnet-based attacks, cyber physical malware-based attacks, cross-vm attacks, and IoT covert channel attacks. We hope that this book will serve the interests of many of the cybersecurity enthusiasts including undergraduates, postgraduate, and doctoral students.

The first chapter on "An Android-Based Covert Channel Framework on Wearables Using Status Bar Notifications" focuses on covert channel attacks on Internet of Things (IoT) devices using notifications. The authors in this chapter show cases of novel covert channel attacks where instead of using global shared resources, attack is performed using common status notifications to users. The chapter shows a detailed description of threat model, types, and motivations of covert channel attacks. Later in the chapter, authors describe a novel Android-based covert channel attack which is based on status bar notifications. Authors also discuss various important parameters behind the success of these attacks. Authors also describe the performance of the covert channel attacks based on throughput analysis and covert analysis. At the end of the chapter, the authors discuss a set of open research directions in this area to help the researchers to ponder on newer problems.

The second chapter on "Insider Threat Detection: Machine Learning Way" aims to cover and analyze contributions from machine learning domain to provide solutions to various kinds of insider threats. The authors in this chapter provide various attack launch mechanisms and details the impacts of an insider attack on various domains. The authors also presents interesting state-of-the-art work on insider threat detection which includes methods based on psychology, criminology, and game theory. The chapter covers various case studies covering usages of machine learning techniques in anomaly detection. The chapter also describes some experimental studies on insider threat detection over large datasets with low frequency anomalies. The authors describe methods such as linear regression followed by Cook's and Mahalanobis distance to identify malicious activities of the user. The authors also show usages of neural network and support vector machines to demonstrate detection of an anomalous behavior. The chapter concludes by providing a glimpse of future research directions from natural language processing, behavioral analysis, sentiment analysis, and machine learning areas for insider threat detection.

DDoS attacks are among the top cyber threats for many years. The third chapter of this book on "Distributed Denial of Service Attacks and Defense Mechanisms: Current Landscape and Future Directions" aims to provide a comprehensive description of the state-of-the-art techniques for DDoS attack detection and defense mechanisms. In addition, the authors in this chapter provide a detailed taxonomy of various DDoS attacks to help the reader understand the types of attack methods used to plan the DDoS attacks. The authors provide a detailed description of various launch methods and also give a light to various reasons for success of notorious DDoS attacks. In the later part of the chapter, authors describe various attack characterization, prevention, detection, and trace-back methods. Authors also discuss the attack sophistication and newer trends in the DDoS attacks space and also provide a list of future research directions at the end of the chapter.

Social engineering attacks lead to multiple threats which may in turn lead to many other security attacks such as phishing, drive-by downloads, file and multimedia masquerading, domain typosquatting, and malvertising. The fourth chapter on "Protection Against Semantic Social Engineering Attacks" focuses on various kinds of semantic social engineering attacks. The authors provide a detailed coverage of over 35 diverse types of semantic attacks. The authors in this chapter provide an in-depth coverage to the semantic attack launch methods using a generic attack structure. A major contribution of this chapter is in providing a detailed yet comprehensive treatment to the solutions in the form of a three-dimensional defense framework for the semantic social engineering attacks. We are sure that the readers will benefit from the application of three-dimensional defenses on popular semantic attack cases such as "Podesta Emails" and "WhatsApp QRishing." The authors also provide three important open research directions in the form of emerging threats in "Internet of Everything," Human-as-a-Security-Sensor, and Cyber Hygiene 2.0.

Program obfuscation makes it difficult for the detection methods to understand the program semantics. Chapter 5 of this book aims to provide details about cryptographic program obfuscators. The authors in this chapter introduce the program obfuscation and its importance in general and provide a detailed description of cryptographic program obfuscation. In this chapter, the authors show the practical implementations of point function obfuscators, provably secure under widely used intractability assumptions and in theory-oriented models and definitions of cryptographic program obfuscation. The authors describe different point function obfuscators based on cryptographic hashing, decisional DH, discrete logarithms, decisional residuosity, the LWR problem, and the LWE problem. Later, the chapter provides guidelines to generate application-oriented models and definitions of cryptographic program obfuscations, addressing more practical classes of attacks.

Chapter 6 of this book focuses on "Botnet-Based Attacks and Defense Mechanisms." The authors in this chapter provide an in-depth discussion to botnet lifecycle and give a comprehensive classification of botnets. The authors detail the launching of botnet-based attacks in the form of compromise attacks (initial threats) and follow-up attacks (continuous threats). The authors also provide a list of reasons behind the success of botnet-based attacks. The major contribution of this chapter is to provide a comprehensive solution hierarchy for botnet-driven attacks. We hope that readers would benefit from the list of newer form of botnets such as mobile, social network-based, IoT-based, cloud-based, and crypto-mining-based botnets. At the end of the chapter, the authors provide a number of future research directions related to the botnet-based attacks, newer sophistications, and related possible solutions.

Highly sophisticated attack incidents in the form of cyber-physical malware (CPM) such as "Industroyer" can virtually paralyze nations. Chapter 7 is dedicated to "Catastrophic Cyber-Physical Malware" and provides an in-depth coverage to diverse aspects of CPM based attacks from the perspective software vulnerabilities. The authors in this chapter provide a detailed description of CPM metrics and various phases of CPM-based attack launch. We feel that the contributions made by the authors in this chapter would greatly benefit readers who are interested in newer form of cyber-attacks. The authors detail the needs of security measures related to CPM and provide connections to the national cybersecurity. The authors discuss various risks related to telecommunication infrastructure, industrial control systems, vulnerable mission-critical software, and IoT and provide critical needs for software assurance and practical tools, and cyber-force training. The authors also describe various practical difficulties in detecting CPM malware with the examples such as GPS malware. In addition, authors also discuss challenges related to software assurance. At the end of the chapter, authors provide interesting discussion to the open research directions including threat modeling and describe their DARPA research on software analysis.

The last chapter of this book is on "Cross-VM Attacks: Attack Taxonomy, Defense Mechanisms, and New Directions". The authors in this chapter focus on cloud-based cyber-attack among the virtual machines. The authors in this chapter focus on cross-VM attacks which are mostly side-channel attacks based on shared resources in a multi-tenant cloud environment. The authors provide a detailed description of cross-VM attacks and provide detailed attack taxonomy based on various shared resources in the cloud. The authors detail about five categories (CPU-based, cache-based, memory-based, network-based, and I/O device-based) of cross-VM attacks in their attack taxonomy. In addition, the authors provide an attack model and threat model for cross-VM attacks and various launch methods. The authors also enlist a number of success factors behind these attacks and provide a detailed survey of various mitigation mechanisms. At the end of the chapter, the authors provide a discussion on newer forms of sophisticated cross-vm attacks and a list of open research problems.

Padua, Italy   Mauro Conti
Ajmer, India   Gaurav Somani
Seattle, WA, USA   Radha Poovendran

Acknowledgments

The Editors of this book would like to thank:

- Prof. Sushil Jajodia, George Mason University, USA, and Series Editor, Advances in Information Security (Springer)
- Susan Lagerstrom-Fife, Springer
- Caroline Flanagan, Springer
- Anonymous reviewers
- Authors of various chapters in the book
- University of Padua, Italy
- Central University of Rajasthan, India
- University of Washington, USA

Contents

Contributors

Dilara Acarali School of Mathematics, Computer Science and Engineering, City, University of London, London, UK

Irfan Ahmed Department of Computer Science, University of New Orleans, New Orleans, LA, USA

Kemal Akkaya College of Electrical and Computer Engineering, Florida International Univeristy, Miami, FL, USA

Hidayet Aksu College of Electrical and Computer Engineering, Florida International Univeristy, Miami, FL, USA

Payas Awadhutkar Department of Electrical and Computer Engineering, Iowa State University, Ames, IA, USA

Sunny Behal Department of Computer Science, Shaheed Bhagat Singh State Technical Campus, Ferozepur, Punjab, India

Sajal Bhatia School of Computing, Sacred Heart University, Fairfield, CT, USA

Sanjay Chaudhary School of Engineering and Applied Science, Ahmedabad University, Ahmedabad, Gujarat, India

Giovanni Di Crescenzo Perspecta Labs, Basking Ridge, NJ, USA

Kyle Denney College of Electrical and Computer Engineering, Florida International Univeristy, Miami, FL, USA

Ratnik Gandhi School of Engineering and Applied Science, Ahmedabad University, Ahmedabad, Gujarat, India

Ryan Heartfield University of Greenwich, London, UK

Benjamin Holland Department of Electrical and Computer Engineering, Iowa State University, Ames, IA, USA

Suresh Kothari Department of Electrical and Computer Engineering, Iowa State University, Ames, IA, USA

EnSoft Corp., Ames, IA, USA

George Loukas University of Greenwich, London, UK

Jon Mathews EnSoft Corp., Ames, IA, USA

Muttukrishnan Rajarajan School of Mathematics, Computer Science and Engineering, City, University of London, London, UK

Mehul S. Raval School of Engineering and Applied Science, Ahmedabad University, Ahmedabad, Gujarat, India

Ganesh Ram Santhanam Department of Electrical and Computer Engineering, Iowa State University, Ames, IA, USA

A. Selcuk Uluagac College of Electrical and Computer Engineering, Florida International Univeristy, Miami, FL, USA

Gulshan Kumar Singh Department of Computer Science and Engineering, Central University of Rajasthan, Ajmer, India

Gaurav Somani Department of Computer Science and Engineering, Central University of Rajasthan, Ajmer, India

Ahmed Tamrawi EnSoft Corp., Ames, IA, USA

About the Editors

Mauro Conti is Full Professor at the University of Padua, Italy, and Affiliate Professor at the University of Washington, USA. He obtained his Ph.D. from Sapienza University of Rome, Italy, in 2009. After his Ph.D., he was a Postdoc Researcher at Vrije Universiteit Amsterdam, The Netherlands. In 2011, he joined as Assistant Professor at the University of Padua, where he became Associate Professor in 2015, and Full Professor in 2018. He has been Visiting Researcher at GMU (2008, 2016), UCLA (2010), UCI (2012, 2013, 2014, 2017), TU Darmstadt (2013), UF (2015), and FIU (2015, 2016). He has been awarded with a Marie Curie Fellowship (2012) by the European Commission and with a Fellowship by the German DAAD (2013). His research is also funded by companies, including Cisco and Intel. His main research interest is in the area of security and privacy. In this area, he published more than 200 papers in topmost international peer-reviewed journals and conference. He is Area Editor-in-Chief for *IEEE Communications Surveys & Tutorials*, and Associate Editor for several journals, including *IEEE Communications Surveys & Tutorials*, *IEEE Transactions on Information Forensics and Security*, and *IEEE Transactions on Network and Service Management*. He was Program Chair for TRUST 2015, ICISS 2016, WiSec 2017, and General Chair for SecureComm 2012 and ACM SACMAT 2013. He is Senior Member of the IEEE.

Gaurav Somani is an Assistant Professor in the Department of CSE at Central University of Rajasthan, India. Earlier, he served as a lecturer at the LNMIIT, Jaipur, INDIA. He has completed his Ph.D. in CSE at MNIT, Jaipur; MTech from DAIICT, Gandhinagar, India; and BE from the University of Rajasthan, India. His research interests include Cloud computing, virtualization, distributed computing, and network and system security. He is a recipient of Teacher Fellowship from University Grants Commission (UGC), INDIA. He has published several papers and served as a reviewer in various top journals and conferences. Some of his top papers are published at *IEEE Transactions on Dependable and Secure Computing*, *Computer Communications*, *Computer Networks*, *Future Generation Computer Systems*, *IEEE International Conference on Cloud Computing*, and *IEEE*

Cloud Computing. He has edited a book *Research Advances in Cloud Computing* (Springer) with Sanjay Chaudhay and Rajkumar Buyya and this volume, *Versatile Cybersecurity* (Springer), with Mauro Conti and Radha Poovendran. He is also a guest editor of a special issue of *Journal of Software: Practice and Experience* on "Integration of Cloud, IoT and Big Data Analytics." He has been a part of program committees of various conferences and was a keynote and tutorial chair for ICISS 2016. He is a member of IEEE.

Radha Poovendran is a Professor and Chair of the Department of Electrical Engineering at the University of Washington since 2000. His research areas are wireless security and cyber-physical systems security. He is a recipient of the NSA Rising Star Award (1999), NSF CAREER award (2001), ARO YIP (2002), ONR YIP (2004), PECASE (2005), Kavli Faculty Fellow of the National Academy of Sciences (2007). He is also a recipient of the UW EE Outstanding Teaching Award (2002) and Outstanding Research Award (2002) as well as the Graduate Mentor Award (2006) from the Office of the Chancellor of the University of California, San Diego. He is a co-author of multiple best paper awards, including 2010 IEEE/IFIP William C. Carter Award winning paper. He is a fellow of the IEEE for contributions to security of Cyber-Physical Systems. In May 2016, he received a Distinguished Alumni Award of the ECE Department of the University of Maryland.

An Android-Based Covert Channel Framework on Wearables Using Status Bar Notifications

Kyle Denney, A. Selcuk Uluagac, Hidayet Aksu, and Kemal Akkaya

Abstract Covert channels circumvent security measures to steal sensitive data undetectable to an onlooker. Traditionally, covert channels utilize global system resources or settings to send hidden messages. This chapter introduces covert channels and focuses on a novel covert channel on Android-based Internet of Things (IoT) devices. Particularly, we were able to make a covert channel using notifications a user gets from everyday applications. The chapter will also present this covert channel by discussing the framework, evaluating the performance, and demonstrating the functionality and flexibility of the proposed model.

1 Introduction

By 2020, it is estimated that there will be 50 to 100 billion devices connected to the Internet [8, 9, 18]. All of these devices traditionally communicate *overtly* using established communication protocols (i.e., TCP/IP), but it is possible to have these devices communicate *covertly* without detection.

Covert communication is the art of using typical communication standards and transforming them into a way that only two parties are aware of the message. This is different from encryption where the message is disguised in a way where an onlooker cannot discern the meaning. With covert channels, the onlooker is completely unaware the message exists in the first place.

This chapter will discuss how covert channels occur in computer systems. We start with a general overview of covert channels in Sect. 2. In Sect. 3, we discuss the timeline of covert channels and how they developed into their current state. Section 4 highlights a covert channel model we introduce that works on Android-based IoT systems, written in a way to show how covert channels may be developed in any computer system. Section 5 discusses the results of our proposed covert

K. Denney (✉) · A. S. Uluagac · H. Aksu · K. Akkaya
College of Electrical and Computer Engineering, Florida International Univeristy, Miami, FL, USA
e-mail: kdenn016@fiu.edu; suluagac@fiu.edu; haksu@fiu.edu; kakkaya@fiu.edu

© Springer Nature Switzerland AG 2018
M. Conti et al. (eds.), *Versatile Cybersecurity*, Advances in Information
Security 72, https://doi.org/10.1007/978-3-319-97643-3_1

1

channel on a live testbed. We discuss possible ways to eliminate our covert channel in Sect. 6. Finally, Sect. 7 discusses where future development in covert channels may be headed–discussing both future attack models and future defenses to covert channels.

2 Background

Covert channels [2, 4, 16] are a way to steal sensitive information in manners undetectable to a third-party onlooker. Essentially, these channels abuse freely-available resources in a system to create novel means of communications. For instance, a *storage covert channel* [16] can alter values of a system resource using a predetermined codebook. A seperate process, knowing the codebook, can detect these changes and interpret the encoded message. This allows processes to work together to send messages surreptitiously within the system. The rest of this section will describe the history and traditional methodology behind covert channels.

2.1 Traditional Threat Model

Covert channels were first described by Lampson [13] to show how processes that were not intended for communication can be used to send hidden messages. Over time, various forms of covert channels were introduced [1–4, 16, 20]. This subsection introduces the concept of covert channel and describes how the different types of channels may be used by attackers in networks.

The process introduced by Simmons is a model we still use today to describe covert channels [19]. He describes a process similar to prisoners attempting to escape a prison. In this model, as shown in Fig. 1, Alice and Bob are two prisoners that plan to escape their confinement under the watch of a warden, Wendy. Alice and Bob must come up with a way to communicate without Wendy finding out. If Wendy discovers their communication, Alice and Bob are thrown into solitary confinement. In order to escape prison, Alice and Bob must communicate with messages that look innocent to Wendy, but actually contains information about escaping.

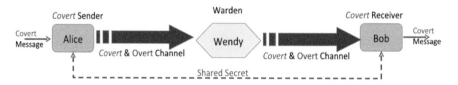

Fig. 1 Covert channel conceptual model [16]

This analogy can be translated to how covert channels work. Two applications must be able to send hidden information between each other without the warden, generally a firewall or antivirus software, discovering the communication. To hide the communication, covert channels generally use resources that are universally given to processes to use at will. Traditionally, there are two ways to communicate using these resources: *timing-based* or *storage-based*.

2.2 Types of Covert Channels

Timing-based covert channels communicate by using the time to send messages. A covert mechanism commonly used in these channels is the systematic delaying of packets being sent across the network. One covert sender will send packets across the network and delay them intentionally. The amount of the delay corresponds to a symbol that is part of the message. The covert receiver will detect these symbols and interpret the message.

On the other hand, *storage-based covert channels* work by altering values in system resources. Storage-based channels operate in intervals that are known between the two processes – typically a time with the least chance of user-interference. When the channel is operating, the covert sender process will change the value of a resource, like the volume setting, to correspond to a symbol in the message. The covert receiver process will read the changes in the values and interpret the message from there.

2.3 Motivations for Using Covert Channels

As with most security concepts, covert channels can be used offensively and defensively. For example, an attacker may establish a covert channel on a system in order to steal data undetected to the system administrators. Imagine the attacker implanting a covert channel on a military base: once established, he can use this covert channel to steal military secrets from the base without high-command knowing his presence.

On the other hand, covert channels are very important for defensive purposes. Take a military unit lost in enemy lands, for instance. Their entire mission can be compromised once the enemy knows of their presence. If the unit uses traditional communication methods to relay information, the enemy would be able to uncover their existence. Even if the unit uses encryption, the enemy could infer the intentions of their messages and detect the unit. However, through the use of covert channels, the unit will be able to remain undetected to the enemy while gaining crucial information from their commanders.

The fact that covert channels can be used for either purpose makes it especially important for research to be done in creating new covert channels and uncovering ways to mitigate existing covert channels.

3   Use Cases of Covert Channels

Covert channels are used throughout computer networks to send messages surreptitiously. Typically, if a system can connect to a network, a covert channel can be developed. In this section, we look at the fields that can be affected by covert channels and examples for each field. We start with the first covert channels and work our way up the timeline to covert channels on today's systems.

As mentioned before, covert channels were first introduced by Lampson in 1973 [13]. His work, "A Note on the Confinement Problem" focused on monolithic systems. He noted that it was possible to obtain information on who called an individual program by utilizing resources and system calls not designed for information sending. At the time, Lampson's work only defined covert channels operating on a single system or mainframe; using the channel to uncover information that was privileged and inaccessible to users. However, it quickly became understood that these covert channels could be used across multiple networked devices.

Once computer systems became networked together, covert channels increased their potential [20]. Researchers examined that it was possible to hide information in packet headers to discretely send information. The first instance of a timing channel was introduced by Girling [12] where he noted it was possible to systematically delay packets to hide information. From there, it quickly became realized that it is possible to create a covert channel on practically any networking protocol as one can either: (1) create a timing channel by systematically delaying the protocol packets or (2) create a storage channel by hiding information in the protocol packet headers.

Since a covert channel can be introduced on practically any networked device, they can have a potentially massive impact on the world. With 50 to 100 billion devices connected to the Internet in the near future [8, 9], the amount of data transferred in covert channels will be massive. For instance, the covert channel showcased in this chapter uses the notification class on Android used to notify a user of an incoming message from an application. Since notifications are used universally on all Android devices, this covert channel impacts the full spectrum of Android devices – including IoT devices that utilize the Android Wear operating system. As of May 2017, Google announced it has over 2 billion active Android devices running in the world [15]. This means the covert channel we discuss has a high potential to affect millions of users.

4 A Novel Covert Channel over Android-Based Notifications

In this section we introduce our proposed covert channel model. We show how it is possible to create a covert channel using the notifications that show on an Android system when one receives an SMS message or email.

Starting with an introduction to the Android operating system, we then move on to how the notifications themselves are created on an Android device. We showcase how one can manipulate these notifications to create both a timing and storage channel. Going step-by-step through the creation of both models, we also show how a covert channel may be developed on any system or protocol.

4.1 Android OS

The Android operating system is based on Linux, with much of the security designs and features being extensions of Linux. The main Android platform is a Java Virtual Machine running on top of the Linux kernel. What makes Android different from Linux is that each application running on Android is awarded the same privilege level – meaning that every application, including Google applications, have the same limitations and privileges.

When an application is running, it is given a unique user ID with unique privileges it can access from the system (these are awarded by the user in the form of permissions). For instance, applications that are given the Wi-Fi permission are allowed to use the phone's Internet connection – all others are barred from this access.

Since each application is its own user on the device, applications are not allowed to talk to each other directly. This technique is called *sandboxing* and is a typical way to increase the security of a device. Essentially, sandboxing works by giving each application a unique user ID. That user ID is then paired with its own set of permissions and system resources and then applications are not allowed to share information between each other. To get around this, additional permissions must be granted based on the type of communication the two applications would like to perform.

Covert channels can attempt to subvert these sandboxing methods [10, 11]. Applications may form either a timing-based or a storage-based covert channel with each other in order to share their own privileged information. One application can write information by altering a system resource while the second application can read that information as the resource is changed. Since system resources are universally given to applications, these attacks circumvent the security measures Android employs.

4.1.1 Android Notifications and Android Wear

The covert channel framework that is presented in this paper uses the *notification* mechanism available on Android-based wearables. Notifications are messages that are displayed to the user to give information about an application that is running. Examples of notifications would be a new SMS message, notice that a file finished downloading, or information about a new system update for the device itself. In this sub-section, the structure of a notification is described and the functionality of notifications across devices is introduced as it is an important concept to understand the covert channel technique introduced in this paper.

Traditionally, the status bar holds all of the notifications that appear on an Android smart phone. When an application needs to tell the user of something important, it creates a notification and displays it on the status bar. The basic structure of a notification includes a notification ID which is used by the smart device to distinguish different notifications, a title that displays at the top of a notification, and the text that gives more information to the user.

Starting in Android 4.3, support for Android wearables was introduced [5]. Using the Android Wear application, a smartphone can sync with a smartwatch. The two devices can then share information such as notifications between each other and make a more user-friendly experience by being more integrated with the user's life.

In order for notifications to be pushed from the phone to the wearable (or vice versa), a notification listening service on the wearable needs to be implemented. When the user gives the BIND_NOTIFICATION_LISTENER_SERVICE permission to an application, the application is allowed to access information about every notification that appears on the status bar. If the user has a wearable device synced with their smart device, the permission allows for all notifications across both devices to be read. *Since all notifications appear on both devices, it does not matter which device the application is installed on for it to read the notifications.*

Note that many applications on the Android marketplace today utilize this permission. Applications can sync with many devices and send notifications from a phone to other personal devices such as a computer or tablet. Moreover, with a simple search for 'notification reader' application on the Google Play Store, a myriad of applications appear that advertise a more user-friendly experience by sharing notifications across devices. Unfortunately, when an application advertises that devices can work together, the user is more inclined to give permissions such as the BIND_NOTIFICATION_LISTENER_SERVICE to the application.

4.2 Threat Model

With this information in mind, we can use these notifications in Android systems to develop a covert channel. First, we must establish the threat model we will be using for this covert channel. Imagine a rogue employee at a company who wishes to steal company secrets. He can sync his Android watch to his work tablet and establish a covert sending application on the tablet and a covert receiving application on the watch. From there, he can make a covert channel that sends messages by hiding the data in notifications. The tablet can create notifications and the watch will read these notifications and infer the hidden data from within. Below we will describe methods to create this covert channel.

4.3   Covert Channel Framework

The covert channel that is introduced in this paper uses Android Wearable notifications to send information between applications on the same device, or even across multiple devices. We first describe the general framework, then introduce how we use the framework to make both storage-based and timing-based covert channels.

The first application we make is the covert sending application. The covert sender is responsible for creating notifications that will be used for the covert channel. It creates notifications with specific notification ID values that have pre-established meaning.

The second application, the covert receiver, is responsible for reading these notifications and determining the hidden message. This receiving application is assumed to have the BIND_NOTIFICATION_LISTENER_SERVICE permission enabled, allowing it to read notifications on the Android system. The receiver can read the notification ID values and infer the hidden message by comparing it to the pre-established codebook.

Below we describe how this can be done using both a timing-based and a storage-based covert channel methodology.

4.3.1   Previous Work

We have previously published works with this covert channel framework [6, 7]. In past works, our framework was only a storage channel framework. In this chapter, we expand on the framework to function as both a timing and storage channel. Additionally, we improve on the storage channel model to have a higher throughput, which we will analyze in later sections.

4.3.2   Timing-Based Framework

Here we describe how a timing-based covert channel can be achieved using notifications.

In the timing-based framework, the sending and receiving applications first have to establish a timing codebook. For our purposes, we established the receiver to look for a notification at every t intervals. We also created 3 notification ID values to be read: $start$, $stop$, and $message$. These ID values are arbitrary as long as both applications know what the corresponding values are.

To establish the covert communication, the sending application creates a notification with the *start* value. When the notification is read by the receiving application, it starts a timer that reads for notifications every *t* intervals.

The sender, with a timer of its own, then takes the message it wants to send and converts it into its hexadecimal data. The sender then reads the current data value in the stream and waits for the appropriate *t* intervals (e.g., if the data value is A, the sender waits 10 *t* intervals; the sender also waits a full 16 *t* intervals if the data value is 0). When the sender has waited the appropriate time, it creates a notification with the *message* value and then moves on to the next data value in the stream and repeats the process.

When the receiving application reads the *start* notification, the application starts looking for notifications with the *message* value every *t* intervals. If the application does not detect a notification, it increases a counter. This counter counts up until either a notification is finally read or the counter counts up to 16. The value of the counter whenever it is reset is added to the receiving application's message stream.

When the message is complete, the sending application creates a notification with the *stop* value. The receiving application reads this notification and stops its timer and counter. The receiver then stores the entire message it collected and the covert message is complete.

Figure 2 describes the covert channel model for the timing channel framework. The sending application creates notifications with specific time intervals in between. Then, the receiving application reads these altering timing values to interpret the hidden message.

4.3.3 Storage-Based Framework

The framework for a storage-based covert channel is similar to the timing-based framework. Here, we again use a *start* and *stop* notification to initialize and terminate the covert message respectively. However, this time, the *message* notification varies in value.

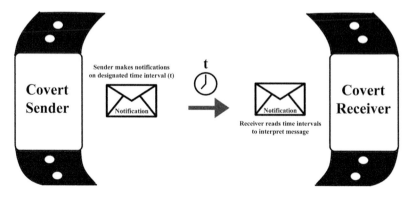

Fig. 2 Design of the timing-based covert channel

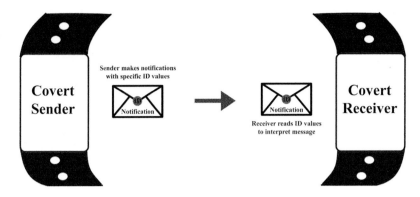

Fig. 3 Design of the storage-based covert channel

Once the covert message has started, the covert sender reads the current value in the message stream and inputs that value directly into the *message* ID value. The receiver then reads the value of the notification and adds it to its message stream.

Figure 3 describes the covert channel model for the storage channel framework. The sending application creates notifications with ID values corresponding to the predetermined codebook. Then, the receiving application reads these altering ID values to interpret the hidden message.

5 Success of the Covert Channel

In this section, we demonstrate the feasibility and functionality of the novel wearable covert channel framework and evaluate its performance on real wearable devices focusing on the two covert channel techniques introduced in the framework.

In our model, a rogue employee (Bob) may use this covert channel set up to steal sensitive data from a work phone by using a paired smart watch. Bob can install the covert sender on his company phone and the covert receiver on the watch. Bob can use the covert sender to encode the sensitive data into either notification-based model–creating notifications on his work phone. The Android Wear application will then send any notifications made on Bob's work phone to his paired smart watch. The smart watch will then receive any notifications sent from the Android Wear application.

By installing the covert receiver on the smart watch, it is possible for Bob to listen to all the incoming notifications on the smart watch. The covert receiver then picks up the message originating from the covert sender on the work phone, storing the sensitive data on the smart watch without the company's knowledge.

To test the functionality and the feasibility of this covert channel model, a Samsung Galaxy S5 was used as the work phone and a Sony SmartWatch 3 was used as a wearable device. The Galaxy phone holds a 2.5 GHz quad-core processor with 2 GB of RAM and the watch a 1.2 GHz quad-core processor and 512 MB of RAM. The devices used in our testbed are shown in Fig. 4.

Fig. 4 First covert channel technique testbed (left: Samsung Galaxy S5; right: Sony SmartWatch 3)

5.1 Throughput Analysis

In this subsection, we analyze the throughput of each covert channel model. By calculating how quickly notifications can be sent, we will be able to calculate how much data can be sent by both models. From there, we can determine which model has a higher throughput by comparing the two results.

5.1.1 Timing-Based Throughput

To have a high throughput, we need as low of a time interval between notifications sent as possible. To measure this, we first need to calculate how quickly the phone can make notifications as well as how fast the watch can read incoming notifications. From there, we can calculate the shortest time interval notifications can be sent at where the message is still discernible.

First, we measured how quickly the phone can make new notifications. We found that our phone could make about 19 notifications per second. To test how quickly the watch could read notifications, we had the phone repeatedly send notifications as quickly as it could (19 notifications per second) for an extended period. On the watch end, we simply made a counter that incremented every time it processed a notification from the phone. The ratio of how many notifications the watch processed to how many notifications were actually made gives us how many notifications per second the watch is capable of receiving. In our case, we found the watch was able to process just over 6 notifications per second, which we round down to 6 to ensure every notification is read during transmission.

By inverting our ratio of 6 notifications per second, we find that the lowest time interval between two notifications being processed is 1/6th of a second. That means our t value for transmission is also 1/6th of a second.

To calculate our final throughput, we assume the slowest possible message sent (a series of straight zeros) making new data being sent every 2.6 s. Dividing the amount of data sent (16 bits) by the maximum sending rate (2.6 s) gives us our final throughput of 6.15 bps. As Claudio et al. discuss [14], even a low bit rate covert channel is enough to share "reasonable amounts of data on the smartphone." Given the timing channels they analyze are 3.70 and 4.88 bps, we can conclude that ours at 6.15 bps is also sufficient.

5.1.2   Storage-Based Throughput

The throughput of the storage-based model is much easier to calculate. Here, we had to simply take how quickly notifications are being sent by how much data can be sent per notification.

We have our speed of 6 notifications per second from analyzing the throughput of the timing-based model before, so we only have to determine how much data can be sent per notification. Notification ID values use the unsigned integer type, making each notification sent worth 4 bytes of data. This gives us around 24 bytes per second (192 bps) for the throughput of the storage-based model; exponentially faster than the timing-based model.

5.2   Covert Analysis

In this subsection, we discuss how covert each model actually is. We do this by analyzing how much system resources each model takes up as well as having a brief discussion on how easily an onlooker may uncover the communication through simple observation.

5.2.1   Pattern Recognition

To hide the communication occurring in our proposed covert channel, we use the *cancel()* function provided to notification creation. This function allows an application to remove a notification it created from the status bar of Android device. We call this function immediately after the covert sender makes a notification for transmission to ensure that an onlooker cannot physically see the notifications appear on the smart device. However, if one looks at the system logs, all the notifications still appear and communication can continue unaltered.

Since the notifications are still present on the system, it is still possible for a warden-type application to detect the covert communication by analyzing incoming notifications on the smart device.

To counter this warden, we can implement measures to mask the patterns one can discern from the covert communications. For instance, instead of the storage model sending notifications at a set pace, we can randomize the time between notifications as that will have no impact on the transmission. For the timing model, we can randomize the time interval after every transmission. Essentially, any measure that can change the transmission pattern without affecting the actual transmission can be introduced to our model to prevent a warden from recognizing the communication occurring.

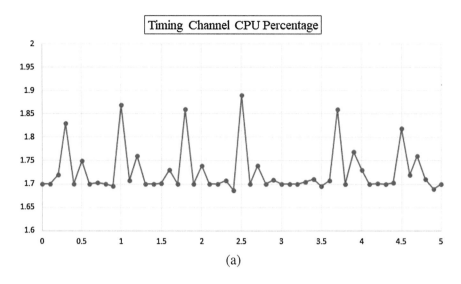

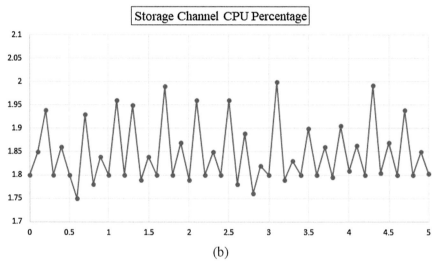

Fig. 5 CPU readings of (**a**) Timing and (**b**) Storage covert channel models

5.2.2 CPU Usage

We set up a simple test to see if there is any noticeable CPU usage from the covert sender. We monitored the CPU usage on our Galaxy device from the covert sender while the sender relayed a message to the covert receiver. Figure 5 has the CPU percentages of the covert sending application for both the timing and storage channel models (with A referring to the timing model and B referring to the storage

Table 1 Analysis summary of storage and timing channels

	Timing	Storage
Throughput	6.15 bps	192 bps
Data per notification	1 bit	4 bytes
CPU usage (average)	1.75%	1.85%

model, respectively). For simplicity's sake, we set the notification rate to 1/5th of a second and set the length of the test over 5 s to read the patterns more clearly.

As expected, the CPU usage spikes whenever a notification is created. This can be clearly seen in the timing model, as there is a heartbeat pattern whenever a notification is created: a large spike for the creation of the notification and a smaller spike for when the *cancel()* function is called to wipe the notification from the phone. While not as clear, this is still present in the storage model.

5.3 Analysis Summary

To conclude the analysis portion of our work, we include a table to compare and contrast the efficacy of both the timing and storage channel frameworks. Table 1 compares the two frameworks in their throughput, amount of data encapsulated in each notification, and average CPU usage respectively.

6 Discussion and Prevention

In this section, we discuss the pros and cons of both covert channel models. We also discuss methods to prevent the proposed covert channels and how effective these prevention models can be.

6.1 Prevention

In fact, there are no current solutions to prevent this proposed covert channel. However, this chapter proposes solutions that diminish, or stop entirely, the success of this covert channel.

A simple way to stop the proposed storage channel is to change the way the notification class handles notification ID values. Instead of allowing an application to create its own ID value for a notification, Android OS should randomly assign an ID value to every created notification. The new notification would still be attributed to the appropriate application, but it prevents this covert channel from operating properly.

However, this does not stop the timing channel from operating. Another solution to prevent both models is through simple intrusion detection. An antimalware software installed on an Android device could be programmed to detect newly created notifications. If one application is creating an unreasonable number of notifications, it would be flagged as a rogue application and proper authorities would be notified.

6.2 Comparison

Overall, the proposed storage channel model is a more well-rounded model compared to the timing channel. Below, we discuss the various criteria we used to come to this conclusion.

In our throughput analysis, we established that the storage channel is capable of sending more information at once. At its maximum throughput, the timing channel was only capable of 6.15 b/s, which is minuscule compared to the storage channel at 20 B/s. From the CPU usage section above, we established that it is simple to spot the pattern of an application sending repeated notifications over time. The timing channel model especially falls prey to this pattern recognition as there is no simple way to break up a system dependent on time. For the storage channel, we can simply send the notifications over a longer span of time, thereby making it harder for an onlooker to discern a pattern. However, the timing channel has more potential for longevity. It is rather simple for Google to shutdown the capability for the storage channel to operate by forcing notifications to have randomized ID values. There is no similar option for Google to take to stop the timing channel, as notifications will always have to be sent at times specified by the calling application. Therefore, the operability of the timing channel is practically ensured in all future Android releases.

7 Trends and Future Work

Since covert channels can exist on practically any computer system, we need to know what new technologies can be used to establish covert channels and what we can do to prevent them from occurring. This section will look at what new research in covert channels may look like in the near future.

7.1 Imminent Threats

As noted, practically any new technology that can be networked can be used to create covert channels. However, we note that current popular technology trends will have the most focus for covert channel development.

The covert channel we showcase only works on Android devices at the moment, but notifications exist on practically all modern devices from smart phones, to personal computers, to IoT devices. In order to improve this covert channel, one would need to develop a universal system that allows the covert channel to work on notifications from all of these devices.

As the case with our covert channel model, more covert channels will be introduced in IoT technologies. Similarly, we believe that covert channels in Cyber-Physical Systems (CPS) will be especially popular due to the nature of a CPS (e.g., stealing information about the energy grid undetected would be especially valuable).

Another research area – especially with its increased popularity in recent months – is uncovering covert channels in Bitcoin and other altcoins. Due to the history of Bitcoin, it is likely that covert channels are currently well-established to communicate in the criminal undergrounds. Research here would be done to prove how these covert channels can operate in order to work on the harder problem: detecting and diminishing the covert channel.

7.2 Future Defenses

Typically, once a covert channel is detected, it is very simple to stop it from occurring. One can simply add a detection system that flags when covert communications are likely happening and stop the process that is operating on the covert channel. However, future research can be done to help automate the detection instead of relying on manual eradication.

As mentioned earlier, covert channels are likely well-established in the Bitcoin network. The real challenge would be detecting and eradicating covert channels currently in place. Due to the nature of Bitcoin and how anonymous each transaction is, it would be more difficult than a traditional network to detect a covert channel in place. Research in this area would be finding ways to determine patterns in blockchain transactions in order to detect possible storage or timing channels in the blockchain network.

Neural networks and machine learning techniques can be used to determine typical covert channel patterns and then implemented on computer systems to automatically flag potential covert channels. Work on this concept was introduced by Shrestha et al. [17] to automatically detect timing channels, but this idea may be extended to include storage channels.

8 Conclusion

Covert channels are an effective means to send information undetected. They have widespread use throughout the Internet and can be used in a variety of ways. As more and more technologies are introduced, the need to understand how covert channels operate is important in order to prevent information from being stolen in these new technologies.

This chapter introduced covert channels and how they are traditionally implemented. We then showcased a model for a timing and storage channel in Android-based IoT systems that work on real and current implementations. We conclude this chapter with discussing where future trends in covert channel development and prevention are headed.

Acknowledgements This work is partially supported by the US National Science Foundation (Awards: NSF-CAREER-CNS-1453647, NSF-1663051, REU-CNS-1461119). The views in this document are of the authors, not of the funding agencies.

References

1. Al-Haiqi, A., Ismail, M., Nordin, R.: A new sensors-based covert channel on android. The Scientific World **2014** (2014)
2. Ambrosin, M., Conti, M., Gasti, P., Tsudik, G.: Covert ephemeral communication in named data networking. In: Proceedings of the 9th ACM Symposium on Information, Computer and Communications Security, ASIA CCS '14 (2014)
3. Caviglione, L., Gaggero, M., Lalande, J.F., Mazurczyk, W., Urbanski, M.: Seeing the unseen: Revealing mobile malware hidden communications via energy consumption and artificial intelligence. IEEE Transactions on Information Forensics and Security **11**(4), 799–810 (2016). DOI 10.1109/TIFS.2015.2510825
4. Chandra, S., Lin, Z., Kundu, A., Khan, L.: Towards a systematic study of the covert channel attacks in smartphones. SECURECOMM 2014 (2014)
5. Comstock, J.: 1 in 5 americans owns a wearable, 1 in 10 wears them daily. Mobi Health News (2014). URL http://mobihealthnews.com/37543/pwc-1-in-5-americans/-owns-a-wearable-1-in-10-wears-them-daily/
6. Denney, K., Uluagac, A.S., Akkaya, K., Bhansali, S.: A novel storage covert channel on wearable devices using status bar notifications. In: 2016 13th IEEE Annual Consumer Communications Networking Conference (CCNC), pp. 845–848 (2016). DOI 10.1109/CCNC.2016.7444898
7. Denney, K., Uluagac, A.S., Akkaya, K., Saputro, N.: Demonstration of a novel storage covert channel on android smartwatch using status bar notifications
8. Drucker, P.F.: Internet of Things position paper on standardization for IoT technologies (2015). URL http://www.internet-of-things-research.eu/pdf/IERC_Position_Paper_IoT_Standardization_Final.pdf
9. Evans, D.: The Internet of Things: How the next evolution of the Internet is changing everything (2011). URL https://www.cisco.com/web/about/ac79/docs/innov/IoT_IBSG_0411FINAL.pdf
10. Gasior, W., Yang, L.: Exploring covert channel in android platform. In: Cyber Security (CyberSecurity), 2012 International Conference on (2012)

11. Gasior, W.C., Yang, L.: Network covert channels on the android platform. Cyber Security and Information Intelligence Research 2011 (2011)
12. Girling, C.G.: Covert channels in lan's. IEEE Transactions on Software Engineering **SE-13**(2), 292–296 (1987). DOI 10.1109/TSE.1987.233153
13. Lampson, B.W.: A note on the confinement problem. Communications of the ACM **16** (1973)
14. Marforio, C., Ritzdorf, H., Francillon, A., Capkun, S.: Analysis of the communication between colluding applications on modern smartphones. In: Proceedings of the 28th Annual Computer Security Applications Conference, pp. 51–60. ACM (2012)
15. Popper, B.: Google announces over 2 billion monthly active devices on android (2017). URL https://www.theverge.com/2017/5/17/15654454/android-reaches-2-billion-monthly-active-users
16. Radhakrishnan, S., Uluagac, A., Beyah, R.: Realizing an 802.11-based covert timing channel using off-the-shelf wireless cards. In: Global Communications Conference (GLOBECOM), 2013 IEEE, pp. 722–728 (2013)
17. Shrestha, P.L., Hempel, M., Rezaei, F., Sharif, H.: A support vector machine-based framework for detection of covert timing channels. IEEE Transactions on Dependable and Secure Computing **13**(2), 274–283 (2016). DOI 10.1109/TDSC.2015.2423680
18. Sikder, A.K., Aksu, H., Uluagac, A.S.: 6thsense: A context-aware sensor-based attack detector for smart devices. In: 26th USENIX Security Symposium (USENIX Security 17), pp. 397–414. Vancouver, BC (2017)
19. Simmons, G.J.: The prisoners' problem and the subliminal channels. In: D. Chaum (ed.) Advances in Cryptology, pp. 51–67. Springer US (1984)
20. Zander, S., Armitage, G., Branch, P.: A survey of covert channels and countermeasures in computer network protocols. IEEE Communications Surveys Tutorials **9**(3), 44–57 (2007). DOI 10.1109/COMST.2007.4317620

Insider Threat Detection: Machine Learning Way

Mehul S. Raval, Ratnik Gandhi, and Sanjay Chaudhary

Abstract The chapter aims to cover and analyse contributions from machine learning to detect an insider threat. It presents various launch mechanisms and details impact of an insider attack on various sectors. Presenting state-of-the-art for detecting insider threat based on psychology, criminology and game theory, the chapter also covers case studies showing use of Machine Learning for anomaly detection. In real life, malicious events are low in number. The chapter will showcase detection of such a low occurring anomaly from a large dataset accurately. The chapter specifically focuses on USB device insertion or removal event and apply linear regression followed by Cook's and Mahalanobis distance to identify malicious activities of the user. Subsequently, it applies Neural Network and Support Vector Machine to login activities of a user to successfully demonstrates detection of an anomaly behaviour. It concludes discussing future directions that uses combination of methods from natural language processing, behavioural analysis, sentiment analysis, and machine learning for insider threat detection.

1 Introduction

Identification of an adversary is one of the fundamental questions in cybersecurity, which is hard to solve. In today's technological era the boundary between "friend" and "rival" is growing fuzzier. The world is separated by borders, but the Internet is diminishing boundaries. Attacks on individuals, organizations, Governments can be planted anywhere on the Internet and executed to cause harm of unprecedented scale. This demands knowledge of various types of attacks, their execution and scale of their impact. The following subsections defines the insider attack, most common mechanism for its launch and sectors which are impacted by this attack.

M. S. Raval (✉) · R. Gandhi · S. Chaudhary
School of Engineering and Applied Science, Ahmedabad University, Ahmedabad, Gujarat, India
e-mail: mehul.raval@ahduni.edu.in; ratnik.gandhi@ahduni.edu.in;
sanjay.chaudhary@ahduni.edu.in

© Springer Nature Switzerland AG 2018
M. Conti et al. (eds.), *Versatile Cybersecurity*, Advances in Information
Security 72, https://doi.org/10.1007/978-3-319-97643-3_2

1.1 Attack, Launch and Impact

Usually, attacks which are hidden and persisting for a long time, are most damaging. Such attacks gradually bleed social, financial, and political infrastructure. On a large scale, a country's general election can be rigged [29], or a referendum can be manipulated. On a smaller scale, an attacker can influence an outcome of a tender process of a company [8]. Generally, databases of various systems or organisations are one of the most important IT assets. This makes them one of the most vulnerable points for an insider attack. The other vulnerable points are file servers, mobile devices, endpoint devices, business applications and network. Customer identity data is the most targeted entity followed by sensitive financial data, intellectual property and company's data. The type of tactics used by perpetrators to break through are as follows [8]: (1) hacking; (2) use of malware; (3) through stolen or weak password; (4) snooping during social events; (5) physical harm.

Most organizations and Governments build a defense against the outside actors but worry little about an "insider threat". The access authorization and the user being insider/outsider is defined by the organization. Typically, behaviour of these persons is to cause harm to people, system, data, organization, and business. The other form of insider threat [31] including activities of non-malicious actors: there are careless and naïve users causing an accidental security breach. It occurs when organization for which they work has not clearly communicated IT policies. The second category includes users who deliberately ignore the IT policy. The last category of users, will deliberately breach and cause willful harm. The chapter will focus on a malicious and willful insider. Formally, insider and insider threat are defined as follows [7, 31]:

Insider Personnel with an authorized access to resources and data of an organization.

Insider threat It's an action by an insider to harm and place organization or its resources at risk.

Insiders collude and organize crimes with multiple insiders in different sections of organization(s). They bypass the security processes and remain undetected. Such users/persons are categorized as active [37] insiders. An insider may masquerade and cause physical damage [5]. There could be a passive insider [37] who would provide only information. However, insiders tend to remain hidden and use deceit for activities. In most cases insider targeted the following [2]:

- stealing information for identity theft;
- modifying credit-worthiness to give higher credit score;
- creating fake credentials.

Insiders primarily copies or modifies customer data during working hours. They use authorized access to bypass integrity checks for copying, modifying or deleting data. The methods used by insiders to cause a breach are as follows:

1. Use social engineering to obtain credentials or password, e.g., after leaving organization to convince ex-colleague(s) to run a search on the database(s) to collect information. This can be used to perform insider trading for some other company.
2. Authorized use of systems e.g., an insider working for a bank steals record and sells it to conspirators.
3. Bypass security procedures laid out by organization e.g., in accounts section of a company two persons collude to issue a pay-cheque.
4. Compromise accounts e.g., an insider working for a bank modifies customer account in exchange for money.
5. The endpoint devices used in IT infrastructure is reported to be the most favoured tool to launch an insider attack [30]. This choice is followed by use of mobile devices and network to launch insider attacks.

According to a report [1], 1.4 billion data records have been compromised in 2016. It is an increase of 86% compared to 2015. In the same year, Yahoo! reported breach of 1.5 billion users account. The leading data breach is through identity theft followed by account access-based breach [1]. The trend is to attack large datasets with personally identifiable information (PII) and 25% of such data breach is due to inside actors [8]. In a study [2], 24 instances of breach due to insiders were covered. It reported two types of insider criminal activity with losses running into several million dollars:

- Insider colluding with external agency or groups.
- Multiple insiders in an organization form group and participate in unlawful activities.

In a damaging case, an insider stole $48 million from city tax office over a period of two decades [2]. In another case, a manager at motor vehicles department caused a loss of a quarter million dollars [2]. A software engineer was arrested with thousands of technical documents and was convicted of stealing trade secrets [32]. There are reports of insider selling social security number (SSN) records at $15–$20 per record [2]. Another paper [3] showed that insider can potentially steal million data records from a credit card, insurance, or healthcare company. Quoting US Justice Department survey, authors in [4] reported that high percentage of cyber-incidents are due to insiders. The CERT division at Carnegie Mellon University [5] maintains a summary of various reports and [6] covers more than 1000 insider cases and describes a practice that organization may undertake to prevent and detect an insider threat.

Top industries impacted by insider threat are public healthcare, finance, retail and accommodation [8]. Malicious insider attack includes IT sabotage [7], i.e., use of organization's information systems to cause harm; theft of intellectual properties (IP); fraud by using IT infrastructure for illegal modification of data for personal gain or cause identity threat. It has been reported in [2] that most insiders committed a crime for financial gains. In fact, the crime involving insider holding a managerial position went off for the longer duration and scale of losses were larger. One can study an interesting case of insider attack in bank Société Générale causing a trading loss of $7 billion [33, 34]. Among other charges, the trader was convicted for illegal access to bank computers. The trader joined the bank in the year 2000 and was promoted in the year 2005. According to bank reports, fictitious trading began in late 2006 and early 2007 with small transactions. The reports indicated that trader managed to remain undetected for 2 years using the trading knowledge gained earlier. The trader was a technologist [33] and managed to stay below bank surveillance radar.

The insider attack industry survey [30] has following important findings and it reaffirms some of the above discussion:

1. Personnel with access to sensitive data e.g., IT admin, poses the biggest threat followed by threats from contractors or consultants and regular employees.
2. It was observed that insider attacks have increased in last year i.e., 2017.
3. The remediation cost from insider attack is also increasing and it is also difficult to quantify such cost.

Some of the broad findings on illicit insider activities in US financial sectors covering 80 cases are as follows [9]:

1. "Low and slow" mode cause the most damage and took a long time to detect. On an average, the start of the fraud took place after 5 years of employment and it took 32 months for the organization to detect it. The early detection has minimized actual impact.
2. The means employed for attack are not very sophisticated. Very few subjects had a high technical role or conducted fraud using specialized means. In many cases, insider used authorized to access and used non-technical means to bypass set process.
3. Fraud caused by managers ($200,105 on average) is more damaging and longer as compared to non-managers ($112,188 on average). The attacks by higher echelon organization lasted twice as long compared to non-managers. The accountants were most damaging and were caught after many months.
4. Most cases came into limelight due to audit, complaint by customer or suspicion from the team member.
5. Very few cases used software and logs to detect insider activity.
6. Personally-identifiable information was the prime target for insider attacks.

The above discussions showcased the gravity of the situation when an attack is launched by an insider. It would be interesting to study motivation for an insider to launch an attack against their own organisation.

1.2 Motivations for Attacks

Motivation represents gains made by insider through an attack and it could be internally or externally induced. Some of the primary and secondary factors driving motivations are [38]: money, divided loyalties, revenge, disgruntlement, coercion, thrill and recognition. A report [30], listed broad motivations for an insider to subvert an organization are: (1) monetization of sensitive data; (2) fraud and sabotage; (3) IP theft and espionage [39]. The subversion happens when individuals and organization goals are misaligned. Certain strata of people in the organization will then follow their own interest.

In recent years, there is a significant change in the relationship between an organization and individuals. A couple of decades back one would enter an organization and serve for many years. That mindset, in today's era, is gone and both the organization and individuals focus on high short-term gains. The motivation for subversive activities has been classified into three categories [35, 36], namely; (1) political; (2) greed; (3) anger. The political reasons are often overlooked but they are a major cause of concern [36]. Some of the political reasons are [35]: (1) user feels a threat to their jobs; (2) there is a change of management and working conditions; (3) dislike towards the control and leadership; (4) fear of losing importance in a group and the organization. An interesting article discussed political reasons for a software project to fail [34]. It has been argued that software projects are fragile and heavily influenced by a subversive behaviour.

The second motivation is greed; it can range from taking printer pages, stationary to pilfering the data. The third motivation is anger towards the organization. The previous two could be driven by the latter. Anger can also lead to an act of vandalism and causing physical harm to resources. This can also happen after termination of the employee. An organization must utilize not only technological means but also use intangible factors like behaviour, psychology, language, culture, history to thwart insider.

1.3 Dimensions of Understand Insider Risk

The four dimensions to understand risk due to insider threat are [31]: (1) The organization; (2) The IT system; (3) The individual; (4) The environment. The organization is at the centre as it sets the procedure and grants access rights to employees. This governs boundaries to decide which actors should be treated as insiders and types of access to them. The organization also lays security policies which can be used to trigger ambiguous behaviours. This helps to define subversive actions. Most importantly organization defines a culture which impacts a great deal of insider's behaviour. In case of the IT system, centralized computing structure benefits as it is less risky. Its restricted scope limits number of people accessing the IT system. However, such a structure is extremely restrictive in ubiquitous computing era. Every employee in the organization should have multiple endpoint devices that are hooked to the IT system. This has enlarged scope of IT system and it now serves a large set of people with different privileges. As discussed in [31], the risk of insider threat varies depending on the role of the IT system.

An insider with a malicious intention has received significant attention from the research community. A personality style of an employee can also be a behavioural indicator of a malicious user [40]. These styles do not mean absolute malevolent attitude, but they may provide a potential pointer. Some personality style discussed in [40] are self-centered, arrogant, manipulative, cold, grandiose, self-deception, and defensive. It has been shown by researchers that non-malicious actors can also cause harm to the organization. However, the intent plays the most important role in deciding response to an insider action. A malicious actor should be severely reprimanded and non-malicious one should be dealt in an appropriate manner. This means that the organization policy must be flexible to deal with different flavours of insiders.

The environment is very intangible, and it is governed by society, culture, ethics, rules, and law of the land. The conservative environment increases the chance of insider action. A value system in an organization and individuals is shaped by the environment in which they live; e.g., views towards anti-piracy varies across countries. The alienation of organization policy from the norms observed by the law or prevailing in societal practice may increase the risk of insider threat.

1.4 Contribution of the Chapter

The chapter proposes to use Machine Learning (ML) for an insider threat detection. It highlights that an insider threat detection needs inputs from technical as well as social sciences. It covers existing protective mechanism in place to defend against insider threats. Various insider threat models i.e., agent-based, game theoretic, system dynamics, Bayesian network and network analysis are discussed through state-of-the-art review.

In real life, malicious events are rarely reported and to top it up they are low in number. Therefore, the chapter uses CERT dataset and presents a case study for detection of the malicious insider. The goal is to accurately detect USB device insertion or removal anomaly from a large dataset. One can identify insider threat by learning normal or baseline behaviour to segregate anomaly. The chapter covers three different approaches for the anomaly detection:

1. Use of linear regression and distance measures (Cook's and Mahalanobis).
2. Four-layer Artificial Neural Network (ANN).
3. Support Vector Machine (SVM) with different kernels.

It culminates with future directions that suggest combination of methods from natural language processing, behavioural analysis, sentiment analysis and machine learning for insider threat detection.

1.5   Chapter Organization

The chapter is organized as follows: Sect. 2.2: existing defence mechanism in place by the organization, Sect. 2.3: approaches for insider threat detection with the focus on approaches using machine learning for anomaly detection. Sect. 2.4, covers the case study on CERT dataset and use of Linear Regression, ANN, and SVM for insider detection. Discussions and conclusions are finally drawn in Sect. 2.5.

2   The Defence Against Insider Threat

It is necessary to address threat, vulnerabilities, and consequences of security risks as they are important to understanding insider threat. The goal for any insider threat research should be, to have effective detection, prevention, mitigation, punishment and remediation. The commonly used defensive means against Insider threat is covered in this section. Many protective mechanisms are placed by an organization to defend against insider threat. Some of the commonly employed means are as follows [37]:

- employee screening by Human Resource (HR) department;
- activity monitoring and auditing;
- security processes like physical security, material and device control, counterintelligence;
- hard and soft access controls;
- create an organizational policy for dealing with insider threat;
- provide training to users.

The devices and infrastructure used for information consumption have dramatically changed over years. However, the defence mechanisms have not kept pace with these changes, e.g., it is believed that securing the network periphery or by controlling devices will protect the network. The structure and policy of an organization are treated as static entities while their surroundings are rapidly changing. A single click by a user or plugging a bad USB stick can trigger malware attack. The technology is becoming personal and this means that attacks can be more personalized. Current security mechanisms are static, and they must evolve and deliver at the level of personal security as well [36]. The bottom line is that human in the loop is the key. The growing number of insider attacks is an indicator that the current protection techniques are expensive, interfering, and they are not working. It is important to consider a systemic approach which is more holistic [37]. It is important that along with technical angle, the system must influence insider's individualities.

2.1 Policies and Procedures for Negative Work-Related Events

After an attack(s) it is also important to find the perpetrator(s), what damage has been done, what was the motive. These are difficult questions to answer. The organizations can store and process data during impact. Based on learning, one can design strategies and policy to minimize the impact of attacks. The studies [7, 9] indicate that management must evolve a policy to deal with 'negative work-related event'. They further recommend laying down procedures for account management, password policy, checking system admins, tracking system integrity, providing remote access, reviewing system logs and disaster recovery plans. The modern-day recovery should be a good mix of technical and psychological component [37]. In another interesting study [38] on insider threat made the following observations about behavioural traits of an insider or a saboteur:

1. They act in a peculiar way during stress.
2. Their behaviour changes during the subversive event.
3. They may violate rules before the onset of an attack.
4. Most often organization fails to observe the signs of acting out.

2.2 Multimodal Approach for Insider Detection

The studies [7, 9, 38] recommends that early detection of an insider attack or its occurrence can be negated with the comprehensive participation of every stakeholder i.e., management, employees, IT team, HR team, and security personnel. Resorting to the only technical solution has limitations. Detection, response, IT and organization's de jure and de facto policies and procedures play a very important role in preventing insider attack. Many organizations also provide security awareness training to their employees. It had been observed that many threats are detected by employees of the organization [9, 30]. The training creates a community which is aware of events; both within and outside an organization. It can prevent insider attacks and protect employees. In case of very high stakes, an outsider would need cooperation from employees. Some aware employees can maximize deterrence against a malicious insider.

There are several organizations involved in understanding insider threat such as Pacific Northwest National Laboratory (PNNL), Carnegie Mellon University/Software engineering institute (CERT) program, US air force research laboratory [42]. The researchers are working on to develop cognitive workshops and game-based training for carrying out relevant experiments. There are projects dedicated to cyber and behavioural modeling to predict malicious insider activities. The CERT program does a comprehensive study on cybercrime in US infrastructure and communicates results to Government, Industry, and public at large.

3   Approaches in Insider Detection

The section covers various approaches for insider detection. It covers modelling-based approaches and discuss insider threat as anomaly detection through log analysis. An example is provided for understanding of the reader. The section then weaves through different approaches for insider detection and the organization is shown in Fig. 6.

The modelling-based approaches [68, 70, 75] for insider threat detection can be classified as follows and shown in Fig. 1.

Early methods took a sequential approach to deal with insider threat [41]. The protection begins by excluding the potential adversaries, limiting their access and their need to know things. In case an adversary penetrates, the approach is focused on detecting, delaying and then responding to malicious attempts. In case adversary launches a successful attack, the strategy is to minimize the loss. The block diagram in Fig. 2 shows a sequential approach in [41].

3.1   Systemic View for Insider Threat Detection

In sequential approach, each phase operates independently, i.e., in a piecewise mode and it has a varying degree of effectiveness. The systemic view in insider defence is missing and the approach [41] does not throw light on the interactions between

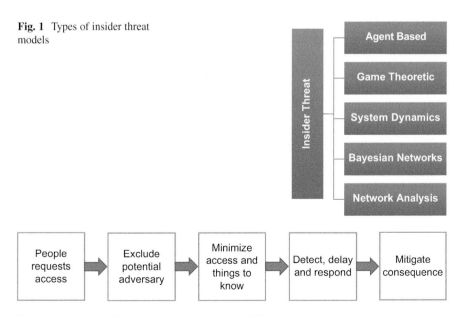

Fig. 1 Types of insider threat models

Fig. 2 Insider protection through sequential phases [41]

each block. It is important to understand interaction and interdependencies between all the stakeholders for effective insider threat mitigation. The employee life cycle model based on system dynamics is also developed for minimizing insider threat [37]. It models the evolution of insider within an organization. Based on the need to know bases the information access model is developed to legitimize access to the employees. It also models how a malicious insider may attempt to get an access to information. The employee life cycle model enacts different scenarios based on system parameters and compares it with baseline scenarios. It investigates interactions between employee population and protection measures in the system. This helps to understand existing lacunae and therefore, modulates system to strengthen it. The results generated by model [37] are based on hypothetical data and does not reflect the real-world situation.

One must note that the authentic data indicating scope and impact of the insider threat is difficult to obtain. Usually, correct information is never revealed by the organization due to fear of losing reputation. On the other hand, large data volume is utmost important to build strong models with accurate predictions.

3.2   Insider Threat Detection as an Anomaly Detection

This chapter is focused on machine learning to thwart insider threat using anomaly detection. One can identify insider threat by learning *normal* or *baseline* behaviour to segregate anomaly. One can study how users access the data and identify suspicious behaviour by machine learning. The identification mechanism at data access point provides a good chance of insider threat detection. It is important to look at both, the users and the way they access information. The common abuse which should be flagged may include; account abuse e.g., using superuser account; direct access to sensitive data; excessive database access in comparison to normal behaviour or excessive use of network resources for file transfers; repeated failed logins to many database or systems; user login through another corporate account.

3.2.1   Log Analysis

Log analysis is used for automatic monitoring of big-data generated in the cloud or servers. It is an integral part of forensics which is done with different goals; i.e., establishing evidence for crime; data recovery from server crash; detecting network vulnerability; finding and tracking activities of an insider [71]. It can be used for forensic analysis or as preventive measure [72]. It is important to use appropriate logs based on the event under investigation and a strong analysis improves the chances of detecting an insider threat [73]. Usually a log management is achieved through: (1) Log analysis; (2) Event correlation. Latter requires former to filter unwanted data and execute the actions. It is important to discover cause of an event and find evidence to prove them. The event correlation analyses

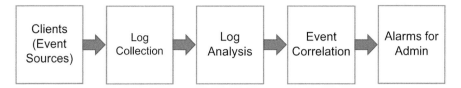

Fig. 3 Typical system architecture for log management

individual information chunk and filter events. It compresses large batch of data into manageable alarms for system or security analyst. Figure 3 shows a typical system architecture for log management.

An event is usually the action identified a system program. Complexity of event varies depending on number of clients in the network. The log collection unit collects data from clients and it paints a complete picture of the system state to an administrator(s). Usually, a basic unit is log file with security and system logs. The log analysis may use a rule or pattern based for recognizing input event type. It may also define scope for event correlation unit which is used to extract knowledge from the information. It decides correlation amongst different events to choose malicious events like insertion of Universal Serial Bus (USB) stick at odd working hours, rebooting of server, network tunnelling request.

Figure 4 reflects popular Machine Learning approaches used for an insider threat detection. The basic algorithms are divided into supervised and unsupervised form of learning. The early example and case-study covered in this chapter focuses on supervised learning with Artificial Neural Network (ANN) and Support Vector Machine (SVM).

The chapter present an early example of anomaly detection to understand some of the assertions about insider threat detection. The later sections deal with exhaustive state-of-the-art reviews and detailed case studies on anomaly detection.

3.3 Early Example

There have been several studies that characterize server log data as time series data and present various algorithms for anomaly detection [23–27]. For example, if the model is applied to network traffic to identify attacks like Denial of Services (DoS), these techniques must then observe potential attacks through logs. The traffic profile can be characterized by parameters such as IP packages, new connections etc. Below, is an example of outlier or anomaly detection on time series data on Yahoo's benchmark dataset [28]. First, linear regression on the data is applied and then statistical methods such as Cook's distance [73] and Mahalanobis distance [74] are used to identify anomalies. Note that points with large Cook's distance have a larger effect on the trend of the data thus can be termed as an outlier if the value is above the threshold (usually chosen 4/n, where n is the number of points in the dataset).

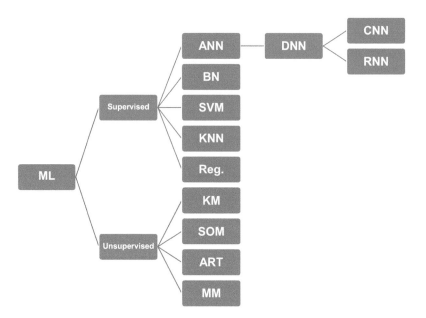

Fig. 4 Hierarchy of ML algorithms. ANN Artificial Neural Network, DNN Deep Neural Network, CNN Convolutional Neural Network, RNN Recurrent Neural Network, BN Bayesian Network, SVM Support Vector Machine, KNN K Nearest Neighbours, Reg. Regression, KM K-Means, SOM Self Organizing Maps, ART Adaptive Resonance Theory, and MM Mixture Models

Cook's distance of data i is given by

$$\frac{\sum_{j=1}^{n}\left(y_j - y_{j(i)}\right)^2}{p \cdot MSE} \tag{1}$$

where, y_j is the jth response, $y_{j(i)}$ is the jth response without considering i, MSE is mean squared error, p is number of coefficients in regression model.

Mahalonobis distance of data Z_i in the matrix $Z = [XY]$ is given by

$$\sqrt{(Z_i - \mu)\, S^{-1}\, (Z_i - \mu)} \tag{2}$$

where, X and Y are vectors of observed dataset, μ is mean of data points and S is the covariance matrix.

$$S = \begin{bmatrix} \mathrm{cov}\,(X, X) & con\,(X, Y) \\ \mathrm{cov}\,(Y, X) & \mathrm{cov}\,(Y, Y) \end{bmatrix} \tag{3}$$

It is clear from Fig. 5b, c that there are less black coloured data points in 5b compared to 5c. This means the Cook's distance can detect most outliers (in fact more than Mahalanobis distance) given in benchmark information. In other words,

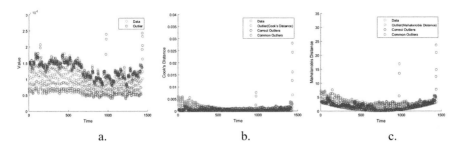

a.   b.   c.

Fig. 5 (**a**) Yahoo time series benchmark dataset with marked data and anomaly points; (**b**) Cook's distance and Mahalanobis distance of Data; (**c**) Outliers – True and False positive (green), Benchmark positive (Black) and both positive (Red)

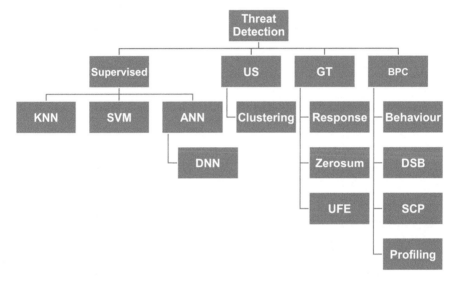

Fig. 6 Organization of literature review. KNN K Nearest Neighbours, SVM Support Vector Machine, ANN Artificial Neural Network, DNN Deep Neural Network, US Unsupervised, GT Game theory, UFE Utility Function and Equilibrium, BPC Behavoiur, Psychology, and Criminology, DSB Deterrence and Social Bond Theory; SCP Social and Crime Prevention

Cook's distance is essentially not missing any malicious activities. On the other hand, there are more green points in 5b compared to 5c and thus there are many more false alarms of malicious activities in Cook's distance approach.

The machine learning for an insider threat detection is covered exhaustively in next few subsections. The organization of literature review is shown in Fig. 6.

3.4 Anomaly Detection Using Supervised Learning

Current systems are unable to detect intrusions hidden in an encrypted payload with non-intrusive means. The paper [44] considers the problem of intrusion and extrusion detection at the network layer in the encrypted environment over the Internet. The motivation comes from the fact that knowledge-based systems are unable to detect attacks on encrypted payloads and behavioural systems suffer from high false alarm rates. Thus, both fail to detect such intrusions. The authors proposed a new architecture of intrusion/extrusion detection system that uses similarity between data in the form of correlations and identifies malicious activities. As the system uses only correlations to identify variations from standard behaviour it does not require a prior learning.

The authors [45] addresses the problem of insider threat using various monitoring and auditing techniques. The work proposes an architecture for handling insider threat, which had three components: decoy document-generation, network, and host-based sensor. The decoy component increases uncertainty during authentication of documents. The network component in conjunction with the decoy is used to trap malicious user and isolate their activities. Finally, the host-based sensor senses malicious activities by auditing user activities. The user of anomaly detection is carried out primarily at host-based level.

The paper [46] proposes a scheme called RADISH (Real-time Anomaly Detection in Streaming Heterogeneity). They use real-time streaming data analytics and machine-learning techniques for identifying normal vs. malicious activities of users. Method primarily uses correlations among multi-stream of data for identifying baseline vs. malicious behaviour. The architecture is multitier, open and offers incremental development of models to perform predictive analytics. The authors show experimental results using K-Nearest neighbour (KNN) for detecting an anomaly in user behaviour. They perform experiments on the r2 dataset of CERT.

The paper [47] focuses on human bio signals and studies balance in access control intent vs. identity for finding malicious activities of users. As knowledge about intent does not translate to exact risk, it is difficult to identify nature of risk in systems. The authors use intent likelihood of the malicious activity execution using brain signal amplitude and categorize activities at various risk levels. For this, they use visual stimulus and perform involuntary electroencephalogram. Intent and intent motivation levels then give information about anomalies against the baseline brain amplitude signals. As one of the significant departure from others, the work capitalizes on the non-identity based measures for detecting malicious activities. The authors also show experiments of their proposed system for 30 real users.

In another approach based on supervised outlier detection, the authors [16] adapt external threat models for insider attacks. They track user activity at all levels of the operating system (OS). The authors adapt method for external threat and tightly integrated them with OS kernel. One must note that the work identifies anomalous records and not the users. The authors [16] identify 7 types of system exploits like; privilege_escalation, removable_media, export_via_email, change_file_extension, encipher-decipher operation, unusual search and malware_installation. They use n-grams, histograms and parameter-based approaches to detect insider threat by supervised outlier detection. The Hamming distance is used on the validation set to find records at a kth greatest distance. The presented results show that n-gram approach does perform well compared to histogram-based approach.

3.4.1 Anomaly Detection Using Deep Neural Networks

An organization's network activity monitoring is also useful for insider threat mitigation. However, volume, velocity, and veracity of data can overwhelm a human observer. The deep learning models scale the analytical capabilities of humans. The authors [18, 19] propose an online deep learning based unsupervised approach to detect an anomaly in network activity from the system logs. It was developed with an aim to help analyst quickly filter through large data volume. The approach decomposes scores into a contribution from individual behaviour features for better analytics. The approaches do not model insider threat behaviour explicitly as it can vary widely. The user activity may vary widely from few seconds to an hour and therefore, quantification of normal behaviour is very difficult. Also, an attacker aims to mimic the normal behaviour.

The authors [18, 19] train Deep Neural Network (DNN) and Recurrent Neural Network (RNN) for malicious activity detection. The authors claimed that time and space complexity of the method are constant functions of stream duration and cache is not infinitely long. The model was trained continuously and adapted to changing pattern. The stream of system log was modelled as interleaved user sequences with metadata. This provides the exact context for an activity on the network. The decisions are made as soon as new data enter the system. In one of the earliest attempts authors [20] trained a single layer neural network to detect intrusion detection. The work [21] is based on RNN to train on Unix command line arguments and predict intrusion. Recently authors in [22] used auto-encoders for online learning setting. An ensemble of anomaly detection methods is fed with logs from web, firewall, and the authors also incorporated analyst feedback.

3.5   Unsupervised Approach for Anomaly Detection

The work [48] focused on the collaborative information system and detection of insider threat. The authors proposed Community Anomaly Detection System (CADS) for detecting the malicious behaviour of users. The method is unsupervised learning approach and uses access logs for identifying threats. The core idea is to design two components (1) relation pattern extractions: for identifying formed communities in the given user pool and (2) anomaly prediction: use statistical methods for identifying a deviation in user behaviour against a pool. The work also performs experiments on 3 months access logs from real electronic healthcare records and show improvement in accuracy with the proposed system. The work [49] was focused on the use of human behaviour parameters (e.g., system logins) as indicators for identifying malicious or non-malicious users. They use regression and correlation for predicting time windows for malicious activities and confirm their observations with experiments on CERT dataset.

3.6   Anomaly Detection Using Game Theoretic Approaches

Game theoretic approaches are becoming popular to model insider threat detection. Game theory is "the study of mathematical models of conflict and cooperation between intelligent rational decisions makers" [69]. It can be used to model behavioural relations and logical decision making in humans and computers. The decision maker must anticipate the response of those affected.

3.6.1   Behavioural Relations and Game Theory

Authors in [10] developed Behavioural Analysis of Insider Threat (BAIT) framework to identify insider threat using behavioural cues. It used bootstrapped algorithms to separate honest and normal users from anomalous users. Their model considers the following conditions; training dataset is imbalanced, the size of training data is very small, the attacks are carried out by humans' independent of past attacks, and attacks are happening along the normal behaviour. The authors used 35 round game and recruited users on Amazon Mechanical Turk. They proposed a suite of seven algorithms based on Support Vector Machine (SVM) and Multinomial Naive Bayes. The authors used linear kernels, polynomial kernels, and Radial Basis Function (RBF) kernels and used cross-validation during testing. Series of features were developed for training and validation. Some of their interesting observations are: malicious users are likely to be more active, they fetch significantly more sensitive information and send more data out of the organization, they fetch significantly less unclassified data. However, some of the hypothesis could not be validated statistically.

The work [57] presented a case study of an insider cyber-threat about a long-term fraud. It also presented a simulation model to support the case study. They examined the motives and trade-offs that organizations make in considering their internal security systems. Their perspective places a counterbalance on the literature that studies organizations and insider play a zero-sum game and thus motivating investment in security.

The works [58–59] considered human behaviour and discuss game-theoretic models. Authors [58] presented a game-theoretic agent model that can be used for bargaining or negotiations, while the latter result [59] discusses uses of game theory to model bounded rationality and various risk attitudes. The authors used cognitive theories (coordination games) and machine learning model for predicting human behaviour and presented their results. The work in [59] also discusses that in real-life behaviour, most people do not follow strict rationality and thus only game-theoretic models are insufficient for modelling human behaviour – they suggested the use of hybrid models.

The paper [60] talked about human adversaries with bounded rationality. They used game theory to model adversarial decision making and apply optimization techniques for avoiding adversarial actions. The paper defined a subjective utility function and through experiments with 547 human subjects showed that human behaviour can be modelled accurately with Stackelberg security games. They further showed their experiments with security intelligence expert and observed that their algorithm for modelling human behaviour outperforms existing other approaches.

3.6.2 Zero Sum Stochastic Game

The set of works [52–55] present models for analysing the security problem from the perspective of Game Theory. Most of these works considered bounded rationality of the players and computed Quantal Response Equilibrium. The work [56] models the insider threat scenario as an "insider game" – a two players zero-sum stochastic game between the insider malicious user and system administrator. The models allowed inferring the strategy by an insider and decided the best counter move strategy for defence. The paper described a simplistic two players zero-sum stochastic game and compute Nash equilibrium strategy using non-linear programming. As a Nash equilibrium defines an optimal strategy of the players – an equilibrium outcome of the game means the insider will play the best strategy against a defender while the defending administrator will also opt for a best defence strategy given insiders optimal strategy. The authors suggested that the game will be in equilibrium and an insider will not be able to take any further malicious action.

3.6.3 Utility Functions and Equilibrium

Interesting results [61, 62] modelled interaction between an insider and Intrusion Detection System (IDS) as an extensive form game which uses Neumann-Morgenstern utility function. The paper focused on Quantal Response Equilibrium (QRE) as the players in these games displayed bounded rationality. With the use of QRE, authors predicted behaviour of players in the game and suggested actions by IDS to protect the system. The paper proposed a detailed model for the proposed system. An important difference between [61, 62] being latter focused more on algorithm design for efficient computation of equilibrium solution using cutting-plane algorithms. The paper considers modelling of malicious user with game theory and information fusion-based algorithms. The paper [63] builds dynamic Bayesian network model for considering multiple information of user behaviour and avoids the use of IDS. Their model fused multiple information using junction tree algorithm. The game is modelled based on this information and a QRE equilibrium is considered as a solution. The authors further perform experiments and showed improved equilibrium convergence with high precision (at an added cost of computation time).

3.7   Anomaly Detection Using Behaviour, Psychology, Criminology and User Profiling

Detecting a malicious insider using machine learning is very challenging due to following reasons [10]. The number of detected malicious insider is very small as compared to honest users. Hence this produces imbalanced data set which may generate biased results in favour of majority i.e., non-malicious users. The public domain also does not have exhaustive testing and training dataset. Malicious users are synthetically generated based on the past attacks for improving datasets. There is no comprehensive study which targets behaviour of the potential insider. The user activity is also very unpredictable in terms of time variation. Several interesting theories from social science, behavioural analysis, and criminology are presented to map behaviour of an insider in [50]. Some of the specific interesting theories are general deterrence theory; social bond theory, social learning theory; theory of planned behaviour; situational crime prevention. They are relevant to an organization planning to build threat prevention mechanism.

3.7.1   Anomaly Detection Using Behavioural Analysis

Authors [11] presented a monitoring tool for file and directory location, file content analysis and file integrity check. The file and directory location would point to misuse of the server by looking at the placement of file in specific type of directory. The content analysis points to the specific signature of a worm or a virus and integrity check helps to detect the compromised target. The authors also developed an Evaluated Potential Threat (EPT) metric to characterize user behaviour. In [12] insider threat security architecture (ITSA) had been presented. The paper carried a hypothetical example of a database admin of an insurance company who went rogue. The threat agent is aiming at stealing money from the company. A bogus claim of $100 K was inserted in the database but security policy auditing prevented the payment. The administrator reduces a claim by $1–$ 99,999 and deletes all traces of manipulation for logs. The ITSA framework has a security alarm to capture such malicious behaviour and it alerts authority about administrator's action.

The authors [13] defined insider threats and presented approaches for threat mitigation using technology, sociology or their combination. They concluded that single strategy to mitigate threat will not work and the combination of techniques is required. Authors in [14] used access control strategies to prevent insider attack. The implementation of access control poses a significant challenge for the organization in service sector like finance, healthcare. The access control interferes with routine activities of users. The authors concluded that prevention can minimize risk as the size of attack's space is reduced.

3.7.2   Deterrence and Social Bond Theory

The general deterrence theory of criminology [64] suggests that people make choice based on the perceived benefit weighted against the associated cost. The choice is independent of work to be done for achieving objectives. The focus on deterrence can be brought in by education and outreach activities within the organization to all the stakeholders. Specifically, the penalties and cost associated with misuse could be highlighted. This step is subsequently followed by prevention, detection, and remedial steps. The social bond theory [65] suggests that the probability of insider misusing the system depends on social bonds with associates. A person is more likely to cause harm if associates have criminal outlook and antisocial behaviour. This can be captured by observing person's interest and interaction with the social environment. For example, working with colleagues, types of projects in which person is associated, commitment to excellence, spending time with family and so on.

3.7.3   Social and Crime Prevention Theories

The social learning theory is also like social bond theory and suggests that person is more likely to commit a crime if he or she remains associated with a criminal. The theory of planned behaviour [66] differentiates intentions for insider crime and its execution. The intentions represent formulation phase which is shaped by the perception of others on the action. The prevailing social norms may inhibit certain actions, or they may also support the action. There are also control factors which checks whether a person has a belief to control behaviour and goal realization. During the execution phase, the insider will wait for the opportunity to strike based on intentions. Situational crime prevention theory [67] suggests that insider crime can occur when a person has a strong motive and opportunity. The crime prevention can be achieved by either denying opportunity to a malicious user or killing the motive for a crime. The state-of-the-art discussed in this section is based on learning from the above theories.

Authors in [15] combined psychology and computational approach using Bayesian nets to conquer insider threat. They used 12 signals; disgruntlement, accepting criticism, anger management, disengagement, disregard for authority, performance, stress, confrontational behaviour, personal issues, self-centeredness, lack of dependability, and absenteeism to detect trace of insider. One may note that each of these 12 indicators are not a good measure individually, but their combination can be a good indicator of future events. The authors used artificial neural network with above indicators to develop the models and the results are validated by two human experts. The work used synthetic data for 100 employees and injected 'threat agents'. The experiments gave a fairly good performance with ability to work with missing values. However, several questions remained unanswered; like, value of 12 indicators for each user; source of data for such indicators was not revealed; the experiments were done using synthetic dataset which may not scale to real world.

3.7.4 Job and Role-Based User Profiling

The work [43] addresses the problem of insider threat to organizations by proposing an automated system. One of the important contributions of this work is the proposal of a job and role-based profiling of users. The authors proposed tree structured profile for jobs, roles of users and compared with their activities during the period. The paper proposed feature extraction technique (Principle Component Analysis) for identifying important information from user activities. These activities are compared for deviations which are further assessed on variance over multiple attributes; e.g., against peers to identify malicious activities. The paper also details the architecture of insider threat detection system and presents their experiments over synthetic data. As the system identifies anomalous behaviour based on comparison with peers' activities it cannot identify malicious behaviour due to collusion.

In [17] system focused on insider detection based on a violation of access privilege ("need to know") by a user. Usually, user at each level has associated rights and privileges. It may also have clearance to view some other level e.g., secret or top_secret. The authors [17] also discussed an interesting case of an FBI analyst who was arrested for downloading and printing information about a country for which he had "no need to know". The Wikileaks episode is also an example of such privilege misuse. The approach is based on the principle that user should look at information which they need to know without going out and snooping for data. The ELICIT system was tested on an intranet with four thousand users for a year. The ethical hacker team generated synthetic insiders on basis of attacks by real-world spies and achieved good results. The system used three important steps: data collection using information units; anomaly detection; Bayesian ranking which amalgamates 76 different type of activity for each user. The 76 detectors used rules, parametric and nonparametric density estimation for sensing anomaly. The alerts are fused to generate a single score using 3 layers Bayesian ranking network. The authors focused on browsing, searching, downloading, and printing activities of a user.

The ELICIT system [17] suffered from few problems; (1) training and validation data set are identical; the past behaviour can be captured very well but it is unable to detect unknown new behaviour; hardcoding of past behaviour is requiredinto the detectors. The ELICIT team conducted additional experiments with management, administrative and technical staff [51]. The participants were randomly assigned role as a benign user or malicious user. The role described a person in financial turmoil and must deliver the most valuable information for personal gains. The benign user is given an opportunity to participate with high profile team and it was suggested that excellent performance yields promotion and pay hike. The malicious user was given an opportunity for a new job on a precondition that user will fetch important information from the previous employer. The team monitored the participant activities and it revealed significant patterns in malicious behaviour.

4 Case Studies on Insider Threat Defence Mechanism Based on Machine Learning

This section is dedicated to cover the case studies for an insider threat detection. It is well known that occurrence rate for anomaly is very low and therefore the challenge is to detect it accurately in a large dataset. The examples in this section focus on USB device insertion or removal event. The first use-case apply linear regression and then apply Cook's and Mahalanobis distance measures to identify malicious activities of the user. Next, the section covers application of ANN and SVM to login for anomaly detection.

4.1 The Dataset

The r2 dataset is a synthetic dataset created by the CERT Insider Threat Center at CMU's SEI. They are numbered r1–r6 according to the generator version that was used to create them. This chapter uses the r2 dataset having 1000 employees' activity records over 494 days, resulting in more than 430 million events (see Tables 1 and 2 for a snapshot of logon/logoff and device insert/remove activities respectively). Out of 375 thousand events/activities, six sessions (of user ONS0995) are known to be malicious. In real life, malicious event/activity are low in number. The machine learning systems' aim is to accurately find such low occurring anomalies from a large dataset. The chapter is focused on USB device insertion or removal event. It also captures couple of instances when a user logs in/off on an odd day of the week and it is labelled as malicious activity. A device insert/remove event is labelled as malicious if the user is not known to do it regularly and does it once or twice in the entire lifespan of the recorded activity data.

Table 1 Snapshot of user's logon/logoff activity record on a time of day on a specific device in r2 dataset

Unique log ID	Date and time	User ID	Device ID	Activity
{X0W9-Q2DW16EI1074QDVQ}	01-02-2010 05:02	WCR0044	PC-9174	Logon
{C2O4-Z2RH12FQ-9176MUEL}	01-02-2010 05:19	WCR0044	PC-9174	Logoff
{U1J8-P4HX02EV-5327GONH}	01-02-2010 06:22	WCR0044	PC-5494	Logon
{F1N9-G4ZL24LA-8747VGHG}	01-02-2010 06:33	LRG0155	PC-0450	Logon
{Y1Q0-U9BN24NB-1906LMVT}	01-02-2010 06:42	RHM0148	PC-8152	Logon
{G0X9-D1CU68SO-7422ISZT}	01-02-2010 06:42	WCR0044	PC-5494	Logoff
{D5U9-A2FE85KK-5132LDYI}	01-02-2010 06:45	BHV0556	PC-6254	Logon
{P5F3-Y0IL09UW-7775RLVD}	01-02-2010 06:51	ACM0931	PC-5571	Logon
{A1G5-M6FR43QP-0895LMPK}	01-02-2010 06:51	BNB0746	PC-2503	Logon

Table 2 Snapshot of device insert/remove activity record on a time of day on a specific device in r2 dataset

Unique log ID	Date and time	User ID	Device ID	Activity
{B2N6-M3YR26LS-3736SJVC}	02-01-2010 07:09	BKM0103	PC-8475	Insert
{Z5G2-G3US81EZ-9888TTVS}	02-01-2010 07:10	BAC0081	PC-6369	Insert
{H7I7-K5NG29TQ-9568YUER}	02-01-2010 07:10	CBA0214	PC-6187	Remove
{K4Y0-K3LN28EH-3959UZOV}	02-01-2010 07:11	XDB0054	PC-5634	Insert
{M6P5-D6PL11OV-2511DOFF}	02-01-2010 07:16	PCH0681	PC-0726	Remove
{A0D5-Z8LM89JG-3484PYUS}	02-01-2010 07:16	GSH0070	PC-5143	Insert
{Z2T8-I7RE18DN-1683HFUU}	02-01-2010 07:17	DCW0021	PC-3621	Remove
{E0R2-J8NJ98LS-4629HVDB}	02-01-2010 07:18	CBA0214	PC-6187	Insert
{G6H6-U5TI86UX-8376RFTC}	02-01-2010 07:20	DKR0925	PC-5885	Insert

4.2   Environment

The environment (Table 3) shows the dataset, malicious and non-malicious users, parameters for their activities in the network, hardware, and software specifications used for the insider threat detection.

4.3   Regression and Distance Measurement on Login Activities

As the activities and other details in the dataset are non-numeric, the given dataset is modified as follows: if a user logs in over a weekday the value of that event is 1. If a user login over a weekend, then the value is 2. Similarly, the 'device inserted' parameter is modified such that if a USB device is inserted during a session then the value of the parameter corresponding to that session is 2 otherwise it is 1. The number of these activities are added and plotted against time (see Fig. 7 for more details). A linear regression is applied on this time-series data and Cook's distance

Table 3 The environment for insider threat detection

Data Set	r2.1
Users	HBN0033, FEA0006, ABT0551, ONS0995
Malicious username	ONS0995
Number of anomalies	6
Parameters	login time (with respect to the start time) login day (whether user logins on weekday of weekend) device inserted (when a USB device is inserted)
Software	OS: Microsoft Windows 8.1 Pro Matlab R2016b
Hardware	Processor: Intel(R) Core(TM) i7-4770 CPU @ 3.40GHz, 3401 MHz, 4 Cores, 8 Logical Processor(s) RAM: 8.00 GB

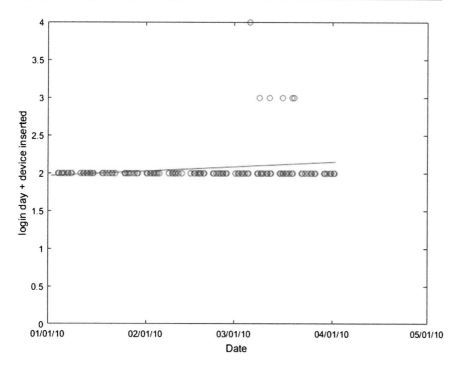

Fig. 7 Login and device inserted activity on a particular day by user ONS0995

is used for computing anomalous activities of a user. Figure 7 shows login and device inserted activity of user ONS0995 and Table 4 shows corresponding Cook's distance against linear regression. Points P1–P6 are outliers and Table 4 also shows

Table 4 Login and device inserted activity of user ONS0995 and its Cook's distance against linear regression

Activity	P1	P2	P3	P4	P5	P6	Other points
Cook's distance	0.314	0.0782	0.0869	0.100	0.111	0.114	10^{-3} to 10^{-5}

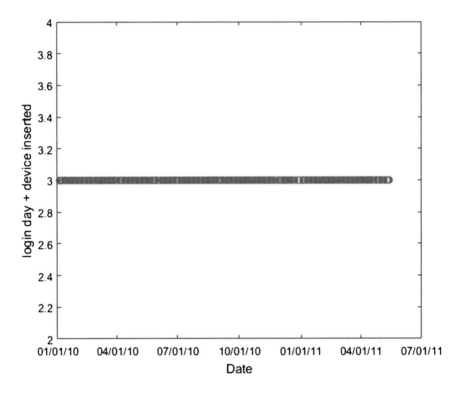

Fig. 8 Login and device inserted activity on a day by user ABT0551

Cook's distance of other points as well. The detection confirms with the synthetic data benchmark published by CERT which identifies these data points as malicious.

The plot in Fig. 8 shows login and device inserted activities of another user ABT0551who regularly logs in/off and use USB drive.

Figure 9 shows device insert/remove activity of four users; one anomalous and three non-anomalous. On each user activity linear regression followed by Cook's distance is applied to identify malicious activities.

4.3.1 Result Analysis with Cook's Distance

The Cook's distance (as given by Eq. (1)) measures the impact of a data point on the least-squares regression solution. It is used for finding an outlier, as point with larger Cook's distance is worthy of closer scrutiny during analysis. It can be observed from

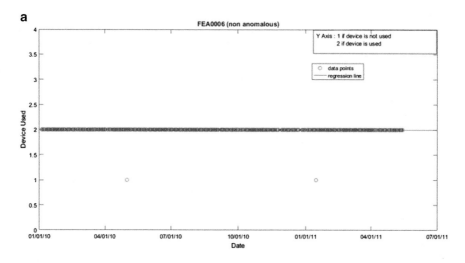

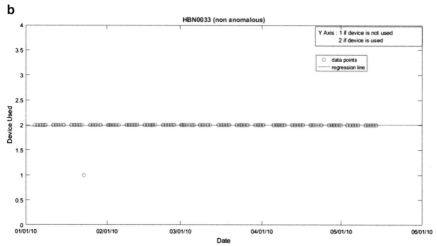

Fig. 9 Anomaly detected based on device insert/remove activity of users (**a**) FEA0006 and (**b**) HBN0033. It must be noted that (**a**) and (**b**) shows false positive anomalies

Fig. 7 (activity for a day) and Table 3 that malicious activities of user ONS0995 is captured by computing Cook's distance with respect to Linear Regression. It can be seen that outliers (P1–P6) in Fig. 7 has significantly larger Cook's distance as compared to normal data points (10^{-3}–10^{-5}). In case of a non-malicious user and there is very little impact of removing points on regression solution i.e., Cook's distance with respect to the regression will be very small. One such case is shown for user ABT0551 in Fig. 8. The Cook's distance for all points for this user is close to zero (10^{-3}–10^{-5}). This does not flag any warning for the user ABT0551 but the system analyst will be notified for the activities of the user ONS0995.

The analysis has been able to detect 100% anomalies for the user ONS0995. The accuracy is computed by comparing correct detection with the available ground truth in the CERT r2 dataset. The detection also falters and generates false positives as seen in Fig. 9a, b. Two false positives anomalies are seen for the user FEA0006. This happens because the user is not using a USB device on those days. The accuracy dips down to 99.71% due to 2 false positive outliers for a given 707 activities. Similarly, plot for the user HBN0033 shows one false positive for 194 activities, resulting into 99.48% accuracy. The average accuracy of Cook's distance-based anomaly detection for four users is 99.79%. It can also be observed that very small number of anomalies are captured from large number of activities.

4.3.2   Result Analysis with Mahalanobis Distance

It is known that the Mahalanobis distance (as given by Eqs. (2) and (3)) transforms and projects the data in a space where the distance between malicious and non-malicious activities are maximized. It is unit-less, scale-invariant and considers the correlations of the data set. Unlike the Cook's distance which considers data in Euclidean space, the data in transformed space in the Mahalanobis approach is expected to reduce errors. Further, the Mahalanobis distance approach has higher accuracy when expected number of anomalies are less. This, typically, happens in case of insider threat situations. Figure 10 similar experiments using the Mahalanobis distance and it obtained similar results as the Cook's distance. It can be observed that (outliers or malicious activities) has significant distance even in the transformed space. All six outliers are correctly captured by this distance measure as well. It resulted into 100% accuracy for user ONS0995. As noted earlier due to non-usage of USB drive by the user FEA0006 on two days resulted into false positives.

4.4   Neural Network on Login Activities

Like the regression experiments on the r2 dataset, in this subsection, ANN is applied for identifying anomalies of malicious activities of a user based on device insert/remove activities. The results are generated using 2 hidden layers neural network (excluding the input and output layer) with 4 and 16 neurons respectively. The malicious user is observed looking for binary results using the MLPClassifier defined in Scikit-learn, with parameters solver = 'lbfgs', alpha = 1e-5, max_iter = 1000, hidden_layer_sizes = (4,16), random_state = 0, shuffle = True in python v2.7.14.

```
Parameters: user id (a unique number to different user)
login time (With respect to the start time)
login day (whether user logins on weekday of weekend)
device inserted (if and when a USB device is inserted)
```

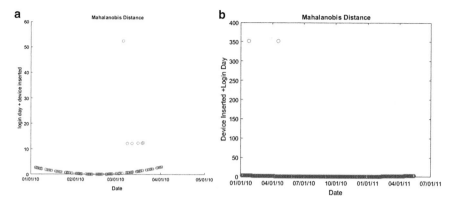

Fig. 10 Mahalanobis distance-based anomaly detection of device insert/remove activity of users (**a**) ONS0995 (**b**) FEA0006. Note that (**a**) identifies all anomalies correctly while (**b**) has two false positives

```
    Size of training data of all the users = 1324 (including
4 anomalous activities of user ONS0995)
    Size of testing data of all the user = 331
    Neural Network Classification of activities (0 being
non-malicious and 1 is malicious activity):
```

It can be observed by comparing Fig. 11a, b that this method gave an accuracy of 100% where it could detect the two anomalies in test dataset when trained with 4 anomalous cases. In Fig. 11a, b '0' indicates non-malicious activities and '1' represents malicious activities.

4.5 SVM on Login Activities

The SVM classifier was applied on the activity data of user ONS0995 with the following configuration and it obtained interesting results with different kernels (−see Fig. 12 for further details). This work is on the similar lines as the algorithms developed in [10] where the authors used linear, rbf and poly kernels with SVM for anomaly detection. The malicious user is observed using the SVM library defined in Scikit-learn. Three different kernels 'linear', 'rbf' and 'poly' were implemented with 'poly' (degree 2) and 'linear' kernel giving the best classification. The SVM is clearly able to differentiate the 6 malicious events performed by this user.

Figure 12a, c shows that the second order Polynomial kernel and Linear-SVC kernel could correctly classify all six anomaly of user ONS0995 data. As evident from Fig. 12b, d, the Linear kernel and surprisingly RBF kernel fail to correctly separate malicious and non-malicious classes.

It can be seen from case studies presented in the chapter, i.e., (1) Linear regression and distance measurement; (2) application of ANN and SVM can

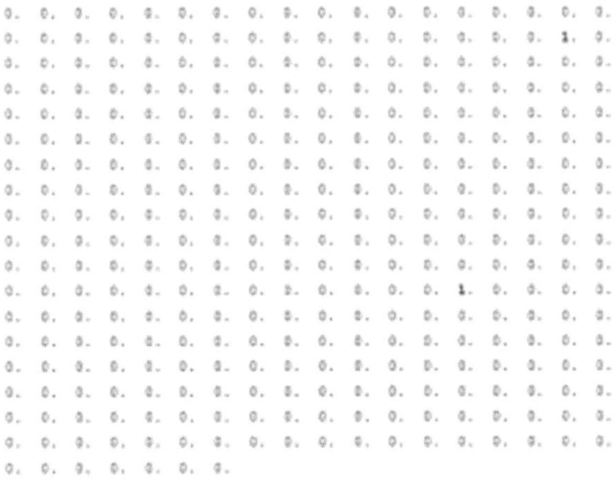

Fig. 11 (a) Ground truth labels for ANN. (b) Actual classification decisions by ANN

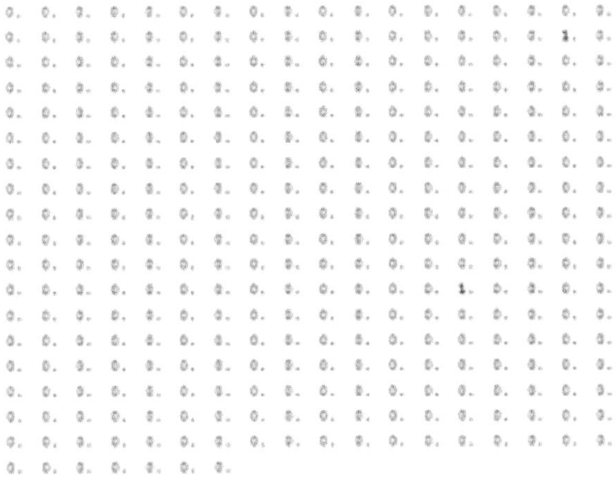

(a)

(b)

successfully detect malicious activities from the available user logs. This shows that a log file monitoring is one of the powerful technique to thwart an insider threat. Many cases of fraud by an insider, e.g., in city tax office [2], IT organization [32], and bank [33, 34] could have been avoided if the log monitoring and analysis mechanism would have been followed actively. As recorded in survey [30] IT team may have a lax approach towards the log analysis, but its active usage can mitigate the risk of an insider threat.

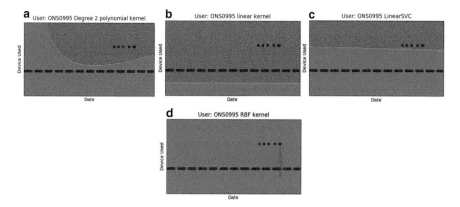

Fig. 12 Applying various SVM Kernel on user ONS0995's activity data: (**a**) Polynomial kernel of degree 2 (**b**) Linear kernel (**c**) Singular Value Classification (SVC) based Linear kernel (**d**) Radial Basis Function(RBF) kernel

5 Discussion and Future Research Directions

Insider threat seems to be on a growing spree across organizations. The impact and its effectiveness are posing a greater threat to organizations. Initially, the chapter presented insider threat launch and its impact. It was found that there are many definitions of insider threat and there is little standardization in defining these terms. The impact of a non-malicious insider can also harm the interest of organization, but the chapter is focused on willful insider. The top industries impacted by insider threat are public, healthcare and finance, retail and accommodation. Some of the important findings were that person with access to sensitive information poses the greatest threat. Low and slow mode causes the gradual but greatest damage. An insider attempts to mimic the normal behaviour and tries to remain below the radar. Many detected episodes of insider threat remain unreported due to perceived damage to organization's reputation. The common methods employed by insiders are social engineering, misuse authority during access, bypass security processes in place and compromise account through hacking. Major motivations for insiders are monetization, sabotage, fraud, IP theft and espionage.

The risk mitigation under insider threat revolves around four important entities; the organization; the IT system; the individual(s); the environment. Some of the entities are tangible and some are intangible e.g., an environment which is governed by many factors like society, culture, ethics, rules, and law of the land. The goal for any insider threat detection is detection, prevention, mitigation, punishment, and remediation. The threat management is complicated by the fact that devices, infrastructure, data's volume, veracity, and velocity have dramatically changed over the years. Insider threat defence is unable to keep pace with such changes. But defence mechanism converges on the understanding that human in the loop is the key to solve an insider threat. The early detection of the insider attack requires participation by every stakeholder i.e., management, employees, IT team, HR team and security personnel. The chapter covers insider threat detection as anomaly detection. The base behaviour of the user is coded and any behaviour in violation of it will flag an alarm. The chapter covers state-of-the-art review in modelling-based approaches with the use of machine learning to detect insider threat as an anomaly. It was observed that only technical approach towards solving the problem is ineffective. Thus, the chapter looks at approaches which combine behaviour, psychology, criminology with machine learning. Specifically, modelling human behaviour based on the application of general deterrence theory; social bond theory, social learning theory; theory of planned behaviour; situational crime prevention seems to be the key.

Solving the problem of insider threat using machine learning way has its own set of challenges. In total population numbers of malicious users are very small. The definition of what constitutes baseline behaviour is highly variable. This directly impacts the performance of insider threat defence mechanism. Many instances went unreported or they are reported incorrectly. Both scenarios generate faulty results by data-driven approaches to machine learning. There is a lack of training and testing public domain dataset generated from the real world. The work depends heavily on simulated datasets which may not generate good models. The algorithms generate good results for the past learning but fail badly on encountering a new situation. The past work based on psychology seems to be promising for intrusion detection, but they have not been rigorously tested. The emergence of deep learning may use a fusion of natural language processing, behavioural analysis, and sentiment analysis [18]. The deep learning architecture also holds promise for a variety of streaming task. The comparison of Long Short-Term Memory (LSTM) network with DNN is also required to map large-scale temporal patterns. The online scenario can also be quantified in term of adapting sampling rate as per the data stream. This can reduce number of potential anomaly miss. It seems feedback in LSTM can be explored to generalize the insider detection model. The greatest advantage seems to be end-to-end learning for DNN and LSTM which eliminates the need for handcrafted features. This can significantly narrow down the search space for analysts.

The supervised form of learning requires training data, and in several scenarios, one may have to respond in real time. This leads to idea of active log monitoring. The case study presented in the chapter can help to actively monitor and detect malicious behaviour. However, monitoring simple and specific patterns cannot be effective. For example, use of camouflage can fool the log monitoring. This warrants advance design models to estimate user behaviour. This needs a very strong behaviour analytic framework dedicated for log analysis.

6 Conclusion

The chapter showcased three important machine learning algorithms (regression, neural network, and SVM) and applied them to CERT r2 dataset. These algorithms are broadly classified as supervised and unsupervised learning. These algorithms can effectively be deployed in the defence mechanisms to stand against insider attack. Despite biased dataset, the machine learning algorithms performed very well. Further, it must be noted that the number of false negatives i.e., a user is malicious but not reported by the presented algorithms are very low, essentially nil. This means that at times due to false positives i.e., a non-malicious user is reported as malicious; the algorithms may question a good user for its activities, but a malicious user is never missed. For example, in the case of r2 dataset, the report mentions that the user ONS0995 was terminated after observing its malicious activities.

There is a significant bias in the data presented for the algorithms. Considering significantly less activity by a malicious user there are very small data samples. Moreover, after termination of a user, its activities cease to exist, resulting in an even lesser number of data samples of malicious activities. This produces a bias in data towards non-malicious samples. Considering the results of various experiments presented, it must also be clear that the machine learning algorithms are sensitive to data bias. Thus, the choice of algorithm or model must be done with sufficient care. On a positive note, the algorithms presented allowed automation for the insider threat detection and they can be scaled for larger data. Also, once the choice of data feature is made these algorithms are independent of data being processed and thus can be considered for any type of data for identifying malicious activities.

Some of the important lessons for use of log analysis are as follows. One must note that log analysis is a very complex process and depends on several sub processes. Like in case of anomaly detection it is necessary to understand pattern in the data. Mere naïve understanding can generate false positives, e.g., false positive for the user FEA0006 in r2 dataset. It is also essential to have a robust data normalization process to smooth the log analysis e.g., converting dates to uniform format. It is useful during correlation analysis when connections are not apparent from the single log but correlating multiple records may help discovering underlying patterns. For example, one can collate logs from servers, firewalls, network devices, and client software for preventive as well as forensic analysis. Collective log analysis can also help to form alerts for the system administrator.

Acknowledgments We would like to thank Ativ Joshi and Pratik Paladia for helping with the experiments. We also express gratitude to unknown reviewers for insightful comments in improving the quality of this chapter.

References

1. http://www.gemalto.com/press/Pages/Gemalto-releases-findings-of-2016-Breach-Level-Index.aspx
2. Chris King, "Spotlight On: Malicious Insiders and Organized Crime Activity", Technical note, CMU/SEI-2012-TN-001, Jan. 2012.
3. G. Fyffe, "Addressing insider threat," Network Security, vol. 2008, no.3, pp. 11–14, 2008.

4. S. L. Pfleeger and S. J. Stolfo, "Addressing the insider threat," IEEE Security & Privacy, vol. 7, no. 6, pp. 10–13, 2009.
5. E. Cole and S. Ring, Insider Threat: Protecting the Enterprise from Sabotage, Spying, and Theft: Protecting the Enterprise from Sabotage, Spying, and Theft. Syngress, 2005.
6. http://www.cert.org/insider-threat/research/Case-Analysis-and-Best-Practices.cfm
7. Collins. Matthew, Theis. Michael, Trzeciak. Randall, Strozer. Jeremy, Clark. Jason, Costa. Daniel, Cassidy. Tracy, Albrethsen. Michael, and Moore. Andrew, "Common Sense Guide to Mitigating Insider Threats, 5th Edition," Software Engineering Institute, Carnegie Mellon University, Pittsburgh, Pennsylvania, Technical Report CMU/SEI-2016-TR-015, 2016. http://resources.sei.cmu.edu/library/asset-view.cfm?AssetID=484738
8. 2017 data breach investigations report executive summary, http://www.verizonenterprise.com/verizon-insights-lab/dbir/2017/
9. Adam Cummings, Todd Lewellen, David McIntire, Andrew P. Moore, Randall F. Trzeciak, "Insider Threat Study: Illicit Cyber Activity Involving Fraud in the U.S. Financial Services Sector," Software Engineering Institute, CMU/SEI-2012-SR-004, July 2012.
10. A. Azaria, A. Richardson, S. Kraus and V. S. Subrahmanian, "Behavioral Analysis of Insider Threat: A Survey and Bootstrapped Prediction in Imbalanced Data," in *IEEE Transactions on Computational Social Systems*, vol. 1, no. 2, pp. 135–155, June 2014.
11. G. Magklaras and S. Furnell, "Insider threat prediction tool: Evaluating the probability of it misuse," Computers & Security, vol. 21, no. 1, pp. 62–73, 2001.
12. G. Jabbour and D. A. Menasce, "The insider threat security architecture: a framework for an integrated, inseparable, and uninterrupted self-protection mechanism," in Computational Science and Engineering, 2009. CSE'09. International Conference on, vol. 3. IEEE, 2009, pp. 244–251.
13. J. Hunker and C. W. Probst, "Insiders and insider threats an overview of definitions and mitigation techniques," Journal of Wireless Mobile Networks, Ubiquitous Computing, and Dependable Applications, vol. 2, no. 1, pp. 4–27, 2011.
14. S. Sinclair and S.W.Smith,"Preventative directions for insider threat mitigation via access control," in Insider Attack and Cyber Security. Springer, 2008, pp. 165–194.
15. L. Greitzer and D. A. Frincke, "Combining traditional cyber security audit data with psychosocial data: towards predictive modeling for insider threat mitigation," in Insider Threats in Cyber Security. Springer, 2010, pp. 85–113.
16. A. Liu, C. Martin, T. Hetherington, and S. Matzner, "A comparison of system call feature representations for insider threat detection," in Information Assurance Workshop, 2005. IAW'05. Proceedings from the Sixth Annual IEEE SMC. IEEE, 2005, pp. 340–347.
17. M. A. Maloof and G. D. Stephens, "ELICIT: A system for detecting insiders who violate need-to-know," in Recent Advances in Intrusion Detection. Springer, 2007, pp. 146–166.
18. Majumder, Navonil, Soujanya Poria, Alexander Gelbukh, and Erik Cambria, "Deep Learning-Based Document Modeling for Personality Detection from Text." IEEE Intelligent Systems 32.2 (2017): 74–79.
19. Tuor, Aaron, Samuel Kaplan, Brian Hutchinson, Nicole Nichols, and Sean Robinson. "Deep Learning for Unsupervised Insider Threat Detection in Structured Cybersecurity Data Streams.", AAAI-17 Workshop on Artificial intelligence for cyber security, pp. 224–230, 2017.
20. Ryan, Jake, Meng-Jang Lin, and Risto Miikkulainen. "Intrusion detection with neural networks." In Advances in neural information processing systems, pp. 943–949. 1998.
21. Debar, Herve, Monique Becker, and Didier Siboni. "A neural network component for an intrusion detection system." In Research in Security and Privacy, 1992. Proceedings., 1992 IEEE Computer Society Symposium on, pp. 240–250. IEEE, 1992.
22. Veeramachaneni, Kalyan, Ignacio Arnaldo, Vamsi Korrapati, Constantinos Bassias, and Ke Li. "AI$^{2:}$ training a big data machine to defend." In Big Data Security on Cloud (Big Data Security), IEEE International Conference on High Performance and Smart Computing (HPSC), and IEEE International Conference on Intelligent Data and Security (IDS), 2016 IEEE 2nd International Conference on, pp. 49–54. IEEE, 2016.

23. Nousiainen, Sami, Jorma Kilpi, Paula Silvonen, and Mikko Hiirsalmi. Anomaly detection from server log data. Technical report, 2009.
24. Rodriguez, Aitor, and Mario de los Mozos. "Improving network security through traffic log anomaly detection using time series analysis." Computational Intelligence in Security for Information Systems 2010 (2010): 125–133.
25. Zhu, Xia. Resilient control and intrusion detection for scada systems. University of California, Berkeley, 2011.
26. Andrysiak, Tomasz, Łukasz Saganowski, Michał Choraś, and Rafał Kozik. "Network traffic prediction and anomaly detection based on ARFIMA model" In International Joint Conference SOCO'14-CISIS'14-ICEUTE'14, pp. 545–554. Springer, Cham, 2014.
27. Model, ARIMA-GARCH. "Detection of Network Attacks Using Hybrid." In Dependability Problems and Complex Systems: Proceedings of the Twelfth International Conference on Dependability and Complex Systems DepCoS-RELCOMEX. July 2–6, 2017, Brunów, Poland, vol. 582, p. 1. Springer, 2017.
28. https://webscope.sandbox.yahoo.com/catalog.php?datatype=s&did=70
29. https://www.dni.gov/files/documents/ICA_2017_01.pdf
30. https://haystax.com/blog/ebook/insider-attacks-industry-survey/
31. Predd, Joel, Shari Lawrence Pfleeger, Jeffrey Hunker, and Carla Bulford. "Insiders behaving badly." IEEE Security & Privacy 6, no. 4, pp.66–70, 2008.
32. https://www.huffingtonpost.com/2012/08/29/hanjuan-jin-motorola_n_1840833.html
33. https://en.wikipedia.org/wiki/J%C3%A9r%C3%B4me_Kerviel
34. Epstein, Jeremy. "Security lessons learned from Société Générale" IEEE Security & Privacy 6, no. 3, pp. 80–82, 2008.
35. Rost, Johann. "Political reasons for failed software projects" IEEE Software 21, no. 6, pp. 103–104, 2004.
36. Thompson, Hugh. "The human element of information security" IEEE Security & Privacy 11, no. 1 pp. 32–35, 2013.
37. Duran, Felicia, Stephen H. Conrad, Gregory N. Conrad, David P. Duggan, and Edward Bruce Held. "Building a system for insider security." IEEE Security & Privacy 7, no. 6, pp. 30–38, 2009.
38. Band, S.R., Cappelli, D.M., Fischer, L.F., Moore, A.P., Shaw, E.D. and Trzeciak, R.F., 2006. Comparing insider IT sabotage and espionage: A model-based analysis (No. CMU/SEI-2006-TR-026). CARNEGIE-MELLON UNIV PITTSBURGH PA SOFTWARE ENGINEERING INST.
39. Herbig, K. "Changes in espionage by Americans 1947–2007," Monterey, CA, Defense Personnel Security Research Center. 2008.
40. Turner, James T., and Michael Gelles. Threat assessment: A risk management approach. Routledge, 2012.
41. "Insider Analysis", Module 23, The 19th International training course, SAND2006-1987C, Sandia National laboratories, 2006, pp. 214–287.
42. Greitzer, Frank L., Andrew P. Moore, Dawn M. Cappelli, Dee H. Andrews, Lynn A. Carroll, and Thomas D. Hull. "Combating the insider cyber threat." IEEE Security & Privacy 6, no. 1, pp. 61–64, 2008.
43. Legg, Philip A., Oliver Buckley, Michael Goldsmith, and Sadie Creese. "Automated insider threat detection system using user and role-based profile assessment." IEEE Systems Journal 11, no. 2 (2017): 503–512.
44. Koch, Robert, Mario Golling, and Gabi Dreo Rodosek. "Behavior-based intrusion detection in encrypted environments." IEEE Communications Magazine 52, no. 7 (2014): 124–131.
45. Bowen, Brian, Malek Ben Salem, Shlomo Hershkop, Angelos Keromytis, and Salvatore Stolfo. "Designing host and network sensors to mitigate the insider threat." IEEE Security & Privacy 7, no. 6 (2009): 22–29.
46. Böse, Brock, Bhargav Avasarala, Srikanta Tirthapura, Yung-Yu Chung, and Donald Steiner. "Detecting Insider Threats Using RADISH: A System for Real-Time Anomaly Detection in Heterogeneous Data Streams." IEEE Systems Journal (2017).

47. Almehmadi, Abdulaziz, and Khalil El-Khatib. "On the possibility of insider threat prevention using intent-based access control (IBAC)." IEEE Systems Journal 11, no. 2 (2017): 373–384.
48. Chen, You, Steve Nyemba, and Bradley Malin. "Detecting anomalous insiders in collaborative information systems." IEEE transactions on dependable and secure computing 9, no. 3 (2012): 332–344.
49. Mills, Jennifer U., Steven MF Stuban, and Jason Dever. "Predict insider threats using human behaviors." IEEE Engineering Management Review 45, no. 1 (2017): 39–48.
50. Theoharidou, Marianthi, Spyros Kokolakis, Maria Karyda, and Evangelos Kiountouzis. "The insider threat to information systems and the effectiveness of ISO17799." Computers & Security 24, no. 6 (2005): 472–484.
51. Caputo, Deanna, Marcus Maloof, and Gregory Stephens. "Detecting insider theft of trade secrets." IEEE Security & Privacy 7, no. 6 (2009): 14–21.
52. Jajodia, Sushil, Anup K. Ghosh, V. S. Subrahmanian, Vipin Swarup, Cliff Wang, and X. Sean Wang, eds. Moving Target Defense II: Application of Game Theory and Adversarial Modeling. Vol. 100. Springer Science & Business Media, 2012.
53. Pita, James, Manish Jain, Milind Tambe, Fernando Ordóñez, and Sarit Kraus. "Robust solutions to Stackelberg games: Addressing bounded rationality and limited observations in human cognition." Artificial Intelligence 174, no. 15 (2010): 1142–1171.
54. Roy, Sankardas, Charles Ellis, Sajjan Shiva, Dipankar Dasgupta, Vivek Shandilya, and Qishi Wu. "A survey of game theory as applied to network security." In System Sciences (HICSS), 2010 43rd Hawaii International Conference on, pp. 1–10. IEEE, 2010.
55. Alpcan, Tansu, and Tamer Basar. "A game theoretic approach to decision and analysis in network intrusion detection." In Decision and Control, 2003. Proceedings. 42nd IEEE Conference on, vol. 3, pp. 2595–2600. IEEE, 2003.
56. Liu, Debin, XiaoFeng Wang, and Jean Camp. "Game-theoretic modeling and analysis of insider threats." International Journal of Critical Infrastructure Protection 1 (2008): 75–80.
57. Rich, Eliot, Ignacio J. Martinez-Moyano, Stephen Conrad, Dawn M. Cappelli, Andrew P. Moore, Timothy J. Shimeall, David F. Andersen et al. "Simulating insider cyber-threat risks: a model-based case and a case-based model." In Proceedings of the 23rd International Conference of the System dynamics Society, pp. 17–21. The System Dynamics Society, 2005.
58. Kraus, Sarit, Penina Hoz-Weiss, Jonathan Wilkenfeld, David R. Andersen, and Amy Pate. "Resolving crises through automated bilateral negotiations." Artificial Intelligence 172, no. 1 (2008): 1–18.
59. Rosenfeld, Avi, Inon Zuckerman, Amos Azaria, and Sarit Kraus. "Combining psychological models with machine learning to better predict people's decisions." Synthese 189, no. 1 (2012): 81–93.
60. Nguyen, Thanh Hong, Rong Yang, Amos Azaria, Sarit Kraus, and Milind Tambe. "Analyzing the Effectiveness of Adversary Modeling in Security Games." In AAAI. 2013.
61. Kantzavelou, Ioanna, and Sokratis Katsikas. "A game-based intrusion detection mechanism to confront internal attackers." Computers & Security 29, no. 8 (2010): 859–874.
62. Yang, Rong, Albert Xin Jiang, Milind Tambe, and Fernando Ordonez. "Scaling-up Security Games with Boundedly Rational Adversaries: A Cutting-plane Approach." In IJCAI, pp. 404–410. 2013.
63. Tang, Ke, Mingyuan Zhao, and Mingtian Zhou. "Cyber insider threats situation awareness using game theory and information fusion-based user behavior predicting algorithm." Journal of Information & Computational Science 8, no. 3 (2011): 529–545.
64. Pratt, Travis C., and Francis T. Cullen. "The empirical status of Gottfredson and Hirschi's general theory of crime: A meta-analysis." Criminology 38, no. 3 (2000): 931–964.
65. Hirschi, Travis. "Social bond theory." Criminological theory: Past to present. Los Angeles: Roxbury (1998).
66. Ajzen, Icek. "From intentions to actions: A theory of planned behavior." In Action control, pp. 11–39. Springer Berlin Heidelberg, 1985.
67. Clarke, Ronald VG. "Situational" "Crime Prevention: Theory and Practice." The British Journal of Criminology 20, no. 2 (1980): 136–147.

68. https://insights.sei.cmu.edu/sei_blog/2016/09/modeling-and-simulation-in-insider-threat.html
69. Myerson, Roger B. Game theory. Harvard university press, 2013.
70. Krawczyk, Bartosz. "Learning from imbalanced data: open challenges and future directions." Progress in Artificial Intelligence 5, no. 4 (2016): 221–232.
71. Haixiang, G., Yijing, L., Shang, J., Mingyun, G., Yuanyue, H., & Bing, G. (2017). Learning from class-imbalanced data: Review of methods and applications. Expert Systems with Applications, 73, 220–239.
72. Azaria, Amos, Ariella Richardson, Sarit Kraus, and V. S. Subrahmanian. "Behavioral analysis of insider threat: A survey and bootstrapped prediction in imbalanced data." IEEE Transactions on Computational Social Systems 1, no. 2 (2014): 135–155.
73. Cook, R. D. (1977). Detection of influential observation in linear regression. *Technometrics*, 19(1), 15–18.
74. Mahalanobis, Prasanta Chandra (1936). "On the generalised distance in statistics". Proceedings of the National Institute of Sciences of India. 2 (1): 49–55.
75. Ratnik Gandhi, Mehul S Raval, and Sanjay Chaudhary, "Pattern Discovery for Insider Threat", CSI Communications 42, No. 2 (2018): 31–33.

Distributed Denial of Service Attacks and Defense Mechanisms: Current Landscape and Future Directions

Sajal Bhatia, Sunny Behal, and Irfan Ahmed

Abstract Societal dependence on Information and Communication Technology (ICT) over the past two decades has brought with it an increased vulnerability to a large variety of cyber-attacks. One such attack is a Distributed Denial-of-Service (DDoS) attack which harnesses the power of a larger number of compromised and geographically distributed computers and other networked machines to attack information-providing services, often resulting in significant downtime and thereby causing a denial-of-service to legitimate clients. The size, frequency, and sophistication of such attacks have exponentially risen over the past decade. In order to develop a better understanding of these attacks and defense system against this ever-growing threat, it is essential to understand their modus operandi, latest trends and other most widely-used tactics. Consequently, the study of DDoS attacks and techniques to accurately and reliably detect and mitigate their impact is an important area of research. This chapter largely focuses on the current landscape of DDoS attack detection and defense mechanisms and provides detailed information about the latest modus operandi of various network and application layer DDoS attacks, and presents an extended taxonomy to accommodate the novel attack types. In addition, it provides directions for future research in DDoS attack detection and mitigation.

S. Bhatia (✉)
School of Computing, Sacred Heart University, Fairfield, CT, USA
e-mail: bhatias@sacredheart.edu

S. Behal
Department of Computer Science, Shaheed Bhagat Singh State Technical Campus, Ferozepur, Punjab, India
e-mail: sunnybehal@sbsstc.ac.in

I. Ahmed
Department of Computer Science, University of New Orleans, New Orleans, LA, USA
e-mail: iahmed4@uno.edu

© Springer Nature Switzerland AG 2018
M. Conti et al. (eds.), *Versatile Cybersecurity*, Advances in Information Security 72, https://doi.org/10.1007/978-3-319-97643-3_3

1 Introduction

Advances in Information and Communication Technology (ICT) over the past two decades has significantly transformed the manner in which data is stored, accessed and communicated, mainly over the network. The variety of services supported by ICT are exponentially expanding and in recent years have even included the control and monitoring of critical infrastructure system such as water, gas, and power. This constant evolution of ICT paired with its ubiquitous nature has brought with it an ever-increasing dependence for storing, processing and transferring information. As a result, any disruption in these systems, even for a relatively short period, directly and adversely affects nearly all key functionalities of a modern society.

A situation, often resulting from a deliberate and malicious attempt by an adversary to intentionally disrupt the normal operations of a service provider (or a server) and render the resources unavailable to its intended clients is known as a Denial-of-Service (DoS) attack. The National Information Assurance Glossary provided by the Committee on National Security Systems (CNSS) gives a more general definition and identifies DoS as [1]:

> Any (series of) actions that prevent any part of an [information system] from functioning.

A DoS attack against an online service provider can target its computing resource such as CPU, memory, or a networking resource such as bandwidth or both. The effects of such an attack can range from a minor delay in service response time to complete inaccessibility. These attacks at times can also have financial implications on organizations heavily dependent on the availability of their services. A report by Amazon suggests that a 100 ms delay in response time can potentially drop their overall sales by approximately 1% [2]. A Distributed Denial-of-Service (DDoS) attack is a distributed variant of the DoS attack where an array of geographically dispersed compromised machines (a.k.a. zombies, bots, slaves) are controlled by an attacker (aka bot-master) and used against a specific target to cause a denial of service. A network of such compromised machines (or bots) is called a *botnet*. In a DDoS attack, individual capability of each compromised machines is utilized and aggregated for use against a common victim, thereby magnifying the effect. Figure 1 demonstrates the working model of a typical DDoS attack. The bot-master compromises an array of bots, commonly by infecting them with a Trojan or a backdoor program, and takes control of them. These compromised bots are then controlled by the bot-master, often via Command and Control (C&C) channels, and simultaneously used to attack a target server using the public network infrastructure. The sophistication, size, volume, and frequency of DDoS attacks have risen exponentially over the years. To develop a better defense system against this ever-growing threat, it is essential to understand their modus operandi, their latest trends, and most widely-used tactics. The motives behind DDoS attacks ranges from fun to financial gain to pushing forward a political agenda, as in the case of the attacks on Estonia and Georgia [3]. A report Arbor Networks on Worldwide Infrastructure Security indicates ideologically-motivated 'hacktivism' and 'vandalism' as the most readily-identified motivations behind DDoS attacks [4].

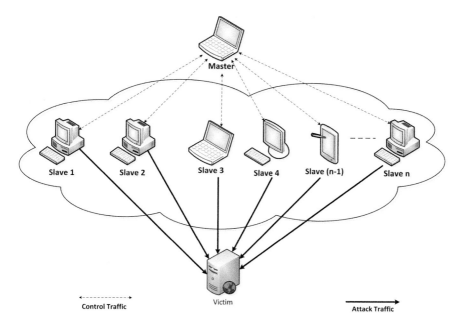

Fig. 1 A typical set-up of a DDoS attack

Moore et al. used their 'backscatter analysis' technique to expose the *worldwide* prevalence of DDoS activity [5]. Their proposed techniques was based on the hypothesis that the attacker often forges or spoofs the source IP address of the packets prior to sending them to the victim. Spoofing of source IP is performed to conceal identity of location. Upon receiving a request from spoofed IP, a response is sent from the victims machine to what is believed to be a genuine host. As the IP address is randomly selected during the spoofing process, the entire IP address space becomes equally likely to receive a response, a phenomenon they referred to as backscatter. Using this backscatter analysis and monitoring the number of replies sent to non-existent IPs over a three-week period 12,805 attacks against an approximately 5,000 distinct Internet hosts from more than 2,000 unique organizations were observed. This widespread nature of DDoS attacks, mainly originating from China, is conformed by a report from Prolexic [6]. A more recent study by Imperva Incapsula shows an increased number of short-lived repeat DDoS attacks such as hit-and-run pulse-wave attacks, Bitcoin as one of the most targeted industries, high-rate and persistent network layer attacks on the rise, and continuous growth of Botnet activity from India and Turkey [7].

The continuous evolving nature, complexity, frequency and magnitude of DDoS attacks implies that the study of such attacks including their detection, characterization, defense and mitigation remain an active area of research and investigation. This chapter focuses on the pertinent DDoS attack detection techniques, defense methods, and launching mechanisms. It also presents an extended taxonomy of

DDoS attacks to include recent attacks, and provides future research directions. Section 2 presents an extended taxonomy of DDoS attacks and describes different methods and mechanisms used to launch DDoS attacks. Section 3 outlines the various reasons for success of these attacks. Section 4 describes in detail some of the pertinent work done in DDoS attack defense methods. The section focuses on attack prevention, detection, traceback, and characterization and mitigation. Finally, Sect. 5 discusses the impact, sophistication and future trends in DDoS attacks and provide directions for research in this important and constantly evolving area.

2 DDoS Attack Taxonomy and Launch Methods

DDoS attack detection research has, not surprisingly, been viewed as a two-dimensional problem – the 'type of attack' and the 'target of attack', as shown in Fig. 2. The classification of DDoS attacks based on the 'target of attack' not only foreshadows the possibility of an attack on any networked system, but also highlights the fact that the magnitude of its impact invariably depends on the resources (computational and communicational) available to the attackers.

In order to exhaust the available resources, an adversary can initiate an attack by overwhelming the target by sending large number of spurious requests. This category of attack is known as the high-rate flooding attack or brute force attack or volumetric attack. These attacks often require attackers to gather sufficient resources both bandwidth and computing to overwhelm the target. Accumulating these computational and networking resources might have been difficult in the past, but with the recent advancements in attacking softwares, availability of high-speed networks, and accessibility of compromised bots that can be 'hired' for as low as $150 per day, it is not particularly difficult [8]. TCP, ICMP, UDP, and HTTP flooding are some of the common types of high-rate flooding attacks.

Contrary to these high-rate flooding attacks, semantic attack exploit the design or implementation flaws of an application or a protocol to cause a denial of service. This can make a semantic attack more challenging to execute as compared to a high-rate flooding attack as it requires the adversary to have comprehensive under-standing of the application or protocol being targeted. Semantic attacks are more stealthy in nature and can be launched successfully even with a disproportionate distribution of resources (network bandwidth and processing capacity) between an attacker and the victim. The 'Ping of Death' is a classic example of a semantic attack, executed by sending malformed ICMP packets to the target [9]. Suriadi et al. [10] proposed an application layer semantic attack by exploiting the SOAP format and thereby allowing deeply nested XML to be successfully embedded into the transmitted message, and forcing the XML parser within the service to process the document often causing memory exhaustion and leading to a DoS attack.

It is to be noted that both high-rate flooding and semantic attacks can occur either at the network or application layer of the TCP/IP stack. A TCP SYN flooding attack is an example of a network layer attack exhausting the available network bandwidth

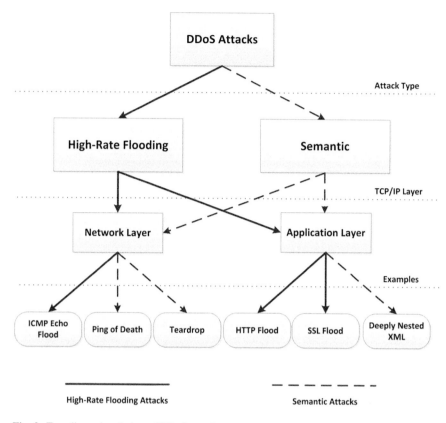

Fig. 2 Two-dimensional view of DDoS attacks

of the victim, while an HTTP flood attack is an example of an application layer flooding attack targeting the application running on the target. Similarly, a deeply nested XML attack and a teardrop attack are examples of application and network layer semantic attack respectively.

2.1 DDoS Attack Taxonomy

Many authors have tried to classify DDoS attacks based on attack launching mechanisms. Jelena et al. [11] classified DDoS attacks (a) by degree of automation wherein they can be categorized into manual, semi-automatic and automatic DDoS attacks, (b) by exploited vulnerability wherein they can be categorized according to type of protocol or type of vulnerability used, (c) by attack rate dynamics wherein they can be categorized into continues or variable rate attacks, (d) by level of impact wherein they can be categorized into disruptive or degrading in nature. Further,

Lee et al. [12] classified DDoS attacks into bandwidth or resource depletion attacks according to the type of network resource overwhelmed. Bhuyan et al. [13] extended the taxonomy of DDoS attacks originally proposed by [11] and [12]. They classified DDoS attacks based on the type of architectural model used by the attackers into agent-handler, IRC based, and peer to peer (P2P) based DDoS attacks. According to the authors, there are mainly two types of DDoS attacks in existence (a) network (Layer 3/4) DDoS attacks that target the network and transport layers. These attacks overwhelm and consume whole of the network level resources of a target network or a webserver, (b) application (Layer 7) DDoS attacks exploit a vulnerability in a web-based application. These attacks overwhelm and consumes the resources of a webserver or a database powering a web-based application and shut down its services. Attackers often mimic legitimate user behavior and use authentic ways to launch application layer attacks which make them harder to detect. Xiang et al. [14] characterized DDoS attacks into (a) high-rate DDoS (HR-DDoS) attacks, when the traffic rate of attack flows is more than the legitimate traffic flows, and (b) low-rate DDoS (LR-DDoS) attack when traffic rate of attack flows is similar or less than the legitimate traffic flows [15].

Though the existing set of taxonomies of DDoS attacks are complete in themselves but they did not fit into the ever changing modus operandi of DDoS attackers. The percentage of IoT and mobile devices have increased manifolds over the years [16]. It has changed the trend and type of DDoS attacks being launched nowadays. So, the existing taxonomies of DDoS attacks need to be extended to incorporate these new diversified types of DDoS attack methods as shown in Fig. 3 and described below:

Fig. 3 DDoS attack methods

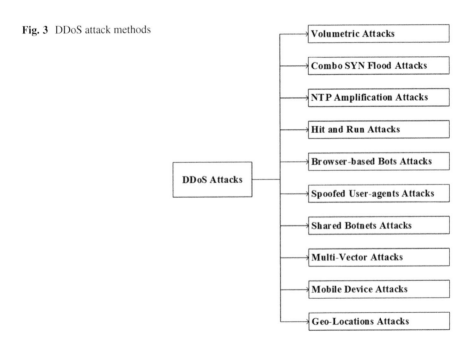

- **Volumetric attacks:** Such type of DDoS attacks overwhelms the available network bandwidth of a target network with a flood of data packets. These attacks overload the targeted network or server with very high volumes of traffic congestion and cause a denial of service to legitimate users. Such attacks can crash down any business or web service within a few minutes. Examples of volumetric attacks include TCP SYN attack, ICMP attack, Smurf attack, etc. Such network-layer attacks are designed to overwhelm bandwidth, networking resources, and applications that are unable to absorb the increased traffic volumes.

- **Combo SYN Flood Attacks:** In a traditional TCP SYN attack, the requester sends multiple SYN messages to the targeted server without receiving or transmitting ACK messages. As the resources of a web server are limited, it begins dropping out of new connection requests and ultimately, resulting in a denial of service. A combo SYN flood is composed of two types of TCP SYN attacks – one with regular SYN packet size, and the other with larger SYN packet size above 250 bytes. The conventional SYN attack exhausts the server resources (e.g., CPU), whereas the larger packet size in SYN attack causes network saturation. Such attacks can quickly consume the resources of a target server, or of intermediate network devices such as firewalls and load balancers. As per the latest DDoS attacks report from Imperva [16], out of all network layer DDoS attacks occurred nowadays, 75% are Combo SYN flood attacks.

- **NTP Amplification Attacks:** Such DDoS attacks have been used extensively in recent times. The attackers exploit MONLIST feature of Network Time Protocol (NTP) which is used by computers to synchronize their clocks over the internet. Attackers then send redundant MONLIST requests to NTP servers using destination IP of the victim. In this way, a huge volume of useless traffic is sent by the NTP server towards the novice target and overwhelmed it with multiple data packets. There are around 400,000 NTP servers deployed across the Globe that can potentially be exploited using an NTP amplification attack. As per the latest DDoS attacks report from Imperva [16], it is one of the leading attack vectors nowadays and has surpassed frequently accessed SYN flood attacks.

- **Hit and Run Attacks:** In such type of DDoS attacks, attackers randomly generate short packet bursts over an extended period; for days or even weeks. These sophisticated attacks are specifically designed to elude slow-reacting DDoS defense solutions. Such attacks are prevalent among attacker community because of their ease of deployment and low cost. They typically last for 20–60 min in duration. After causing some collateral damage to a target server, such attacks usually occur again after another 12–48 h. They force the anti-DDoS defense solution to be active all the time and can easily elude the existing preventions mechanism such as DNS rerouting and tunneling.

- **Browser-based bot attacks:** Browser-based bots typically become active during a legitimate web browsing session and are sneakily installed on credulous user systems upon visiting a malicious website. Such bots are called Bad bots, and can easily emulate the normal user browsing behavior to elude current DDoS defense solutions. These bots primarily target the application layer and can easily crash down a web server with mere 50–100 requests per second. Such attacks are difficult to prevent and detect.

- **Spoofed User Agents:** There are Good bots in existence as well, such as Google-bots or Facebook-bots that cannot be stopped to install and, that are critical to ensuring the proper functioning of websites. Bad bots mimic and spoof Good bots to dodge detection. Attackers use this method to pass through low-level filters and proceed to inflict chaos on target webserver. Some of the common spoofed user-agents are Mozilla/5.0 Baiduspider/2.0, MSIE 6.0, Googlebot/2.1, and Linux i686.
- **Shared Botnets:** Nowadays, even a novice and non-technical user can use publically available Botnets either on rent or on sharing basis to launch diversified DDoS attacks. The same machine is sometimes compromised by more than one Botnet. It leads to the generation of sophisticated volumetric attacks with dissimilar traffic patterns which not difficult to identify but also elude the existing DDoS defense system which works on the principle of flow similarity. The trend of latest DDoS attacks is to use more and more shared botnets as they can be accessed cheaply and easily without any technical knowledge.
- **Multi-Vector Attacks:** Traditionally, DDoS attack traffic is composed of a single attack type or a vector. However, the modus operandi of DDoS attacks has been changed drastically using multiple vectors to disrupt the services of a web server. A multi-vector DDoS attack is a blend of (a) volumetric attacks; (b) state exhaustion attacks; and (c) application layer attacks. As per the recent report of Imperva [16], over 81% of DDoS attacks occurred nowadays are multi-vector attacks. Being a combination of different suave techniques, such attacks are difficult to detect and mitigate; and have more success rate as compared to traditional single vector DDoS attacks.
- **Mobile Device Attacks:** The number of mobile users has increased dramatically over the last few years. The cheaper internet bandwidth and faster connectivity leads to more chances for mobile devices to be compromised and inadvertently used to launch mobile DDoS attacks. Mobile phones and tablets are not unaffected by the ever-growing malware as they have weaker security protection as compared to PCs. Lack of awareness of installing anti-virus application, freely available vulnerable mobile applications further adds up the chances of being compromised. So, there is a need to customize existing DDoS defense solutions with the additional layer of complexity in mitigating mobile device attacks. Further, freely available new tools, such as Low Orbit Ion Cannon (LOIC) and High Orbit Ion Cannon (HOIC) intentionally use the mobile devices to participate in ongoing attacks.
- **Geolocations DDoS Attacks:** The presence of insecure IT infrastructure, vulnerable hosting environments, and internet-connected devices have given rise to a series of geolocations DDoS attacks. A DDoS attack may originate in one country but may use the unprotected infrastructure of another country, and later amplified by other environments. The extensive use and deployment of less secure IoT devices have further increased the chances of geolocations DDoS attacks. However, the implementation of sturdier guidelines and security policies

could suggestively lessen the frequency of such kind of DDoS attacks. As per the latest DDoS attacks report from Imperva [16], 52% of the DDoS attacks originate from only ten countries including India, China, Iran, Indonesia, US, Thailand, Turkey, Russian, Vietnam, and Peru.

2.2 DDoS Attack Launch Methods and Mechanisms

DDoS attacks are primarily launched either manually with human coordination or automated using botnets. Manually coordinated attacks require a significant human intervention to be successful and are generally 'ideologically-motivated'. These attacks involve a large army of volunteers, with a common purpose, using their individual machines and a pre-shared tool. Depending on the number of volunteers orchestrated by an attacker, the computing capacity of their individual machines, and the complexity of the attacking tool being used, the aggregated traffic volume targeted to the victim machine can exhaust the available resources and render it unavailable to its intended clients. A recent example of a manually coordinated attack was *Operation Payback*, a name given to attacks launched by a group called *Anonymous* against commercial websites (Mastercard, PayPal,and Amazon) and anti-piracy organizations after they withdrew their ties with WikiLeaks [17–19]. These attacks were launched using a modified version of LOIC (Low Orbit Ion Cannon) tool, an open-source stress testing utility. LOIC was modified and extended to add a new feature called 'Hivemind' which was used to connect volunteers' LOIC tool to 'AnonOps' (a communication platform used by Anonymous) to receive attack instructions [20]. The modified tool had to be later installed on volunteers' machine to enable them to participate in the attack. The Anonymous group also created a web-page requiring volunteers to visit and click on the attack button [20].

Contrary to manually coordinated attacks, automated or Semi-automated DDoS Attacks, usually rely on exploiting network protocol and misusing them to amplify and/or obfuscate network traffic directed towards a victim. These attacks can be fully or semi automated and are generally launched using Botnets. Using browser-based bots is a common launch method in this category of DDoS attacks. Browser-based bots typically become active during a legitimate web browsing session and are sneakily installed on credulous user systems upon visiting a malicious website. Such bots are called Bad bots, and can easily emulate the normal user browsing behavior to elude current DDoS defense solutions. These bots primarily target the application layer and can easily crash down a web server with mere 50–100 requests per second.

Amplification and reflections are two most commonly used attack mechanisms to launch DDoS attacks. An 'Amplification-based DDoS attack' consists of an attacker, an amplification network, and a target victim. An amplification network is a network of host machines which allows broadcast messages to be sent. Any amplification network, when used for communication via a reply-based protocol like ICMP, is potentially prone to amplification-based DDoS attacks. When a packet from a spoofed IP is sent to the broadcast address of such networks, a response from every host is triggered and directed towards the intended victim. Smurf attack is a classic example of a DDoS attack launched using amplification.

Similar to an amplification-based attack, an adversary can also exploit a reply-based protocol such as DNS to launch a 'reflection-based DDoS attack' comprising of an attacker, a set of reflectors (reflective network) and a target host. A reflector can be any machine responding to an incoming request with a response sent to the source IP of that request [21]. Common examples of reflectors are web servers, DNS servers and mail servers because they send reply packets to incoming requests. Reflection-based attacks make use of a set of reflectors rather than a single host (broadcast address) in amplification-based attacks to initiate a response and cause the desired effect. A DNS Reflector Attack is a classic example of a reflection-based attack. This attack mechanism was used against Spamhaus, a provider of anti-spam DNS-based Blocklists and Whitelists [22]. Both these attack launch techniques when coupled with the distributed nature of botnets, renders such fully or semi automated DDoS attacks extremely difficult to detect and mitigate.

3 Reasons for Success

The use of latest technology, high level of sophistication, freely available user-friendly attack tools, cheaper Botnets-for-hire services, and advanced tactics have led to the multidimensional growth of DDoS attacks over the years. The traditional cyber security methods like Firewalls, Intrusion Prevention Systems (IPS), Intrusion Detection Systems (IDS), and Router Access Control Lists (ACL's) are unable to provide an ideal solution against DDoS attacks. Some of the reasons can be summarized as follows:

1. Firewalls perform state-level monitoring of each incoming connection. When a DDoS attack occurs, a high volume of network packets travels towards a specific destination. For each malicious network packet, a new connection or network flow is established at a Firewall resulting in exhaustion of more legitimate connections in the connection table which is limited in size. It, in turn, causes exhaustion of Firewall resources and leading to degradation of its performance. The Firewalls can shut down specific flows associated with attacks, but cannot perform anti-spoofing tasks similar to a Router. Firewalls are unable to discriminate between legitimate and DDoS attacks due to a similarity of network traffic and legitimate connection setups in application layer DDoS attacks.
2. The IDS/IPS solutions have some anomaly-detection capabilities. They can recognize malicious network packets with valid protocols. They are widely used along with traditional firewalls to block the attack traffic automatically. But they often generate a high number of false positives and false negatives and requires manual configurations specific to a network.

3. Both IDS/IPS and Firewalls are deployed close to the protected web server. They are not the first line of defense where DDoS attacks can be filtered before reaching to the target web server. However, DDoS mitigation techniques can be deployed on the edge routers for early detection.
4. IDS/IPS techniques can be used to detect some known types of DDoS attacks because the majority of them followed signature-based detection approach. However, the signature-based techniques cannot detect zero-day attacks. Even mitigation function is not provided by any of the available IDS/IPS.
5. DDoS attack traffic cannot be filtered by router access control lists (ACLs) alone as they use valid network protocols. Routers can be configured to stop trivial DDoS attacks (e.g., a ping attack) by filtering the nonessential protocols and can also prevent invalid IP addresses through ingress/egress filtering. However, they are typically ineffective against more sophisticated spoofed and application-level DDoS attacks using valid IP addresses.

Apart from the reasons above, there are various other reasons as mentioned below that lead to the successful launching of DDoS attacks and makes these attacks extremely challenging to defend.

- **Automated, user-friendly attack tools:** Availability of user-friendly and freely available attack tools and cheaper Botnets-for-hire services give flexibility to the attackers to launch a variety of diversified DDoS attacks without any technical knowledge. These tools automatically recruit and launch attack traffic with just one click without having any technical knowledge about them.
- **No common characteristics of DDoS streams:** Attackers are becoming more intelligent nowadays. To elude the current DDoS defense deployments, they mimic the characteristics of legitimate traffic and regularly alter the attack patterns. Such a similarity of both types of traffic makes the characterization and filtering very difficult.
- **Hidden identity of participants:** Another important characteristic of DDoS attacks is that they use the technique of IP spoofing to hide, where the attackers make use of fake but legitimate IPs to send the packets to the target. In this way, the attackers try to defeat existing resource-sharing mechanisms which works with valid IP address and also it makes the process of traceback the actual identity of attackers very difficult. In the absence of IP spoofing, malicious IPs could potentially be differentiated from the legitimate ones, and their traffic could be filtered accordingly.
- **Huge volume of traffic:** Under a DDoS attack, a vast number of redundant packets are sent towards the victim to overwhelm its network and server resources which makes the process of traffic profiling tough. Under this considerable network traffic volumes, the defense solutions can merely perform per-packet processing and start dropping the legitimate packets and lead to denial of service to legitimate users.
- **Large number of unwitting and geographically distributed participants:** A DDoS attack involves recruiting of a large number of geographically dispersed attack nodes to generate a massive volume of aggregated attack traffic towards

a victim. It is possible because of the availability of a large pool of unsecured hosts sitting in homes, school, business and governments around the world. The impact of DDoS attack could be controlled if somehow attackers are not able to recruit many agents. But with the ever-increasing number of internet and mobile users over the years, this pool of novice agents being distributed over the globe has also increased manifolds. So, even if we found some ways to secure these novice systems, it requires a long time to deploy such practices in reality to limit the impact of DDoS attacks.

- **Persistent security holes on the Internet:** All the Internet traffic passes through a set of well-connected routers called autonomous systems (ASs) before reaching out to the target. These specialized high-speed ASs are provisioned to forward huge Internet traffic from one hop to another. If some of these ASs become heavily congested or crash down by attackers, the whole of the Internet would slog to cessation and would have a distressing consequence on global connectivity.
- **No administrative domain cooperation:** Since there is no centralized control of the Internet infrastructure and low administrative cooperation between ISPs, deploying a DDoS defense on different parts of the Internet is practically a difficult problem to address. Moreover, to tackle huge volume of DDoS traffic, large amount of resources is also required which cannot be managed by a single victim alone, so a pragmatic DDoS defense solution requires a complete defense infrastructure with autonomous control.

4 DDoS Attack Defense Methods

Many DDoS defense schemes have been proposed in the literature for defending against DDoS attacks but an effective solution is not available till date. Even the attackers also consistently upgrade their skills to circumvent existing countermeasures. The architecture of a typical DDoS defense system is shown in Fig. 4.

As shown, a complete DDoS defense solution is composed of a number of modules namely: Traffic monitoring and analysis, Prevention, Detection, Traceback, Characterization and Mitigation modules. All these modules work in collaboration with each other to defend from a DDoS attack. Accordingly, Peng et al. [23] has classified the DDoS defense methods into following four categories:

- Prevention
- Detection
- Traceback
- Characterization and Mitigation

Traffic monitoring and analysis module sample the network traffic as per the relevant network traffic features. This sampled network traffic is then given as input to the proposed detection algorithm. Attack prevention methods stop the attack traffic before reaching out the specified target. Attack detection method refers to

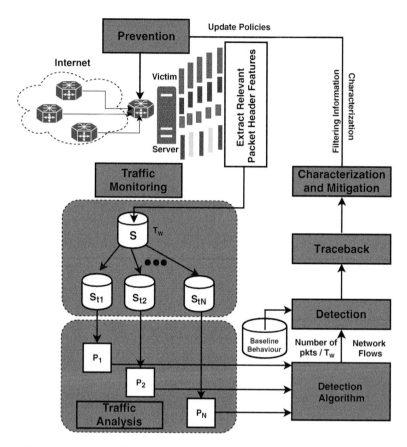

Fig. 4 Modules of a typical DDoS defense system

the detection of attack traffic when it occurs. Traceback of the attack source or its identification is the process of identifying the actual sources of the attack packets. Attack mitigation or response is the last step of a DDoS defense in which techniques are applied to minimize the impact of ongoing attack.

It is worth mentioning that the successful DDoS defense deployments depends on its placement along with the underlying logic of various defense modules [24]. As per [15, 25], a DDoS defense can be deployed at source-end, intermediate network, and victim-end. However, each of these possible deployment location has its own merits and demerits. Traditional security approaches such as Router ACLs, firewalls, IDS/IPSs are not able to protect from against DDoS attacks effectively that has lead to the absence of a perfect solution to combat against DDoS attacks till date; some of the reasons may be the decentralized nature of Internet, collateral damage, lack of collaboration among ISPs, the absence of latest real datasets, infrastructure changes, and obsolete methods used for validation purpose, and deployment issues, etc. [25–30]. The prominent approaches proposed by the fellow researchers for the efficient working of these modules are summarized in subsequent sections.

4.1 Prevention Methods

A prevention is always better than a cure. Attack prevention is the first step to stop an attack before it cause damage to the critical infrastructures and services of a network. Prevention methods aim to fix the security vulnerabilities that are exploited by DDoS attackers to launch attacks. Prevention methods are implemented with a packet filtering technique that is used to drop the malicious incoming packets.

Ingress means the packets that are coming towards the local area network and egress means the packets that are leaving from a local area network as shown in Fig. 5. In the year 1998, Senie et al. [31] proposed an ingress/egress filtering method to prevent DDoS attacks at the edge level routers of the protected network with the aim to allow only those network packets with a pre-specified IP address range. But such methods can be easily eluded by the sophisticated attackers by making use of IP spoofing technique. In this technique, attackers alter the source IP address space in the IP packet headers so that victims are unable to discriminate the attack packets from normal ones. Further, Park et al. [32] extended the concept of ingress filtering originally proposed by [31] to be deployed beyond a LAN. They implemented their proposed Router based packet filtering (RPF) method at the core of the Internet. Their proposed scheme works on the principle that only a limited number of source networks called autonomous systems (ASs) would send traffic on a specific link. Based on this information, traffic with spoofed IP address range can be discarded easily. This technique was then complemented by Li et al. [33] by using a source address validity protocol (SAVE) to store information regarding legitimate source IPs on each interface of the routers and block all other IPs. This scheme continuously propagates updated messages of valid source IPs from source to destination locations. But this scheme requires changes in the well-established routing protocols and universal deployment for better prevention which was very difficult to achieve.

In 2003, Peng et al. [34] proposed a novel scheme to filter attack traffic based on the history of IP addresses. In their scheme, every victim maintained its own list of IP addresses under normal working of a network i.e. under no attack. During a DDoS attack, only those IPs are allowed to send traffic which are available in the previously maintained IP address database. However, such scheme was vulnerable to any sophisticated DDoS attack that mimics legitimate traffic behavior. To overcome this problem, Kim et al. [35] proposed a statistical filtering mechanism called PacketScore, in which every network packet is given a score based on the selected traffic features. Their proposed scheme declared a packet as legitimate packet if the computed score is less than a dynamically computed threshold otherwise declare as attack packet without any human intervention. Their proposed scheme works well for non-spoofed DDoS attacks but the approach itself was vulnerable to performance degradation when the number of attributes used to compute packet score increased.

Further, Liu et al. [36] proposed a hybrid filter-based prevention method called a StopIt to overcome the limitation of IP spoofing. They proposed a passport method by making use of a secure source authentication system. It enable each destination

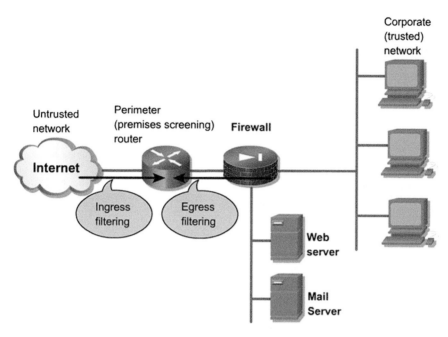

Fig. 5 Prevention of DDoS attacks using Ingree/Egress Filtering

target to install a network filter that blocks the undesirable attack traffic as it receives. However, their proposed method is vulnerable to flooding DDoS attacks. To prevent from such situations, the proposed framework can be configured in such a way that only the requests from nodes within a local AS or from other StopIt servers need to reach to a StopIt server but such manual configurations for an AS with large number of nodes is a very challenging.

Some authors like Saifullah et al. [37] proposed a weight-fair throttling mechanism at the upstream routers to prevent a high profile web server from DDoS attacks. They used a leaky bucket congestion control algorithm to control the network traffic volume destined for a target server based on the connection count. In their proposed scheme, the survival capacity is kept at low initially to protect the target server from any sudden burst of attack traffic. The capacity is increased in each subsequent rounds of the algorithm based on the feedback from the server. The updated capacity is then forwarded to its child routers which then propagated it further to all the routers.

Apart from preventing network layer DDoS attacks, some authors like Saleh et al. [38] proposed a Flexible, Collaborative, Multi-layer DDoS framework for preventing application layer DDoS attacks. Their framework blocks the source IPs based on pre-built black lists. However, their framework suffer produced low FNR. In some recent works, Muharish et al. [39] used neural network learning algorithms and statistical analysis to design a novel packet filtering system. They applied a self-organized-map neural network clustering technique to characterize and classify the different types of traffic. Further, Kalkan et al. [40] proposed a distributed,

Table 1 Comparison of prevention methods

Authors/ year	Deployment type	Working mode	Parameters	Prevention mechanism
Senie et al. 1998	Source-end	Distributed	src/dst IPs	Ingress/egress filtering
Park et al. 2001	Intermediate	Distributed	No. of autonomous systems src/dst IPs	Extension of ingress filtering implement Router based filtering (RBF) BGP routing information
Li et al. 2002	Intermediate	Distributed	src IPs	Proposed a source address validity protocol (SAVE) to overcome the limitations of RBF empower routers to store IPs at local level
Peng et al. 2003	Victim-end	Centralized	src/dst IPs	Filtering based on history of src/dst IPs
Kim et al. 2006	Victim-end	Distributed	src/dst IPs, ports TCP flags, TTL packet size, protocol	Packets are scored based on traffic features
Liu et al. 2008	Intermediate	Distributed	src/dst IPs	Automated characterization Selective packet discarding Overload control
Saiffulah et al. 2009	Intermediate	Distributed	Network traffic volume at upstream routers	Weighted-fair throttling
Saleh et al. 2015	Victim-end	Distributed	Entropy	Multi-layer defense framework
Muharish et al. 2016	Victim-end	Centralized	src/dst IPs, ports Packet transfer rate packet length, count	Applied a self-organized-map neural network clustering technique to characterize and classify the different types of traffic
Kalkan et al. 2016	Victim-end	Distributed	src/dst IPs protocol, packet size No. of packets	Compute score of each connection based on traffic features a realtime filtering mechanism

proactive and collaborative realtime filtering mechanism called ScoreForCore against application layer DDoS attacks. Their proposed scheme compute score of each connection based on the extracted relevant packet header features under normal network conditions. i.e. under no attack. When the network is under attack, the score of each incoming connection is compared with baseline score of connections. Their proposed scheme detect known attacks with 100% accuracy whereas it detect novel unknown attacks with 80% detection accuracy (Table 1).

It is clear from the above discussion of various network level and application level prevention mechanisms that all of the prevention schemes require wider geographical deployment to be more efficient but due to the openness and decentralization of Internet, it is very difficult to implement them.

4.2 Detection Methods

Mainly, DDoS attack detection methods can be categorized based on two approaches: (a) signature-based detection and (b) anomaly-based detection. Signature based approach match a known pattern with the pattern of incoming packets whereas anomaly based approach match the pre-built network traffic model with the incoming network traffic behavior in real-time. As mentioned in [23], anomaly-based detection approach has some inherent limitations as mentioned below:

- **Sophisticated attackers can monitor the network traffic to train their detection systems** There is a possibility that sophisticated attackers can monitor the network traffic to predict the traffic volume, number of source/destination IPs, and source/destination port numbers. This information can then be used by the attackers to launch variety of DDoS attacks in such a way so that there is a minimal deviation in the network traffic features which could effect the working of an anomaly based detection system.
- **Inappropriate selection of threshold values can lead to high false positive rates** Since network traffic is highly dynamic in nature, it is very difficult to set the baseline network traffic parameters. These parameters are used to set the crucial optimal threshold values for the efficient working of an anomaly based detection system. Further, the absence of benchmarked datasets for representing normal traffic also make this selection very difficult.
- **Difficult to extract both qualitatively and precisely appropriate features of legitimate and anomalous network behavior** Existing research have used diversified set of packet header features for the detection of attack traffic but to reduce the overall complexity of computing all of these packet header features, it is necessary to use only those packet header features that are sufficient to detect DDoS attacks.

Fellow researchers have proposed many isolated but effective solutions to detect different types of DDoS attacks. We have summarized these prominent DDoS attack detection methods in Table 2. These methods have been compared on an identified set of attributes such as type of attack detected (LR-DDoS/HR-DDoS), type of deployment (source-end/intermediate/victim-end), detection mode (centralized/distributed), type of network header parameters used, detection metric used, validation mechanism (simulation/emulation/realtime/datasets), datasets used and detection layer (network/application).

Table 2 Comparison of detection techniques for DDoS defense

Authors/ year	Attack type	Deployment type	Detection mode	Parameters	Detection metric	Validation technique	Datasets used	Detection layer
Gil et al. 2001	HR-DDoS	Victim-end	Distributed	Packet rate	CPU cycles Memory size	Realtime	Click tool	Network layer
Feinstein et al. 2003	HR-DDoS	Victim-end	Distributed	src/dst IP src/dst Ports	Shannon Entropy Chi-Square	Simulation	NZIX Bell Labs Ohio University	Network layer
Akella et al. 2003	HR-DDoS	Intermediate	Distributed	src/dst IP packet rate		Simulation	Abiline Backbone Trinoo, TFN	Network layer
Jin et al. 2004	LR-DDoS	Victim-end	Distributed	TCP flags	Correlation Covariance	Simulation	dec-pkt-1 dec-pkt-2	Network layer
Mirkovic et al. 2005	LR-DDoS HR-DDoS	Source-end	Distributed	packet rate connection size	No. of failed transactions No. of dropped packets	Emulation	UCLA Cleo attack tool	Network layer
Zhang et al. 2006	HR-DDoS	Intermediate	Distributed	src/dst IP, ports protocol,drop rate packet size,TTL	Legitimate traffic	Simulation		Network layer

Chen et al. 2007	HR-DDoS	Victim-end	Distributed	change point detection	CUSUM DETER	Emulation		Network layer
Kumar et al. 2007	LR-DDoS	Victim-end	Distributed	src/dst IPs, ports protocol	Shannon Entropy	Simulation		Network layer
Lu et al. 2007	LR-DDoS	Victim-end	Distributed	src/dst IP, Port TCP SYN/FIN(RST) pkt rate	Correlation	Simulation	Auckland university	Network layer
Nychis et al. 2008	HR-DDoS	Victim-end	Centralized	src/dst IPs,ports flow size in/out Degree	Shannon Entropy Correlation	Simulation CMU-2008	GEANT, Internet2	Network layer
Li et al. 2008	HR-DDoS	Victim-end	Centralized	src/dst IPs, ports protocol no. of packets	Euclidian distance Cluster Analysis	Simulation	2000 DARPA	Network layer
Chonka et al. 2009	HR-DDoS	Victim-end	Centralized	flow similarity	Chaos Theory Lypanuv Exponent	Simulation	2000 DARPA	Network layer

(continued)

Table 2 (continued)

Authors/ year	Attack type	Deployment type	Detection mode	Parameters	Detection metric	Validation technique	Datasets used	Detection layer
Xia et al. 2010	LR-DDoS HR-DDoS	Victim-end	Centralized	flow similarity no. of packets	SIC dropped packets	Simulation		Network layer
Sangkatsanee et al. 2011	HR-DDoS	Victim-end	Centralized	src/dst IPs, ports protocol, packets	Shannon Entropy Information gain	Realtime	RLD'09 Weka tool	Network Layer Application layer
Xiang et al. 2011	LR-DDoS	Victim-end	Centralized	src/dst IP protocol	Renyi Entropy Renyi Divergence	Real Datasets	1998 MIT Lincoln CAIDA 2007 attack	Network layer
Karimazad et al. 2011	HR-DDoS attacks	Victim-end	distributed	src/dst IPs no. of packets packets size	RBF Neural network	Simulation	UCLA	Network layer
Das et al. 2011	HR-DDoS	Victim-end	Centralized	no. of requests request pattern	DSB Index Clustering	Simulation	1999 KDD LBNL University campus	Network Layer Application layer

					JDR		Synthetic	
Wang et al. 2012	LR-DDoS	Victim-end	Distributed	src/dst IP, Port protocol packet length,rate	Entropy	Realtime	Synthetic	Network layer Application layer
Tellenbach et al. 2012	HR-DDoS	Victim-end	Centralized	src/dst IPs, ports Correlation	Tsallis entropy	Simulation	Netflow Data Flame attack tool	Network layer Application layer
Franccois et al. 2012	HR-DDoS	Intermediate	Distributed	No. of packets Score	Shannon entropy KL Divergence	Simulation	1999 DARPA Router Adjacency Dataset	Network layer
Bhatia et al. 2012	HR-DDoS	Victim-end	Centralized	src/dst IPs no. of packets CPU Load Memory/CPU Usage	Shannon entropy Correlation	Realtime	CAIDA 2007 1998 MIT Lincoln	Network layer Application layer

(continued)

Table 2 (continued)

Authors/ year	Attack type	Deployment type	Detection mode	Parameters	Detection metric	Validation technique	Datasets used	Detection layer
Beitollahi et al. 2012	LR-DDoS	Victim-end	Centralized	Request/ download rate up/down time page access rate src IP, no. of packets	Shannon entropy	Simulation	Clarknet www server	Application layer
Shiales et al. 2012	LR-DDoS	Victim-end	Centralized	packet inter arrival time	Fuzzy logic	Real Datasets	1999 DARPA Hping, BlackEnergy tools	Application layer
Ni et al. 2013	HR-DDoS	Victim-end	Centralized	No. of requests	Shannon entropy SVM Classifier	Simulation	Changzhov www server logs Mydoom Botnet	Application layer
Ma et al. 2014	HR-DDoS	Victim-end	Centralized	src/dst IPs	Tsallis entropy Lyapunov Exponent	Simulation	1998 MIT Lincoln	Network Layer
Jun et al. 2014	HR-DDoS	Victim-end	Centralized	src/dst IPs, ports protocol	Shannon entropy	Simulation		Network layer

Spognardi et al. 2014	HR-DDoS	Victim-end	Centralized	flow	Renyi's entropy KL divergence	Realtime	Net flows	Application layer
Basicevic et al. 2015	LR-DDoS HR-DDoS	Victim-end	Centralized	src/dst IPs, ports in/out Degree no. of packets	Tsallis Entropy Renyi's entropy Correlation	Realtime		Network layer
Dorbala et al. 2015	HR-DDoS	Victim-end	Centralized	src/dst IPs, ports no. of packets packet size,protocol	Manhattan distance KNN classifier	Real datasets	2000 DARPA 2007 CAIDA	Network layer
Sachdeva et al. 2016	HR-DDoS	Victim-end	Distributed	src/dst IPs protocol	Shannon entropy	Simulation	1998 FIFA 2007 CAIDA	Network layer Application layer
Bhuyan et al. 2016	HR-DDoS	Victim-end	Centralized	src/dst IPs, ports protocol no. of packets	Renyi's entropy Shannon entropy	Real datasets	1998 MIT Lincoln 2007 CAIDA	Network layer
Joldzic et al. 2016	HR-DDoS	Victim-end	Distributed	src/dst IPs	Shannon entropy	SDN technique	–	Network layer

In 2001, Gil et al. [41] proposed a heuristic data-structure called MULTOPS to detect HR-DDoS attacks by analyzing the packet rate in both the directions. MULTOPS is basically a tree of nodes that contains packet rate statistics for subnet prefixes at different aggregation levels. Their idea works on the assumption that the packet rates between two nodes in both the directions are comparative during the normal network conditions i.e. without attack. A significant deviation in the packet rates indicate a bandwidth level DDoS attack. However, their proposed method may fail to detect an attack in the cases where

- malicious packets uses randomized spoofed source IP addresses, and
- a large number of disproportional flows destined towards a specific target.

For example, there is a huge disproportion among the incoming and outgoing packet rates in case of real audio/video streams, on-line movies and news. Such situations would results in increase in false positive rates. Their proposed scheme also require router reconfigurations and new memory management schemes which is again a challenging issue.

Further, Feinstein et al. [42] presented a statistical detection approach based on computing entropy and frequency sorted distributions (chi-square). It had been observed that there were anomalies in the packet header attributes of DDoS attack traffic. After the detection phase, they also proposed some filtering rules for mitigating the impact of DDoS attacks. The drawback of this approach is that there is a minimum interaction between the detection and response module which lead to high false positive and false negative rate.

Akella et al. [43] proposed an ISP level detection mechanism where each router detects traffic anomalies using normal traffic profiles of baseline network behavior. Their proposed method works on the principle that routers usually exchange messages with other neighboring routers to take detection decisions. A router analyze the messages received from other routers and declare the traffic as an attack or legitimate traffic. The main advantage of their scheme is that it produce low FPR and FNR.

Some authors like Jin et al. [44] used the concept of two-variable correlation covariance model to detect different types of DDoS attacks. They compute a covariance matrix distance function to detect traffic anomaly. The attacker nearest router focused on detection of LR-DDoS attacks whereas victim nearest router focused on detecting HR-DDoS attacks. They performed multivariate analysis be considering the six control flags of TCP header to detect SYN flooding DDoS attacks.

To remove the limitations of this work, Jelena et al. [45] proposed an anomaly based distributed model called a D-WARD which continuously monitor the bidirectional traffic flows between the target network and Internet to identify HR-DDoS attacks. Whenever there is a noticeable periodic deviation from the normal flow patterns, attack is declared. They deployed their proposed system at the edge routers of a network and monitor the incoming and outgoing traffic of the network. If there is a significant deviation in the incoming and outgoing packet rates, their proposed system decrease the packet rate. They validated their proposed system in

Emulab, legitimate traffic was taken from UCLA dataset. They generate different types of network layer DDoS attacks using cleo attack tool. False negatives can also occur because of the distributed nature of DDoS traffic and use of a vast number of zombies to launch attacks. Furthermore, some legitimate flows like real time UDP flows do exhibit asymmetry.

Further, Chen et al. [46] extended their idea to propose a distributed change point (DCP) detection architecture to detect HR-DDoS attacks. They used change aggregation trees (CAT) to work in collaboration with edge routers to detect deviations in the network traffic. The computational server construct CATs using the traffic pattern changes at attack-transit routers which represent the attack flow patterns. They observed that in the case a DDoS attack, traffic feature deviation is more. The main feature of change point monitoring method is that it is stateless and requires less computational overhead. The principal objective of this scheme was to determine a point of time when a change happens. It uses CUMSUM approach to detect SYN flooding attack. This approach works effectively if all the networks packets route through the same edge router. However, traffic in autonomous system routed through different edge routers.

Few authors [25, 47, 48] have proposed an ISP level distributed approaches to defend from DDoS attacks. For example, Kumar et al. [25] distribute the computational overhead of computing detection metric at the edge POPs of an ISP level topology. Lu et al. [47] deployed a local analyzer at edge router(s) of an ISP which communicates with a global analyzer. used machine learning algorithm, CUSUM algorithm and spatial correlation of DDoS attack traffic to detect DDoS attacks at ISP level. They also used simulation based experiments to validate their approach. Their proposed approach predicts the next network state using maximum a posteriori (MAP) criteria. They also used a variant of expectation-maximization (EM) algorithm for optimizing searching over large no. of candidate structures. Their framework detect both LR-DDoS and HR-DDoS attacks. Franccois et al. [48] presented an approach named FireCol to detect HR-DDoS attacks. Their proposed system comprised of an intrusion prevention system located at edge routers of an ISP. They form a virtual protection ring around the hosts to defend and collaborate by exchanging selected traffic information.

In 2016, Sachdeva et al. [26] extended the work of [25] to differentiate the attack traffic from behaviorally similar FE traffic. They used an ensemble of cluster entropy and source IP entropy to discriminate the two. They observed that in the case of flash events traffic cluster entropy is small whereas it is more in the case of attack traffic.

Some authors [49, 50] have also used correlation coefficient between different packet header features (source/destination IPs/ports, and the number of distinct destination/source IP pairs) to detect different types of DDoS attacks.

Many authors [14, 15, 51–56] have used information theory based metrics to detect different types of DDoS attacks. Xiang et al. [14] proposed a collaborative detection algorithm using generalized entropy metric to differentiate an LR-DDoS attack from legitimate traffic. Bhuyan et al. [15] extended the idea of [14] to compute extended entropy metric based on packet header features of source IP and incoming packet rate to detect HR-DDoS attacks.

Wang et al. [51] proposed a multistage anomaly detection framework to detect LR-DDoS attacks at an early stage. They deployed their framework at the monitors close to the attack sources i.e. on edge routers and quantitatively analyze the deviations in traffic features. They define a network traffic state (NTS) to represent the state of the network traffic at each monitoring point. Then they compute a joint deviation rate (JDR) which is a combination of the variations of multiple traffic features. Their proposed detection efficiently detects both LR-DDoS and HR-DDoS attacks. The authors claimed that their proposed approach needs only three-time windows to extract malicious IP addresses from the start time of a DDoS attack. They launch a variety of network layer and application layer flooding DDoS attacks using the botnet executables to generate attack datasets in an experimental testbed synthetically. However, their proposed framework did not detect attacks when the attack traffic rate is similar to legitimate traffic.

Bhatia et al. [52, 57] proposed a novel ensemble based detection model which combine the results of network traffic analysis with the server load analysis for detecting HR-DDoS attacks. They compute various packet header features like the number of new source IPs, the total number of source IPs, number of packets per IP from the network traffic in each sampling interval, and a set of server specific parameters of CPU utilization, CPU load and real memory usage for each type of network traffic. They differentiate the different kinds of HR-DDoS attacks on network and application layer using a feature correlation matrix. They found that there is a strong correlation between the different types of network flows. For validating their proposed scheme, the authors performed a set of real experiments to launch the ICMP, HTTP, and SSL attacks by simulating the traffic traces of CAIDA, FIFA and MIT datasets.

Ma et al. [53] analyzed the variation of Lyapunov exponent in combination with Tsallis entropy to detect anomalies in the network traffic. They proposed an exponent separation detection algorithm to verify the feasibility of combining the source and destination entropy variations to detect HR-DDoS attacks. They used the detection system evaluation parameters of true positive rate, false positive rate, and ROC curve to check the efficiency of their proposed detection scheme. They validate their proposed approach by simulating the HR-DDoS attack scenario from MIT Lincoln dataset. Jun et al. [54] proposed a flow entropy and packet sampling based detection scheme to detect HR-DDoS attacks. Their proposed detection system measures the entropy of each flow, the entropy of source port and the number of packets/sec. Spognardi et al. [55] proposed a flexible DDoS defense framework called a fast network analyzer (FAN), which analyze the aggregated network traffic to identify HR-DDoS attacks. They compute a number of information theory metrics such as Shannon entropy, Renyi entropy and KL divergence metrics using traffic features of timestamp, duration, number of packets and transmitted bytes. They found that KL divergence is best for analyzing huge amount of network traffic. Basicevic et al. [56] compute Tsallis detection metric to detect HR-DDoS attacks. They found that Tsallis entropy produce low FPR and high detection accuracy as compared to Shannon entropy in detecting DDoS attacks.

Some authors like Sangkatsanee et al. [58] identified 12 essential features of a network traffic such as source(destination) IPs and port numbers, protocol, packet rate, TCP flags for detecting HR-DDoS attacks. In some recent works, Joldzic et al. [59] proposed a novel software defined networking (SDN) based scalable solution called TIDS (transparent intrusion detection system) for detecting network layer flooding based DDoS attacks. They used Shannon entropy metric for the detection of malicious traffic.

Further, many authors [60–62] have proposed schemes to detect application layer DDoS attacks. Beitollahi et al. [60, 61] proposed a novel ConnectionScore technique to detect and mitigate application layer DDoS attacks. They compared the connection score of malicious connections during the attack with the threshold scores computed during the non-attack period. The connection score is calculated by using various statistical attributes like request/download rate, uptime/downtime, browsing behavior (page classification, page access rate and page popularity), hyperlink fraction click, hyperlink depth, source IP address distribution, arrival distribution rate of users. The connections with low scores are identified as malicious connections; thereby the server retakes bottleneck resources from them. They validate their proposed detection scheme by simulating the real traffic traces of clarknet www server and some benchmark attack tools in Emulab environment. Ni et al. [62] compute entropy of HTTP GET requests per source IP (HRPI) to detect application layer HR-DDoS attacks. They approximate an AAR auto regressive model and a SVM support vector machine classifier to identify DDoS attacks. They observed that HRPI is highest in FEs and least in attack traffic even lesser than the legitimate traffic.

Besides above discussed detection methods, many authors have also proposed efficient DDoS attack detection methods using novel techniques such as:

- Machine learning and neural networks
- Chaos theory
- Fuzzy logic
- and wavelet analysis

Lee et al. [63] performed machine learning based cluster analysis based method for the proactive detection of DDoS attacks. They separate the DDoS attack into different phases and identified various precursors required for the proactive detection of attacks. They proposed a hierarchical type of clustering detection scheme which is often used to classify plants and animals. They proposed detection system compute the Euclidian distance between the entropy values of various precursors and apply WARD's minimum variance method to find the linkage between them. To optimize the number of precursors, they use principal component analysis (PCA) method. They validate their detection scheme by simulating the 2000 DARPA IDS dataset.

Chonka et al. [64] proposed a chaos theory based model to distinguish a HR-DDoS attack based on flow similarity. They developed a neural network based system to detect anomalous traffic. Xia et al. [65] proposed a fuzzy logic based method to identify LR-DDoS and HR-DDoS attacks in real time. Their proposed approach works in two phases. In the first phase, a time series based statistical analysis of network traffic is performed using discrete wavelet transform. A schwarz information criterion (SIC) is used to find the deviations in Hurst parameter. In the second phase, the identification of attack packets and evaluation of the approach is performed by counting the number of dropped packets. The authors validate their proposed method using NS2 simulations, testbed experiments and publically available Internet traffic traces. Karimazad et al. [66] proposed a Radial Basis Function (RBF) neural networks based DDoS detection method. They deployed the proposed scheme to edge routers of the victim network. They defined a network flow consisting of seven traffic features to activate a RBF neural network in each time window. In the case of a DDoS attack, the malicious IPs are forwarded to the filtering module and generate alarm signal for further actions. Otherwise, traffic is forwarded to the downstream routers.

Das et al. [67] proposed a clustering based detection scheme for unsupervised anomaly detection using feature-based analysis of HTTP GET requests traffic. They used three different HTTP flooding attack scenarios of random flooding, shrew flooding, and blast flooding to compute legitimate access pattern and pattern disagreement between request arrivals. Based on these values, they compute a DSB index which then clusters the incoming requests as normal or malicious. They monitor the university campus traffic for making baseline behavior and then, validate their detection scheme using the KDD cup99, and synthetically generated datasets.

Shiaeles et al. [68] proposed a realtime detection and traceback approach for defending against DDoS attacks by constructing a fuzzy estimator using mean packet inter arrival times. They validate their proposed scheme using publically available DARPA dataset and synthetically generated dataset using a real experimentation setup. They used automated botnet attack tools namely Hping and Black Energy for generating encrypted application layer malicious traffic. The authors claimed that their proposed method can detect DDoS attacks and traceback malicious IPs at an early stage before the impact reached at the target server. The reporting results show over 80% success rate of the proposed approach. However, it is vulnerable to more false positives in the case IP spoofing. However, they did not discriminate the legitimate looking FEs from HR-DDoS attacks. Dorbala et al. [69] proposed a scalable implementation of a clustering and classification algorithm for detecting the HR-DDoS attacks. They calculate interval summary based on per second traffic analysis of existing real datasets. An interval summary constitutes the number of packets, average packet length, the number of TCP, UDP and ICMP packets, distinct source and destination IPs and port numbers. They classify different types of network packets using a K- nearest neighbor classification algorithm. They compute information theory based Manhattan distance metric between the various elements of a cluster. They validate their proposed approach using real datasets of DARPA and CAIDA. Firstly, they train the proposed detection system using half of the dataset records and then, apply the detection algorithm on the remaining half of the dataset records. Their proposed detection system detect HR-DDoS attacks with 99.5 precision, and 100% detection accuracy when computed with a tolerance factor $k = 5$.

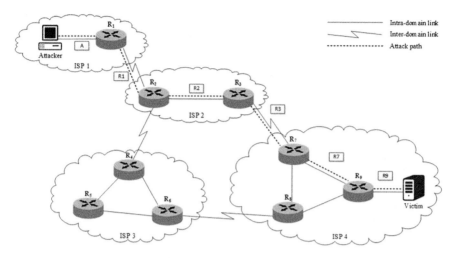

Fig. 6 A typical Traceback mechanism of a DDoS defense

4.3   Traceback Methods

Most of the DDoS attacks are characterized by a high incoming rate of network packets with random and valid source IPs. However, these source IPs are often spoofed. To identify the source of such fake network packets requires tracing the packets back to the source hop by hop. The current traceback approaches necessitate the dreary unrelenting responsiveness and support of each intermediate ISP which is not a trivial task.

Once an attack is detected, the next step is to identify the attack sources and to block the attack traffic. As per [70], traceback is defined as a mechanism of identifying actual sources of a packet sent over the Internet (Fig. 6). Mathematically, let $C = h_1 + h_2 + h_{n-1} \ldots . h_n$ be a connection chain between the hosts h_n (i = 1 to n). Given a hosts h_n (i.e. IP Address), the traceback problem is to identity recursively the identities of $h_{n-1}, h_{n-2} \ldots h_1$ in an automated way. This section summarizes the prominent work done in this area as shown in Table 3.

Burch et al. [71] proposed a generalized traceback scheme without having dependence on the cooperation of intervening ISPs. Their proposed scheme flood the network links with traffic bursts to identify the attack path. However, this scheme is less effective because in the case of a typical DDoS attack, only a small proportion of attack traffic converge from a single link, so there would not be any significant changes in the total attack traffic by flooding a single link. To improve this limitation, Savage et al. [72] proposed a IP traceback scheme based on probabilistic packet marking (PPM). In this scheme, each router is required to embed its IP address in the incoming packets while they travel through that router. Based on this embedded information, the victim can predict the attack transmission path. However, it is very difficult reconfigure the existing well established IPv4

Table 3 Comparison of traceback techniques for a DDoS defense

Authors/year	Parameters	Traceback mechanism
Burch et al. 2000	Packet rate	Flooding of network links to identify attack paths
Savage et al. 2001	src IPs	IP traceback using Probable Packet Marking (PPM)
		Need to re-configure IPv4 scheme on each router
Dean et al. 2002	src IPs, TOS	Used an algebraic approach to insert partial path information
	ID	low computational comlexity
Al et al. 2006	Path coverage ratio	Combines packet marking and packet logging techniques
	Attack source localization distance ratio	
	Detection % age	
Yu et al. 2011	Entropy variations	Use entropy variations in legitimate and attack traffic
Wu et al. 2011	Misidentified normal edge ratio	Proposed an approach based on protection agent and sentinels
	Misidentified attack edge ratio	they apply a C4.5 algorithm to construct a decision tree using
	Entropy, Flow similarity	TCP SYN and ACK flag rate
Xiang et al. 2011	Information distance	Compute information distance based on variation in entropy values of
		local and forwarded traffic to its immediate upstream routers
Rajam et al. 2011	Ant density	Deterministic packet marking based on Ant colony optimization
		Compute ant density of all possible paths
		Low computational and memory overhead
Saleh et al. 2015	Entropy	Traceback based multi-layer defense framework
Bhuyan et al. 2016	Entropy	Traceback and filtering based on EEM metric
		compute entropy difference based on in-traffic and out-traffic from a router

protocol as there are no field reserved for the tracking purposes. Their scheme is also independent of any cooperation from intervene ISPs.

Dean et al. [73] proposed an alternative coding scheme to remove the limitations of PPM approach. They applied an algebraic approach to insert the partial path information so as to reduce the number of packets required to reconstruct the attack path. Authors in [74] proposed a hybrid scheme which combines the packet marking and packet logging schemes called a distributed link list traceback (DLLT) and probabilistic pipelined packet marking (PPPM). The first scheme preserves the marking information at the intermediate routers so that it can be collected using a linked list approach when required. The second scheme target to disseminate the source IPs of routers that were involved in marking packets by embedding them into the packets going to the victim. In this way, the scheme avoid the need for long term storage at the intermediate routers.

Yu et al. [75] used the entropy variations of legitimate and attack traffic to propose a new traceback scheme. In comparison to the existing IP traceback methods, their proposed strategy is more efficient in terms of less memory intensive, scalable and independent of any specific attack traffic patterns. Wu et al. [76] designed a system that can detect and traceback the origins of network layer HR-DDoS attacks sources quickly. Their proposed scheme consists of two subsystems namely protection agent and sentinels. The protection agent is located in the Victim (for detection purpose) and sentinels are located in routers (for traceback purpose). Then they apply a decision tree technique using the attributes TCP SYN and ACK flag rate, as the tests to detect abnormal traffic. They adopt the C4.5 algorithm to construct the decision tree which is based on the concept of entropy. Then they use a flow similarity algorithm to isolate the attack flows for trace back purpose. They also used an AI based classifier for detecting DDoS attacks. The authors evaluate their proposed scheme by measuring detection metrics such as false negative rate, false positive rate, false classification ratio, and detection latency.

Further, Rajam et al. [77] proposed an IP traceback mechanism for large scale distributed systems based on deterministic packet marking. Unlike other marking schemes, it reduces the computational and memory overheads. They applied their proposed scheme to secure online voting system, which in turn improves the security processed involved in the distributed systems. Saleh et al. [38] proposed service traceback oriented architecture (STBOA) to trace back the actual attacking IP source. They validate their proposed framework using simulation based experiments. Singh et al. [78] systematically reviewed a number of IP traceback schemes. They concluded that IP traceback does not play a significant role in defending against DDoS attacks. Rather, it only allows to identify the path that the attack flows follows. However, it can be integrated with other defense modules to provide the enhanced mitigation mechanisms.

4.4 Characterization and Mitigation Methods

Mitigation techniques primarily deal with flooding based DDoS attacks. Tolerating DDoS attacks concentrates on controlling the intentional and malicious traffic. Whereas mitigation is defined as the process of minimizing the impact of a DDoS attack. It can be achieved by deploying different filtering and rate limiting methods on the incoming network traffic. The main aim is to dropping out the attack traffic as much as possible whereas keeping the legitimate traffic intact. A mitigation framework requires the communication among different modules of a defense system including detection, characterization and traceback. A considerable amount of research effort has been carried in literature for tolerating and mitigating DDoS attacks as summarized in Table 4.

Floyd et al. [79] stated that flooding DDoS does not observe end to end congestion control. Due to this role of router scheduling and queuing algorithm is very important in tolerating against DDoS attacks. Their proposed mechanism identify and restrict the bandwidth allocation to high-bandwidth flows in the situation of congestion. The proposed scheme utilize the history of dropped packets from queues with RED (Random Early Detection) queue management.

Mahajan et al. [80] propose a mitigation framework called Aggregate Congestion Control (ACC) agent for routers to identify aggregates responsible for the network congestion. ACC agent identify the congestion signature using the history of dropped packets in a time window of k seconds and then filter the useless traffic accordingly. Further, routers cooperate with upstream routers using a pushback scheme to share the filtering information. Peng et al. [34] proposed an integrated framework for mitigation and traceback. They improve the pushback mechanism by introducing selective pushback a router based system to defend against DDoS attacks. DDoS attacks are treated as a congestion control problem. The main issue is to identify the congestions and then pushback a packet filter to the router closed to the source that causes the congestion. Source information is obtained using the probabilistic packet marking (PPM). By filtering the packets using the source information filtering of malicious traffic is achieved while protecting the legitimate traffic.

Zhang et al. [81] proposed a distributed collaborative approach to defend against HR-DDoS attacks. Their proposed system is deployed at an intermediate network. The proposed scheme uses a gossip based communication mechanism to exchange traffic information between independent Internet devices to collect, analyze and predict the network attacks. This compiled information is then shared among these devices so as to use it for detecting and stopping DDoS attacks more effectively and accurately at the local level. The proposed scheme uses an overlay network for the dissemination of attack information. Lu et al. [47] described a perimeter-based anti-DDoS system. Their proposed system is deployed at the edge routers of an ISP level network. Anti-DDoS extracts the relevant traffic features in first phase and then apply a spatial correlation method for the detection. The proposed scheme detect and characterize the attack packets with accuracy and without rendering the embedded logic of routers.

Wang et al. [82] proposed a distributed mitigation and filtering mechanism based on a pushback and resource regulation methods to mitigate the effect of DDoS attacks. They assume that all the routers cooperate with victim to share critical information used in implementing the defense strategy. A Pushback mechanism based on the improved aggregate-based congestion control (IACC) algorithm is applied to routers for defending bandwidth HR-DDoS attacks, whereas resource regulation is applied to victim for defending resource consumption HR-DDoS attacks. Devi et al. [83] used a set of host-network based metrics to detect HR-DDoS attack. They compute various server level statistics like the CPU and memory usage, packet loss, latency, link utilization and throughput in an experimental testbed. They also proposed a DDoS mitigation algorithm based on the interface based rate

Table 4 Comparison of mitigation and characterization techniques for DDoS defense

Authors/year	Deployment location	Detection mode	Parameters	Mitigation/Characterization approach
Floyd et al. 1997	Victim-end	Centralized	No. of dropped packets	Identify, classify and restrict bandwidth allocation to high-bandwidth flows while in congestion using TCP flows
Mahajan et al. 2002	Intermediate	Distributed	Aggregates, flows	Aggregates based congestion control (ACC) using a pushback mechanism. ACC agent identify the congestion signature using the history of dropped packets
Peng et al. 2003	Intermediate	Distributed	src IPs	IP history based dropping of network packets
Zhang et al. 2006	Intermediate	Distributed	No. of dropped packets	Gossip based communication to exchange traffic information between intermediate network nodes using overlay network
Lu et al. 2007	victim-end	distributed	src/dst IP, Port TCP SYN/FIN(RST) pkt rate	Correlation
Wang et al. 2008	Intermediate	Distributed		A distributed mitigation and filtering mechanism based on a pushback and resource regulation methods improved ACC is applied to routers for defending bandwidth HR-DDoS attacks resource regulation is applied to victim for defending resource consumption HR-DDoS attacks

(continued)

Table 4 (continued)

Authors/ year	Deployment location	Detection mode	Parameters	Mitigation/Characterization approach
Devi et al. 2012	Source-end	Distributed	CPU/Memory Usage packet loss, Latency Link utilization, throughput	Interface based Rate Limiting mechanism
Wei et al. 2013	Victim-end	Centralized	Flow, Packet count	Pearson coefficient is used to find relationship relationship between flows using packet count
Zhou et al. 2014	Victim-end	Centralized	src IPs, Packet rate web page frequency	Correlation based detection and characterization
Bedi et al. 2015	Victim-end	Distributed	Packet loss Throughput	Active queue management (AQM) using deterministic weighted fair scheduling (DFS) Dynamically self-adjust buffer usage depending on congestion
Behal et al. 2018	victim-end	Distributed	src IPs, Packet rate	Information distance based characterization and rate limiting mechanism
Wang et al. 2018	victim-end	Distributed	Sketch data structure	Modified Hellinger distance based characterization using whitelists and blacklists of user profiles

limiting (IBRL). Based on the deviations in the observed parameters, their proposed mitigation scheme is activated so as to mitigate the impact of ongoing DDoS attacks.

Gupta et al. [84] proposed dynamic and auto responsive approach for defending against DDoS attack. Various design principles and evaluation results of the proposed framework that autonomously detects and accurately characterizes a wide range of flooding DDoS attacks have been highlighted. Detection of attacks is performed using the low volume based approach that observe abrupt change in the network traffic in the ISP domain. Characterization of attack traffic and normal traffic is performed using total number of the bytes arrival for each flow during monitoring period. The flows that crosses predefined thresholds are classified as either suspicious or attack traffic flows depending on detection from threshold values. Wei et al. [85] proposed a rank correlation-based detection (RCD) approach for detecting LR-DDoS attacks. The simulation results show that RCD can characterize the attack flows from legitimate flows with efficacy.

Zhou et al. [86] observed that the ratio of source IP entropy and click rate entropy of a web page is high in the case of DDoS attacks. Bedi et al. [87] observed that none of the schemes provide an effective solution against the congestion occurred due to flooding DDoS attacks. Under HR-DDoS attack situation, the network resources including routers, links, web server etc. gets overwhelmed and the mitigation systems gets crashed before taking any action to mitigate the situation.

Such kind of problems occur because majority of the DDoS defense methods are deployed primarily at the victim-end. The mammoth network traffic volume generated during DDoS attacks and deficient computational resources at the victim-end, makes defense solution vulnerable to these attacks. Such limitations have lead to the development of many distributed solutions and have shift the trend to more economical Software Defined Technique (SDN) and cloud based DDoS defense solutions [24, 59, 88–90]. All of these novel distributed systems tend to distribute the computational complexity among multiple computational devices with the objective of early detection of malicious traffic.

5   Impact, Sophistication and Future Trends

Usually, the prominent websites are the prime victims of DDoS attacks and suffer interruptions in their services. Such interruptions in the services often have substantial financial implications. The revenue loss has amplified to $209 million in the first quarter of 2016, as compared to $24 million for all of 2015 [91]. According to a recent report by the security firm Imperva Incapsula [16], a single hour of a DDoS attack can cost up to $20,000. A study by the Ponemon Institute [92] also witnessed that the average company's cost for every minute of downtime during a DDoS attack is around $22,000. As majority of DDoS attacks lasts for more than six hours, the incurred losses can reach a high dollar value in a relatively short time. Besides revenue losses, these attacks can also result in financial losses including the cost of investigation and responding to attacks, expenses related to loss in customer support and public relations, and potential financial penalties and lawsuits.

Increased Sophistication, Persistence and Magnitude Global DDoS threat landscape Q4 report [16], indicates that the trend of sophisticated DDoS attacks has shifted from spoofing based network layer DDoS attacks to legitimate TCP connections based application layer DDoS attacks. These attacks sends redundant HTTP GET requests to consume web server's resources such as bandwidth, memory, CPU cycles, file descriptors, and buffers. 2017 also saw an increase in attack duration with an average DDoS attack lasting for 1.2 h with the largest reported attack lasting 5.5 days. The third quarter also showed the number of attacks lasting more than 6 h increased to 7.5% compared to 0.8% in the preceding quarter [16]. Over the years, the conventional DDoS attacks have not only grown in sophistication but have dramatically expanded in their magnitude. As per WISR report [93], the traffic volume of DDoS attacks has touched to 650 Gbps in 2016 as compared to 500 Gbps in 2015 and 350 Gbps in 2014.

DDoS and IoT Devices: The Perfect Match? Apart from using the traditional compromised desktop and workstation systems, the attackers have started making use of less secured Internet of Things (IoT) devices as the launching pad, mainly owing to their astonishing rate of proliferation and their inherent insecurity [94]. Recently Twitter, Spotify, and Amazon suffer interruptions in their services for almost two hours on Oct 21, 2016, because of the large number of unsecured internet-connected digital devices, such as home routers and surveillance cameras. The attackers employed thousands of such devices that had been infected with malicious code to launch a series of DDoS attacks. The Mirai botnet, which harnessed the high CPU capability and high-bandwidth uplinks of hundreds of thousands of IoT devices such as DVRs and CCTV cameras has set new records for DDoS attack size, reaching towards 1 Tbps. With more and more IoT devices coming online every day (Gartner forecasts that there will be 20.4 billion connected devices worldwide by 2020[1]), the threat of DDoS attacks from increasingly sophisticated IoT botnets will only grow.

DDoS and Software Defined Networking – In recent times, dynamic environments such as SDNs (Software Defined Networking) have been used frequently to implement and validate various DDoS defense mechanisms. SDN seems to be promising approach to remove the limitations of existing traditional DDoS defense solutions but still they are susceptible to diversity of attacks that occur in traditional networks, such as the attacks that target control and data plane [95–97]. By exploiting the vulnerabilities in the controller or the communication links between the switch and controller can lead to several attacks such DDoS [88] and Host Location Hijacking Attacks [98]. So, there are possible attack scenarios that make the current architecture of SDN non-secure, which requires more attention to various security aspects of SDNs.

---

[1]http://www.gartner.com/newsroom/id/3598917

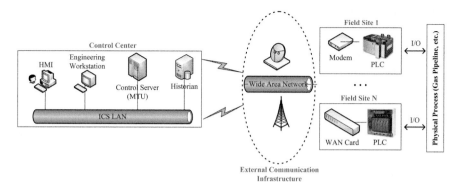

Fig. 7 Overview of an industrial control system environment

DDoS and Blackchain Technology – In some latest works, a company named Gladius has come up with a solution to the DDoS problem by making use of a novel blockchain technology [99]. Gladius provides a decentralized solution to DDoS attacks by allowing participants to rent out their under used network bandwidth in exchange for Gladius tokens. Network participants form "Pools" that monitor requests and traffic to a website, therefore making it harder for any DDoS attacks to occur. Website owners can even switch to larger pools as they grow in return for increased protection. However, currently this technology is in its token sale stage. It would take time before we can have the full-blockchain solution to the crippling effects a DDoS attack.

Industrial Control Systems – a New Target Domain. Industrial control systems (ICS) are classified as a cyber-physical system and are mainly used to control and monitor physical industrial and infrastructure processes such as oil and gas pipeline, power grid, and nuclear plants [100]. Figure 7 provides an overview of a typical ICS environment. It consists of control center and field sites.

The physical processes are located at field sites and are monitored and controlled via sensors, actuators, and programmable logic controllers (PLCs), equipped to communicate with the control center remotely via different proprietary and open ICS protocols such as Modbus, EtherNet/IP, and PROFINET. The control center comprises of several ICS services including human-machine-interface (HMI), Historian and Engineering Workstation. When the data arrives at the control center, the HMI interprets and presents the data in a graphical user interface to a human operator to facilitate in operational decisions. Control engineers use engineering workstation to configure and program PLCs to define how the PLCs should control a physical process.

Industrial control systems run 24/7 for continuous monitoring and controlling of physical processes. These systems run 24/7 and their availability is the main concern in CIA triad. In recent years these systems have been upgraded from the standard serial bus systems to modern TCP/IP based systems, thereby getting connected with larger networks such as corporate network and the Internet, and thus exposing them to cyber-attacks. Attackers target these systems to compromise their availability and sabotage physical processes [101–104]. In particular, they can launch Denial of Service attacks against ICS services, network, and embedded devices such as PLCs at field sites. In particular, they can launch Denial of Service attacks against ICS services, network, and embedded devices such as PLCs at field sites.

- ICS Services – Attacker exploit bugs and vulnerabilities in ICS services to cause denial of service. For instance, ICS-CERT reported that Elipse SCADA application fails when it receives data packets of DNP3 protocol with formatting errors. The vulnerability is found in the DNP Master Driver [105]. Senthivel et al. identify two attack scenarios that crash RSLogix 500 Engineering software when the software attempts to retrieve the control logic from a target PLC [106, 107]. The first scenario involves man-in-the-middle attack between RSLogix and the PLC. It intercepts the control logic traffic and replace a control instruction with noise data such as 0xFFFF. Apparently, RSLogix cannot handle it and crash. In the second scenario, attacker creates a well-crafted control logic program at the binary level. It involves tempering the metadata related to the size of the program. Attacker installs the program to a target PLC. Apparently, the program runs successfully on the PLC but when RSLogix attempts to retrieve it from the PLC, it crashes the software.
- Programmable Logic Controller – A DoS attack on a PLC device exploits a vulnerability in a PLC component, such as firmware. Recently, ICS-CERT reported a similar vulnerability on Siemens SICAM products. Attacker sends crafted packets to port 2404/TCP to cause a target device to go into defect mode [108]. Similarly, attacker sends crafted packets to Siemens SIPROTEC Compact devices at port 50000/UDP to cause a denial of service [109]. To recover the device, a manual reboot is required.
- Network Connectivity – Control operator monitors the physical processes through HMI that receives data from PLCs periodically. A DoS attack targets the communication link between the PLC and the control center using packet flooding to exhaust the bandwidth of the link [110].

In summary, ICS security is a big concern and timely detection and prevention of DDoS attacks in an ICS environment requires the attention of cybersecurity research community. DDoS attacks are not only increasing in size but are becoming more sophisticated in their makeup. This is largely due to a rapid expansion of the contemporary digital world consisting of ever-increasing number of inherently unsecured and connected devices presenting an ideal platform for the attackers to overwhelm disrupt.

References

1. US Committee on National Security Systems, "National Information Assurance (IA) Glossary," CNSS, Instruction 4009, 2006.

2. G. Linden, "Make Data Useful," *Presentation, Amazon, November*, 2006.
3. R. Stapleton-Gray and W. Woodcock, "National Internet Defense—Small States on the Skirmish Line," *Communications of the ACM*, vol. 54, no. 3, pp. 50–55, 2011.
4. C. M. R. Dobbins, "Worldwide Infrastructure Security Report," Arbor Networks, Tech. Rep., 2011.
5. D. Moore, C. Shannon, D. Brown, G. Voelker, and S. Savage, "Inferring Internet Denial-of-Service Activity," *ACM Transactions on Computer Systems (TOCS)*, vol. 24, no. 2, pp. 115–139, 2006.
6. "Prolexic Quarterly Global DDoS Attack Report – Q4 2012," Prolexic, Tech. Rep., 2012.
7. "Global ddos threat landscape q3 2017," https://www.incapsula.com/ddos-report/ddos-report-q3-2017.html, 2017.
8. F. Khan, "Botnet Economy," http://dos-attacks.com/2010/10/26/botnet-economy/, [Online; accessed 23-Sep-2012].
9. M. Kenney, "Ping of Death," http://insecure.org/sploits/ping-o-death.html, Jan 1997, [Online; accessed 26-Sep-2012].
10. S. Suriadi, A. Clark, and D. Schmidt, "Validating Denial of Service Vulnerabilities in Web Services," in *IEEE Computer Society Proceedings of the Fourth International Conference on Network and System Security*.   IEEE Computer Society, 2010.
11. J. Mirkovic and P. Reiher, "A Taxonomy of DDoS Attack and DDoS Defense Mechanisms," *ACM SIGCOMM Computer Communication Review*, vol. 34, no. 2, pp. 39–53, 2004.
12. S. M. Specht and R. B. Lee, "Distributed denial of service: Taxonomies of attacks, tools, and countermeasures." in *ISCA PDCS*, 2004, pp. 543–550.
13. M. H. Bhuyan, D. K. Bhattacharyya, and J. K. Kalita, "Network anomaly detection: methods, systems and tools," *Ieee communications surveys & tutorials*, vol. 16, no. 1, pp. 303–336, 2014.
14. Y. Xiang, K. Li, and W. Zhou, "Low-rate ddos attacks detection and traceback by using new information metrics," *IEEE Transactions on Information Forensics and Security*, vol. 6, no. 2, pp. 426–437, 2011.
15. M. H. Bhuyan, D. Bhattacharyya, and J. K. Kalita, "E-ldat: a lightweight system for ddos flooding attack detection and ip traceback using extended entropy metric," *Security and Communication Networks*, vol. 9, no. 16, pp. 3251–3270, 2016.
16. Imperva, "Global ddos threat landscape q4 report." https://www.incapsula.com/ddos-report/ddos-report-q4-2016.html, 2017, [Online; accessed 25-Aug-2017].
17. C. Labovitz, "The Internet Goes to War," http://asert.arbornetworks.com/2010/12/the-internet-goes-to-war/, 14 Dec 2010, [Online; accessed 23-Sep-2012].
18. T. Bradley, "Operation Payback: WikiLeaks Avenged by Hacktivists," http://www.pcworld.com/businesscenter/article/212701/operation_payback_wikileaks_avenged_by_hacktivists.html, 7 Dec 2010, [Online; accessed 23-Sep-2012].
19. E. Addley and J. Halliday, "Operation Payback Cripples MasterCard Site in Revenge for WikiLeaks Ban," http://www.guardian.co.uk/media/2010/dec/08/operation-payback-mastercard-website-wikileaks, Dec 2010, [Online; accessed 23-Sep-2012].
20. R. Singel, "Operation Payback Cripples MasterCard Site in Revenge for WikiLeaks Ban," http://www.wired.com/threatlevel/2010/12/web20-attack-anonymous/, Dec 2010, [Online; accessed 24-Sep-2012].
21. V. Paxson, "An Analysis of Using Reflectors for Distributed Denial-of-service Attacks," *ACM SIGCOMM Computer Communication Review*, vol. 31, no. 3, pp. 38–47, 2001.
22. "The DDoS that knocked Spamhaus offline," http://blog.cloudflare.com/the-ddos-that-knocked-spamhaus-offline-and-ho, 2013, [Online; accessed 2-Apr-2013].
23. T. Peng, C. Leckie, and K. Ramamohanarao, "Survey of Network-based Defense Mechanisms Countering the DoS and DDoS Problems," *ACM Computing Surveys*, vol. 39, no. 1, p. 3, 2007.
24. V. Gulisano, M. Callau-Zori, Z. Fu, R. Jiménez-Peris, M. Papatriantafilou, and M. Patiño-Martínez, "Stone: A streaming ddos defense framework," *Expert Systems with Applications*, vol. 42, no. 24, pp. 9620–9633, 2015.

25. K. Kumar, R. Joshi, and K. Singh, "An isp level distributed approach to detect ddos attacks," in *Innovative Algorithms and Techniques in Automation, Industrial Electronics and Telecommunications*. Springer, 2007, pp. 235–240.
26. M. Sachdeva, K. Kumar, and G. Singh, "A comprehensive approach to discriminate ddos attacks from flash events," *Journal of Information Security and Applications*, vol. 26, pp. 8–22, 2016.
27. S. Behal and K. Kumar, "Trends in validation of ddos research," *Procedia Computer Science*, vol. 85, pp. 7–15, 2016.
28. S. Bhatia, "Ensemble-based model for ddos attack detection and flash event separation," in *Future Technologies Conference (FTC)*. IEEE, 2016, pp. 958–967.
29. R. Saravanan, S. Shanmuganathan, and Y. Palanichamy, "Behavior-based detection of application layer distributed denial of service attacks during flash events," *Turkish Journal of Electrical Engineering & Computer Sciences*, vol. 24, no. 2, pp. 510–523, 2016.
30. A. Bhandari, A. L. Sangal, and K. Kumar, "Characterizing flash events and distributed denial-of-service attacks: an empirical investigation," *Security and Communication Networks*, 2016.
31. D. Senie and P. Ferguson, "Network ingress filtering: Defeating denial of service attacks which employ ip source address spoofing," *Network*, 1998.
32. K. Park and H. Lee, "On the effectiveness of route-based packet filtering for distributed dos attack prevention in power-law internets," in *ACM SIGCOMM computer communication review*, vol. 31, no. 4. ACM, 2001, pp. 15–26.
33. J. Li, J. Mirkovic, M. Wang, P. Reiher, and L. Zhang, "Save: Source address validity enforcement protocol," in *INFOCOM 2002. Twenty-First Annual Joint Conference of the IEEE Computer and Communications Societies. Proceedings. IEEE*, vol. 3. IEEE, 2002, pp. 1557–1566.
34. T. Peng, C. Leckie, and K. Ramamohanarao, "Protection from Distributed Denial of Service Attacks Using History-based IP Filtering," in *IEEE International Conference on Communications, 2003. ICC'03*, 2003, pp. 482–486.
35. Y. Kim, W. C. Lau, M. C. Chuah, and H. J. Chao, "Packetscore: a statistics-based packet filtering scheme against distributed denial-of-service attacks," *IEEE transactions on dependable and secure computing*, vol. 3, no. 2, pp. 141–155, 2006.
36. X. Liu, X. Yang, and Y. Lu, "Stopit: Mitigating dos flooding attacks from multi-million botnets," Technical Report 08-05, UC Irvine, Tech. Rep., 2008.
37. A. Saifullah, "Defending against distributed denial-of-service attacks with weight-fair router throttling," 2009.
38. M. A. Saleh and A. Abdul Manaf, "A novel protective framework for defeating http-based denial of service and distributed denial of service attacks," *The Scientific World Journal*, vol. 2015, 2015.
39. E. Y. M. Muharish, "Packet filter approach to detect denial of service attacks," 2016.
40. K. Kalkan and F. Alagöz, "A distributed filtering mechanism against ddos attacks: Scorefor-core," *Computer Networks*, vol. 108, pp. 199–209, 2016.
41. T. Gil and M. Poletto, *MULTOPS: a data-structure for bandwidth attack detection*. Defense Technical Information Center, 2001.
42. L. Feinstein, D. Schnackenberg, R. Balupari, and D. Kindred, "Statistical Approaches to DDoS Attack Detection and Response," in *DARPA Information Survivability Conference and Exposition, 2003. Proceedings*, vol. 1. IEEE, 2003, pp. 303–314.
43. A. Akella, A. Bharambe, M. Reiter, and S. Seshan, "Detecting ddos attacks on isp networks," in *Proceedings of the Twenty-Second ACM SIGMOD/PODS Workshop on Management and Processing of Data Streams*. Citeseer, 2003, pp. 1–3.
44. S. Jin and D. S. Yeung, "A covariance analysis model for ddos attack detection," in *Communications, 2004 IEEE International Conference on*, vol. 4. IEEE, 2004, pp. 1882–1886.
45. J. Mirkovic and P. Reiher, "D-ward: a source-end defense against flooding denial-of-service attacks," *IEEE transactions on Dependable and Secure Computing*, vol. 2, no. 3, pp. 216–232, 2005.

46. Y. Chen, K. Hwang, and W.-S. Ku, "Collaborative detection of ddos attacks over multiple network domains," *Parallel and Distributed Systems, IEEE Transactions on*, vol. 18, no. 12, pp. 1649–1662, 2007.
47. K. Lu, D. Wu, J. Fan, S. Todorovic, and A. Nucci, "Robust and efficient detection of ddos attacks for large-scale internet," *Computer Networks*, vol. 51, no. 18, pp. 5036–5056, 2007.
48. J. François, I. Aib, and R. Boutaba, "Firecol: a collaborative protection network for the detection of flooding ddos attacks," *IEEE/ACM Transactions on Networking (TON)*, vol. 20, no. 6, pp. 1828–1841, 2012.
49. G. Nychis, V. Sekar, D. G. Andersen, H. Kim, and H. Zhang, "An empirical evaluation of entropy-based traffic anomaly detection," in *Proceedings of the 8th ACM SIGCOMM conference on Internet measurement*. ACM, 2008, pp. 151–156.
50. B. M. Tellenbach, "Detection, classification and visualization of anomalies using generalized entropy metrics," Ph.D. dissertation, ETH ZURICH, 2012.
51. F. Wang, H. Wang, X. Wang, and J. Su, "A new multistage approach to detect subtle ddos attacks," *Mathematical and Computer Modelling*, vol. 55, no. 1, pp. 198–213, 2012.
52. S. Bhatia, D. Schmidt, and G. Mohay, "Ensemble-based ddos detection and mitigation model," in *Proceedings of the Fifth International Conference on Security of Information and Networks*. ACM, 2012, pp. 79–86.
53. X. Ma and Y. Chen, "Ddos detection method based on chaos analysis of network traffic entropy," *Communications Letters, IEEE*, vol. 18, no. 1, pp. 114–117, 2014.
54. J.-H. Jun, D. Lee, C.-W. Ahn, and S.-H. Kim, "Ddos attack detection using flow entropy and packet sampling on huge networks," *of: ICN*, pp. 185–190, 2014.
55. A. Spognardi, A. Villani, D. Vitali, L. V. Mancini, and R. Battistoni, "Large-scale traffic anomaly detection: Analysis of real netflow datasets," in *E-Business and Telecommunications*. Springer, 2014, pp. 192–208.
56. I. Basicevic, S. Ocovaj, and M. Popovic, "Use of tsallis entropy in detection of syn flood dos attacks," *Security and Communication Networks*, vol. 8, no. 18, pp. 3634–3640, 2015.
57. S. Bhatia, "Detecting distributed denial-of-service attacks and flash events," Ph.D. dissertation, Queensland University of Technology, 2013.
58. P. Sangkatsanee, N. Wattanapongsakorn, and C. Charnsripinyo, "Practical real-time intrusion detection using machine learning approaches," *Computer Communications*, vol. 34, no. 18, pp. 2227–2235, 2011.
59. O. Joldzic, Z. Djuric, and P. Vuletic, "A transparent and scalable anomaly-based dos detection method," *Computer Networks*, vol. 104, pp. 27–42, 2016.
60. H. Beitollahi and G. Deconinck, "Tackling application-layer ddos attacks," *Procedia Computer Science*, vol. 10, pp. 432–441, 2012.
61. H. Beitollahi, G. Deconinck, "Connectionscore: a statistical technique to resist application-layer ddos attacks," *Journal of Ambient Intelligence and Humanized Computing*, vol. 5, no. 3, pp. 425–442, 2014.
62. T. Ni, X. Gu, H. Wang, and Y. Li, "Real-time detection of application-layer ddos attack using time series analysis," *Journal of Control Science and Engineering*, vol. 2013, p. 4, 2013.
63. K. Lee, J. Kim, K. H. Kwon, Y. Han, and S. Kim, "Ddos attack detection method using cluster analysis," *Expert Systems with Applications*, vol. 34, no. 3, pp. 1659–1665, 2008.
64. A. Chonka, J. Singh, and W. Zhou, "Chaos theory based detection against network mimicking ddos attacks," *IEEE Communications Letters*, vol. 13, no. 9, 2009.
65. Z. Xia, S. Lu, J. Li, and J. Tang, "Enhancing ddos flood attack detection via intelligent fuzzy logic," *Informatica*, vol. 34, no. 4, 2010.
66. R. Karimazad and A. Faraahi, "An anomaly-based method for ddos attacks detection using rbf neural networks," in *Proceedings of the International Conference on Network and Electronics Engineering*, 2011, pp. 16–18.
67. D. Das, U. Sharma, and D. Bhattacharyya, "Detection of http flooding attacks in multiple scenarios," in *Proceedings of the 2011 international conference on communication, computing & security*. ACM, 2011, pp. 517–522.

68. S. N. Shiaeles, V. Katos, A. S. Karakos, and B. K. Papadopoulos, "Real time ddos detection using fuzzy estimators," *computers & security*, vol. 31, no. 6, pp. 782–790, 2012.
69. S. Y. Dorbala, R. Kishore, and N. Hubballi, "An experience report on scalable implementation of ddos attack detection," in *International Conference on Advanced Information Systems Engineering*. Springer, 2015, pp. 518–529.
70. R. K. Chang, "Defending against flooding-based distributed denial-of-service attacks: a tutorial," *IEEE communications magazine*, vol. 40, no. 10, pp. 42–51, 2002.
71. H. Burch and B. Cheswick, "Tracing anonymous packets to their approximate source," in *LISA*, 2000, pp. 319–327.
72. S. Savage, D. Wetherall, A. Karlin, and T. Anderson, "Network support for ip traceback," *IEEE/ACM transactions on networking*, vol. 9, no. 3, pp. 226–237, 2001.
73. D. Dean, M. Franklin, and A. Stubblefield, "An algebraic approach to ip traceback," *ACM Transactions on Information and System Security (TISSEC)*, vol. 5, no. 2, pp. 119–137, 2002.
74. B. Al-Duwairi and M. Govindarasu, "Novel hybrid schemes employing packet marking and logging for ip traceback," *IEEE Transactions on Parallel and Distributed Systems*, vol. 17, no. 5, pp. 403–418, 2006.
75. S. Yu, W. Zhou, R. Doss, and W. Jia, "Traceback of ddos attacks using entropy variations," *IEEE Transactions on Parallel and Distributed Systems*, vol. 22, no. 3, pp. 412–425, 2011.
76. Y.-C. Wu, H.-R. Tseng, W. Yang, and R.-H. Jan, "Ddos detection and traceback with decision tree and grey relational analysis," *International Journal of Ad Hoc and Ubiquitous Computing*, vol. 7, no. 2, pp. 121–136, 2011.
77. V. S. Rajam, G. Selvaram, M. PradeepKumar, and S. M. Shalinie, "Autonomous system based traceback mechanism for ddos attack," in *Advanced Computing (ICoAC), 2013 Fifth International Conference on*. IEEE, 2013, pp. 164–171.
78. K. Singh, P. Singh, and K. Kumar, "A systematic review of ip traceback schemes for denial of service attacks," *Computers & Security*, vol. 56, pp. 111–139, 2016.
79. S. Floyd and K. Fall, "Router mechanisms to support end-to-end congestion control," Technical report, February 1997. URL" http://wwwnrg.ee.lbl.gov/floyd/end2end-paper.html, Tech. Rep., 1997.
80. R. Mahajan, S. Bellovin, S. Floyd, J. Ioannidis, V. Paxson, and S. Shenker, "Controlling High Bandwidth Aggregates in the Network," *ACM SIGCOMM Computer Communication Review*, vol. 32, no. 3, p. 73, 2002.
81. G. Zhang and M. Parashar, "Cooperative defence against ddos attacks," *Journal of Research and Practice in Information Technology*, vol. 38, no. 1, pp. 69–84, 2006.
82. X. Wang, "Mitigation of ddos attacks through pushback and resource regulation," in *Multi-Media and Information Technology, 2008. MMIT'08. International Conference on*. IEEE, 2008, pp. 225–228.
83. S. R. Devi and P. Yogesh, "Detection of application layer ddos attacks using information theory based metrics," *CS & IT-CSCP*, vol. 10, pp. 213–223, 2012.
84. B. Gupta, M. Misra, and R. C. Joshi, "An isp level solution to combat ddos attacks using combined statistical based approach," *arXiv preprint arXiv:1203.2400*, 2012.
85. W. Wei, F. Chen, Y. Xia, and G. Jin, "A rank correlation based detection against distributed reflection dos attacks," *IEEE Communications Letters*, vol. 17, no. 1, pp. 173–175, 2013.
86. W. Zhou, W. Jia, S. Wen, Y. Xiang, and W. Zhou, "Detection and defense of application-layer ddos attacks in backbone web traffic," *Future Generation Computer Systems*, vol. 38, pp. 36–46, 2014.
87. H. Bedi, S. Roy, and S. Shiva, "Mitigating congestion based dos attacks with an enhanced aqm technique," *Computer Communications*, vol. 56, pp. 60–73, 2015.
88. Y. Cui, L. Yan, S. Li, H. Xing, W. Pan, J. Zhu, and X. Zheng, "Sd-anti-ddos: Fast and efficient ddos defense in software-defined networks," *Journal of Network and Computer Applications*, vol. 68, pp. 65–79, 2016.
89. S. Behal, K. Kumar, and M. Sachdeva, "D-face: An anomaly based distributed approach for early detection of ddos attacks and flash events," *Journal of Network and Computer Applications*, 2018.

90. S. Behal, K. Kumar, and M. Sachdeva, "D-fac: A novel ϕ-divergence based distributed ddos defense system," *Journal of King Saud University-Computer and Information Sciences*, 2018.
91. "Twitter, Amazon, other top websites shut in cyber attack," https://ddosattacks.net/twitter-amazon-other-top-websites-shut-in-cyber-attack/, 2016, [Online; accessed 25-Aug-2017].
92. Poneman, "Evaluating the cost of a ddos attack," http://23.235.200.57/~pcninc5/wp-content/uploads/2014/06/Evaluating-The-Cost-of-A-DDoS-Attack.pdf, Dyn, Tech. Rep., 2016, [Online; accessed 25-Aug-2017].
93. Arbor, "Arbor network wisr report https://www.arbornetworks.com/images/documents/wisr2016enweb.pdf," Arbor Networks, Tech. Rep., 2017. [Online]. Available: https://www.arbornetworks.com/images/documents/WISR2016ENWeb.pdf
94. "Ddos attacks, iot, and the future of it security," https://medium.com/ibm-journal/ddos-attacks-iot-and-the-future-of-it-security-b57975dd1b74, 2016.
95. D. Kreutz, F. Ramos, and P. Verissimo, "Towards secure and dependable software-defined networks," in *Proceedings of the second ACM SIGCOMM workshop on Hot topics in software defined networking.* ACM, 2013, pp. 55–60.
96. S. Sezer, S. Scott-Hayward, P. K. Chouhan, B. Fraser, D. Lake, J. Finnegan, N. Viljoen, M. Miller, and N. Rao, "Are we ready for sdn? implementation challenges for software-defined networks," *IEEE Communications Magazine*, vol. 51, no. 7, pp. 36–43, 2013.
97. B. A. A. Nunes, M. Mendonca, X.-N. Nguyen, K. Obraczka, and T. Turletti, "A survey of software-defined networking: Past, present, and future of programmable networks," *IEEE Communications Surveys & Tutorials*, vol. 16, no. 3, pp. 1617–1634, 2014.
98. W. Li, W. Meng *et al.*, "A survey on openflow-based software defined networks: Security challenges and countermeasures," *Journal of Network and Computer Applications*, vol. 68, pp. 126–139, 2016.
99. M. Crosby, P. Pattanayak, S. Verma, and V. Kalyanaraman, "Blockchain technology: Beyond bitcoin," *Applied Innovation*, vol. 2, pp. 6–10, 2016.
100. I. Ahmed, V. Roussev, W. Johnson, S. Senthivel, and S. Sudhakaran, "A SCADA system testbed for cybersecurity and forensic research and pedagogy," in *Proceedings of the 2nd Annual Industrial Control System Security Workshop*, ser. ICSS '16. New York, NY, USA: ACM, 2016, pp. 1–9. [Online]. Available: http://doi.acm.org/10.1145/3018981.3018984
101. I. Ahmed, S. Obermeier, M. Naedele, and G. G. R. III, "SCADA Systems: Challenges for Forensic Investigators," *Computer*, vol. 45, no. 12, pp. 44–51, Dec 2012.
102. I. Ahmed, S. Obermeier, S. Sudhakaran, and V. Roussev, "Programmable Logic Controller Forensics," *IEEE Security Privacy*, vol. 15, no. 6, pp. 18–24, November 2017.
103. I. Ahmed, "Supervisory Control and Data Acquisition (SCADA) Forensics: Network Traffic Analysis for Extracting a Programmable Logic Controller (PLC) System and Programming Logic Files," in *Proceedings of the 69th Annual Meeting of the American Academy of Forensic Sciences*, ser. AAFS '17. AAFS, 2017.
104. N. Kush, E. Foo, E. Ahmed, I. Ahmed, and A. Clark, "Gap analysis of intrusion detection in smart grids," in *Proceedings of the 2nd International Cyber Resilience Conference*, ser. ICRC '11. Australia: secau-Security Research Centre, 2011, pp. 38–46.
105. "ICS CERT Advisory (ICSA-14-303-02) on Elipse SCADA DNP3 Denial of Service," https://ics-cert.us-cert.gov/advisories/ICSA-14-303-02, 2018.
106. S. Senthivel, I. Ahmed, and V. Roussev, "SCADA Network Forensics of the PCCC Protocol," *Digit. Investig.*, vol. 22, no. S, pp. S57–S65, Aug. 2017.
107. S. Senthivel, S. Dhungana, H. Yoo, I. Ahmed, and V. Roussev, "Denial of Engineering Operations Attacks in Industrial Control Systems," in *Proceedings of the 8th ACM Conference on Data and Applications Security and Privacy (CODASPY)*, 2018.
108. "ICS CERT Advisory (ICSA-16-299-01) on Siemens SICAM," https://ics-cert.us-cert.gov/advisories/ICSA-16-299-01, 2018.
109. "ICS CERT Advisory (ICSA-15-202-01) on Siemens SIPROTEC Denial-of-Service Vulnerability," https://ics-cert.us-cert.gov/advisories/ICSA-15-202-01, 2018.
110. S. Bhatia, N. Kush, C. Djamaludin, J. Akande, and E. Foo, "Practical modbus flooding attack and detection," in *Proceedings of the Twelfth Australasian Information Security Conference-Volume 149.* Australian Computer Society, Inc., 2014, pp. 57–65.

Protection Against Semantic Social Engineering Attacks

Ryan Heartfield and George Loukas

Abstract Phishing, drive-by downloads, file and multimedia masquerading, domain typosquatting, malvertising and other semantic social engineering attacks aim to deceive the user rather than exploit a technical flaw to breach a system's security. We start with a chronological overview to illustrate the growing prevalence of such attacks from their early inception 30 years ago, and identify key milestones and indicative trends which have established them as primary weapons of choice for hackers, cyber-criminals and state actors today. To demonstrate the scale and widespread nature of the threat space, we identify over 35 individually recognised types of semantic attack, existing within and cross-contaminating between a vast range of different computer platforms and user interfaces. Their extreme diversity and the little to no technical traces they leave make them particularly difficult to protect against. Technical protection systems typically focus on a single attack type on a single platform type rather than the wider landscape of deception-based attacks. To address this issue, we discuss three high-level defense approaches for preemptive and proactive protection, including adopting the semantic attack killchain concept which simplifies targeted defense; principles for preemptive and proactive protection for passive threats; and platform based defense-in-depth lifecycle designed to harness technical and non-technical defense capabilities of platform providers and their user base. Here, the human-as-a-security-sensor paradigm can prove particularly useful by leveraging the collective natural ability of users themselves in detecting deception attempts against them.

1 Introduction

It is often posited that the user can be the "weakest link" [1] in information security, because even the strongest technical protection can be bypassed or undermined

R. Heartfield (✉) · G. Loukas
University of Greenwich, London, UK
e-mail: r.j.heartfield@gre.ac.uk; g.loukas@gre.ac.uk

© Springer Nature Switzerland AG 2018
M. Conti et al. (eds.), *Versatile Cybersecurity*, Advances in Information
Security 72, https://doi.org/10.1007/978-3-319-97643-3_4

if an attacker successfully manipulates a user into divulging a password, opening a malicious file or visiting a compromised website. We begin by introducing the concept of "semantic social engineering attacks" formalised as *Semantic Attack* [31], which refers to a cyber threat targeting the user-computer interface as an attack vector, circumventing traditional technical security controls through user deception rather than by exploiting technical vulnerabilities. Common examples include phishing emails and websites, drive-by downloads, file and multimedia masquerading, domain typosquatting, malvertising and Trojan horse software to name a few.

Semantic attacks target human nature as a unique and distinct vulnerability in a computer system's security by triggering key emotional, behavioural and cognitive processes designed to elicit specific user response which allows an attacker to defeat a system's information security. Semantic attacks can be highly successful because without the requisite training and conditioning for threat detection (consider an operating system without the defense of antivirus scrutinising each and every system call it is being asked to make), human nature tends towards trust rather than mistrust. As a result, the threat is ubiquitous and the variation between attack vectors (such as their degree of complexity and target platform) is extreme, ranging from state-backed Advanced Persistent Threats employing multi-stage/platform attack vectors to that of script kiddies and pay-as-you-go bots generating automated phishing emails campaigns. Due to the vast problem space, attacks can be technically basic [34, 39, 40], highly complex [41, 60] or a combination of the two [36, 61].

Over the years, numerous defenses have been proposed at scientific research level to target exploitations such as website and phishing attacks [42–45, 62], as well as at commercial level [5, 6, 18–20]. However, they almost always fail to consider the wider problem space in which semantic attacks pose a threat, the result of which is the design of technical mitigations to address very specific attack vectors, lacking the flexibility to detect conceptually similar attacks across different platforms. Furthermore, over the years traditional deception-based attacks, such as phishing emails, spoofed websites and drive-by downloads, have shifted to new platforms in social media [35], cloud applications [36] and near field communications [37], and the advent of the Internet of Things (IoT) [38] will extend considerably the impact of semantic attacks through threats to physical space. The more effective semantic "cyber-physical" attacks prove [2], the larger the threat space becomes.

1.1 A Brief History of Semantic Attacks in Computer Systems

Semantic social engineering attacks first emerged in computer systems as early as 1989 when the *"AIDS Information Introductory Diskette"* Trojan [63] was sent to a mailing group in which Dr Joseph Popp, the Trojan's author, subscribed. To gain access to a computer system, a diskette pertaining to contain information about the AIDS virus deceived the recipients into inserting it into their system. The diskette contained a Cryptovirus [64] which ransomed users for money by encrypting their systems files. Another noteworthy semantic attack appeared a year later, introducing what we call today "Scareware". The malware, aptly named *Nightmare* [7], was distributed via diskettes called "Fish Disks" designed to share applications between *Amiga* computer systems. On execution, every five minutes *Nightmare* would hijack the computer screen for 0.8 s to display a full-screen image of a skull with bullet wound and blood leaking out, whilst playing a loud shriek on the speakers. The malware posed no obvious risk to user data, but the concept of scaring/panicking a user would later be employed by many cyber criminals to force users into opening malware or paying for fraudulent services [46]. In 1995, new attacks were specifically designed to exploit users accessing resources over a new open network, called the Internet. Domain investor John Zuccarini introduced the concept of Typosquatting or Cybersquatting, where cyber criminals would purchase domain names that were similar to those of legitimate websites. Users who mistyped the domain name URL of a legitimate website would be redirected to a malicious or fraudulent website. During the same year, service provider America Online (AOL) experienced growing success with a popular instant messaging tool, which hackers soon realised that it could be exploited, and developed an attack tool that lead to the first use of the term "phishing". *AOHell* [47] contained a "fisher" tool that enabled hackers to steal passwords and financial information by generating instant messages to random AOL users with content such as: "Hi, this is AOL Customer Service. We are running a security check and need to verify your account. Please enter your username and password to continue".

Over the next decade, phishing attacks became widespread. In 2000, the infamous *ILOVEYOU* "worm"[1] contained a malicious visual basic script titled "LOVE-LETTER-FOR-YOU.txt.vbs" [9], initially spreading through corporate Philippine mailing lists and eventually affecting over 45 million computers systems worldwide. This attack was copied a year later in 2001 by the *Anna Kournikova* worm, using the same worm generating script [48]. The same year, the first known phishing attack against a financial institution was discovered, where E-Gold users were targeted with emails tricking them into entering their passwords into phishing websites [10]. Leading up to today, the rapid growth of the Internet, multimedia services and mobile platforms, have enabled semantic attacks to spread further into Android devices [49], peripheral hardware accelerated by direct memory access [11] (e.g., Thunderbolt and Firewire devices), file sharing networks [50], search engine optimisation engines [65] and drive-by malware on websites [51], and the landscape continues to expand. For example, the advent of online social networks and increase in online social media has introduced a paradigm shift in Internet communication where platform functionality promotes openness and information sharing amongst users. This online social paradigm has enabled cyber criminals to take advantage of "friend" recommendations, user "posts" and sharing of media or apps that are replicated and automated with the network [12, 35, 52]. Also concerning is the potential for semantic attacks to result in physical impact, through cyber-physical and IoT systems.

---

[1]Note that here we use the term "worm" to refer to a malware with a semantic attack vector that exhibits automated, self-replicating behaviour, as in [8].

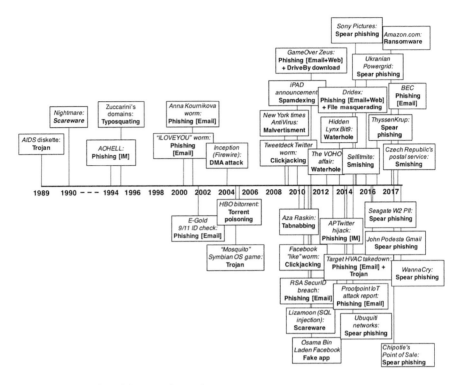

Fig. 1 Timeline of notable semantic attacks

In Fig. 1, we provide a timeline of high-profile semantic attacks identifying the chronological emergence and persistence of different types.

1.2   Characterising the Extreme Diversity in Semantic Attacks

There exist over 35 individually types or variations of semantic attack, existing within and cross-contaminating between different platforms and systems (Table 1).

2   The Scale of the Threat Today: Characterising the Impact of Semantic Attacks

Semantic attack statistics have been dominated by phishing incidents due to their widespread use by cyber criminals and consistent success in breaching computer systems. A 2012 report by Trend Micro identified that over 90% of targeted malware attacks discovered were initiated through spear-phishing [13]. In 2014, *Social*

Table 1 Different types of semantic attack observed in today's computer systems

Attack Pseudonym	Description
Spam	Irrelevant/unsolicited messages sent over the Internet to a large number of users, often containing advertising scams
Phishing	Attempt to obtain access to sensitive information by disguising as a trustworthy entity in an electronic communication
Spear phishing	Phishing attack designed to target a specific person and or organisation
Pharming	Installing malicious code on a personal computer or server, misdirecting users to fake web sites without knowledge or consent
Whaling	Type of phishing attack that targets high-profile end users such as corporate executives, politicians and celebrities
QRishing	Phishing style attack using quick response (QR) codes to distribute malicious file/links
Blue snarfing	Phishing attack enticing users to install malware which grants access to target device via the Bluetooth protocol
Smishing	Phishing style attack sent via mobile short message service (SMS)
URL spoofing	Impersonating a websites URL address such as copying domain name by exploiting bugs in web browsers
DriveyBy download	Implanting a malicious file through programmatic manipulation of scripts on a vulnerable web platform
Waterhole	Targeted version of a DriveBy download attack, typically targeting platforms a victim accesses
File masquerading	Disguising a malicious file to appear as a legitimate file type
Multimedia masquerading	Disguising a malicious application appear as multimedia (e.g., video)
GUI confusion	A mobile application confusing users by impersonating as another app (e.g., banking app) to obtain sensitive information
Adware	Software that automatically displays or downloads advertising material such as banners or pop-ups when a user is online
SSL spoofing	MitM attack that intercepts HTTPS web requests, redirecting the users to malicious and fake HTTPS website
Visual SSL spoofing	Process of using fake SSL verification logos or browser GUI components to visually masquerade as a secure website
Scareware	Malicious program tricking a user into buying/downloading unnecessary often malicious software (e.g., antivirus protection)
Rogueware	Standalone malware program pretending to be a well-known program or a non-malicious one in order to steal sensitive data
Malvertisement	An online advertisement that incorporates or installs malware
WiFi evil twin	A fraudulent WiFi access point that often spoofs other nearby access points that appears to be legitimate
Rogue AP	Wi-Fi access point installed on a network but is not authorized for operation on that network and appears to be legitimate
Trojan horse	Type of malware that is often disguised as legitimate software, such as a game that is actually a key-logger
Self XSS	Operates by tricking users into copying and pasting malicious content into their browsers' web developer console
Typosquatting	Registering similar domain names which rely on typographical errors when inputting a website address into a browser

(continued)

Table 1 (continued)

Attack Pseudonym	Description
Combosquating	Form of typosquatting registering domain names that combine popular trademarks with a string of words or phrases
RansomWare	Type of malicious software designed to block access to a computer system until a sum of money is paid, often using fear tactics
Tabnabbing	A type of phishing where a website changes to impersonate popular websites
Sharebaiting	Enticing web content persuading users to share on their profile, often used to spread fake apps and phishing URLs
Click jacking	Concealing hyperlinks beneath legitimate click-able content, causing the user to perform actions of which they are unaware
Like jacking	Variation on clickjacking in which malicious coding is associated with a Facebook Like button
Touch jacking	Variation of clickjacking which applies to mobile devices where users touch the interface instead of using a mouse or keypad
Cursor jacking	Variation of clickjacking where users are deceived by means of a custom cursor image and the pointer is displayed with an offset
Spamdexing	Manipulation of search engine indexes where a website repeats unrelated phrases to manipulate relevance or prominence
Torrent poisoning	Intentionally sharing corrupt data and malware with misleading file names using the BitTorrent protocol
DNS cache poisoning	Process by which DNS server records are illegitimately modified to replace a website address with a different address
Fake App	Variation of trojan horse, rogueware, scareware on mobile devices where a malicious app masquerades as a legitimate one
Fake plugin	Malicious media plugin typically spread by through a fake video post on social media posting
Madware	Aggressive advertising placement in mobile devices photo albums, calendar entries and notification bar
Browser extension malware	Malicious browser-add similar to Trojan app that steals personal information and/or add browser to attacker botnet

Engineer reported that 90% of the 129 billion emails sent daily are malicious. Clicking on email links accounted for 80% of reported phishing attacks, and phishing itself represented 77% of all socially-based attacks [14]. In 2015, Statista reported that phishing and deception-based attacks accounted for 62% of all cyber attacks experienced by companies world-wide [15], with 59% reported by US companies alone [16]. Furthermore, the average time to resolve this type of attack for a US-based company was 20 days [17], with damages of 12% for medium and 16% for large enterprises' total operating costs. The Anti-Phishing Working Group (APWG) produce yearly statistics related to the current trends across a multitude of different phishing attacks that are reported from around the world to their online phishing repository. We have compiled data from the APWG phishing activity trends report archive [3] for years 2008 to 2016, illustrating in Fig. 2 that the number of phishing reports received by APWG is dramatically increasing.

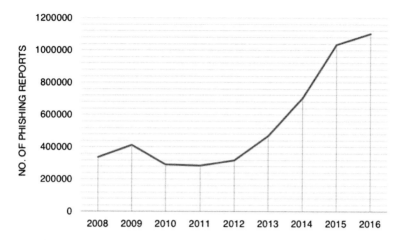

Fig. 2 APWG phishing report statistics for years 2008–2016 [3]

The Internet Security Threat Report, a yearly security study produced by Symantec, expands beyond traditional phishing statistics and organises semantic attacks amongst four categories: mobile and IoT, social media and spam, web threats and targeted attacks. Figures 2, 3 and 4 summarise a number of semantic attacks and threats utilising deception techniques from years 2012 to 2016 [4]. For mobile platforms, from 2012 to 2016 approximately 14.8 million apps were categorised as malware; with a further 22.4 million apps categoried as grayware. Malware and grayware require users to agree to install applications, granting aggressive permissions to the applications on the device, irrespective of whether any further deception techniques are used (e.g., during app usage); which indicates low user awareness of mobile app vulnerabilities where users are likely to be deceived by a lack of perceived threat. Social media attacks were consistently shown to be propagated largely by users manually sharing posts and apps amongst friends and groups, instead of automated "free offerings" (e.g., surveys and malvertisements) that were dominant in 2013; further highlighting the vulnerability of users behaviour in online social network platforms. Spear phishing campaigns were also observed to have consistently increased over the period of 2013 to 2015, whilst the number of recipients per campaign have decreased by an average of 25% each year, which may indicate that attackers are developing methods for spear phishing which require fewer targets for successful exploitation and are more difficult to detect. Whilst spear phishing attacks continue to target the financial sector, attackers are now often targeting the energy and health-care sectors too (Fig. 4).

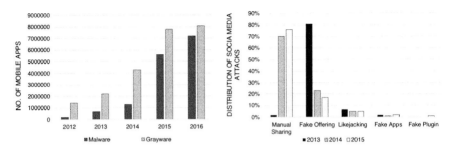

Fig. 3 Classification of mobile apps analysed by Symantec during 2012–2016 (left), Distribution method of social networks and social media scams/attacks by percent from 2013–2015 (right) [4]

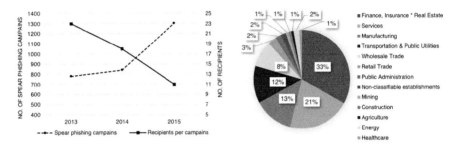

Fig. 4 Number of spear phishing campaigns and average number of attack recipients per campaign from 2013–2015 (left), top industries targeted by spear phishing attacks in 2015, ordered by majority percentage (right) [4]

3 Attacking the Weakest Link: Designing, Developing and Launching Semantic Attacks

Towards a core and collective understanding of semantic attack composition, beyond individual attacks on specific platforms, we start by exploring the specific characteristics which formulate the design, development and distribution of semantic attacks. To illustrate the functional components of a semantic attack, we employ taxonomy in [31], describing the generic schematic structures of semantic attacks, which apply irrespective of specific attack vectors that may be used (e.g., specific platform user interface). Next, we apply this approach on notable real world semantic attacks.

3.1 Generic Attack Structure

Semantic attacks, irrespective of attack vector, follow a generic functional structure in terms of design and delivery [31]. The high-level structure can be seen as

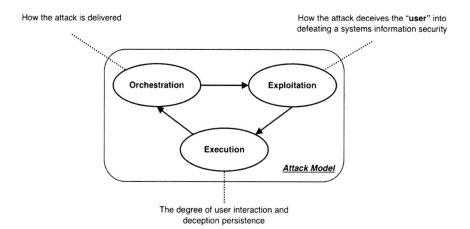

Fig. 5 High-level attack model showing the interactions between each behavioural function within semantic social engineering attacks

comparable to any kind of cyber threat in that it consists orchestration, exploitation and execution. Orchestration consists of user targeting (including information gathering), distribution and automation parameters, exploitation is the application of deception vectors (to elicit compromising user actions) and their technical construction through the user interface, and execution is the functional interaction required by the user during attack runtime and the persistence of the deception vector(s) after the attack is complete. Below, we summarise each of these individual elements as to their functional behaviour in semantic attack design and illustrate the process in Fig. 5.

- **Target description**. *The targeting parameters of the semantic attack.* Typically, this is a target user (an individual or organisation) or target platform. The former constitutes "explicit" targeting, which requires tailored attack delivery and may predetermine the method of distribution, automation and deception vectors to employ after a information gathering phase. By comparison, a specific user interface platform is a form of "promiscuous" targeting, as the attack vector does not control who is exposed, the functionality of the target platform and the behaviours of the users do (e.g., social media sharing).
- **Method of Distribution**. *The means by which a semantic attack reaches a target platform or user.* There are two means of distribution: software or hardware, the latter of which can also result in subsequent software executed distribution. Hardware is always a local distribution vector (e.g., within physical proximity of the user), while software is local (i.e., through a hardware interface) or remote (over a distributed application and network i.e., the Internet). For local hardware interaction, examples include direct memory access peripherals (e.g., Firewire), local hardware with software executed distribution is a system that is

locally interfaced with a target system (as initiated by the user), with physical communication and software execution (e.g., USB flash drives).

- **Method of Automation**. *The degree of attacker supervision of the semantic attack activation and administration.* An attack can be fully automated by predefining all its functional procedures in a format similar to worms, whereby the attack contains all of the procedural code necessary to operate without specific attacker execution, interaction or administration. The degree of automation depends on the functionality of the target platform and the behaviour of its user base. For highly targeted attacks that require tailored deception vectors which are meaningful to specific user(s) or organisational attributes, manual attacker operation may be required. This includes activities such as specifying when the attack is executed, or responding in real-time to user interaction (e.g., instant messaging). The degree of attack automation is dependent on the target description.

- **Deception Vector**. *The deception techniques designed to persuade the target user(s) into performing a compromising action.* The deception techniques developed for a semantic attack effectively represent the human exploitation parameters which persuade the user into performing a compromising action (e.g., clicking on a URL, or opening a executable file). At a high level, deception within a semantic attack has three modes. Firstly, the use of cosmetic, visually convincing deception by masquerading as a legitimate entity (through a specific user computer interface design), secondly behavioural deception by conforming to system convention in respect to expectations of user interface functionality and response to user interaction and thirdly a hybrid combination of cosmetic and behavioural deception.

- **Interface Manipulation**. *The technical implementation of an semantic attacks deception vector(s).* Interface manipulation is the technical means used to establish a semantic attacks deception vector on a target platform's user interface. There are two ways in which this achieved, either through (ab)using legitimate platform functionality or programmatically modifying and or spoofing it in order to change appearance of behaviour.

- **Executions steps**. *The number of functional steps an attack requires the user to carry out in order to execute the exploitation payload.* The primary interaction with a semantic attack is the corresponding user action in response to exposure to its deception vector(s). Depending on the attacks required users actions, this can be a single step (e.g., a single user click) or multiple steps (e.g., multiple users clicks) in order for the attacks exploitation to complete; or as the means direct the user to another semantic attack in the attack chain.

- **Attack persistence**. *The persistent level of deception after user exploitation.* After successful exploitation, it is rare for a deception vector to continuing executing, as typically exploitation is a one-off procedure to forward the user to another semantic attack in a attack chain or as the user action has enabled execution of the intended attack payload. However, in some cases a semantic attack will continually execute deception vectors, as is common with Scareware.

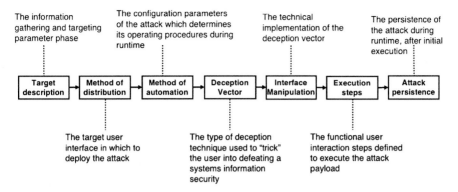

Fig. 6 High-level structure of a semantic social engineering attack illustrated as series of linear steps which together formulate the design, development and execution behaviour of a semantic attack [31]

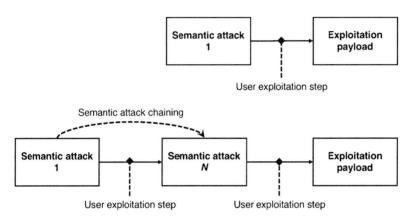

Fig. 7 Attack models for a single phase (top) and multi-phase (bottom) semantic attack. Here each individual attack (e.g. semantic 1 . . . n), is formulated by and therefore contains the linear structured criteria and corresponding parameters defined in Fig. 6

Semantic attacks follow the same functional structure, regardless of whether they are executed as individual semantic attacks or chained together within a multi-phase attack. Each individual semantic attack is distinguished by its functional elements (as per Fig. 6), even if in practice certain parameters, such as the target description and method of distribution, are shared as a consequence of attack chaining. To illustrate this, Fig. 7 provides an abstract example of a single semantic attack against a chain semantic attack model, and Fig. 8 provides examples of how multiple individual semantic attacks form a multi-phase semantic attack through chaining.

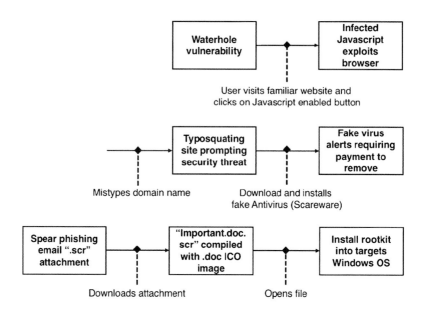

Fig. 8 Examples of single (top) and multi-phase semantic attacks (middle and bottom). Here the waterhole vulnerability is a one step attack requiring that a target simply visit the infected website for the attack to complete. For the typosquating attack, after a user visits the website, they are then prompted with a scareware download, which formulates a second phase semantic attack in the attack chain. For the spear phishing email, the user must download a masqueraded file, which consitutes the second phase semantic attack through user execution of the file to complete the attack

3.2   Semantic Attacks in the Press

In the following attacks, we employ these generic attack structure principles to provide a low-level breakdown of three notable semantic attacks: Spear phishing, QR code phishing and multimedia masquerading on social network platforms.

3.2.1   The Podesta Spear-Phishing E-mails

During the 2016 United States presidential election race, John Podesta, former chief of staff to Bill Clinton (and at the time chairman of the 2016 Hillary Clinton presidential campaign), received an email purportedly from Google with a warning that his Gmail account had received a sign-in attempt from an IP address in Ukraine. It advised Podesta "you should change your password immediately", including a blue "CHANGE PASSWORD" box to be clicked. This attack was part of a chained semantic attack process, whereas once this button was clicked, Podesta's Gmail account was redirected to a Google login phishing page, where his credentials were entered and ultimately stolen, giving the attackers access to over fifty thousand

Table 2 Podesta spear-phishing e-mail attack

Spear phishing e-mail (Fig. 9)	
Target	This specific e-mail had been crafted for John Podesta, using the salutation "Hi John" and using a provocative warning associated to a falsified connection attempt from a politically sensitive country
Distribution	The e-mail was distributed to the user's Gmail inbox through the SMTP protocol from the attacker's own mailservers
Automation	Unlike typical spear phishing attacks which carried out manually, the particular attack parameters seemed to have been programmed automatically as the same attack vector was exposed to multiple political candidates during the US presidential election race
Deception	The attack mimicked both visual and behavioural functionality, by (1) spoofing a legitimate looking Gmail address, (2) copying exactly the Gmail email template, (3) creating what appears to be a genuine Google URL from Bitly shortening service where the attack then leads to a second semantic attack which spoofed the Google webpage used to reset an account passwords. These deception vectors were implemented by (1) pragmatically modifying the SMTP (or registering the corresponding domain if available), (2) copying the source code from the Gmail email template, (3) abusing Bitly's inbuilt functionality to create a custom URL string
Execution	The attack required the target user to perform a single action by clicking on the "CHANGE PASSWORD NOW" button, at which point the exploitation of the email is complete and the user is redirected to a phishing page designed to harvest their account login credentials
Persistence	After the email attack as successful (by clicking on the link in the email body), this attack is completed and exhibits no further persistence as the user is redirected to a phishing website semantic attack as the next stage in the attack chain

emails with highly sensitive exchanges and data related to the Hilary Clinton presidential campaign. In Table 2 we take a closer look at the low-level configuration of this spear phishing email, illustrating the attacks visual deception in Fig. 9.

3.2.2 WhatsApp "Jack" (QRLjacking)

In 2016, ethical hacker Mohamed Abd Elbaset demonstrated how to hack the WhatsApp web connectivity service (which is associated to a WhatsApp account) by employing a variation of QR code phishing (Qrishing). Unlike previous QRishing attacks which opted to generate QR code with malicious URLs, this attack employs the concept of QR link jacking where the attacker creates a legitimate client side browser session to WhatsApp web service to generate a QR code and forwards this legitimate QR code through a phishing webpage to the victim. Here, QR link phishing would normally be logically ordered after a phishing email in a chained set of semantic attacks. If the attacker has access to the victim's network, a phishing email can be replaced by using ARP cache poisoning to forward the victim to the phishing website. On scanning the legitimate QR code, the victim's WhatsApp account on their mobile device registers with the WhatsApp

Fig. 9 Gmail spear phish attack against US former chairman of the 2016 Hillary Clinton presidential campaign. The top email body illustrates the spoofed gmail login alert with a change password button, with the bottom image showing the malicious link obfuscated by the button

service, which subsequently allows the attackers to register their connection to the WhatsApp web application with the victim's accounts. This results in the attacker having full access to any data transmitted from the victim's WhatsApp application on their device (Table 3).

3.2.3   The Case of the Facebook "Hungry Bear"

In 2009, there was an incident in a Berlin zoo where a lady jumped into a polar bear enclosure, which she subsequently survived. Soon, a Facebook multimedia masquerading scam emerged, using a doctored image, which appeared to be clickable video. The video was an image with a superimposed play video icon

Table 3 QRcode phishing link jacking attack

Spear phishing e-mail (Fig. 10)	
Target	Whilst designed for the WhatsApp platform, the recipient is explicitly defined as they must have a WhatsApp account to exploit and the attacker is required to distribute a phishing attack in order to expose the intended target to the QR code
Distribution	The QR WhatsApp authentication code is distributed through a mirrored website that maintains a persistent link to the attacker original client side connection
Automation	The attack is fully automated once established through a looping script mirroring the attackers client connection to WhatsApp web authentication page, requiring no further intervention from the attacker
Deception	The QR code and mirrored phishing website employ a combination of visual and behavioural deception. The QR code is a legitimate web authentication request, which when scanned responds correctly to the user authenticating their WhatsApp mobile account with the web service
Execution	The QR link jacking requires programmatic manipulation of the web authentication page generating the QR code for WhatsApp. The attacker must mirror the web page and create a script to continually update the QR code which is refreshed every 20 s on the WhatsApp web authentication
Persistence	Once the user has been duped into accessing the phishing website created by the attacker which hosts the mirrored QR code, they simply need to scan the QR code to generate an authorisation token which the attack requires to gain access to their account data. After scanning the code the attack execution is complete and the deception vector of the QR code ceases

Facebook video masquerading (Fig. 11)	
Target	The attack targets all Facebook users
Distribution	The fake video is distributed through social media profile timelines, provided as feeds to a profile's subscribers or friends through the Facebook *EdgeRank* algorithm; this increases the virality of the fake video post based on popularity such as post comments and links
Automation	The video masquerading post is automated once launched, whereby user sharing behaviour enables the video to be spread through inbuilt Facebook functionality. The process of redirection to a fake video website also requires no attacker intervention. It is a URL that activates once the image is clicked on
Deception	By superimposing the Facebook specific play video button on the image and augmenting the post with fake comments, the video masquerading attack utilises crude visual deception
Execution	The attack is constructed by simply creating a timeline post from a Facebook account and attaching the doctored image; using standard inbuilt Facebook functionality to embed the image as a hyperlink to an external website
Persistence	Once the fake video image is clicked by a user, the Facebook video deception vector is complete and the victim is forwarded to the secondary semantic attack

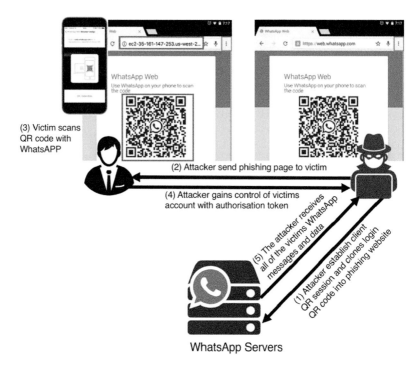

Fig. 10 WhatsApp QR link hijacking attack (initiated via sending a target victim a phishing website link). Here the spoofed QR code is automatically refreshed through the Javascript that has been copied from the legitimate WhatsApp authentication page

button, which redirected users to a secondary semantic attack in the form of a typical scam video webpage coercing the victim into completing a pop-up survey for access to the video and installing malware.

4 Methods for Defense Against Semantic Attacks

The extreme diversity of semantic attacks has led to many types of defenses proposed, often with multiple techniques developed for a single type (especially, phishing emails). Most defense mechanisms aiming to protect against the wider semantic attack space remain experimental products of research without integration or long-term empirical validation. So, the problem space is left with research and commercial tools which address only a small portion of the problem space. Here, we analyse the different defense approaches. We have already shown that individual types of semantic attack, irrespective of attack vector, are composed of the same functional elements. We have illustrated that individual semantic attacks can be used in attack chaining to direct users from one semantic attack to another to deliver

Fig. 11 The "Hungry Bear" Facebook video masquerading. The top image shows the fake Facebook video post of a bear allegedly attacking a woman, which once clicked directs the user to a new web page prompting the user to complete a survey that harvests sensitive user information to watch the spoofed video (bottom image)

the desired attack payload, and that in this composite attack architecture, some attack parameters such as targeting and automation can be shared across attacks. By focusing on both technical and non-technical mitigation concepts, rather than conducting an exhaustive search of the defense literature across all possible attack vectors (of which there are many, see Table 1), here we take a view of defense according to key concepts that would address the wider semantic attack problem space. This is because relying solely on the low-level functionality of any single defense is insufficient as a means for defending against the wider threat space. Here, we consider defense across three complementary dimensions, which may offer a holistic defense architecture against semantic attacks: Semantic attack killchain for targeted defense simplification; principles for preemptive and proactive protection for passive threats; and platform based defense-in-depth lifecycle designed to harness technical and non-technical defense capabilities of platform providers and their user base.

4.1 Semantic Attack Killchain: Defense Simplification

A primary aim for lasting and practical defense against semantic attacks is to address a wide range of attack vectors without introducing considerable complexity. Intuitively, it is possible to limit the number and types of user interfaces in which to target defense mechanisms by focusing defense on initial (i.e., entry) attack vectors, that if mitigated, would serve to kill a wider semantic attack chain. In line with Lockheed Martin's killchain model [70], we refer to this as the semantic attack killchain. For example, consider a phishing email containing a URL to an attack website, where once clicked the user is forwarded to a drive by download resulting in infection with a Trojan horse spyware application. Focusing on the individual semantic attacks in the attack chain (e.g., the drive-by download), rather than its possible permutations (phishing email → attack website → drive-by download → spyware), simplifies the objective of defense. In the above example, the spyware would be thwarted by blocking the phishing email or the attack website or the drive-by download.

Figure 12 illustrates how a semantic attack killchain architecture is constructed. Firstly, the aim is to identify the different entry vectors by which a semantic attack may target and reach an organisation/individual (which may change based on the environment context and platforms used). The purpose is to help establish an indicative threat landscape by highlighting the means by which both single and multi-phase semantic attacks pose a risk to technical security. Determining the potential entry vectors of semantic attacks then simplifies the strategic placement of defence mechanisms to both address semantic attacks that rely on attack chains in order execute certain deception vectors, as well as minimising the number of different defence systems required to be implemented to address such threats specifically. In Fig. 13, an example of how a semantic attack killchain would function is illustrated.

Table 4 provides an indicative list of common user interface platforms required to distribute different semantic attacks. For the instant messaging and website distribution categories, we include functionality observed in modern social media and networking sites, chat forums and message boards, whereas for the Appstore category we include the functionality provided by online webstores, appstore and app marketplaces for mobile devices. The table shows that prevalent user interfaces

Identify entry vector(s)   **Later attack vector(s) / exploitation payload**

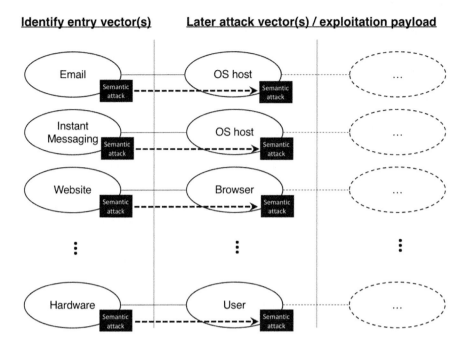

Fig. 12 The semantic attack killchain architecture aims to simplify the object of defence by providing a means to identify key platform entry vectors for semantic attacks. The aim is to design and implement defences which address a wide range of attacks whilst reducing the complexity of security mechanisms employed

are website platforms, followed by email and instant messaging platforms. However, for an attacker to initiate a targeted user attack (Target Description = "Explicit"), direct communication with a specific victim user is always required. Therefore, the sole use of a website or appstore interface as the primary distribution for user targeting becomes impractical for attackers as it limits the types of attack vectors available – especially for targeted attacks (thus introducing the need for an attack chain). For instance, if a website were the primary distribution means for a targeted exploit, the attacker may need to develop a complicated waterhole attack after finding a vulnerable platform that their target visits, ensuring that the deception vector for the target only activates for their specific browser's user agent string; this approach is of course complex and time consuming and therefore of less practicality to threat actors. In the same sense, for an appstore, or network (Net) or hardware (H/W) interface, simplicity is reduced by the need to direct the users through some means to these platform types. As a result, attackers often first rely on an initial unsolicited communication vector as distribution dependency in an attack chain, such as the use of email or instant messages containing a link to the target platform where a secondary semantic attack is positioned. As a basic high-level example of defense simplification against targeted semantic attacks specifically, for

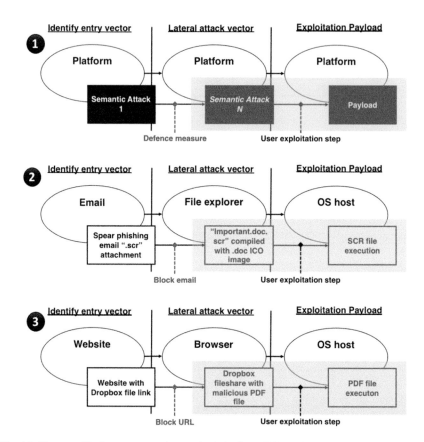

Fig. 13 Here an (1) abstract semantic attack chain from Table 7 is illustrated to show how a semantic attack consisting of multiple phases can be effectively nullified by addressing defence against the attack parameters of its first phase. By example, using the spear phishing threat example from Fig. 8 (2), we can see that by simply blocking the spear phishing attack as the first phase of the semantic attack chain, all subsequent phases and attack vectors can be averted. Equally, by blocking a malicious URL on a website, a malicious Dropbox share hosting PDF file malware can be also be prevented from deceiving the user into downloading and opening the file (3)

unsolicited targeted attacks (e.g., attacker directly contacts the target) the killchain can be reduced from 28 to 9 different attacks. The corresponding attacks and distribution platforms are shown in Table 5. The number can be further reduced if an attacker does not have control of a website for a waterhole and Bluetooth snarfing is mitigated by simply turning off Bluetooth. Further analysis of Table 5 shows that by developing defense mechanisms for email or instant messaging platforms would address 6 of the remaining different semantic attack vectors.

For completeness, in Table 6 we expand beyond the key killchain defences identified in Table 5 by further identifying applicable protection mechanisms that have been proposed for the wider landscape of different semantic attacks (Table 1). While we have no expectation to provide an exhaustive literature characterisation for such a long list of attacks, here, a sample of defense mechanisms and literature

Table 4 Methods of distribution required to **directly** exposure target users to corresponding semantic attacks

Attack vector	E-mail	Instant message	SMS	Appstore	Website	H/W interface	Net interface
Phishing	✓	✓	✓		✓	✓	
Spear phishing	✓	✓	✓			✓	
QRishing	✓	✓		✓	✓	✓	
Bluetooth snarfing							✓
Smishing			✓				
DriveyBy download					✓		
Waterhole					✓		
File masquerading	✓	✓			✓	✓	
Multimedia masquerading		✓		✓	✓		
GUI confusion					✓		
URL spoofing	✓	✓		✓	✓		
Visual SSL spoofing	✓				✓		
Scareware				✓	✓		
Malvertisement				✓	✓		
WiFi evil twin							✓
Trojan horse				✓	✓		
Self XSS	✓	✓			✓		
Typosquatting					✓		
Combosquatting					✓		
Tabnabbing					✓		
Sharebaiting					✓		
Click jacking					✓		
Cursor jacking					✓		
Spamdexing					✓		
Torrent poisoning					✓		
Fake app				✓	✓		
Fake plugin				✓	✓		
Malicious browser add-on				✓	✓		

papers on each of these attacks provides a useful tool for evaluating the current protection mechanisms against these threats. Here, we aim to identify existing approaches to defence that can be employed in unison with the semantic attack killchain to establish a practical and selective means of holistic defence against semantic attacks.

Table 5 Example of reduced semantic attack vectors by killchain platform defense

Attack vector	Primary distribution	Applicable defences
Phishing	Email IM SMS H/W	Machine learning [86, 89, 90, 99] User awareness [77, 78, 85, 88, 95, 98]
Spearphishing	Email IM SMS H/W	Machine learning [84, 86] User awareness [78, 92]
Smishing	SMS	Machine learning [71]
File masquerading	Email IM Website H/W	Integrity checking [83]
Multimedia masquerading	IM Website	Dynamic and static analysis [114]
Bluetooth snarfing	Net	Authentication/platform lock-down [100]
Waterhole	Website	Machine learning [72, 74] Dynamic analysis [73]
URL spoofing	Email IM Website	Machine learning [87, 97] User awareness [77, 78, 85, 88, 95, 98]
Visual SSL spoofing	Email Website	Heuristic scanning [94]

The examples in Table 5 largely agree with recent commercial defense products focusing on messaging platforms. Currently, most major email (Gmail [23], Microsoft Outlook [24], Yahoo [22]) and antivirus (Norton [25], Kaspersky [18], Sophos [20]) providers claim to have integrated robust detection capabilities for email threats.

In general, the utility of the semantic attack killchain can be expanded as a function of defense strategy across multiple and independent platforms, where platform providers aim to simplify their own semantic attack security by focusing protection mechanisms to address specific user interface functionality that would also serve to thwart other potential deception vectors that this may lead to through attack chaining. For instance, in the case of the social networking platform *Facebook*, focusing defense measures on *Facebook Messenger* as a distribution mechanism to plant malicious links to other semantic attacks within *Facebook* (e.g., *Facebook* pages with malicious content, fake Facebook videos, file masquerading etc.) or external phishing websites would serve as a killchain that simultaneously addressed multiple deception-based threats distributed on or via the *Facebook* platform.

Table 6 The application of defence

Attack pseudonym	Primary distribution	Defence category
Spam	Email IM SMS, social media	Machine learning [86, 89–91] User awareness [77, 78, 85, 88, 98] Sandbox [96]
Pharming	Email IM SMS	Machine learning [86, 89, 90] User awareness [77, 85, 88, 95, 98]
Whaling	Email IM SMS	Machine learning [86, 90] User awareness [77, 85, 88, 95, 98]
QRishing	Email Website SMS	Machine learning [106]
DriveyBy download	Website	Machine learning [72, 74] Dynamic analysis [73]
GUI confusion	Mobile app	Machine learning/user awareness [93] Static analysis [82]
Adware	Website, app marketplace	Sandbox [105]
SSL Spoofing	Website	Machine learning
Scareware	Software app	Machine learning [103, 104]
Rogueware	Software app	Sandbox [105]
Malvertisement	Social media, website	Machine learning [115, 116]
WiFi evil twin	Net	Integrity checking [80] User awareness [79]
Trojan horse	Software/App	Sandbox [75, 76]
Rogue AP	Net	Integrity checking (RTT analysis) [107]
Self XSS	Browser	Integrity checking [117]
Typosquatting	Browser	Machine Learning [118] Integrity checking (rule-based) [119]
Combosquating	Browser	Integrity checking (rule-based) [119]
RansomWare	Software app	Sandbox [109] Machine learning [110] Formal methods [111]
Tabnabbing	Website	Machine learning [108]
Sharebaiting	Social media Website	User awareness [81]
Click jacking	Social media Website	Integrity checking [101]
Like jacking	Social media Website	Integrity checking [123, 124]
Touch jacking	Social media (mobile) Website (mobile)	Integrity checking [101, 123, 124]

(continued)

Table 6 (continued)

Attack pseudonym	Primary distribution	Defence category
Cursor jacking	Social media Website	Integrity checking [123]
Spamdexing	Search engine	Machine learning [120, 121] Heuristic scanning [122]
Torrent poisoning	Torrent software	Integrity checking (reputation scoring) [125]
DNS cache poisoning	DNS server	Authentication/integrity checking [102]
Fake app	Mobile app marketplace Side-loaded install	Machine learning/user awareness [93]
Fake plugin	Browser	Dynamic and static analysis [114]
Madware	Mobile app marketplace Side-loaded install	Machine learning/user awareness [93] Static analysis [82]
Browser extension malware	Browser	Static analysis [112] Integrity checking [113]

4.2 Principles for Preemptive and Proactive Protection Against Semantic Attacks

The use of a semantic attack killchain helps to simplify the placement and scope of defense against semantic attacks by reducing to what kind of platforms and where in those platforms to place defenses; with the aim to reduce the diversity of where an attacker can initiate the exposure of a semantic attack on a given platform. However, the killchain method alone cannot cater for the unpredictability of user access to different computer platforms through passive activity. That is, where a user inadvertently exposes themselves to a semantic attack through their computing habits and behaviour. For example, the effectiveness of a semantic killchain blocking certain semantic attacks by placing defenses within an email platform is effectively bypassed if a user chooses them self to access a malicious website or application directly, without being coerced to by an attacker. It is necessary therefore to design defenses to protect against user activity and behaviour which may expose users to passive semantic attack threats. Namely, preemptive (prevention of semantic attack execution) and proactive (detection and treatment of semantic attack exposure) system security. However, it remains a continued challenge to develop best practice preemptive and proactive defense techniques when their exists such extreme diversity between semantic attacks, even when they employ conceptually similar deception vectors across multiple disparate platforms. To address this complexity, it is valuable to revisit the generic semantic attack structure in Sect. 3.1 and analyse each modular component of a semantic attack to develop insights for establishing generic principles of preemptive and proactive defense that are

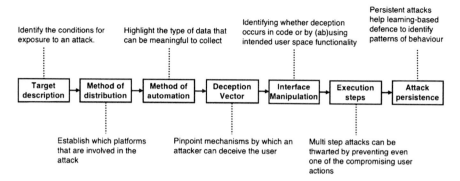

Fig. 14 Defense considerations with the generic semantic attack model. Here, the semantic attack model is employed as a template framework to develop defence measures against key aspects of an attack's construction and behaviour

independent of individual attack vectors. Below, we provide instructional examples for eliciting key parameters that aid the construction of preemptive and proactive defense mechanisms based on each generic semantic attack component, as well providing corresponding examples of defense systems that have been developed in research and commercial platforms. Figure 14 summarises the key defense considerations for each individual component of a semantic attacks structure.

- **Target description**. Distinguish between the different of targeting parameters across a range of semantic attack to identify both distinct and common conditions for exposure. For example, whether a user is at risk due to their identity (so that these attributes can be monitored and evaluated), or whether a users passive computer (whether personal or work related) usage inadvertently exposes them to certain semantic attacks.

  Recent advances in the detection of spear phishing email have demonstrated that by monitoring explicit user attributes and interactions in email content, corresponding meta-data can be learned proactively to generate anomalous behaviour facilitating the detection of spear phishing. For example, in 2015 researchers Stringhini and Thonnard developed a prototype spear phishing classification engine which collected and profiled behavioural features associated to email writing style, composition, communication context (e.g., time/date, email chain, contact interaction) within a support vector machine learning system to detect compromised email accounts. Similarly, commercial security vendor *Barracuda* [21] have introduced a spear phishing detection system called *Sentinel* that monitors an organisations communication history based on specific user email interactions as a context feature-set to train an artificial intelligence system to predict and prevent future attacks.

- **Method of Distribution**. Identify platforms that are involved in an attack to provide defense developers with the insight to choose which remote (e.g., involving a network) or local system to monitor to determine where best place the defense mechanism. Establish patterns in distribution between systems, such as shared functionality (e.g., cross-site advertising plugins) to highlight where functionality supply chains open up a semantic attack distribution vector. Again, guiding developers as to points of vulnerability within a platforms user interface. Stringhini et al. have shown that by monitoring the redirection path taken to reach a web destination effectively identifies attack platforms involved in a malicious website, which are intentionally obfuscated from blacklists [56]. Instead of positioning defense locally on a web browser platform which scrutinises physical website features, the researchers demonstrated that patterns in HTTP redirection can be used as a distributed means of detection through network-based analysis; hence informing developers that such detection may be implemented within network security systems monitoring DNS and HTTP requests.

- **Method of Automation**. The type of automation exhibited dictates to a large degree the response mechanism or the type of data that can be collected for its detection. For instance, an attack that is fully automated is likely to leave a fingerprint of behaviour that can be used to develop attack signatures, whereas an attack that is conducted manually will benefit from focusing on specific attacker behaviour.

  In 2014, an example of measuring automated attack procedures by Ruskov et al. demonstrated how by dynamically monitoring the sequence of actions within a semantic attack can help to model user and attacker behaviour through simulation. This process can then be used to facilitate the development of knowledge-based defense systems that can more efficiently detect deception-based threats through enumeration of automatic attack procedures.

- **Deception Vector**. Establish the different deception vectors possible on a platforms user interface so that developers and researchers can pinpoint the mechanisms by which an attacker can manipulate the visual and/or system behaviour to "trick" the user into committing a compromising action.

  As susceptibility to deception vectors triggers user exploitation, it is generally agreed that semantic attack education is a core element of defense-in-depth against semantic attacks where technical mechanisms fail to prevent or proactively detect threats. As a result, research has explored interactive training through bitesize quizzes, test and games and attack simulations to maximise the effectiveness of learning [57, 58, 62], some of which have empirically proven to reduce susceptibility to deception vectors and have been converted into popular commercial offerings, with examples including PhishGuru [26], Anti-Phishing Phil and Phyllis [27] and PhishMe's Simulator [28] applications. However, most commercial solutions for security awareness training focus almost exclusively on phishing emails and websites, which constitute only a small portion of different semantic attacks possible deception vectors. Where research has explored further deception vectors in other attacks, these remain largely as prototype products. Moreover, the type of awareness training can vary just as much as the diversity of different semantic attacks if training is based on specific attack vectors rather than general concepts of good cyber hygiene; the prior of which can become outdated quickly. Therefore, where possible it is important that embedded awareness training and user interface security indicators are integrated both individually and across interdependent platforms based on generic semantic attack principles rather than specific attack vectors.

- **Interface Manipulation**. Identify whether the deception vector occurs in code or by abusing intended user space functionality, to shape the design of a defense system and to narrow down its scope.

To prevent or detect deception vectors without relying on the effectiveness of user awareness training requires platform developers to pinpoint vulnerabilities in the user interface where it may be (ab)used to execute deception vectors, whether through programmatic manipulation or intended user space functionality. In both cases, preemptive functions have been explored in research [53] for the android operating system to block malicious apps executing visual and behavioural deception through spoofing a legitimate applications appearance. The preemptive defense was implemented by capturing and analysing application program interface calls to the android graphic user interface to classify malicious behaviour. In the commercial space, the use of sandbox environments has gained popularity to interrogate the legitimacy of user interface functionality, for example as to whether certain functions result in potentially malicious behaviour. For instance, most modern web browsers employ sandbox technologies to isolate prevent website JavaScript coding from manipulating browsers' visual and behavioural properties, examples include the presentation of URLS in the address bar and the format of visual user security indicators such as the level of websites transport layer security. In the majority of cases commercial security technologies focus on preemptive programmatic manipulation rather than the misuse of normal user functionality.

- **Executions steps**. Execution steps: An attack that relies on more than one step can potentially be detected more easily than a single-step one and before it completes by looking for traces of its initial steps. It may also be thwarted by preventing even one of the compromising actions that a user needs to be deceived into committing.

Recent advances and greater uptake in the FIDO authentication protocol [29] has demonstrated robust proactive defense against phishing attacks, by enforcing two-factor authentication integrated between multiple architectures. Successful deception will not always result in user account compromise as the FIDO protocol employs temporal session keys generated by a second factor of authentication always available to the user (typically biometric).

- **Attack persistence**. Contrary to one-off deception attempts, persistent ones may have a high chance of succeeding in their target but could also help a learning-based defense system (or platform user) to gradually identify its pattern of behaviour and report or block it.

Whilst persistent deception for a singular semantic attack is uncommon, for Scareware attack vectors in particular persistent deception forms part of the exploitation payload. In 2011, Shahzad and Lavesson [54] proposed a machine learning approach based on mining variable length instruction sequences as a means for detection of persistent attack behaviors. In 2013, Microsoft demonstrated high detection accuracy in a prototype system that identified

Table 7 Summary of preemptive and proactive defenses based on generic semantic attack components

Attack component	Mechanism	Preemptive	Proactive	Practicality	Maturity
Target description	Integrity checking	✓	✓	P + O	Medium
Method of distribution	Platform monitoring	✓	✓	P + O	Low
Method of automation	Threat modelling		✓	O	Medium
Deception vector	User awareness training	✓	✓	O	Low
Interface manipulator	Platform sandbox		✓	P+O	High
Execution steps	Cross platform AAA		✓	P+O	High
Attack persistence	Machine learning classification	✓	✓	P + O	Low

persistent patterns in visual scareware deception through image detection with Logistic Regression using stochastic gradient descent [55].

Table 7 summarises the types of preemptive and proactive defenses, according to the generic functional elements of a semantic attack, their practicality for both the personal (P) user and organisational (O) operating environment, including their general maturity as defense solutions at the time of writing.

4.3 Platform-Based Defense-in-Depth Lifecycle

A defense-in-depth lifecycle for user platforms is intended to provide a multi-faceted framework approach for effectively implementing semantic attack defense. Its primary aim is to establish key roles and responsibilities for different components of a system (e.g., platform provider, security, developer and users) that contribute holistically to defense against semantic attacks. The platform defense lifecycle does not just represent a specific software or hardware platform providers' (e.g., social media or app vendor, email or website host), but also includes any organisational context providing access to user-interface platform(s) for their incumbent user base. In both scenarios, the lifecycle applies as a framework to provide through life defense for preemptive and proactive defense measures against semantic attack threats by establishing the ecosystem of responsibility which can be utilised to harness different defense capabilities through each functional element of the lifecycle.

In Fig. 15, we illustrate three key roles: platform developer, platform security and platform user, which form each element of a platforms defense lifecycle against semantic attacks. Whilst each role is distinct in its own right (e.g., contribution to defense and dependencies for its utilisation), this is not intended to indicate an

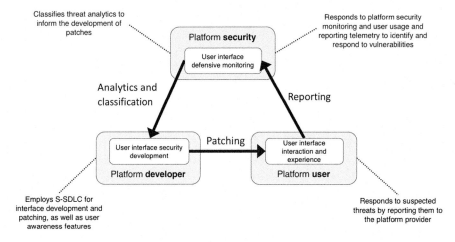

Classifies threat analytics to inform the development of patches

Platform **security**

User interface defensive monitoring

Responds to platform security monitoring and user usage and reporting telemetry to identify and respond to vulnerabilities

Analytics and classification

Reporting

User interface security development

Patching

User interface interaction and experience

Platform **developer**

Platform **user**

Employs S-SDLC for interface development and patching, as well as user awareness features

Responds to suspected threats by reporting them to the platform provider

Fig. 15 The semantic attack defence life cycle consists of three continuously interacting defence functions: secure platform development, user threat reporting and platform security systems; which in combination aim to provide holistic and complementary preemptive and proactive protection against semantic attacks

implicit separation of the particular role amongst different entities, as each role in the lifecycle can exist in the same organisation. As an example, *Facebook* is a independent social network platform which implements internal functions for each role described, but for the *Facebook* platform and users only. However, within an organisational environment, each role may serve as a holistic function across all platforms that the organisation hosts or makes available to their user base. So, the lifecycle is intended as a high-level functional model that is applicable across multiple contexts to describe how to combine the capabilities of each type of platform role for defense against semantic attacks. Below, we elaborate on each role as to their defense function:

- **Platform developer**. Developers are responsible for programming both the internal and user interface functionality of a platform that is both secure and resilient to technical threats or abuse of intended user space functionality that would result in deception vectors for semantic attacks. Platform developers can employ the Secure Software Development Life cycle (S-SDLC) framework to design and integrate security considerations systematically into the core requirements and design of the platforms architecture, as well as utilise threat classification from system and user security telemetry. The following S-SDLC life cycle stages provide indications of activities to be carried out when introducing new user interface functionality or applying security patches against deception based threats.

    – *Requirements*: Define intended user space functionality and its expected limitations to establish any possible attack surface through misuse. This requires documenting system-to-system and system-to-user interactions which form the platforms system of interest, then identifying how and if these interactions affect other related platforms within the deployment environment.

– *Design*: Develop user interface threat models which consider different elements of the platforms design. Highlight potential weak spots in the user interface that may be targets for misuse or vulnerabilities in data representation and transfer (within and externally from the platform) which can be used to inject toward or extract data from target users.

– *Coding*: Build programmatic determinism through static code analysis to establish confidence that the platforms programmatic features do not force the platform to exhibit visual or behavioural deception vectors if targeted by spoofed or injected data on the user interface (e.g., where a graphic or physical button may be (ab)used through normal user usage).

– *Testing*: Utilise "fuzzing" based test within user interface scenarios where different types of behaviour are arbitrarily executed as means to elicit anomalous system responses or situations which can form the basis for a deception vector.

– *Release/Maintain*: Implements processes and procedures from the platforms security monitoring capability as part of continual integration to support the delivery of telemetry based patching (both system and user awareness based) against internal as well as external platform vulnerabilities.

- **Platform security**. The security role within the platform defense lifecycle is responsible for both implementing preemptive security measures (e.g., to prevent technical vulnerability exploitation or platform misuse), as well supporting proactive defenses through monitoring and collecting system and user telemetry to aid in the detection of unknown or emergent threats. The latter of which feeds into preemptive defense through activation of security rules (e.g., blocking an activity), as well as providing crucial platform analytics and classification data that is forwarded to platform developers to produce platform patches and or to develop future secure user interface functionality. For semantic attacks, unlike traditional platform security controls such as intrusion detection systems or firewalls, the platform security requires to monitor and respond to key measurable elements of the user interface via telemetry produced by the platform itself and by the user base who access it.

- **Platform user**. Sole reliance on platform security alongside external technical defense mechanisms provided by platform users is often insufficient as a means of defense for detecting the vast range of semantic attacks, especially when deception vector utilises legitimate user space functionality [33]. It is imperative that outside of technical controls employed, that user telemetry is also harnessed. Here, the contribution of platform users for semantic attack defense is twofold. Firstly, platform users generate activity that can be analysed to determine if their behaviour is consistent with malintent or victimisation. Platform-based user activity creates meta-data that has been shown to be useful in a number contexts where human activity can be used for establishing situational awareness in natural disasters [59]. From a security standpoint, the same method can be used to identify where user activity is consistent with exploitation by a semantic attack or indeed the construction of one. The second utility of platform users is their ability to report security threats, where a growing trend in platform security to address semantic attacks is to provide a means for users to report suspected threats. Most major email and browser platforms now provide inbuilt mechanisms for users to report phishing attacks or malicious content, with various external security companies developing enterprise platforms, such as *PhishMe Reporter* and *Wombat Security PhishAlarm*. In general, with access to both types of user telemetry (passive platform usage and active threat reporting), platform security and developers are provided with rich analytics that can be used to classify and intercept suspected threats in online platform defense systems or through patching of vulnerabilities in the user interface.

4.4   Defense in Hindsight

Taking in to consideration the three dimensions of defense we have discussed, here we evaluate how these defense approaches would have provided defense against the three real world semantic attacks illustrated in Sect. 3.2.

- **Podesta Emails**.

  - *Semantic Attack killchain*: By detecting and blocking the Google phishing email, the Google login phishing website which was used to capture user credentials would have been thwarted. Therefore, to prevent this exploitation it would have required only that the email was blocked or detected as malicious to prevent compromise.
  - *Principles of preemptive and proactive defense*: If the email account in question had enabled mails two form factor authentication mechanisms then on redirection to the attackers phishing login page and input of login credentials the attackers would still have been unable to successfully access the email account.
  - *Defense-in-depth lifecycle*: This particular email template was spoofed directly from Google and was not the first time it had been used or reported as phishing. Therefore, if first phishing report had been forward by Google's platform security to their Gmail platform security developers the combination of the emails content, images and domain name (i.e., not being an official Google email address) would have served as key features to create a detection signature. Which could have subsequently been built into Gmails phishing detection engine. Here, the combination of user reporting, Gmail's security analyst (or system) forwarding the report details and classification to developers, and security system updates by developers would have prevented the email ever having reached John Podesta's email account.

- **WhatsApp QRishing**.

  - *Semantic Attack killchain*: As this specific attack it is dependent on either a phishing email, instant message or SMS in order to coerce the user in to accessing the supposed WhatsApp URL detecting the attack through these initial methods of distributions would prevent the user from being persuaded into visiting the phishing webpage.

- *Principles of preemptive and proactive defense*: A combination of standard phishing defenses analysing the integrity of webpage content (e.g., use of logos, scripts and redirection from site mirroring) alongside common phishing website awareness training (e.g., domain highlighting) would provide both a preemptive and proactive defense measure against this threat.
- *Defense-in-depth lifecycle*: Through a user reporting mechanism this particular threat to WhatsApp web application would have alerted the platform security team of the QR code authentication vulnerability. As a result, prompting developers to patch the system to enforce a secure means for authentication through a secondary authentication mechanism only accessible to the legitimate user, as well as instead exploring ways to protect to their web platform by prevent third party mirroring of their website scripts generating the QR code.

- **The case of the "Hungry Bear"**.

  - *Semantic Attack killchain*: Multimedia masquerading serves as the first attack in a chain, spreading through Facebook via user activity ("liking" and manually sharing the video). However, the subsequent phishing website and fake survey attack chain could have been thwarted by focusing defense on the redirection behaviour of the post to external platforms outside Facebook.
  - *Principles of preemptive and proactive defense*: Much like the *Facebook EdgeRank* algorithm analyses features associated to social interaction to suggested friends, posts, advertisements and material it believes certain users are interested in, by monitoring post behaviours alongside textual information and responses from affected users, this attack could be proactively identified by developing machine learning models that match patterns of anomalous redirection activity. For example, collecting data associated to the post video nature (such as title text), user comments asking how to view the video on *Facebook*, alongside the URL redirection provides features that can be fed into a learning algorithm to classify the post's malicious and deceptive behaviour.
  - *Defense-in-depth lifecycle*: The combination of platform security measures monitoring both platform functionality activity and that of its user base would have served as crucial telemetry to *Facebook* security teams for classifying this as a suspected malicious post automatically, in turn, highlighting to platform developers the need to embed security measures in certain post configuration (e.g., an image post with an embedded URL) before users are redirected to external platforms automatically. Alongside technical detection, providing user notification requesting for confirmation of external website would highlight the nature of the post to users and indicate anomalous activity.

5   Open Research Challenges

5.1   Emerging Threats in the Internet of Everything

Historically, semantic attack exploits in computer systems were limited to traditional Internet communications such as messaging and web application platforms. However, in IoT, the threat landscape includes vehicles, industrial control systems, and even smart home appliances. The result of this is that the impact is not limited to cyberspace (such as stealing information, compromising a system, crashing a web service etc.), but is branching into physical space too. Early examples can be observed through physical damage dealt by malware in manufacturing plants, rail signalling, water treatment plants and even nuclear facilities. We anticipate that cyber-physical systems, such as industrial control systems and vehicles, will soon become realistic targets for user deception. The potential impact in physical space makes them attractive targets, and the limited diversity of human-system interaction, makes it difficult for the users to detect misbehaviour. For instance, consider the Tire Pressure Monitoring System (TPMS) on a modern automobile. It consists of a sensor inside the tire, which monitors tire pressure and periodically transmits that data wirelessly to an electronic control unit (ECU) on the in-vehicle network of the automobile. If the tire pressure is below a threshold, this is displayed on the driver's dashboard as a tire pressure warning. Rouf et al. [68] have shown from as early as 2010 that spoofing these messages can be relatively straightforward. So, an attacker can wirelessly transmit fake TPMS data to the ECU and trigger a fraudulent warning. The driver-system interface does not provide anything more than a visual display of the warning. So, there is no way for the driver to tell that this is a deception attempt rather than a legitimate safety issue, and as such will probably decide to pull over as soon as possible.

While the potential of attacks on vehicles captures the public's interest, it is cyber-physical systems in industrial control that have been targeted several times in high-profile incidents in the past. The exploitation was almost always highly technical, but usually the initial point of entry was standard spear-phishing and in some cases watering hole attacks. In 2014, a German steel mill was attacked via spear-phishing, with the aim to capture user credentials, gain access to the back office and from there to the control network, ultimately damaging a blast furnace. In 2015, 80,000 homes in Ukraine lost power when phishing emails deceived employees of the electricity provider into clicking on an attachment in an email, purportedly from the Prime Minister of Ukraine [69].

Smart home IoT systems also constitute attractive targets as deception devices. Most commonly, they involve access to cloud, voice-activated artificial intelligence (such as Alexa or Siri) and workflow automation services, such as IFTTT and Stringify. Each one of these can be compromised by deceiving a user or with the purpose to deceive a user. A simple example would be to inject audio commands (e.g. "Alexa, purchase item X") in an audio or video file sent to a user via email. In fact, a similar incident (albeit not an attack by design) occurred in 2016, when a 6-year old girl asked Alexa Can you play dollhouse with me and get me a dollhouse? and Alexa actually did order a $160 dollhouse. Then, when a news presenter repeated this on TV while covering the story, several Amazon Echos in people's homes attempted to order further dollhouses. At the same time, any breach of confidentiality relating to the smart home can lead to breach of physical privacy and thus be useful information in the hands of attackers building a picture about a household's pattern of life. Data sniffed from sensors or smart meters can tell when someone is in or out during the week, and even how they look or sound like if their Internet-connected camera is compromised. The impact can be further accentuated if the breach of privacy extends to users' smart wearables, especially when they relate to health, as attackers can use information on likely medical conditions to target them convincingly. Consider the impact that ransomware would have if it were designed for wearable or implantable medical devices. Protecting against semantic attacks in cyber-physical context has not been explored yet.

5.2   Human-as-a-Security-Sensor

By their very nature, semantic attacks are challenging for autonomous technical defenses to detect and prevent. In recent years, the focus on user awareness training has shifted to actively involving users as human sensors spotting and reporting suspected attacks. As alluded to in Sect. 4.3, the user plays a crucial role in the platform defense-in-depth lifecycle against semantic attacks, supplementing technical defense mechanisms with human detection efficacy. In [32], we established the concept of Human-as-a-Security-Sensor by demonstrating how one's ability to detect different semantic attacks can be predicted. We then showed experimentally how predictive modelling can be integrated into a real-world technical system to actively engage and empower users to report detection of different semantic attacks across a range of platforms in real-time; outperforming all technical defense systems compared against [33]. Moreover, there are now examples of security vendors and public organisations advocating and actively employing human security sensor functions to augment defense against semantic attacks, such as the "human sensor" publicised phishing detection platform *PhishMe Reporter* and the University of Oxford CERT team's phishing reporting portal [30]. However, to realise this concept's long term benefits, there is a need to extend to a wider range of threats (other than phishing) and to find effective means of encouraging users to take part. Furthermore, in IoT space, the means by which to report suspected threats may be less intuitive or "safe" as that of a laptop or mobile device user interface. If a deception vector is executed within the user interface of an industrial control system or vehicle, it may be dangerous to stop any activity to report a suspected threat and similarly dangerous to ignore a suspected deception as false. Taking the example of spoofed tire pressure warnings again, if onboard vehicle security fails to detect the deception, the driver has to make the decision whether to report the suspected deception and ignore the tire pressure warnings or pull over as per the attacker's aim. The Human-as-a-Security-Sensor paradigm harbours great potential for augmenting existing technical defenses in the fight against semantic attacks, but finding a consolidated and secure means of reporting threats against multi-platform user interfaces is a complex challenge.

5.3 Cyber Hygiene 2.0

Perhaps the most common advice for stepping up the security of an individual or organisation is to protect themselves against basic cyber threats by keeping their software and operating system up to date, avoiding unsafe websites or email attachments from people they do not know, and other basic measures collectively referred to as "cyber hygiene". The aim is prevention, and it is without doubt that such measures do improve overall security posture. However, as threats gradually become more advanced, and this is certainly the case for semantic attacks, individual users need to be equipped with recommendations on not only how to prevent, but also how to identify and respond to less basic attacks that have not been thwarted through prevention. Here, researchers can make use of the early steps that have been taken in the field of neuroscience, for instance using fMRI to show that the areas that exhibit the most brain activity when a user successfully distinguishes between a phishing and a legitimate website are those associated with decision-making, attention, and problem-solving [67], or using mindfulness to improve attention when facing a phishing attempt [66]. We anticipate that the next phase for cyber hygiene efforts will be in the form of simple techniques and habits that can help detect threats rather than relying on successful prevention.

6 Conclusion

Semantic attacks have been posing a significant and sustained threat to computer information security for almost 30 years, with a cryptovirus appearing as early as 1989 and scareware existing since 1990. The basic principles in deceiving users have remained largely the same, yet the threat has not been thwarted. On the contrary, all statistics point to a continuous increase in the number and diversity of semantic attacks and worsening impact. We argue that the ineffectiveness of the very large number of technical security approaches developed is that they look at each type of attack in isolation. For example, the deception logic and the nature of the tell-tale signs of phishing in email and in social media are the same. Yet, the two cannot be addressed by the same technical security mechanism. In response to this challenge, we have discussed three high-level defense approaches, which can be attractive areas for further exploration in addressing the wider semantic attack space. Wholly unsurprisingly for a type of threat that is based on user deception, the key in defense is again the human, whether as developer of user interfaces or as a user acting as human sensor, but not making the same mistake of attempting to detect threats in isolation. The human users are best placed to thwart deception attempts against them if this capability can be leveraged as part of technical defense systems.

References

1. Schneier, B., 2011. Secrets and lies: digital security in a networked world. John Wiley and Sons.
2. Loukas, G., 2015. Cyber-physical attacks: A growing invisible threat. Butterworth-Heinemann.
3. APWG, 2018. APWG Phishing Attack Trends Reports. https://apwg.org/resources/apwg-reports/.
4. Symantec, 2018. Security Center Archived Publications - Internet Security Threat Reports https://www.symantec.com/security-center/archived-publications.
5. FirstCyberSecurity, 2009. Protecting your brand online and creating customer confidence. http://www.firstcybersecurity.com/main/IPRiskMReview.pdf.
6. Webroot, 2013. Webroot real-time anti-phishing service. http://www.webroot.com/shared/pdf/WAP-Anti-Phishing-102013.pdf.
7. Amiga Fish-Disk Database, 1990. Fish-disk 448 content: Nightmare. http://amiga-fish.erkan.se/amiga-fish-disk-448-contentNightMare/.
8. Cisco, 2017. Viruses, worms, trojans, and bots. https://www.cisco.com/c/en/us/about/security-center/virus-differences.html.
9. M. Bishop, 2000. Analysis of the iloveyou worm. Internet:http://nob.cs.ucdavis.edu/classes/ecs155-2005-04/handouts/iloveyou.pdf.
10. Financial Cryptography, 2005. GP4.3 - growth and fraud - case 3 - phishing, 2005. http://financialcryptography.com/mt/archives/000609.html.
11. M. Dornseif, 2004. 0wned by an ipod, 2004. Presentation. https://www.slideshare.net/KarlFrank99/owned-by-an-ipod
12. G. Cluley, 2011. Osama bin laden death video scam spreads virally on facebook. https://nakedsecurity.sophos.com/2011/05/02/osama-binladen-death-video-scam-spreads-virally-on-facebook/.
13. TrendLabs, 2012. Spear-phishing email: Most favored apt attack bait. Technical report, TrendLabs - APT Research Team. http://www.trendmicro.com/cloud-content/us/pdfs/securityintelligence/white-papers/wp-spear-phishing-email-most-favoredapt-attack-bait.pdf.
14. Social Engineer (2014). The social engineering infographic. http://www.social-engineer.org/social-engineering/socialengineering-infographic/
15. Statista, 2015. Types of cyber attacks experienced by companies worldwide as of August 2015. http://www.statista.com/statistics/474937/cyber-crime-attacks-experienced-by-global-companies/.
16. Statista, 2015. Average number of days to resolve a cyber attack on companies in the united states as of august 2015. http://www.statista.com/statistics/193463/average-days-toresolve-a-cyber-attack-in-us-companies-by-attack/.
17. Statista, 2015. Share of cyber crime damages caused to u.s. companies through phishing and social engineering in 2015. http://www.statista.com/statistics/193465/financial-damagecaused-by-phishing-for-us-companies/.
18. Kaspersky, 2017. Kaspersky internet security 2017. https:www.kaspersky.co.uk/internet-security
19. Avast, 2017. Safezone browser. https://www.avast.com/f-safezone.
20. Sophos, 2017. Intercept X tech specs. https://www.sophos.com/en-us/products/intercept-x/tech-specs.aspx.
21. Barracuda, 2017. Evolution of Spear Phishing. https://assets.barracuda.com/assets/docs/dms/Barracuda_Sentinel_WP_Evolution_Spear_Phishing_US.pdf
22. Yahoo, 2017. Secure your inbox. https://uk.antispam.yahoo.com/.

23. Engadget, 2017. Google beefs up gmail security to fight phishing attempts. https://www.engadget.com/2017/05/31/google-gmail-security-fight-phishing/.
24. Microsoft, 2017. Office 365 email anti-spam protection. https://support.office.com/en-us/article/https://support.office.com/en-us/article/Office-365-email-anti-spam-protection-6a601501-a6a8-4559-b2e7-56b59c96a586
25. Symantec, 2017. Norton security review 2017: Top antivirus provider with fully furnished internet security suites. https://fatsecurity.com/review/norton.
26. Wombat Security, 2017. PhishGuru Simulated Phishing Attacks. https://www.wombatsecurity.com/security-education/phishguru-simulated-phishing-attacks
27. Wombat Security, 2017. Security Awareness Training Modules https://www.wombatsecurity.com/security-education/security-awareness-training-modules
28. PhishMe, 2017. PhishMe Simulator. https://phishme.com/product-services/simulator-2/
29. FIDO alliance, 2017. How FIDO Works. https://fidoalliance.org/how-fido-works/
30. University of Oxford, 2016. Information security - report an incident. https://www.infosec.ox.ac.uk/report-incident.
31. Heartfield, R. and Loukas, G., 2016. A taxonomy of attacks and a survey of defence mechanisms for semantic social engineering attacks. ACM Computing Surveys (CSUR), 48(3), pp. 37.
32. Heartfield, R., Loukas, G. and Gan, D., 2016. You are probably not the weakest link: Towards practical prediction of susceptibility to semantic social engineering attacks. IEEE Access, 4, pp. 6910–6928.
33. Heartfield, R., Loukas, G. and Gan, D., 2017, June. An eye for deception: A case study in utilizing the human-as-a-security-sensor paradigm to detect zero-day semantic social engineering attacks. In Software Engineering Research, Management and Applications (SERA), 2017 IEEE 15th International Conference on (pp. 371–378). IEEE.
34. Jordan, M. and Gouday, H., 2005. The signs, and semiotics of the successful semantic attack. In 14th Annual EICAR Conference (pp. 344–364).
35. Huber, M., Mulazzani, M., Weippl, E., Kitzler, G. and Goluch, S., 2011. Friend-in-the-middle attacks: Exploiting social networking sites for spam. IEEE Internet Computing, 15(3), pp. 28–34.
36. Heartfield, R. and Loukas, G., 2013. On the feasibility of automated semantic attacks in the cloud. In Computer and Information Sciences III (pp. 343–351). Springer, London.
37. Madlmayr, G., Langer, J., Kantner, C. and Scharinger, J., 2008, March. NFC devices: Security and privacy. In Availability, Reliability and Security, 2008. ARES 08. Third International Conference on (pp. 642–647). IEEE.
38. Weber, R.H., 2010. Internet of Things–New security and privacy challenges. Computer law and security review, 26(1), pp. 23–30.
39. Dhamija, R., Tygar, J.D. and Hearst, M., 2006, April. Why phishing works. In Proceedings of the SIGCHI conference on Human Factors in computing systems (pp. 581–590). ACM.
40. Drake, C.E., Oliver, J.J. and Koontz, E.J., 2004, August. Anatomy of a Phishing Email. In CEAS.
41. Huber, M., Mulazzani, M. and Weippl, E., 2010, September. Who on earth is Mr. Cypher: automated friend injection attacks on social networking sites. In IFIP International Information Security Conference (pp. 80–89). Springer, Berlin, Heidelberg.
42. Aburrous, M., Hossain, M.A., Thabatah, F. and Dahal, K., 2008, April. Intelligent phishing website detection system using fuzzy techniques. In Information and Communication Technologies: From Theory to Applications, 2008. ICTTA 2008. 3rd International Conference on (pp. 1–6). IEEE.
43. Chou, N., Ledesma, R., Teraguchi, Y. and Mitchell, J.C., 2004, February. Client-Side Defense Against Web-Based Identity Theft. In NDSS.
44. Huang, H., Zhong, S. and Tan, J., 2009, August. Browser-side countermeasures for deceptive phishing attack. In Information Assurance and Security, 2009. IAS'09. Fifth International Conference on (pp. 352–355). IEEE.

45. Kumaraguru, P., Rhee, Y., Acquisti, A., Cranor, L.F., Hong, J. and Nunge, E., 2007, April. Protecting people from phishing: the design and evaluation of an embedded training email system. In Proceedings of the SIGCHI conference on Human factors in computing systems (pp. 905–914). ACM.
46. Giles, J., 2010. Scareware: the inside story. New Scientist, 205(2753), pp. 38–41.
47. Rekouche, K., 2011. Early phishing. arXiv preprint arXiv:1106.4692.
48. Kabay, M.E., 2001. Viruses and worms: more than a technical problem. Ubiquity 2001. ACM
49. Leavitt, N., 2005. Mobile phones: the next frontier for hackers?. Computer, 38(4), pp. 20–23.
50. Kong, J., Cai, W. and Wang, L., 2010, February. The evaluation of index poisoning in bittorrent. In Communication Software and Networks, 2010. ICCSN'10. Second International Conference on (pp. 382–386). IEEE.
51. S. Doherty, J. Gegeny, B. Spasojevic, and J. Baltazar, 2013. Hidden lynx - Professional hackers for hire. Symantec Security Response. https://www.symantec.com/content/dam/symantec/docs/security-center/white-papers/hidden-lynx-hackers-13-en.pdf
52. Irani, D., Balduzzi, M., Balzarotti, D., Kirda, E. and Pu, C., 2011, July. Reverse social engineering attacks in online social networks. In International Conference on Detection of Intrusions and Malware, and Vulnerability Assessment (pp. 55–74). Springer, Berlin, Heidelberg.
53. Bianchi, A., Corbetta, J., Invernizzi, L., Fratantonio, Y., Kruegel, C. and Vigna, G., 2015, May. What the app is that? deception and countermeasures in the android user interface. In Security and Privacy (SP), 2015 IEEE Symposium on (pp. 931–948). IEEE.
54. Shahzad, R.K. and Lavesson, N., 2011, August. Detecting scareware by mining variable length instruction sequences. In Information Security South Africa (ISSA), 2011 (pp. 1–8). IEEE.
55. Seifert, C., Stokes, J.W., Colcernian, C., Platt, J.C. and Lu, L., 2013, May. Robust scareware image detection. In Acoustics, Speech and Signal Processing (ICASSP), 2013 IEEE International Conference on (pp. 2920–2924). IEEE.
56. Stringhini, G., Kruegel, C. and Vigna, G., 2013, November. Shady paths: Leveraging surfing crowds to detect malicious web pages. In Proceedings of the 2013 ACM SIGSAC conference on Computer and communications security (pp. 133–144). ACM.
57. Asanka, N., Love, S. and Scott, M., 2012. Designing a mobile game to teach conceptual knowledge of avoiding'phishing attacks'. International Journal for e-Learning Security, 2(1), pp. 127–132.
58. Sheng, S., Magnien, B., Kumaraguru, P., Acquisti, A., Cranor, L.F., Hong, J. and Nunge, E., 2007, July. Anti-phishing phil: the design and evaluation of a game that teaches people not to fall for phish. In Proceedings of the 3rd symposium on Usable privacy and security (pp. 88–99). ACM.
59. Aulov, O. and Halem, M., 2012. Human sensor networks for improved modeling of natural disasters. Proceedings of the IEEE, 100(10), pp. 2812–2823.
60. Marforio, C., Francillon, A. and Capkun, S., 2011. Application collusion attack on the permission-based security model and its implications for modern smartphone systems. Technical Report. ETH Zurich.
61. Selvaraj, K. and Gutierrez, N.F., 2010. The rise of PDF malware. Symantec Security Response. https://www.symantec.com/content/en/us/enterprise/media/security_response/whitepapers/the_rise_of_pdf_malware.pdf.
62. Kumaraguru, P., 2009. Phishguru: a system for educating users about semantic attacks. Carnegie Mellon University.
63. Bates, J., 1990. Trojan horse: AIDS information introductory diskette version 2.0. Virus Bulletin, pp. 3–6.
64. Young, A. and Yung, M., 1996, May. Cryptovirology: Extortion-based security threats and countermeasures. In Security and Privacy, 1996. Proceedings., 1996 IEEE Symposium on (pp. 129–140). IEEE.
65. Howard, F. and Komili, O., 2010. Poisoned search results: How hackers have automated search engine poisoning attacks to distribute malware. Sophos Technical Papers, pp. 1–15.

66. Jensen, M.L., Dinger, M., Wright, R.T. and Thatcher, J.B., 2017. Training to mitigate phishing attacks using mindfulness techniques. Journal of Management Information Systems, 34(2), pp. 597–626.
67. Neupane, A., Saxena, N., Maximo, J.O. and Kana, R., 2016. Neural Markers of Cybersecurity: An fMRI Study of Phishing and Malware Warnings. IEEE Transactions on Information Forensics and Security, 11(9), pp. 1970–1983.
68. Ishtiaq Roufa, R.M., Mustafaa, H., Travis Taylora, S.O., Xua, W., Gruteserb, M., Trappeb, W. and Seskarb, I., 2010, February. Security and privacy vulnerabilities of in-car wireless networks: A tire pressure monitoring system case study. In 19th USENIX Security Symposium, Washington DC (pp. 11–13).
69. Koppel, T., 2015. Lights out: a cyberattack, a nation unprepared, surviving the aftermath. Broadway Books.
70. Hutchins, E.M., Cloppert, M.J. and Amin, R.M., 2011. Intelligence-driven computer network defense informed by analysis of adversary campaigns and intrusion kill chains. Leading Issues in Information Warfare and Security Research, 1(1), pp. 80.
71. Joo, J.W., Moon, S.Y., Singh, S. and Park, J.H., 2017. S-Detector: an enhanced security model for detecting Smishing attack for mobile computing. Telecommunication Systems, 66(1), pp. 29–38.
72. Cova, M., Kruegel, C. and Vigna, G., 2010, April. Detection and analysis of drive-by-download attacks and malicious JavaScript code. In Proceedings of the 19th international conference on World wide web (pp. 281–290). ACM.
73. Jayasinghe, G.K., Culpepper, J.S. and Bertok, P., 2014. Efficient and effective realtime prediction of drive-by download attacks. Journal of Network and Computer Applications, 38, pp. 135–149.
74. Lu, L., Yegneswaran, V., Porras, P. and Lee, W., 2010, October. Blade: an attack-agnostic approach for preventing drive-by malware infections. In Proceedings of the 17th ACM conference on Computer and communications security (pp. 440–450). ACM.
75. Blsing, T., Batyuk, L., Schmidt, A.D., Camtepe, S.A. and Albayrak, S., 2010, October. An android application sandbox system for suspicious software detection. In Malicious and unwanted software (MALWARE), 2010 5th international conference on (pp. 55–62). IEEE.
76. Brickell, E.F., Hall, C.D., Cihula, J.F. and Uhlig, R., Intel Corp, 2011. Method of improving computer security through sandboxing. U.S. Patent 7,908,653.
77. Cone, B.D., Irvine, C.E., Thompson, M.F. and Nguyen, T.D., 2007. A video game for cyber security training and awareness. Computers and Security, 26(1), pp. 63–72.
78. Heartfield, R. and Loukas, G., 2018. Detecting semantic social engineering attacks with the weakest link: Implementation and empirical evaluation of a human-as-a-security-sensor framework. Computers and Security, 76, pp. 101–127.
79. Heartfield, R., Loukas, G. and Gan, D., 2016. You are probably not the weakest link: Towards practical prediction of susceptibility to semantic social engineering attacks. IEEE Access, 4, pp. 6910–6928.
80. Darknet, 2015. EvilAP Defender Detect Evil Twin Attacks. (2015). http://www.darknet.org.uk/2015/04/evilap-defender-detect-evil-twin-attacks/.
81. Heartfield, R. and Loukas, G., 2016, June. Evaluating the reliability of users as human sensors of social media security threats. In Cyber Situational Awareness, Data Analytics And Assessment (CyberSA), 2016 International Conference On (pp. 1–7). IEEE.
82. Bianchi, A., Corbetta, J., Invernizzi, L., Fratantonio, Y., Kruegel, C. and Vigna, G., 2015, May. What the app is that? deception and countermeasures in the android user interface. In Security and Privacy (SP), 2015 IEEE Symposium on (pp. 931–948). IEEE.
83. Dhanalakshmi, R. and Chellappan, C., 2010, July. Detection and recognition of file masquerading for e-mail and data security. In International Conference on Network Security and Applications (pp. 253–262). Springer, Berlin, Heidelberg.
84. Stringhini, G. and Thonnard, O., 2015, July. That ain't you: Blocking spearphishing through behavioral modelling. In International Conference on Detection of Intrusions and Malware, and Vulnerability Assessment (pp. 78–97). Springer, Cham.

85. Aggarwal, A., Rajadesingan, A. and Kumaraguru, P., 2012, October. PhishAri: Automatic realtime phishing detection on twitter. In eCrime Researchers Summit (eCrime), 2012 (pp. 1–12). IEEE.
86. Basnet, R., Mukkamala, S. and Sung, A.H., 2008. Detection of phishing attacks: A machine learning approach. In Soft Computing Applications in Industry (pp. 373–383). Springer, Berlin, Heidelberg.
87. Bhardwaj, T., Sharma, T.K. and Pandit, M.R., 2014. Social engineering prevention by detecting malicious URLs using artificial bee colony algorithm. In Proceedings of the Third International Conference on Soft Computing for Problem Solving (pp. 355–363). Springer, New Delhi.
88. Asanka, N., Love, S. and Scott, M., 2012. Designing a mobile game to teach conceptual knowledge of avoiding'phishing attacks'. International Journal for e-Learning Security, 2(1), pp. 127–132.
89. Bergholz, A., Chang, J.H., Paass, G., Reichartz, F. and Strobel, S., 2008, August. Improved Phishing Detection using Model-Based Features. In CEAS.
90. Dong-Her, S., Hsiu-Sen, C., Chun-Yuan, C. and Lin, B., 2004. Internet security: malicious e-mails detection and protection. Industrial Management and Data Systems, 104(7), pp. 613–623.
91. Drucker, H., Wu, D. and Vapnik, V.N., 1999. Support vector machines for spam categorization. IEEE Transactions on Neural networks, 10(5), pp. 1048–1054.
92. Stembert, N., Padmos, A., Bargh, M.S., Choenni, S. and Jansen, F., 2015, September. A study of preventing email (spear) phishing by enabling human intelligence. In Intelligence and Security Informatics Conference (EISIC), 2015 European (pp. 113–120). IEEE.
93. Malisa, L., Kostiainen, K. and Capkun, S., 2017, March. Detecting mobile application spoofing attacks by leveraging user visual similarity perception. In Proceedings of the Seventh ACM on Conference on Data and Application Security and Privacy (pp. 289–300). ACM.
94. Corbetta, J., Invernizzi, L., Kruegel, C. and Vigna, G., 2014, September. Eyes of a human, eyes of a program: Leveraging different views of the web for analysis and detection. In International Workshop on Recent Advances in Intrusion Detection (pp. 130–149). Springer, Cham.
95. Kumaraguru, P., 2009. Phishguru: a system for educating users about semantic attacks. Carnegie Mellon University.
96. Lee, K., Caverlee, J. and Webb, S., 2010, April. The social honeypot project: protecting online communities from spammers. In Proceedings of the 19th international conference on World wide web (pp. 1139–1140). ACM.
97. Lee, S. and Kim, J., 2012, February. WarningBird: Detecting Suspicious URLs in Twitter Stream. In NDSS (Vol. 12, pp. 1–13).
98. Sheng, S., Magnien, B., Kumaraguru, P., Acquisti, A., Cranor, L.F., Hong, J. and Nunge, E., 2007, July. Anti-phishing phil: the design and evaluation of a game that teaches people not to fall for phish. In Proceedings of the 3rd symposium on Usable privacy and security (pp. 88–99). ACM.
99. Xiang, G., Hong, J., Rose, C.P. and Cranor, L., 2011. Cantina+: A feature-rich machine learning framework for detecting phishing web sites. ACM Transactions on Information and System Security (TISSEC), 14(2), p.21.
100. Pandeym T. and Khare, P, 2017. Bluetooth Hacking and its Prevention. http://www. lnttechservices.com/sites/default/files/resources/pdf/whitepapers/2017-12/Bluetooth-Hacking-and-its-Prevention.pdf
101. Shamsi, J.A., Hameed, S., Rahman, W., Zuberi, F., Altaf, K. and Amjad, A., 2014, January. Clicksafe: Providing security against clickjacking attacks. In High-Assurance Systems Engineering (HASE), 2014 IEEE 15th International Symposium on (pp. 206–210). IEEE.
102. Larson, M., Massey, D., Rose, S., Arends, R. and Austein, R., 2005. DNS security introduction and requirements. IETF. https://tools.ietf.org/html/rfc4033
103. Shahzad, R.K. and Lavesson, N., 2011, August. Detecting scareware by mining variable length instruction sequences. In Information Security South Africa (ISSA), 2011 (pp. 1–8). IEEE.

104. Seifert, C., Stokes, J.W., Colcernian, C., Platt, J.C. and Lu, L., 2013, May. Robust scareware image detection. In Acoustics, Speech and Signal Processing (ICASSP), 2013 IEEE International Conference on (pp. 2920–2924). IEEE.
105. BufferZone Pro, 2014. BufferZone-Pro sandbox. http://www.trustware.com/BufferZone-Pro/
106. Alnajjar, A.Y., Manickam, S., Anbar, M., Al-saleem, S. and Elejla, O., 2016. TrustQR: A New Technique for the Detection of Phishing Attacks on QR Code. Advanced Science Letters, 22(10), pp.2905–2909.
107. Beyah, R., Kangude, S., Yu, G., Strickland, B. and Copeland, J., 2004, December. Rogue access point detection using temporal traffic characteristics. In Global Telecommunications Conference, 2004. GLOBECOM'04. IEEE (Vol. 4, pp. 2271–2275). IEEE.
108. Al-Khamis, A.K. and Khalafallah, A.A., 2015, November. Secure Internet on Google Chrome: Client side anti-tabnabbing extension. In Anti-Cybercrime (ICACC), 2015 First International Conference on (pp. 1–4). IEEE.
109. Kharraz, A., Arshad, S., Mulliner, C., Robertson, W.K. and Kirda, E., 2016, August. UNVEIL: A Large-Scale, Automated Approach to Detecting Ransomware. In USENIX Security Symposium (pp. 757–772).
110. Vinayakumar, R., Soman, K.P., Velan, K.S. and Ganorkar, S., 2017, September. Evaluating shallow and deep networks for ransomware detection and classification. In Advances in Computing, Communications and Informatics (ICACCI), 2017 International Conference on (pp. 259–265). IEEE.
111. Mercaldo, F., Nardone, V., Santone, A. and Visaggio, C.A., 2016, June. Ransomware steals your phone. formal methods rescue it. In International Conference on Formal Techniques for Distributed Objects, Components, and Systems (pp. 212–221). Springer, Cham.
112. Bandhakavi, S., King, S.T., Madhusudan, P. and Winslett, M., 2010, August. VEX: Vetting Browser Extensions for Security Vulnerabilities. In USENIX Security Symposium (Vol. 10, pp. 339–354).
113. Ter Louw, M., Lim, J.S. and Venkatakrishnan, V.N., 2008. Enhancing web browser security against malware extensions. Journal in Computer Virology, 4(3), pp. 179–195.
114. Ford, S., Cova, M., Kruegel, C. and Vigna, G., 2009, December. Analyzing and detecting malicious flash advertisements. In Computer Security Applications Conference, 2009. ACSAC'09. Annual (pp. 363–372). IEEE.
115. Li, Z., Zhang, K., Xie, Y., Yu, F. and Wang, X., 2012, October. Knowing your enemy: understanding and detecting malicious web advertising. In Proceedings of the 2012 ACM conference on Computer and communications security (pp. 674–686). ACM.
116. Poornachandran, P., Balagopal, N., Pal, S., Ashok, A., Sankar, P. and Krishnan, M.R., 2017. Demalvertising: A Kernel Approach for Detecting Malwares in Advertising Networks. In Proceedings of the First International Conference on Intelligent Computing and Communication (pp. 215–224). Springer, Singapore.
117. Patil, K., 2016. Request dependency integrity: validating web requests using dependencies in the browser environment. International Journal of Information Privacy, Security and Integrity, 2(4), pp. 281–306.
118. Banerjee, A., Rahman, M.S. and Faloutsos, M., 2011. SUT: Quantifying and mitigating url typosquatting. Computer Networks, 55(13), pp. 3001–3014.
119. Szurdi, J., Kocso, B., Cseh, G., Spring, J., Felegyhazi, M. and Kanich, C., 2014, August. The Long "Taile" of Typosquatting Domain Names. In USENIX Security Symposium (pp. 191–206).
120. Almeida, Tiago, Renato Moraes Silva, and Akebo Yamakami. "Machine learning methods for spamdexing detection." International Journal of Information Security Science 2, no. 3 (2013): 86–107.
121. Geng, G.G., Wang, C.H. and Li, Q.D., 2008, January. Improving Spamdexing Detection Via a Two-Stage Classification Strategy. In Asia Information Retrieval Symposium (pp. 356–364). Springer, Berlin, Heidelberg.

122. Abou-Assaleh, T. and Das, T., 2006, November. Combating spamdexing: Incorporating heuristics in link-based ranking. In International Workshop on Algorithms and Models for the Web-Graph (pp. 97–106). Springer, Berlin, Heidelberg.
123. Shahriar, H., Haddad, H. and Devendran, V.K., 2015. Request and Response Analysis Framework for Mitigating Clickjacking Attacks. International Journal of Secure Software Engineering (IJSSE), 6(3), pp. 1–25.
124. Johns, M. and Lekies, S., 2013, October. Tamper-resistant likejacking protection. In International Workshop on Recent Advances in Intrusion Detection (pp. 265–285). Springer, Berlin, Heidelberg.
125. Sarjaz, B.S. and Abbaspour, M., 2013. Securing BitTorrent using a new reputation-based trust management system. Peer-to-Peer Networking and Applications, 6(1), pp. 86–100.

Cryptographic Program Obfuscation: Practical Solutions and Application-Driven Models

Giovanni Di Crescenzo

Abstract Program obfuscation is about modifying source or machine code into functionally equivalent code that is hard to understand to a human or some other program. Early obfuscation techniques included heuristic non-cryptographic code transformations, many of which however, have been found to be ineffective against sufficiently motivated adversaries. The recent area of cryptographic program obfuscation targets the design and implementation of program obfuscators that are provably secure under a widely accepted intractability assumption, following the standard of modern cryptography solutions. In this chapter we provide a brief summary of the state of the art in cryptographic program obfuscation, focusing on two main aspects: first, there are many implementations of point function obfuscators, satisfying different obfuscation notions, and many of them can be used with practical performance guarantees; second, multiple application-driven obfuscation models and problems can be generated, where practical attack classes can be addressed by leveraging current implementations of point function obfuscators, as well as potential future practical implementations of special-purpose obfuscators.

This work was supported by the Defense Advanced Research Projects Agency (DARPA) via U.S. Army Research Office (ARO), contract number W911NF-15-C-0233. The U.S. Government is authorized to reproduce and distribute reprints for Governmental purposes notwithstanding any copyright annotation hereon. Disclaimer: The views and conclusions contained herein are those of the authors and should not be interpreted as necessarily representing the official policies or endorsements, either expressed or implied, of DARPA, ARO or the U.S. Government. Approved for Public Release, Distribution Unlimited.

G. D. Crescenzo (✉)
Perspecta Labs, Basking Ridge, NJ, USA
e-mail: gdicrescenzo@perspectalabs.com

© Springer Nature Switzerland AG 2018
M. Conti et al. (eds.), *Versatile Cybersecurity*, Advances in Information
Security 72, https://doi.org/10.1007/978-3-319-97643-3_5

1 Introduction

Program obfuscation is about modifying source or machine code into functionally equivalent code that is however hard to understand to a human or some other program. Until about 20 years ago, studies in program obfuscation were motivated mainly by the intention to protect software intellectual property from reverse-engineering attacks. Obfuscation techniques included heuristic code transformations performed by a human or by an obfuscator program, some of them building on transformations similar to those applied during compilation (see, e.g., [15] for a taxonomy of code transformation techniques). Many such techniques, however, have been found to be ineffective against a sufficiently motivated adversary, eventually being capable of developing automated deobfuscation techniques and thus reverse-engineering of the program (see, e.g., [35]).

In the past 20 years or so, the problem of program obfuscation has been attracting a significant amount of research in the modern cryptography literature, as 'cryptographic program obfuscation' might remove the heuristic aspect from obfuscation techniques. Following the success of modern cryptography, where multi-party computation protocols can be designed and proved secure under widely accepted computational intractability assumptions, cryptographic program obfuscation aspires at designing obfuscated programs whose obfuscation enjoys similar provability guarantees. Actually early results in the area conveyed somewhat mixed messages: on the positive side, in [25] it was showed that cryptographic program obfuscation could solve a long-standing open problem in cryptography; while on the negative side, results in [4] implied the very likely impossibility of constructing a single obfuscator for all polynomial-time programs. This still left open the following two main possibilities: (1) constructing a program obfuscator for all polynomial-time programs (i.e., a general-purpose obfuscator) with respect to a less general notion of obfuscation security (and thus, a less general class of attacks); and (2) constructing a program obfuscator for each specific polynomial-time program (a special-purpose obfuscator) with respect to a general notion of obfuscation security.

The line of research (1) has seen much excitement since several other uses of general-purpose obfuscation with respect to this weaker notion of obfuscation were presented (see, e.g., [3] and references therein), potentially solving several long-standing open problems, including some rather surprising ones (e.g., transforming any public-key encryption scheme into a private-key encryption ones). Many candidate general-purpose obfuscator constructions have been proposed based on heuristic constructions of an advanced mathematical objects, called multilinear forms, or approximate versions of them; unfortunately, as of today, many of these candidates have been broken and the future of this research direction has been questioned.

The line of research (2) has actually shown some encouraging progresses, in that recent results show the possibility of constructing obfuscators for restricted families of functions, such as secret verification (aka point) functions, and a few isolated extensions of them, under commonly used, and widely accepted, hardness assumptions. Point functions can be seen as functions that return 1 if the input value is equal to a secret value stored in the program, and 0 otherwise. This line of research has many more chances of being relevant to real-life applications. For starters, commonly used protocols for password-based authentication have been reformulated as instances of point-function obfuscation (the password playing the role of the secret point to be matched). More specifically, the current research literature contains a few theoretical definitions of program obfuscation for point functions (see, e.g., [4, 5]), several constructions of program obfuscators for point functions based on commonly used hardness assumptions, with different performance and security features (see, e.g., [5, 11, 28, 36], as well as several other contributions cited in these cited papers), and implementation efforts showing the practicality of some of these results (see, e.g., [1, 18]). Some of the most relevant results are, in turn, based on other cryptographic primitives (such as deterministic encryption, lossy trapdoor functions, etc.), which have been previously studied in other sequences of papers, even though following the paths of these relationships and understanding the full applicability of these results is a non-trival task for the casual cryptography or security reader. Further specific programs for which special-purpose obfuscators have been proposed include hyperplane membership [13], short-distance matching [19], proxy re-encryption [27], and wildcard-based matching [10]. For none of these latter obfuscators, however, practical implementations have been shown yet.

This chapter can be divided into two conceptual parts, where we show:

1. practical implementations of point function obfuscators, provably secure under widely used intractability assumptions and in theory-oriented models and definitions of cryptographic program obfuscation, and
2. guidelines to generate application-oriented models and definitions of cryptographic program obfuscations, addressing more practical classes of attacks.

In the first part of the chapter (Sects. 2, 3, 4, 5, 6, 7, and 8) we start by considering theory-oriented models and definitions of program obfuscators from the literature, and specialize it to a practice-oriented version that is more suited for implementation, especially with respect to program obfuscators for a large class of functions, including point functions. Then, we consider including 4 of the most used security notions for cryptographic program obfuscators, capturing the following theoretical classes of attacks:

1. learning some information on the obfuscated program significantly better than by just evaluating a black box computing the same program;
2. learning the output of a predicate on input the obfuscated program significantly better than by just evaluating a black box computing the same program;
3. distinguishing the output of a predicate on input the obfuscated program from the output of a predicate on input an obfuscation of a random program within a given class;
4. distinguishing the obfuscated program from an obfuscation of a random program within a given class.

We sort out the intricate literature on this sub-area to select some interesting point function obfuscators from [1, 5, 11, 18, 28, 36], including: (a) at least one satisfying each of these security notions; (b) at least one that is practically efficient and provably secure based on group-theory and no random oracles; (c) at least one based on a lattice-theory assumption, which is resistant to quantum computation attacks. We then report on our implementations of these obfuscators from [1, 18], showing their practical performance, in terms of runtime and storage of the obfuscated program. These implementations apply, wherever possible, a small amount of both design and coding optimizations. Among the former type of optimizations, the computations of certain values are replaced with different and more efficient computations of almost equally distributed values. In one case, a similar distribution is maintained only at the cost of a (much) stronger hardness assumption. Among the second type of optimizations, in group-theory obfuscators, conventional modular exponentiation (often, the most expensive operations in group-theoretic cryptography) is replaced with modular exponentiation via pre-processing, combined with Montgomery multiplication; in lattice-theory obfuscators, probabilistic testing techniques can be used to reduce both storage and runtime.

Overall, our conclusion in this chapter's first part is that implementations of point function obfuscators, provably satisfying different obfuscation notions under widely accepted intractability assumptions, can be used with practical performance (i.e., runtime and storage) guarantees.

In the second part of our chapter (Sect. 10), we present application-driven models for cryptographic program obfuscation identifying research problems in this area as a tuple of points, each point in the tuple being taken from a different 3-dimensional space. We consider a first 3-dimensional space on problem models (with dimensions on program representation models, input models and participant models), a second 3-dimensional space on security requirements (with dimensions on adversary resources, adversary attacks and adversary goals), and a third space on performance requirements (with dimensions on runtime, memory use and storage of the obfuscated program). Definitions of security requirements are driven by (a) adversary goals and security notions based on distinguishing and computing over obfuscated programs; (b) adversary resources such as chosen program inputs and associated outputs, inspection of the program's code, and eavesdropping program inputs and associated outputs; and, most importantly, (c) practical attack classes such as:

1. the adversary making remote calls to the obfuscated program;
2. the adversary stealing or being leaked the obfuscated program and being able to run it in a different computing environment;
3. the adversary intruding in the same computing environment where the obfuscated program resides, observing while it is being run in that environment as well as being able to inspect and run the program.

Variants of these attacks are discussed in various models, where the adversary may target general or secret-based programs, taking low-entropy or high-entropy inputs, in a 2-party or 3-party model. The resulting application-driven research problems enhance the applicability of program obfuscation solutions. As an example for that, we show an obfuscation in the 3-party model for simple function families with low-entropy secrets that does protect the secret (instead, any obfuscation in the 2-party model would not adequately protect the secret against learning or black-box attacks).

Overall, our conclusion in this chapter's second part is that current implementations of point function obfuscators (as well as potential future implementations of special-purpose obfuscators) may soon be leveraged to address practical attack classes with practical performance guarantees.

2 Theory-Oriented Modeling of Cryptographic Program Obfuscation

This section introduces and refines a number of definitions and facts related to the literature's theory-oriented modeling of cryptographic program obfuscation. First, it starts with some basic notations and definitions (in Sect. 2.1); then, it provides functionality, efficiency and security requirements of program obfuscators for point functions (in Sect. 2.2); finally, it quickly recalls known constructions of program obfuscators for point functions (in Sect. 2.3).

2.1 Basic Notations and Definitions

Let $a|b$ denote the concatenation of a and b, and let symbol Z_q denotes the set of integers $\{0, \ldots, q-1\}$.

If S is a set, an element of S^n is an n-component vector with components in S, and an element of $S^{m,n}$ is an m-row, n-column matrix with entries in S.

The expression $y \leftarrow T$ denotes the probabilistic process of uniformly and independently choosing y from set T. The expression $y \leftarrow A(x_1, x_2, \ldots)$ denotes the (possibly probabilistic) process of running algorithm A on input $x_1, x_2, \ldots$ and any necessary random coins, and obtaining y as output. A probability distribution D is also written as $D = \{p_1; p_2; \ldots; p_n : v\}$ to denote the distribution of v after the ordered execution of probabilistic processes $p_1, \ldots, p_n$.

2.2 Modeling Cryptographic Program Obfuscation

The original definition from [4] of cryptographic program obfuscators contained 3 main requirements that can be briefly stated as follows: (program functionality) the obfuscated program behaves like the original program; (polynomial slowdown) the obfuscated program is only polynomially slower than the original program; (virtual black-box obfuscation) the obfuscated program does not leak more to an adversary than access to a black box computing the original program. After recalling a formal version of this definition, the rest of this subsection gives a refined definition of cryptographic program obfuscators, obtained by syntax changes to the original definition and by allowing for some very small error probability of incorrect program output, even when the program input is adversarially chosen after seeing the obfuscated program. The resulting definition is simpler to deal with, from both theory and implementation purposes, and is semantically equivalent for a large class of function families, including point functions. Finally, various security notions are reviewed, including and beyond the original virtual black-box obfuscation (here renamed 'adversary output black-box simulation').

The original definition. We say that the family of functions F admits an obfuscator Obf if Obf is an efficient (possibly probabilistic) algorithm that, on input a description of function $f \in F$ and/or a circuit C_f computing $f \in F$, returns an (obfuscated) circuit oC_f, such that the following two properties are satisfied:

1. (Almost exact functionality): For all f in F, and inputs x, it holds that $oC_f(x) = f(x)$, except possibly with very small probability.
2. (Polynomial slowdown): There exists a polynomial p such that for all f in F, the running time of oC_f is $\leq p(|C_f|)$, where $|C_f|$ denotes the size of circuit C_f.

A refined definition. In practice, it can be unnecessarily complex to implement an obfuscator taking as input a circuit that computes function f, and returns as output another (obfuscated) circuit. Therefore, we perform syntax changes to obtain a definition involving simpler algorithms, from the point of view of implementation, and semantically-equivalent for a large class of function families, including point functions. We then generalize this definition to allow for some small error probability of incorrect program output, even when the program input is adversarially chosen after seeing the obfuscated program. Specifically, we view an obfuscator as a pair of efficient algorithms: an *obfuscation generator* $oGen$ and an *obfuscation evaluator* $oEval$, with the following syntax. On input function parameters $fpar$, including a description of function $f \in F$, $oGen$ returns generator output $gpar$. On input a description of function $f \in F$, generator output $gpar$, and evaluator input x, $oEval$ returns evaluator output y. The pair of algorithms $(oGen, oEval)$ satisfies the following two properties:

1. (Almost exact functionality): For any f in F, with function parameters $fpar$, and any algorithm A, the equality $y = f(x)$ holds with probability $1 - \delta$, for some very small value δ, where y is generated by the following probabilistic steps:

    1. $gpar \leftarrow oGen(fpar)$,
    2. $x \leftarrow A(gpar)$
    3. $y \leftarrow oEval(gpar, x)$.

2. (Polynomial slowdown): There exists a polynomial p such that for all f in F, the running time of $oEval$ is $\leq p(|f|)$, where $|f|$ denotes the size of the (smallest) boolean circuit computing f.

Security notions. Obfuscators (in both the original and refined definition) can satisfy any one of the following different obfuscation security notions (which have to be valid for all functions input to the obfuscation generator chosen according to their specified distribution, for all efficient adversary algorithms, and except possibly with very small probability):

1. *adversary view black-box simulation* [4]: The adversary can read, and thus execute, the evaluator program $oEval(gpar, \cdot)$. Informally speaking, this notion says that no efficient adversary with these capabilities learns any more information than what it can learn by evaluating a black box program that computes function f. A bit more formally, for any efficient adversary with these capabilities, there exists an efficient algorithm, called the simulator, with black-box access to function f, that produces an output indistinguishable from the evaluator program $oEval(gpar, \cdot)$.

2. *adversary output black-box simulation* [4]: The adversary can read, and thus execute, the evaluator program $oEval(gpar, \cdot)$ and is constrained to return a bit at the end of its computation. Informally speaking, this notion says that for any efficient adversary with these capabilities, the adversary's output bit (indicating, for instance, whether the obfuscated program satisfies a certain property or not) could have been produced after evaluating a black box program that computes function f. A bit more formally, the adversary's output bit can be guessed by an efficient algorithm, called the simulator, with black-box access to function f.

3. *real-vs-random indistinguishability* [5]: The adversary can read, and thus execute, an evaluator program $oEval(rr, \cdot)$ which is randomly chosen between the evaluator program obtained after an obfuscation of the program computing function f and the evaluator program obtained after an obfuscation of the program computing a function randomly chosen from F. The adversary is returning a bit at the end of its computation. Informally speaking, this notion says that at the end of its computation, the adversary cannot distinguish the two cases: an obfuscation of the program computing function f from an obfuscation of the program computing a random function from family F.

4. *strong indistinguishability* [5]: As in the real-vs-random indistinguishability, the adversary can read, and thus execute, an evaluator program $oEval(rr, \cdot)$ which is randomly chosen between the evaluator program obtained after an obfuscation of the program computing function f and the evaluator program obtained after an obfuscation of the program computing a function randomly chosen from F. Informally speaking, this notion says that at the end of its computation, no efficient distinguisher algorithm can distinguish the adversary's output in the two cases: an obfuscation of the program computing function f from an obfuscation of the program computing a random function from family F.

All these notions intuitively capture important properties that a program obfuscator should have, and for any two of these notions, their equivalence is either false or unknown. It is not hard to see that an obfuscator satisfying notion 1 also satisfies notions 2, 3, and 4. Moreover, in [5], it was proved that, for the family of point functions, an obfuscator satisfying notion 4 also satisfies notion 3, and that the converse may not hold.

2.3 Cryptographic Point Function Obfuscation

We consider *families of functions* as families of maps from a domain to a range, where maps may be parameterized by some values chosen according to some distribution on a parameter set. Let pF be a family of functions $f_{par} : Dom \rightarrow Ran$, where $Dom = \{0, 1\}^n$, $Ran = \{0, 1\}$, and each function is parameterized by value par from a parameter set $Par = \{0, 1\}^n$, for some length parameter n. We say that pF is the *family of point functions* if on input $x \in Dom$, and *secret value* $s \in Par$, the point function f_{par} returns 1 if $x = s$ and 0 otherwise.

In an obfuscator for the family of point functions, the following holds: the obfuscation generator algorithm $oGen$ takes as input the secret value s; the almost exact functionality property implies that, except with very small probability, the evaluator's output is equal to 1 if $x = s$ and 0 otherwise; and each of the security notions implies a different type of obfuscation of secret value s.

We now summarize a sample of known constructions of point function obfuscators. A first obfuscator, satisfying adversary view black-box simulation, was given in [28], under the random oracle assumption. Previous results, although formulated as different cryptographic primitives, might be restated as point function obfuscators satisfying strong indistinguishability under the Decisional Diffie Hellman assumption [11] or under the existence of claw-free permutations [12]. The obfuscator in [36] satisfies (a weakened version of) adversary output black-box simulation under the existence of a strong type of one-way permutations. Finally, more obfuscators were given in [5], and one of these, based on any deterministic encryption scheme, satisfies real-vs-random indistinguishability, and happens to have several instantiations. This is due to the fact that deterministic encryption schemes can be built using hard problems on lattices [37] or lossy trapdoor functions [7], and the latter have been built using any one of many group-theoretic assumptions (see, e.g., [21]).

In Sects. 3, 4, 5, 6, 7, and 8, we review somewhat improved designs of these obfuscators from [1, 18] and in Sect. 9 we compare their security and performance properties.

3 A Point Function Obfuscator from Cryptographic Hashing

The first obfuscator (from [18, 28]), denoted as $(\text{oGen}_1, \text{oEval}_1)$, for the family of point functions, is based on collision-resistant hashing, modeled in the security analysis as random oracles.

Informal description: This well-known construction is based on a technique often used to store passwords in certain operating systems, which has recently been re-interpreted as an obfuscation of the password verification algorithm. Informally, it goes as follows. The obfuscation generator first concatenates the secret value with a sufficiently-long random string, then applies a cryptographic hash function on this concatenated value, and finally returns the computed hash tag. The obfuscation evaluator does essentially the same computations on the input point (instead of the secret value), and returns 1 if the computed hash tag is equal to the hash tag returned by the obfuscation generator or 0 otherwise. A more formal description follows.

Formal description: Let H denote a collision-resistant hash function (i.e., a function mapping an arbitrary-length input string to a fixed-length output string, such that it is hard for any efficient adversary to find two preimages of the same function output). Scheme $(\text{oGen}_1, \text{oEval}_1)$ goes as follows.

Input to oGen_1: security parameters 1^n, 1^{ℓ_0}, length parameter 1^ℓ, secret value $z \in \{0, 1\}^\ell$,

Instructions for oGen_1:

1. Uniformly and independently choose $r \in \{0, 1\}^{\ell_0}$
2. Compute $v = H(r|z)$, where $v \in \{0, 1\}^n$
3. Set $gpar = (r, v)$ and return: $gpar$.

Input to oEval_1: security parameter 1^n, length parameter 1^ℓ, $r \in \{0, 1\}^{\ell_0}$ and $v \in \{0, 1\}^n$, input value $x \in \{0, 1\}^\ell$

Instructions for oEval_1:

1. compute $v' = H(r|x)$, where $v' \in \{0, 1\}^n$
2. if $v' = v$ return 1 else return 0

Theoretical result. Assuming H behaves like a random oracle, $(\text{oGen}_1, \text{oEval}_1)$ is an obfuscator of the family of point functions, satisfying the adversary view black-box simulation notion. In [28], it was first stated that if H behaves like a random oracle, the value $H(z)$ is a (not composable) obfuscation of secret value z. The known technique of concatenating z with a sufficiently long random string r before hashing makes the scheme composable (i.e., secure even if executed many times, on input related secret strings).

Parameter and primitive settings. Parameter ℓ can be set as needed in the specific application. Parameter n can be set as ≥ 256, to guarantee security against generic "birthday-type" collision attacks; our implementation sets it $=512$. Parameter ℓ_0 is also set as $=512$. H can be any cryptographic hash function that is believed to be secure enough in light of a significant amount of cryptanalysis efforts; thus, including SHA2 and SHA3. Our implementation uses SHA512, which is SHA2 when set it to return $n = 512$ bits as output.

4 A Point Function Obfuscator Based on Decisional DH

The second point function obfuscator (from [11, 18]) we describe, denoted as $(\text{oGen}_2, \text{oEval}_2)$, is based on the Decisional Diffie-Hellman (DH) assumption. We first briefly recall this assumption and the notions of faster computation of modular exponentiation via preprocessing, and then describe the obfuscator and its properties.

Decisional DH assumption: Let p and q be primes such that $p = 2q + 1$ and $|q| = n + 1$. The pair $(Z_p^*, \cdot)$, where $Z_p^* = \{1, \ldots, p - 1\}$ and $\cdot$ denotes product modulo p, is a group and has a q-order subgroup, denoted as G_q. Let g denote a generator of G_q. Efficient algorithms are known to randomly choose primes p, q of this form, and a generator for G_q. The *Decisional DH problem* over G_q asks to efficiently distinguish, given p, q, g, the following two tuples:

1. $(p, q, g, g^a \bmod p, g^b \bmod p, g^{ab} \bmod p)$, and
2. $(p, q, g, g^a \bmod p, g^b \bmod p, g^c \bmod p)$,

for uniformly and independently chosen elements a, b, c from Z_q. The *Decisional DH assumption* over G_q says that no efficient algorithm can distinguish these two distributions, except with very small probability. The *Discrete Logarithm problem* over G_q asks to efficiently compute, given p, q, g, and an element $h \in G_q$, the exponent $x \in Z_q$ such that $g^x = h \bmod p$. The *Discrete Logarithm assumption* over G_q says that no efficient algorithm can solve the Discrete Logarithm problem, except with very small probability. The Decisional DH assumption implies the Discrete Logarithm assumption. Even if the converse is known not to hold in some other groups, no polynomial-time algorithm is known to solve the Decisional DH problem in subgroup G_q. A survey of the Decisional DH problem can be found in [8].

Modular exponentiation with preprocessing: The pair of algorithms (ModExpPreproc, ModExpCompute) denotes a scheme for faster computation of modular exponentiation, using preprocessing, and defined as follows. On input a base u and a modulus p, the algorithm ModExpPreproc computes some auxiliary information $aux_{u,p}$. On input a base u, a modulus p, an exponent d, and auxiliary information $aux_{u,p}$, the algorithm ModExpCompute computes a value v, such that $v = u^d \bmod p$. Here, the goal is to use auxiliary information $aux_{u,p}$ to compute v faster than using a standard modular exponentiation algorithm, such as the textbook square-and-multiply algorithm. A survey of such faster methods was given in [24]. Some of these methods reduce exponentiation to an arbitrary exponent to a sequence of multiplications of simpler and pre-computed exponentiations to specific exponents. In the implementation described here, one of these methods is further optimized by efficient variants of modular multiplications (i.e., performing Montgomery modular multiplications [9]).

Informal description: First, the obfuscation generator computes a first value as a random power of generator g, a second value as an exponentiation of the first value to the secret value, and returns both values; then, the obfuscation evaluator exponentiates the first value to the input point (instead of the secret value), and returns 1 if the computed group element is equal to the second value or 0 otherwise. This basic idea is extended by replacing one modular exponentiation with a random subgroup value computable using only one modular multiplication in the chosen group, and by computing all other exponentiations by carefully distributing the technique of exponentiation with preprocessing between the obfuscation generator and evaluator. A formal description of (oGen₂, oEval₂) follows.

Input to oGen₂: length parameter 1^n, secret value $z \in \{0, 1\}^n$

Instructions for oGen₂:

1. Randomly choose primes p, q such that $p = 2q + 1$, $|q| = n + 1$
2. Randomly choose generator g of q-order subgroup G_q of Z_p^*
3. Randomly choose $u \in G_q$
4. Compute $(aux_{u,p}) = \text{ModExpPreproc}(u, p)$
5. Consider z as an element of G_q
6. Compute $v = \text{ModExpCompute}(u, p, z, aux_{u,p})$
7. Return: $(aux_{u,p}, (u, v))$.

Input to oEval₂: security parameter 1^n, input value $x \in \{0, 1\}^n$ and the output from *oGen*, containing auxiliary information $aux_{u,p}$ for faster computation of exponentiation modulo p in base u, and pair (u, v).

Instructions for oEval₂:

1. Consider x as an element of G_q
2. Compute $v' = \text{ModExpCompute}(u, p, x, aux_{u,p})$
3. If $v' = v$ then return: 1 else return: 0.

Theoretical result. Under the Decisional DH assumption, (oGen₂, oEval₂) is an obfuscator of the family of point functions with (almost) uniformly distributed secret values, according to strong indistinguishability obfuscation notion of [5] (which generalizes the oracle hashing secrecy from [11]). This follows by a generalization of the proof from [11] that the basic version of this construction is an oracle hashing scheme for random secret inputs under the Decisional DH assumption.

Parameter and primitive setting. Parameter n can be set as $=2048$, to guarantee security against known discrete logarithm finding algorithms. In algorithm $initO_2$, to perform the generation of prime p, along with prime q, and of generator g for the q-order subgroup G_q of Z_p, we used procedures from the OpenSSL library. The scheme (ModExpPreproc, ModExpCompute) can be any pair of algorithms from [24]. In one such schemes, algorithm ModExpPreproc precomputes exponentiations modulo p in the same base u and for specific exponents (e.g., powers of 2 and combinations of them). Later, based on these pre-computed values, algorithm ModExpCompute computes exponentiations modulo p in the same base u and for an arbitrary exponent, as a suitable sequence of multiplications modulo p.

5   A Point Function Obfuscator Based on Discrete Logarithms

The third obfuscator (from [18, 36]), denoted as (oGen$_3$, oEval$_3$), for the family of point functions, is based on the Discrete Logarithm assumption. First, we briefly recall this assumption, and then describe the obfuscator and its properties.

Discrete Logarithm assumption over Z_p^*: Let p be an $(n + 2)$-bit prime, and let g be a generator of the group Z_p^*. The *Discrete Logarithm problem over* Z_p^* asks to compute x, given p, g, y such that $y = g^x \bmod p$, for a random $x \in \{0, \ldots, p - 1\}$. The *Discrete Logarithm assumption over* Z_p^* says that no efficient algorithm can compute x with more than negligible, in n, probability. For any $x \in \{0, \ldots, p - 1\}$, the function MostSigBit(x) returns 0 if $1 \leq x \leq (p - 1)/2$ and 1 if $(p - 1)/2 < x \leq p - 1$. As for the obfuscator from Sect. 4, we use scheme (ModExpPreproc, ModExpCompute) for faster computation of modular exponentiation.

Informal and formal description: The starting idea of this scheme is as in [36], using two main tools: a one-way permutation (i.e., a permutation that can be efficiently computed but is conjectured to be hard to invert when computed on a random input); and a hard-core predicate for this one-way permutation (i.e., a predicate function that returns a single hard-core bit, is efficiently computable from the input to the one-way permutation and is hard to guess given only the output of the one-way permutation). The obfuscation generator works in $3n$ iterations, and computes at each iteration the output of a one-way permutation on input the output from the previous iteration, and a hard-core bit associated with the current evaluation. The input in the first iteration is the secret value z. At the end of all iterations, it returns the $3n$ hard-core bits. The obfuscation evaluator performs the same computation of $3n$ hard-core bits, using as input in the first iteration the input value x. At the end, it returns 1 if the computed hard-core bits are equal to those returned by the obfuscation generator or 0 otherwise. This basic idea is instantiated by setting the one-way permutation as exponentiation modulo a prime p (which is often conjectured to be a one-way permutation over Z_p^*), and by setting the hard-core bit as the most significant bit of the discrete logarithm exponent (which has been proved to be a hard-core bit for exponentiation modulo p, under the same conjecture). Then, all modular exponentiations are computed by carefully distributing the technique of modular exponentiation with preprocessing between the obfuscation generator and evaluator, similarly as done for our obfuscator in Sect. 4.

A formal description of (oGen$_3$, oEval$_3$) follows.

Input to oGen$_3$: length parameter 1^n, secret value $z \in \{0, 1\}^n$.
Instructions for oGen$_3$:

1. Randomly choose prime $p \in \{0, 1\}^{n+1}$
2. Randomly choose a generator g of Z_p^*
3. Compute $aux_{g,p} = $ ModExpPreproc(g, p)
4. Consider z as an element of Z_p^* and set $w_1 = z$
5. For $i = 1, \ldots, 3n$,

$\quad\quad$ compute $w_{i+1} = \mathrm{ModExpCompute}(g, p, w_i, aux_{g,p})$
$\quad\quad$ compute $v_i = \mathrm{MostSigBit}(w_{i+1})$
6. Set $v = (v_1 | \cdots | v_{3n})$
7. Return: $(aux_{g,p}, v)$.

Input to oEval$_3$: security parameter 1^n, input value $x \in \{0, 1\}^\ell$ and the output from *oGen*, containing auxiliary information $aux_{g,p}$ for faster computation of exponentiation modulo p in base g, and $3n$-bit vector v.
Instructions for oEval$_3$:

1. Consider x as an element of Z_p^* and set $w_1' = x$
2. For $i = 1, \ldots, 3n$,
$\quad\quad$ compute $w_{i+1}' = \mathrm{ModExpCompute}(g, p, w_i', aux_{g,p})$
$\quad\quad$ compute $v_i' = \mathrm{MostSigBit}(w_{i+1}')$
3. Set $v' = (v_1' | \cdots | v_{3n}')$
4. If $v' = v$ then return 1 else return: 0.

Theoretical results. Under the Discrete Logarithm assumption, (oGen$_3$, oEval$_3$) is an obfuscator of the family of point functions, according to (a weak version of) the adversary output black-box simulation notion [4]. This follows by combining the following: (1) the proof in [36] that the generalized construction is an obfuscator under a strong one-way permutation assumption; (2) an instantiation of the strong one-way permutation using exponentiation modulo a large prime, based on the Discrete Logarithm assumption; (3) an instantiation of the hard-core predicate for the one-way permutation using the most significant bit, based on the Discrete Logarithm assumption and a result from [6].
Parameter and primitive setting. To guarantee security against known discrete logarithm finding algorithms, we set $n = 2048$. In algorithm $initO_3$, to perform the generation of prime p and generator g for Z_p^*, we used procedures from the OpenSSL library. The scheme (ModExpPreproc, ModExpCompute) can be any scheme from [24].

6 A Point Function Obfuscator from Decisional Residuosity

This section presents an obfuscator from [5, 7, 17, 18, 21, 31], denoted as (oGen$_4$, oEval$_4$), for the family of point functions, based on the Decisional Residuosity (DR) assumption. We first briefly recall this assumption, and then describe the obfuscator and its properties.
DR assumption: Let p, q be ℓ-bit primes and let $N = pq$. The DR (modulo N^2) problem asks to efficiently distinguish, given N, a random value in $Z_{n^2}^*$ from a random n-th residue in $Z_{n^2}^*$ (i.e., a value $y = x^N \bmod N^2$, for some random $x \in Z_{n^2}^*$). The DR assumption says that no efficient algorithm can distinguish the two distributions, except with negligible probability.

Informal description: The starting idea of this scheme combines results in [5, 7], where a point function obfuscator is constructed from any deterministic encryption [5], and the latter is constructed from any pairwise-independent hash function and lossy trapdoor function [7]. Finally, the construction of a lossy trapdoor function from [21] is used, in turn based on the public-key cryptosystem from [17] (a variant of the one in [31]). The resulting obfuscation evaluator only performs two modular exponentiations, and one of them can be computed using preprocessing, similarly as done in Sect. 4.

Formal description: For any x, let $t = minH(x)$ denote the min entropy of string x; that is, x is sampled from a distribution that returns no value with probability $> 2^{-t}$. We now give a formal description of $(oGen_4, oEval_4)$.

Input to $oGen_4$: security parameter 1^n, length parameter 1^ℓ, accuracy parameter ϵ, secret value $z \in \{0, 1\}^\ell$, and min-entropy parameter t, such that $minH(z) \geq t \geq n + 2\epsilon$, and $\ell = (n - 2)s + n/2 - 1$, for some integer $s \geq 1$.

Instructions for $oGen_4$:

1. Randomly choose primes p, q such that $|p| = |q| = n/2$
2. Set $N = pq$
3. Randomly choose $r \in Z_N^*$
4. Set $c = (1 + N)r^{N^s} \bmod N^{s+1}$
5. Write z as (u_0, u_1), where $u_0 \in Z_{N^s}$ and $u_1 \in Z_N^*$
6. Randomly choose pairwise independent hash function $piH : Z_{n^s} \times Z_n^* \to Z_{n^s} \times Z_n^*$
7. Set $(v_0, v_1) = piH(u_0, u_1)$, where $v_0 \in Z_{N^s}, v_1 \in Z_N^*$
8. Set $aux_{c, N^{s+1}} = \text{ModExpPreproc}(c, N^{s+1})$
9. Set $w_0 = \text{ModExpCompute}(c, N^s, v_0, aux_{c, N^{s+1}})$
10. Set $w = w_0(v_1)^{N^s} \bmod N^{s+1}$
11. Return: $(t, piH, \epsilon, c, N, s, w)$

Input to $oEval_4$: security parameter 1^n, length parameter 1^ℓ, input value $x \in \{0, 1\}^\ell$ and $oGen_4$'s output, containing min-entropy parameter t, pairwise independent hash function piH, accuracy parameter ϵ, auxiliary information $aux_{c, N^{s+1}}$ for faster computation of exponentiation modulo N^{s+1} in base c, value $c \in Z_{N^{s+1}}$, integer N, integer s, and value $w \in Z_{N^{s+1}}$.

Instructions for $oEval_4$:

1. Write z as (u_0', u_1'), where $u_0 \in Z_{N^s}$ and $u_1 \in Z_N^*$
2. Set $(v_0', v_1') = piH(u_0', u_1')$, where $v_0' \in Z_{N^s}, v_1' \in Z_N^*$
3. Set $w_0' = \text{ModExpCompute}(c, N^{s+1}, v_0', aux_{c, N^{s+1}})$
4. Set $w' = w_0'(v_1')^{N^s} \bmod N^{s+1}$
5. If $w' = w$ then return 1 else return 0.

Theoretical properties. Under the Decisional Residuosity (modulo N^{s+1}) assumption, the pair $(oGen_4, oEval_4)$ is an obfuscator for the family of point functions, according to the real-vs-random obfuscation indistinguishability definition of [5], and where the point has min entropy at least $n + 2\epsilon$. This is obtained by combining the following: (1) the proof in [5] that an obfuscator based on any deterministic encryption scheme satisfies the real-vs-random indistinguishability obfuscation notion; (2) the result in [7] saying that a deterministic encryption scheme can be obtained by applying a pairwise-independent hash function to the input, and then a lossy trapdoor function to its output; (3) the construction in [21] of a lossy trapdoor function based on Damgaard-Jurik's cryptosystem [17] (a variant of Paillier's cryptosystem [31]). The pairwise-independent hash function is used to apply the Leftover Hash Lemma from [26].

Parameter and primitive setting. Parameter s can be set depending on what ℓ is needed in the specific application, and our implementation only requires an essentially unrestricted $\ell < 2^{31}$. Parameter ϵ can be set as 128, to guarantee that the statistical distance between the distribution of piH's output and a uniformly distributed string of the same length, is $\leq 2^{-128}$. Parameter t can be set as $t = n + 2\epsilon$. For the generation of $n/2$-bit primes p, q, we used procedures from the OpenSSL library. Function piH can be any pairwise-independent hash function, including the 1-degree polynomial over $GF(2^\ell)$ [14], which we implemented using [34].

7 A Point Function Obfuscators Based on the LWR Problem

In this section we describe an obfuscator, denoted as $(\text{oGen}_5, \text{oEval}_5)$, for the family of point functions (with almost uniformly distributed secrets), using an assumption related to the LWR problem. The obfuscator is obtained in [1] by first combining results in [5, 30, 37] and then performing various design optimizations. We first briefly recall the definition of the LWR problem and its related assumptions, and then present the obfuscator and its properties.

Learning With Rounding assumption. Let A^T denote the transpose of matrix or vector A. Let p, q be primes, and, for any vector $v = (v_1, \ldots, v_m)$, let $\lfloor v \rfloor_p$ denote the vector whose i-th element is the closest integer to $(q/p)v_i$, for $i = 1, \ldots, m$. Let $Z_q^{n,m}$ denote the set of $n \times m$-matrix with elements in $\{0, \ldots, q-1\}$, and let $Z_q^n = Z_q^{n,1}$, for any positive integers n, m. Consider the following two distributions:

1. $D_0 = \{A \leftarrow Z_q^{n,m}; s \leftarrow Z_q^n; b = \lfloor A^T s \rfloor_p : (A, b)\}$
2. $D_1 = \{A \leftarrow Z_q^{n,m}; b \leftarrow Z_p^m : (A, b)\}$

The *LWR problem* asks to efficiently distinguish, whether a sample (A, b) came from D_0 or D_1. The *LWR assumption* says that the distributions D_0 and D_1 are indistinguishable to any efficient algorithm, except with negligible probability. The LWR assumption has been introduced in [2], as a variant of the LWE assumption, previously introduced in [33], and has been used in some cases to potentially improve the design of cryptographic primitives and protocols based on the LWE assumption. In [2] it is also conjectured that in light of known algorithmic attacks, the LWR assumption seems to hold if $q/p \geq \sqrt{n}$ is an integer and p is polynomial in n. We also consider a modified LWR assumption, also called *public-seed*

LWR assumption, which assumes the hardness of the LWR problem when matrix A is pseudo-randomly generated with publicly known seed. The variant of this assumption based on LWE has been discussed in detail in [22], and similar conclusions can be reached in the LWR case. Specifically, the public-seed LWR assumption does not appear to be significantly stronger than the LWR assumption.

Informal Description. We start with the obfuscator from any deterministic encryption scheme, as described in [5]. Then, we instantiate the deterministic encryption scheme with the one from [37], based on the LWR assumption. Next, we use two design optimizations from [18]: first, the key generation for the deterministic encryption algorithm only generates the public key, and not the secret key, since the latter is never used by the obfuscator; second, we generate a uniformly distributed public key, instead of the one returned by the scheme in [37], in turn based on lattice key generation approaches from [30]. The latter simplification is possible since the distribution of the public key was proved in [30] to be statistically indistinguishable from uniform. Finally, we use three design optimizations from [1]: (1) both the obfuscation generator and the obfuscation evaluator use a pseudo-random (instead of random) matrix M with published seed as the public key, and (2) the obfuscation generator stores $H(b)$ instead of a target vector b, and the obfuscation evaluator uses $H(b')$ instead of a generated vector b' in its test checking equality between a generated and a target vector, where H denotes a collision-resistant hash function; (3) inspired by probabilistic testing techniques, we expect that it suffices to run the evaluator's equality test only on a randomly chosen subset of the matrix A's rows, of size much smaller than the original number of rows; then, since matrix A is pseudo-randomly generated, one might as well modify the obfuscator so that it only returns a much reduced number of rows. Optimizations (1) and (2) reduce storage, but slightly increase running time, while optimization (3) further reduces both storage and running time.

Formal description: Let H be a collision-resistant hash function. We now give a formal description of (oGen₅, oEval₅).

Input to oGen₅: dimension parameters 1^n, 1^m, domain parameter 1^q, factor parameter δ, rounding parameter p, statistical security parameter 1^λ, and secret vector $z \in \{0, 1\}^n$.

Instructions for oGen₅:

1. Set $v = (n + \lambda)/\log q$
2. Pseudo-randomly choose M from $Z_q^{v,n}$ starting from a random seed s
3. Compute vector $u = M \cdot z$
4. Compute rounded vector $b = \lfloor u \rceil_p$
5. Compute tag $w = H(b)$
6. Return: (s, w)

Input to oEval₅: dimension parameters 1^n, 1^m, domain parameters t, 1^q, factor parameter δ, rounding parameter p, statistical security parameter 1^λ, input vector $x \in \{0, 1\}^n$, and the output from $oGen_5$, containing seed s and $w \in \{0, 1\}^\ell$.

Instructions for oEval₅:

1. Set $v = (n + \lambda)/\log q$
2. Pseudo-randomly generate $M' \in Z_q^{v,n}$ using seed s
3. Compute vector $u' = M' \cdot x$
4. Compute rounded vector $b' = \lfloor u' \rceil_p$
5. Compute tag $w' = H(b')$
6. If $w' = w$ then return 1 else return: 0.

Theoretical result. Under the public-seed LWR assumption, and using results from [5, 37], in [1] it is proved that (oGen$_5$, oEval$_5$) is an obfuscator for the family of point functions (with almost uniformly distributed secrets), according to the adversary view black-box simulation definition.

Parameter setting. Parameters for scheme (oGen$_5$, oEval$_5$) are set in [1] by slightly improving some constants in those recommended by [37]. Specifically, all parameters are set as a function of the dimension n and a parameter δ, and settings for n, δ are determined so to approximately minimize other parameters, including performance metrics, while subject to the following two constraints:

1. $n >= \log(q/\sigma) * 33.1$, for $\sigma = 5$, and
2. q/p is an integer $\geq \sqrt{n}$.

Constraint 1 is based on analysis in [23], which provides a lower bound on n, guaranteeing that the strongest known attacks to the LWE problem, and also applicable to LWR, are as successful as breaking a 128-bit cryptographic primitive. Constraint 2 is based on a conjecture in [2], saying that, in light of the strongest known attacks to LWE, and also applicable to LWR, the LWR problem seems to remain hard as long as $q/p \geq \sqrt{n}$ is an integer and p is polynomial in n. This set of parameters is then generated starting from $n = 1336$. The resulting settings are:

1. $n = 1336$,
2. $\delta = 0.521$,
3. $m = 285707$ (the dimension of the ciphertext),
4. $p = 170396512836$
5. $q = 6304670974932$, where $q/p = 37$, and
6. $v = \lceil (n + \lambda)/\log p \rceil = 40$, where $\lambda = 128$.

An alternative set of parameter settings can be generated starting with the larger value $n = 2048$, in case the above conjecture appears too optimist in the future, using analogue formulae to derive all other parameters from n, δ.

8   A Point Function Obfuscator Based on the LWE Problem

In this section we present an obfuscator from [1], denoted as (oGen$_6$, oEval$_6$), for the family of point functions (with almost uniformly distributed secrets), using an assumption related to the LWE problem. We first briefly recall the definition of the LWE problem and its related assumptions, and then present the obfuscator and its properties.

Learning With Error assumption. Let A^T denote the transpose of matrix or vector A, let q be a prime, let $\cdot$ denote matrix-vector product mod q, and let $+$ denote vector sum mod q. Let $G_{\mu,\sigma}$ denote the probability density of the Gaussian distribution with mean μ and standard deviation σ. For any set $S \subseteq Z$, let $dG_{S,\mu,\sigma}$ denote the probability density of the *discrete Gaussian distribution* with mean μ and standard deviation σ, with assigns to any $x \in S$ the probability $G_{\mu,\sigma}(x) / \sum_{z \in S} G_{\mu,\sigma}(z)$. We note that $dG_{Z_q,\mu,\sigma}$ can be efficiently sampled [20].

Now, consider the following two distributions:

1. $D_0 = \{A \leftarrow Z_q^{n,m}; s \leftarrow Z_q^n; e \leftarrow dG_{Z_q,0,2\sqrt{n}}; b = A^T \cdot s + e : (A,b)\}$
2. $D_1 = \{A \leftarrow Z_q^{n,m}; b \leftarrow Z_q^m : (A,b)\}$

The *LWE problem* asks to efficiently distinguish, whether a sample (A,b) came from D_0 or D_1. The *LWE assumption* states that the distributions D_0 and D_1 are indistinguishable to any efficient algorithm, except with negligible probability. The LWE assumption has been introduced in [33] and has been used to design various cryptographic primitives and protocols since then. The literature includes both research on attack efforts, and on its relationship to other well studied assumptions on lattices, such as bounded-distance decoding and shortest-vector finding. (See [29, 30, 32] for detailed bibliographies and problem overviews). We also consider a modified LWE assumption, also called *public-seed LWE assumption*, which assumes the hardness of the LWE problem when matrix A is pseudo-randomly generated with publicly known seed. This assumption has been discussed in detail in [22], where it is suggested that it might not be significantly stronger than the LWE assumption.

Informal Description. Although similar to the obfuscator in Sect. 7, the approach used by obfuscator (oGen$_6$, oEval$_6$) is not based on a deterministic encryption scheme and in fact is inherently probabilistic. On input an n-bit secret string z, the generator algorithm uses the LWE assumption to embed the secret into a random matrix A and a vector b computed as $A \cdot z + e$, for some short Gaussian error e. Note that by the LWE assumption, vector b is computationally indistinguishable from a random vector of the same structure. On input an n-bit string x, the evaluator algorithm computes vector b' as $A \cdot x$, and returns 1 if the vector $b' - b$ is short with respect to some norm (e.g., the L^1 norm), and 0 otherwise. As for the obfuscator in Sect. 7: (1) matrix A is pseudo-randomly generated by both generator and evaluator, using the same short random seed, which is returned as output by the generator and then taken as input by the evaluator; and (2) the generator only returns a much reduced number of rows for matrix A. We refer the reader to [1] for a formal description.

Theoretical results. Under the public-seed LWE assumption, in [1] it is proved that (oGen$_6$, oEval$_6$) is an obfuscator for the family of point functions (with almost uniformly distributed secrets), according to the adversary view black-box simulation definition.

9 Security and Performance Comparisons

Security comparisons. Table 1 contains the security notions satisfied by the presented obfuscators and the hardness assumptions under which the obfuscators satisfy these security notions.

Performance comparisons. Table 2 contains the generator runtime, evaluator runtime and storage complexity of the presented obfuscators. The implementation of the first 4 obfuscators was performed on a Dell 2950 processor (Intel(R) Xeon(R) 8 cores: CPU E5405 @ 2.00GHz, 16GB RAM), without parallelism. The implementation of the last 2 obfuscators was performed on an 8-core x8664 machine, with 2 CPU GHz and 3990.05 BogoMIPS. In all cases, both the secret and the input length were chosen as $= 2048$.

Remarks The 6 point function obfuscators can be mapped to uncomparable points in a multi-dimensional space based on the following attributes: evaluator runtime, storage, security notion, hardness assumption, as well as quantum-resistant security. While (oGen$_1$, oEval$_1$) has the slowest evaluator runtime, it also assumes that the hash function behaves like a random oracle (a very strong assumption that turned out to be false for some older hash functions). Obfuscators (oGen$_i$, oEval$_i$), for $i = 2, 3, 4$, are the only ones satisfying strong indistinguishability, adversary output black-box simulation, and real-vs-random indistinguishability, respectively. Obfuscators (oGen$_j$, oEval$_j$), for $j = 5, 6$, are the only ones satisfying a security notion under a quantum-resistant hardness assumption.

Table 1 Security notions and hardness assumptions

Obfuscator	Security notion	Hardness assumption
(oGen$_1$, oEval$_1$)	Adv view bb simulation	Random Oracle
(oGen$_2$, oEval$_2$)	Strong indistinguishability	Decisional DH
(oGen$_3$, oEval$_3$)	Adv output bb simulation	Discrete Log
(oGen$_4$, oEval$_4$)	Real-vs-random indistinguishability	Decisional Residuosity
(oGen$_5$, oEval$_5$)	Adv view bb simulation	Learning with Rounding
(oGen$_6$, oEval$_6$)	Adv view bb simulation	Learning with Errors

Table 2 Performance of the 6 point function obfuscators (oGen$_i$, oEval$_i$), for $i = 1, \ldots, 6$

Obfuscator	Generator runtime	Evaluator runtime	Storage
(oGen$_1$, oEval$_1$)	0.0004 s	0.0002 s	1 KB
(oGen$_2$, oEval$_2$)	0.0734 s	0.0139 s	1 MB
(oGen$_3$, oEval$_3$)	76.46 s	12.09 s	0.22 GB
(oGen$_4$, oEval$_4$)	0.1317 s	0.1005 s	2.4 MB
(oGen$_5$, oEval$_5$)	0.0178 s	0.144 s	<100 B
(oGen$_6$, oEval$_6$)	0.5580 s	0.3271 s	<250 B

10 Application-Driven Modeling of Cryptographic Program Obfuscation

Our treatment of application-driven modeling for cryptographic program obfuscation identifies research problems in this area as a tuple of points, each point in the tuple being taken from a different 3-dimensional spaces. In particular, we focus our dicussion on two 3-dimensional spaces that contain the seemingly most interesting problem variables. In a first 3-dimensional space, based on problem models, we consider dimensions on program representation model, input entropy model and participant model. In a second 3-dimensional space, based on security requirements, we consider dimensions on adversary resources, attacks and goals. Here, identified practical attack classes include remote calls, program theft, and system intrusion. One could consider yet another 3-dimensional space, based on performance requirements, with most interesting dimensions being running time, storage complexity, and memory usage of the evaluator program.

Most tuples generated using points in these 3-dimensional spaces have not been investigated in the literature or even posed as open problems. In the rest of this section, we describe all the mentioned dimensions and 3-dimensional spaces, and discuss which problems in these spaces have been studied in the literature or are currently open problems.

Program Representation. The formalism used to represent programs can be important to determine what features of a program need to be obfuscated or not. Certain program parameters, such as input length, might often be leaked to an adversary without compromising the secrecy desired in the application at hand (as is most typically the case with encryption). Most interestingly, programs can be parameterized by additional secret values or have sensitive logic or both.

In some applications, it might be of greater interest to obfuscate these secret values while it might be not a problem to reveal the program's logic. For instance, consider the family of point functions, defined as $pF = \{f_s \mid s \in \{0, 1\}^n\}$, where s is a secret string, and $f_s : \{0, 1\}^n \to \{0, 1\}^n$ maps an input $x \in \{0, 1\}^n$ to 1 if $x = s$ or to 0 otherwise. For such family, it is of interest to obfuscate secret s while allowing the capability of evaluating f_s, and it may be not important or of less interest to hide the logic (i.e., conditional, equality, etc.) used by function f_s. Applications captured by this program representation include password/passphrase verification, password managers, and, more generally, secret-based entity authentication.

In other applications, it might be of greater interest to obfuscate the sensitive logic than parameter values. For instance, consider the family of all polynomial-time functions over n-bit inputs, defined as $aF = \{f \mid Dom(f) = \{0, 1\}^n\}$, where f can be any polynomial-time computable function. For such family, it might be of interest to obfuscate the function's logic (i.e., the structure and gates of the circuit computing f), while allowing the capability of evaluating f, and it may be not important or of less interest to hide parameters (i.e., the input length or any auxiliary input values) used by function f. Several applications related to protection of program logic and any related intellectual property are captured by this program representation.

Input Model. The amount of entropy in the program's input can be important to determine if the program can be securely obfuscated or not against adversaries with certain resources or interaction models. In particular, consider a program with a *low-entropy input* and an adversary capable of unlimited evaluations of this program on inputs of its choice. By evaluating the program on all candidate inputs, the adversary can efficiently determine the entire program's input/output behavior, regardless of whether the program is obfuscated or not. If the program's input has low entropy, this adversary can efficiently learn the program and thus bypass any obfuscation. Note that in the literature the definition of low-entropy input is often left unspecified or limited to an asymptotic statement (i.e., an input's entropy is low if it is at most logarithmic in the security parameter). On the other hand, the definition of *high-entropy input* is usually identified with the value of the security parameter (i.e., the entropy amount for which exhaustive search attacks are actually impractical). While it is true that there are many applications, especially when it comes to cryptography programs, where inputs have high entropy, it is also true that in many non-cryptographic applications, inputs might have low entropy. In the latter case, to allow any obfuscation approach to maintain desired security properties, one needs to resort to a weaker model for the adversary's resources and/or interaction with the program. (See, for instance, participant, adversary resource and adversary attack models below.)

Participant Model. As the most basic participant model for cryptographic program obfuscation, one can consider 2 logical entities:

1. a *program deployer*, in charge of generating the obfuscated program, and
2. a *program evaluator*, being allowed to evaluate the program (obfuscated by the program deployer).

Figure 1 depicts the interaction between the two parties, as considered in most literature papers in the area. In some applications, however, the obfuscated program

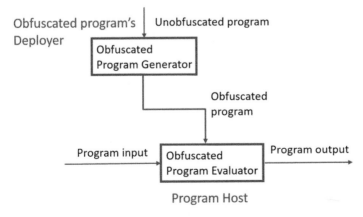

Fig. 1 2-party participant model for cryptographic program obfuscation

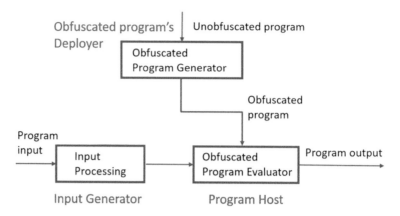

Fig. 2 3-party participant model for cryptographic program obfuscation

is hosted with a server and the input to the program is generated from an additional input source. Thus, one can extend the above 2-participant model into a model with 3 logical entities, defined as follows:

1. a *program deployer*, in charge of generating the obfuscated program,
2. an *input generator*, in charge of generating inputs to the obfuscated program, and
3. a *program host*, being allowed to store the obfuscated program. (Note that an adversary corrupting or intruding into the program host is expected to be also capable of evaluating the program.)

Figure 2 depicts the interaction between the three parties as a natural extension of the interaction between the two parties shown in Fig. 1.

Adversary resources. We identify three main types of program resources that an adversary may use during its attacks:

1. program inputs, chosen by the adversary, and corresponding outputs,
2. program inputs, chosen by a honest user, and corresponding outputs; and
3. a description of the (obfuscated) program's code.

Without knowing further details on how resources of type (2) are generated and the relative state of knowledge of honest users and adversaries with respect to program secrets, it is unclear whether these are less or more valuable (to the adversary) than resources of type (1). For instance, if a honest users generates inputs according to a distribution that somehow depends on program secrets, these inputs and their corresponding outputs might have not been obtained by an adversary with no knowledge of the program secrets. We also note that in practical attacks resources of different types might more or less naturally compose. For instance, access to a resource of type (3), a description of the obfuscated program's code, would directly allow an adversary resources of type (1), as the adversary can use this description to run the program on inputs of its choice and thus see the corresponding outputs.

Table 3 Security notions and hardness assumptions

Adversary attack classes	Adversary resources classes
Remote call	Program inputs, chosen by adversary, and corresponding outputs
Code theft	Description of (obfuscated) program's code
	Program inputs, chosen by adversary, and corresponding outputs
System intrusion	Description of (obfuscated) program's code
	Program inputs, chosen by adversary, and corresponding outputs
	Program inputs, chosen by honest program users, and corresponding outputs, all eavesdropped by adversary

Adversary attacks. We identify three main types of attack that an adversary may run, in order of increasing strength:

1. *remote call* to program functionality, according to which the adversary can remotely execute the program on chosen inputs and receive corresponding outputs;
2. *program theft*, where the adversary can inspect the program's code, run the program with chosen inputs and receive corresponding outputs; and
3. *system intrusion*, according to which the adversary can inspect the program's code, and eavesdrop program executions with inputs chosen by honest users and their corresponding outputs.

There is a natural mapping between these three types of adversary attacks and the three types of program resources available to the adversary, as shown in Table 3.

Adversary goal. Similarly as for other cryptographic primitives, one can define various goals for an adversary attacking an obfuscated program. To protect against such goals, researchers have identified various security notions in the literature. Goals and identified notions in the literature include the following:

1. *distinguishing* a random obfuscation of the given program from information computable in polynomial time given access to *a virtual black-box* computing the same function (with associated security notions identified in [4, 11, 25]);
2. *distinguishing* a random obfuscation of the given program from a random obfuscation of a *randomly chosen program within the defined class* (with associated security notions identified in [5, 25]);
3. *distinguishing* a random obfuscation of *any two programs computing the same given function* (with associated security notions identified in [4]);
4. *computing*, on input a random obfuscation of a program, *an unobfuscated version of the same program* (with associated security notions identified in [16]).

Models and security requirements. Models in cryptographic program obfuscation can be identified as points in a 3-dimensional space (pictorially depicted in Fig. 3), consisting of the previously discussed 3 dimensions: program representationmodel (secret-based programs, general programs, etc.), input entropy model (low-entropy, high-entropy, etc.) and participant model (2-party, 3-party, etc.).

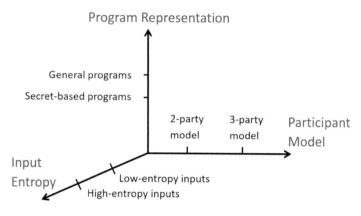

Fig. 3 Problem space for cryptographic program obfuscation

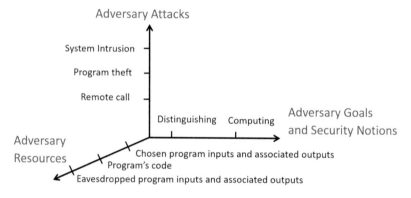

Fig. 4 Security requirement space for cryptographic program obfuscation

Security requirements in cryptographic program obfuscation can be identified as points in a 3-dimensional space (pictorially depicted in Fig. 4), consisting of the previously discussed 3 dimensions: adversary resources (chosen program inputs and associated outputs, program's code, eavesdropped program inputs and associated outputs, etc.), adversary attacks (remote access, program theft, system intrusion, etc.) and adversary goals (on distinguishing the obfuscated program from virtual black boxes, obfuscations of random programs in the class, or other obfuscations for the same program, or computing unobfuscated versions of the same program, etc.).

Performance requirements in cryptographic program obfuscation can be identified as points in a 3-dimensional space, consisting of the previously mentioned 3 dimensions: running time, storage and memory use of the evaluator program.

State of the art and open problems. By taking a model from the 3-dimensional space in Fig. 3, a security requirement from the 3-dimensional space in Fig. 4, and a desired level of performance with respect to the above mentioned performance requirements, one can generate a meaningful research problem for cryptographic program obfuscation. Most of these research problems have not yet been considered in the literature. More specifically, with respect to models, the literature has focused so far on the obfuscation of general programs, as well as various secret-based programs, including point functions, with high-entropy inputs in the 2-party model. With respect to attack classes, the literature has only considered program theft, for which several different security notions have been defined including those for point functions discussed in Sect. 2.2. With respect to performance requirements, the literature has mainly considered running time of the evaluator program, and practical runtime has been achieved by point function obfuscators, as discussed in Sect. 9.

Application-driven Solutions: a simple example. As a simple example of the increased applicability of the models introduced in this section, we discuss how to design a cryptographic program obfuscator of a program that checks equality between an input bit and a secret bit. More formally, define the *family of bit equality functions* as $beF = \{f_b | b \in \{0, 1\}\}$, where b is a secret bit, and $f_b : \{0, 1\} \to \{0, 1\}$ maps an input $x \in \{0, 1\}$ to 1 if $x = b$ or to 0 otherwise.

Note that for any obfuscation of such program in the most common 2-party model, the secret bit b is easily learnable from the obfuscated program by an adversary that can run the obfuscated program on inputs of its choice. (The adversary runs the obfuscated program on a bit x, obtains an output bit y, and returns x if $y = 1$ and $1 - x$ if $y = 0$, which is a correct guess for secret bit b).

On the other hand, in the 3-party model, one can construct an obfuscator for beF, starting from any block cipher BC, as follows. Let k denote a random key shared by the obfuscated program generator and the input generator. On input secret bit b, the obfuscated program generator computes a nonce $r_0 | R = BC(k, 0)$, for some bit r_0, and returns $c = BC(k, b|r)$. On input a bit x, the input generator computes the same nonce $r_0 | R = BC(k, 0)$, with the same bit r_0, and returns $d = BC(k, x|r)$. On input c, d, the obfuscated program evaluator returns 1 if $c = d$ and 0 otherwise.

It is not hard to see that this program obfuscator satisfies almost exact functionality, polynomial slowdown and adversary view black box simulation (assuming block cipher BC behaves like a pseudo-random permutation). The almost exact functionality follows from $BC(k, \cdot)$ being a deterministic function that returns the same value when evaluated twice on the same input string. The adversary view black box simulation follows from the pseudo-randomness of BC, as k and r are unknown to the adversary (only attacking the program host).

11 Conclusions

Cryptographic program obfuscation is very promising as it might change the heuristic nature of previous code obfuscation techniques into rigorous and provable solutions, along the paradigm of modern cryptography research. Early negative results on the existence of a single obfuscator for all polynomial-time programs have been recently mitigated by constructions of obfuscators for specific polynomial-time programs. As of today, the literature contains many implementations of point function obfuscators, satisfying different obfuscation notions, many of which can be used with practical performance guarantees. Moreover, the early theory-driven obfuscation models can be enriched with multiple application-driven obfuscation models by which researchers can protect computer programs against practical attack classes by leveraging current implementations of point function obfuscators, as well as upcoming future practical implementations of obfuscators for other specific functions.

References

1. Lisa Bahler, Giovanni Di Crescenzo, Yuriy Polyakov, Kurt Rohloff, and David Bruce Cousins. Practical implementation of lattice-based program obfuscators for point functions. In *2017 International Conference on High Performance Computing & Simulation, HPCS 2017, Genoa, Italy, July 17-21, 2017*, pages 761–768, 2017.
2. Abhishek Banerjee, Chris Peikert, and Alon Rosen. Pseudorandom functions and lattices. In *Proc. of EUROCRYPT 2012*, pages 719–737.
3. Boaz Barak. Hopes, fears, and software obfuscation. *Commun. ACM*, 59(3):88–96, 2016.
4. Boaz Barak, Oded Goldreich, Russell Impagliazzo, Steven Rudich, Amit Sahai, Salil P. Vadhan, and Ke Yang. On the (im)possibility of obfuscating programs. In *Proc. of CRYPTO 2001*, pages 1–18.
5. Mihir Bellare and Igors Stepanovs. Point-function obfuscation: A framework and generic constructions. In *Proc. of TCC 2016-A2*, pages 565–594.
6. Manuel Blum and Silvio Micali. How to generate cryptographically strong sequences of pseudo random bits. In *Proc. of 23rd IEEE FOCS 1982*, pages 112–117, 1982.
7. Alexandra Boldyreva, Serge Fehr, and Adam O'Neill. On notions of security for deterministic encryption, and efficient constructions without random oracles. In *Proc. of CRYPTO 2008*, pages 335–359.
8. Dan Boneh. The decision diffie-hellman problem. In *Algorithmic Number Theory, Third International Symposium, ANTS-III, Portland, Oregon, USA, June 21–25, 1998, Proceedings*, pages 48–63, 1998.
9. Joppe W. Bos and Peter L. Montgomery. Montgomery arithmetic from a software perspective. *IACR Cryptology ePrint Archive*, 2017:1057, 2017.
10. Zvika Brakerski, Vinod Vaikuntanathan, Hoeteck Wee, and Daniel Wichs. Obfuscating conjunctions under entropic ring LWE. In *Proceedings of the 2016 ACM Conference on Innovations in Theoretical Computer Science, Cambridge, MA, USA, January 14–16, 2016*, pages 147–156, 2016.
11. Ran Canetti. Towards realizing random oracles: Hash functions that hide all partial information. In *Proc. of CRYPTO 1997*, pages 455–469.
12. Ran Canetti, Daniele Micciancio, and Omer Reingold. Perfectly one-way probabilistic hash functions (preliminary version). In *Proc. of 13th ACM STOC, 1998*, pages 131–140.
13. Ran Canetti, Guy N. Rothblum, and Mayank Varia. Obfuscation of hyperplane membership. In *Theory of Cryptography, 7th Theory of Cryptography Conference, TCC 2010, Zurich, Switzerland, February 9–11, 2010. Proceedings*, pages 72–89, 2010.
14. Larry Carter and Mark N. Wegman. Universal classes of hash functions. *J. Comput. Syst. Sci.*, 18(2):143–154, 1979.
15. C. Collberg, C. Thomborson, and D. Low. A taxonomy of obfuscating transformations. In *Technical Report 148, Department of Computer Science, University of Auckland*, 1997.

16. Giovanni Di Crescenzo, Jeyavijayan Rajendran, Ramesh Karri, and Nasir D. Memon. Boolean circuit camouflage: Cryptographic models, limitations, provable results and a random oracle realization. In *Proceedings of the 2017 Workshop on Attacks and Solutions in Hardware Security, ASHES@CCS 2017, Dallas, TX, USA, November 3, 2017*, pages 7–16, 2017.
17. Ivan Damgård and Mads Jurik. A generalisation, a simplification and some applications of paillier's probabilistic public-key system. In *Proc. of PKC 2001*, pages 119–136, 2001.
18. Giovanni DiCrescenzo, Lisa Bahler, Brian A. Coan, Yuriy Polyakov, Kurt Rohloff, and David Bruce Cousins. Practical implementations of program obfuscators for point functions. In *Proc. of HPCS 2016*, pages 460–467.
19. Yevgeniy Dodis and Adam D. Smith. Correcting errors without leaking partial information. In *Proceedings of the 37th Annual ACM Symposium on Theory of Computing, Baltimore, MD, USA, May 22–24, 2005*, pages 654–663, 2005.
20. Léo Ducas, Alain Durmus, Tancrède Lepoint, and Vadim Lyubashevsky. Lattice signatures and bimodal gaussians. In *Proc. of CRYPTO 2013*, pages 40–56.
21. David Mandell Freeman, Oded Goldreich, Eike Kiltz, Alon Rosen, and Gil Segev. More constructions of lossy and correlation-secure trapdoor functions. In *Proc. of PKC 2010*, pages 279–295.
22. Steven D. Galbraith. Space-efficient variants of cryptosystems based on learning with errors, 2013.
23. Craig Gentry, Shai Halevi, and Nigel P. Smart. Homomorphic evaluation of the AES circuit. In *Proc. of CRYPTO 2012 (see also updated version on eprint)*, pages 850–867.
24. Daniel M. Gordon. A survey of fast exponentiation methods. *J. Algorithms*, 27(1):129–146, 1998.
25. Satoshi Hada. Zero-knowledge and code obfuscation. In *Advances in Cryptology - ASIACRYPT 2000, 6th International Conference on the Theory and Application of Cryptology and Information Security, Kyoto, Japan, December 3–7, 2000, Proceedings*, pages 443–457, 2000.
26. Johan Håstad, Russell Impagliazzo, Leonid A. Levin, and Michael Luby. A pseudorandom generator from any one-way function. *SIAM J. Comput.*, 28(4):1364–1396, 1999.
27. Susan Hohenberger, Guy N. Rothblum, Abhi Shelat, and Vinod Vaikuntanathan. Securely obfuscating re-encryption. *J. Cryptology*, 24(4):694–719, 2011.
28. Ben Lynn, Manoj Prabhakaran, and Amit Sahai. Positive results and techniques for obfuscation. In *Proc. of EUROCRYPT 2004*, pages 20–39.
29. Daniele Micciancio. Lattice-based cryptography. In *Encyclopedia of Cryptography and Security, 2nd Ed.*, pages 713–715. 2011.
30. Daniele Micciancio and Chris Peikert. Trapdoors for lattices: Simpler, tighter, faster, smaller. In *Proc. of EUROCRYPT 2012*, pages 700–718.
31. Pascal Paillier. Public-key cryptosystems based on composite degree residuosity classes. In *Proc. of EUROCRYPT '99*, pages 223–238, 1999.
32. Chris Peikert. A decade of lattice cryptography. *Foundations and Trends in Theoretical Computer Science*, 10(4):283–424, 2016.
33. Oded Regev. On lattices, learning with errors, random linear codes, and cryptography. In *Proc. of 37th ACM STOC*, pages 84–93, 2005.
34. Gadiel Seroussi. Table of low-weight binary irreducible polynomials. In *Technical Report HPL-98-135*, 1998.
35. Sharath K. Udupa, Saumya K. Debray, and Matias Madou. Deobfuscation: Reverse engineering obfuscated code. In *12th Working Conference on Reverse Engineering, WCRE 2005, Pittsburgh, PA, USA, November 7–11, 2005*, pages 45–54, 2005.
36. Hoeteck Wee. On obfuscating point functions. In *Proc. of 37th ACM STOC 2005*, pages 523–532.
37. Xiang Xie, Rui Xue, and Rui Zhang. Deterministic public key encryption and identity-based encryption from lattices in the auxiliary-input setting. In *Proc. of SCN 2012*, pages 1–18.

Botnet-Based Attacks and Defence Mechanisms

Dilara Acarali and Muttukrishnan Rajarajan

Abstract This chapter considers the threat posed by botnets and the impact of botnet-based attacks on both private domains and the global digital infrastructure. Botnets are widely employed by cyber-criminals for a variety of malicious activities and are frequently observed as a component within large-scale organised cyber-crime campaigns. In addition to this, botnets are a varied and evolving threat, bound to grow in parallel with our increasing dependence on digital services and the Internet, as well as the adoption of upcoming technologies like the Internet-of-Things. Botnets can be considered as attacks in-and-of themselves, as well as platforms for future attacks. With this as the foundational perspective, this study examines how a botnet is defined and classified, how it is built and used, the characteristics of a botnet attack, and the factors contributing towards its success. We then analyse how a botnet provides other attack capabilities for the cyber-criminal. This is supplemented with a discussion of how the threat is adapting to new technologies, followed by a short survey of some outstanding problems to be considered in future research.

1 Introduction

Botnets are a growing problem in our increasingly digital world, underpinning malicious activities such as identify theft, financial fraud, corporate espionage, and even cyber-terrorism. They come in a variety of shapes and flavours, can be deployed on a multitude of platforms, and can vary in functionality and scope, making it difficult to find a single, standardised solution. To provide a general framework for discussion, botnet activities can be considered in two distinct parts

D. Acarali (✉) · M. Rajarajan
School of Mathematics, Computer Science and Engineering, City, University of London, London, UK
e-mail: dilara.acarali@city.ac.uk; r.muttukrishnan@city.ac.uk

© Springer Nature Switzerland AG 2018
M. Conti et al. (eds.), *Versatile Cybersecurity*, Advances in Information
Security 72, https://doi.org/10.1007/978-3-319-97643-3_6

consisting of the initial penetration and infection of a target, followed by the exploitation of that target. To build a foundation for the rest of the study, this section explains how we define botnets and what kind of behaviours we can expect to observe from them.

1.1 Definition of a Botnet and Basic Functionality

At the most basic level, a botnet is defined as a collection of bot clients connected to each other via a control network through which they can send and receive updates and information. The word "bot" (shortened from "robot") refers to a piece of software which is written to carry out some automated tasks on behalf of the user. Legitimate services frequently use bots as part of their routine processes. For example, consumption bots on Twitter curate content for individual users based on their tastes [1]. The overall purpose of a bot is to free the human user from tasks which need to be performed constantly and consistently over time. Malicious bots function on the same principles. The cyber-criminal behind a botnet campaign is commonly referred to as a botmaster or botherder.

Although there are variations from case to case, the key components of a botnet can be summarised as follows: the bot client program, the infection vector, the communication protocol, the control architecture, the control servers, and the botmaster. The infection vector is the means by which the bot client is inserted into a victim system (e.g. worms, viruses or Trojan software). This tends to be defined as part of the malware design. Opposite the client, the command and control servers (referred to as C&C or C2 servers) are distribution and collection points for instructions and information. The communication protocol and control architecture in combination define how messages will be sent and received. Finally, the botmaster is the human brain and the driver behind the botnet, and their intentions or aims determine how it will be used.

Similarly, we can abstract the activities of a botnet into a generalised lifecycle (Fig. 1), which may begin with initial conception and design [2] or at the point of the first successful infection [3]. For practical purposes, we will focus on the second scenario here. Once executed, the malware performs its initial setup, and then enters the rally stage. This is where a previously isolated bot attempts to connect to the C&C network. Once this connection is achieved, the cycle moves into the secondary injection stage, in which relevant binaries and tools are gathered and installed on the host [3]. The bot is now ready for use and will be provided with commands via the C&C network. When the relevant command comes through, the cycle moves into the attack phase [3]. Note that when the attack ends, the botnet will probably fall back into waiting mode, ready for the next round of activity.

A botnet's main functionality comes from its ability to exploit the resources (e.g. memory, RAM, bandwidth, or data) of existing domains and devices to carry out large-scale tasks. Denial-of-Service (DoS) attacks and spam campaigns are both examples. To achieve this, the bot malware needs to propagate to as many

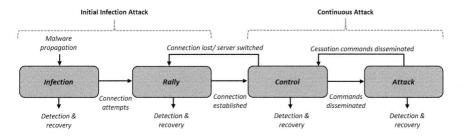

Fig. 1 Botnet lifecycle based on stages proposed by [3] with alignment to the 2-part attack

networked devices as possible, thereby increasing this pool of exploitable resources. Additionally, a bot provides a back-door into the victim system, thereby allowing a botmaster to gain access to potentially sensitive data and environments. It is the flexibility and range of botnets that make them an attractive option for cyber-criminals.

These functionalities are also what distinguish botnet attacks from others. The attack is not a one-off situation, but rather a continuous one. As long as a piece of bot malware remains within a network (and its C&C servers are online), that network should be considered under attack. The difficulty in dealing with this scenario is that there may be no visible symptoms whilst bots operate intermittently or stay dormant until their next update. In propagation modelling, the analogy applied to malware is that of an infectious disease. Bot malware can be thought of as a specialised strain that weakens a body's immune system, making it more vulnerable to future health problems or other illnesses. The network's functionality and integrity is compromised by the presence of this infection.

1.2 Botnet Classifications

Botnets can be classified in terms of their command dissemination style, broadly defined as either push- or pull-based (Fig. 2a). Commands originate from the botmaster, who plants them into the C&C network. C&C servers may then "push" messages out for the clients to receive. This was the typical approach of earlier botnets [4], but has also been used in more recent theoretical mobile setups [5]. In contrast, pull-based spread involves each client individually polling the C&C server to receive an update. Perimeter defences like firewalls contain default rules to block all unknown incoming web traffic. The pull-based approach is effective in getting around this issue, thanks to the client (who is internal to the network perimeter) initiating the connection. Examples of botnets which use pull-based methods are Storm [6], Zeus [7], and Asprox [8]. Meanwhile, GameOver Zeus is reported to use a hybrid push/pull approach for contingency [9].

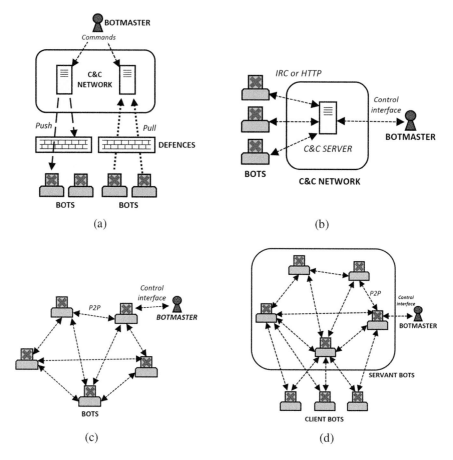

Fig. 2 Botnet classifications, including command dissemination style and architectures. (**a**) Push vs. pull-based dissemination (**b**) Centralised botnet (IRC- or HTTP-based) (**c**) Decentralised botnet (P2P-based) (**d**) Hybrid botnet (combined P2P- and HTTP-based) [10]

Botnets may also be classified by architecture, which refers to the way their client-server relationships are organised. Early botnets used solely centralised architectures (Fig. 2b), where many clients connect to a few central servers. This approach is simple and straightforward, but also vulnerable thanks to the single point-of-failure in its design [11]. Silva et al. [3] lists early examples of centralised botnets including EggDrop (first detected in 1993), GTBot (1998), SDBot and Agobot (2002), and Spybot (2003). The alternative is a decentralised architecture (Fig. 2c), where many clients connect to many servers, and the same devices may act as both clients and servers depending on the situational requirement [11]. This clearly eliminates the single point-of-failure, making the botnet more robust, discrete and resistant to takedown attempts [11].

Hybrid architectures have emerged more recently (Fig. 2d), featuring both centralised and decentralised elements to make the botnet easy to maintain and sturdy against adversaries [11]. This can also be used to obfuscate C&C networks behind layers of clients, making it harder to identify or trace them. For example, [14] reported that Waledac uses a decentralised hierarchical topology made up of spammer nodes, repeater nodes, and 3 layers of servers, combining centralised top-level C&Cs with a decentralised client node layout.

The C&C categories described so far tend to align with the use of particular protocols, providing another angle for classification. Centralised architectures use IRC or HTTP. For instance, EggDrop, AgoBot, and the Chuck Norris botnet are all IRC-based [3, 17]. However, this protocol has fallen out of favour after being targeted by network defenders and was replaced with HTTP, widely used in modern botnets including Rustock [12], Clickbot.A [13], Waledac [14], Koobface [16], Asprox [8], and Dirt Jumper [18]. HTTP-based C&C communication is effective in enabling bot flows to blend in with benign web traffic, and is often combined with pull-based dissemination to overcome defences. Meanwhile, P2P protocols are obvious choices for decentralised architectures, allowing bots to act as peers to exchange data symmetrically within overlay networks. Examples of P2P-based botnets are Storm and Nugache [6], Sinit, Phatbot, SpamThru, and Peacomm [22]. Custom protocols may also be used, like Mariposa's UDP-based Iserdo Transport Protocol [15].

The final classification method is based on malware family, which can be defined in two ways. In the first, botnets belonging to the same family are built using separate instances of the same malware [23]. For example, two botmasters may have access to the same binaries, and launch their own separate campaigns [23]. This is relevant where malware code is known to be highly accessible via underground forums or the black market [7]. The second definition is a group of separate malware codes, which appear to have a single progenitor. Zeus is a famous example of this. After first appearing in 2007, the malware was made public in 2011 [24] leading to the appearance of many derivatives, including GameOver Zeus, Citadel, and Shylock [24]. This is significant to our understanding of botnet evolution.

To summarise, Table 1 lists some botnets along with their classifications.

1.3 The Two-Part Attack

The botnet lifecycle establishes separate stages for spreading, rallying, awaiting commands, and performing attacks [3]. In this study, we further abstract these stages into two parts; the initial compromise and the continuous threat (Fig. 1). The first refers to the process of infiltration and infection, whilst the second refers to the cycle of attacks and waiting periods. From a defensive perspective, our intention is to frame the botnet with two opportunities for mitigation, where missing the opportunity to stop the infection opens the pathway to many future attacks.

Table 1 Summary of classification methods for a selection of botnets

Botnet	Classification method		
	Push/Push	Architecture	Protocol
Storm [6]	Pull	Decentralised	P2P
Nugache [6]	Pull/Push	Mixed	P2P/IRC
Rustock [12]	Pull	Centralised	HTTP
Clickbot.A [13]	Pull	Centralised	HTTP
Waledac [14]	Pull	Decentralised	P2P
Mariposa [15]	Pull	Centralised	UDP
Koobface [16]	Pull	Centralised	HTTP
Chuck Norris [17]	Push	Centralised	IRC
Asprox [8]	Pull	Centralised	HTTP
Zeus [7]	Pull	Centralised	HTTP
Dirt Jumper [18]	Pull	Centralised	HTTP
GameOver Zeus [9]	Pull/Push	Decentralised	P2P
Kelihos [19]	Pull	Decentralised	P2P
Citadel [20]	Pull	Centralised	HTTP
ZeroAcess [21]	Pull	Decentralised	P2P

The initial compromise attack is designed to discreetly implant malware into a node of the target network. Bots take great care to stay hidden at this stage, as the ultimate success of the botnet depends on it. Examples of obfuscation methods used are packing (Storm [6], Citadel [20]), encryption (Citadel [20], Mariposa [15]), rootkits (Nugache [6]), and registry amendments (Nugache [6], Dirt Jumper [18], Citadel [20]). These may also double as methods to weaken the host, making it more malleable. Successful detection and mitigation of this propagation process reduces the later impact of a botnet presence in the network.

A person with an infectious disease can become more vulnerable to further health issues, becoming a health-hazard to others in the process. The concept of the continuous threat is similar to this, as a compromised network (with even a single bot) is now in a weakened state with an increased chance of receiving new infections from unrelated malware and of propagating binaries on to others. The continuous threat also encompasses the possibility of the compromised network being used as a weapon in attacks against third-parties.

There are several benefits to considering botnet threats in this manner. Firstly, the distinction allows us to approach the two attacks separately and in a way befitting of their characteristics. We cannot approach single-host infections the same way we approach a DDoS attack, for example. However, both are botnet-related issues that need to be addressed as such. Secondly, it provides two opportunities for dealing with the problem. If the original infection can be resolved, no further action is needed. If not, there is still an opportunity for damage limitation, provided that the correct understanding and defensive strategies are in place.

2 Domain Impact

Despite the level of compromise, if the malware is well-designed, network users and analysts may be none the wiser. Bot presence may only become apparent once the botnet is offensively engaged. This section explores some of the ways in which an infected network may be directly impacted by the its unwelcome guests.

Maintaining stealth is crucial to a successful bot infection. Hence, the executed bot binary makes various changes to the host system. For example, Nugache installs a rootkit driver to System32 of Windows operating systems, which is then loaded into the kernel [6]. Both Nugache and Dirt Jumper make modifications to the system registry [6, 18]. These changes have an overall weakening effect on the host (and consequently, the wider network), perhaps re-opening previously dealt-with vulnerabilities, causing other malicious processes to go unnoticed, or introducing new exploits.

During the rally stage, bots register with the C&C and authenticate themselves, usually providing information on the host. This allows the botmaster to gain an overview of the variation of nodes recruited. These messages may contain details of hardware, operating system version, and patch levels – all potentially valuable in planning further attacks [8]. Additionally, many bots including Shylock, SpyEye, and Tinba contain keylogging and screen-capture modules used to steal user information [25]. Botmasters may sell this and network details on to other adversaries for future exploitation. Furthermore, captured user credentials enable a botmaster to personally manoeuvre into secure environments in the network.

Another impact of bot infection is the draining of a victim's resources, including physical memory, RAM, processing power, and bandwidth. Botnets are designed to use the collective power of many machines to reach some end goal. An example is the launch of DDoS attacks. Whilst the target may be a third-party, the continuous stream of messages sent out by bots can negatively affect the source network too, especially if multiple infections are present. In mobile botnets, C&C traffic may cause devices to hit data usage limits resulting in additional fees [26]. Alternatively, users of infected nodes may notice their devices running more slowly as bot processes operate in the background.

Discussion so far has focused on instances of a single botnet malware, but the presence of multiple unique malware infections is also possible. This could result in competitive behaviour for the finite resources available, and to the doubling of traffic generated. If analysts then become suspicious, this is a hindrance to both botnets. An example of possible competitive behaviour is the disabling or removal of one malware by another when the two exist on the same host [27]. Alternatively, botnets may collaborate with each other, providing access to core sets of nodes, as reported by [23], who observed separate botnets belonging to the same families with large areas of population overlap.

Case studies reveal that bots often spread laterally through the network resulting in localised clusters of infected hosts. This propagation may be driven by automated worms which scan the local network or via viruses and Trojans delivered through

Table 2 Methods used by botnets as part of initial and continuous attacks

Techniques	Used by
Initial compromise stage	
Binary obfuscation	Chuck Norris [17], Citadel [20], SpyEye [25]
Client testing	Citadel [20], Mariposa [15], Miner [28]
File system manipulation	Zeus [7], DirtJumper [18], Citadel [20]
Registry manipulation	Nugache [6], Rustock [12], Waledac [14]
Hardcoded C&Cs	Asprox [8], DirtJumper [18], Miner [28]
Fast-fluxing	Mirai [29], Waledac [14], Asprox [8]
DGA/domain-fluxing	Carberp [25], GameOver Zeus [25], Kraken [30]
Continuous threat stage	
Trojans	Storm [6], Nugache [6], Koobface [16]
Social engineering	Asprox [8], Chuck Norris [17], Miner [28]
Drive-by-downloads	JiFake [31], Plankton [31], Asprox [8]
DDoS	DirtJumper [18], Mirai [29], Kelihos [19]
Data theft	Zeus [25], SpyEye [25], Citadel [25]
Web-injects/fake pages	Tinba [25], Bugat [25], Asprox [8]
Click-fraud	Clickbot.A [32], ZeroAccess [21]

messaging channels (e.g. internal email) as spam. Mariposa reportedly checks for
P2P applications and if found, copies itself to the shared folder to propagate [15].
When a bot infection is detected, it should always be assumed that there are others
in the vicinity Table 2 summarises behaviours observed in various botnets.

In summary, a botnet infection can weaken a domain's defence against other
threats, expose the network structure, and diminish productivity by causing slow
connections and interrupted services. As even minor infections can quickly grow,
botnet mitigation should be a top priority for all organisations, large and small.

3   Launching the Attack

The way in which an attack is initiated provides details as to its design, function,
and purpose. Here we discuss the launch stages of both the initial compromise
and continuous threat, demonstrating both the short-term and long-term effect of
a botnet on the target domain.

3.1   The Initial Threat: Compromise Attack

During the infection stage, botnets expand through the propagation activities of
individual bots. The characteristics of this process are largely defined by the
chosen propagation vector, defined as the bot binary delivery method. Choice of

vector depends on the connectivity capabilities of targets – the more channels, the more possibilities. Malware may be delivered through LANs, the Internet, WiFi, Bluetooth, and even USB devices. Bot binaries piggyback on infectious malware, the choice of which has an impact on the rate and speed of spread. For example, botnets using worm-based propagation may expand faster than those using Trojans. This is because worms are self-activated and self-replicating (e.g. Chuck Norris botnet [17]), whereas Trojans require user interaction to execute and share them (e.g. GameOver Zeus [9]).

Once the bot binary is executed, it goes through a setup process. If the binary is highly obfuscated, it first needs to be unpacked and decrypted (e.g. Mariposa [15]). Next, it will create new directories in system folders and make copies of itself or important files. This allows the binary to launch from within the system folders, giving it the illusion of being part of the OS [6, 7]. The Zeus bot also copies the MAC details of nearby system files to further blend in [7]. The registry is edited to manipulate system processes (e.g. Dirt Jumper [18] and Citadel [20]), and some bots like Nugache install rootkits in the operating system kernel to help them stay hidden [6]. The Citadel bot also goes to the additional step of removing its binary files after installation [20]. These details can vary between families and implementations, making detection difficult without a priori knowledge.

After installation, the bot must rally to the C&C network to register and authenticate itself. This often includes the use of a unique ID (e.g. iKee.B [32] and Clickbot.A [13]) as well as details on the host system. For instance, Mirai bots send the IP, port, and login credentials of the victims [29], whilst Miner bots report on connectivity and speed testing results [28]. These details give the botmaster an overview of node capabilities and statuses, which may then be used to devise attacks or adapt propagation strategies. Bot binaries may be hardcoded with lists of C&C domain names or IPs [18] that are queried sequentially until one can be resolved. However, these C&Cs are easily detected by defenders through binary analysis. Botnets may employ expendable proxies (allowing bots to register and pull-down instructions to access the main C&Cs) to get around this. The rally process typically generates a large amount of erroneous DNS traffic, especially if servers have been migrated or taken offline. This characteristic can be used for detection [30].

Fluxing may be used to minimise detection risk or to protect the C&C network from exposure. Fast-fluxing is where DNS records are periodically updated to rapidly change the IP that a domain name resolves to, thereby obfuscating the true location of C&C servers. Waledac uses this approach, employing its upper tier nodes to act as DNS servers [14]. Double-fluxing adds the cycling of authoritative name server IPs, as observed in Asprox, which uses layered double-fluxing to create a "hydra-flux" setup [8]. Alternatively, botmasters may replace hardcoded lists with a domain name generation algorithm (DGA). Bots use DGAs to generate sets of possible domains, and test each one until a resolving IP is found. This is known as domain-fluxing. DGAs are pseudo-random, taking a seed value shared by the botmaster to ensure that matching domains can be achieved [30]. This behaviour was observed in Zeus, Conficker, and Kraken [9, 30].

The botmaster now has access to system resources, visibility of some users, and the ability to move stealthily through the network. The stage is set for follow-up attacks.

3.2   The Continuous Threat: Follow-Up Attacks

The continuous threat can be considered as either (a). the activities of a previously-initialised botnet (at macro scale), or (b). the activities of a single activated bot (at micro scale). Whichever is chosen, a variety of attack options are available to the botmaster at this stage.

One option is a Denial-of-Service (DoS) attack, where a large number of connection requests are sent to a target server with the intention of overwhelming its capacity. Distributed-DoS (DDoS) consists of requests generated by many devices, thereby increasing the total force of the attack [33]. Dirt Jumper reportedly has 4 different types of DDoS capability, including HTTP flood made up of standard HTTP requests, synchronous flood consisting of batches of 150 requests, downloads flood designed to consume bandwidth, and POST flood aimed at overloading the processing capacity of servers [18]. Large-scale DDoS attacks were also reported for Mirai in 2016 [33]. Alternatively, botnets may deliver ransomware, which once installed 'locks' the device, blocking user access. The authors then demand a ransom to unlock the system [34]. These types of attacks are designed to cause disruption to services.

User data is a precious commodity, and can be farmed via client bots. A keylogger records the keystrokes of a user, whilst screen capture tools record an image of the desktop. Harvested data is then sent back to the C&C. Examples of this behaviour have been observed in Carberp, Tinba, and Bugat [25]. Another method of data theft is a man-in-the-browser attack, where a web browser is hijacked with script injections allowing form details submitted by the user to be intercepted by the malware [25]. Bots may also manipulate browsers to redirect users to malicious replicas of legitimate web pages for social engineering.

Click-fraud is the manipulation of the online ad system to generate revenue for botmasters. Search engines maintain ad networks, agreeing with advertisers to host their content and serving it to users when certain keywords are triggered in search queries. Clicking an ad takes users to a landing page for which search engines receive payments-per-click. Third-parties (known as syndicates) are also allowed to display ads, receiving a cut of the earnings for the traffic they generate. Syndicates may then employ sub-syndicates, and so on, to extend ad visibility. Click-fraud exploits this system by generating fake traffic to the landing page. Clickbot.A sets up its own search engines (called doorways) which are registered as syndicates [13]. Bots are provided with a list of keywords to query, receiving ad URLs to be clicked [13]. ZeroAccess has a built-in auto-clicking module which runs in the web browser, opening hidden windows to access C&C-provided URLs (which are periodically updated) [21]. An additional module also redirects users themselves to ad landing pages when they perform searches [21].

4   Reasons for Attack Success

Botnets operate in phases with attacks formed of sequential steps. This means that many factors may have impact on attack success along the way. In this section, we identify and discuss some of these factors.

4.1   Pre-Existing Vulnerabilities

Exploitation of software is one of the most common approaches used by malware to infect or attack systems. ZeroAccess uses the BlackHole exploit kit for propagation [21], whilst [31] reports that some Android bots use root exploits for privilege escalation. In the underground community, exploitable areas of code are actively sought out and shared. Therefore, continuous use of old software leaves devices, and subsequently networks, vulnerable as flaws and loopholes become known amongst cyber-criminals. Delaying or disabling of scheduled updates can increase the chances of contracting a botnet infection. However, even with defensive measures in place, all software inevitably contains vulnerabilities that, despite extensive testing and review, can go unnoticed. Therefore, networks should contain layers of defence including scheduled backups, perimeter defences (where applicable), and failover systems.

   Probability of attack success is greatly impacted by the behaviour of users. Some botnets rely on user negligence to spread. For example, iKee.B and Mirai both used default login credentials to gain access to target devices [29, 32]. Others count on users lacking the vigilance or skills needed to differentiate between legitimate and malicious applications and services. For instance, Clickbot.A uses Trojans disguised as games [13], Asprox uses a fake Flash Player and anti-virus package [8], and Koobface sends malicious URLs from fake Twitter/Facebook accounts [16]. Each of these approaches require user interaction to reach their goal. From an enterprise perspective, employees may circumvent security policies and guidelines by using company devices for personal tasks (expanding the attack surface), connecting unsecured devices to the network via USB (used by Mariposa for propagation [15]), or not using encryption for sensitive data.

4.2   Malware Variability

Malware increases its chances of success when it manages to deviate enough from known attacks. This is because defences tend to be heavily based on previous experiences. At the initial infection stage, propagation vectors vary wildly. Some vectors observed in the past include drive-by-downloads (Asprox [8]), spam mail (Waledac and Storm [14], Dirt Jumper [18]), instant messaging (SpyEye and

Citadel [25], Mariposa [15]), social networks (Kelihos [19], Koobface [16]), and social engineering (Asprox [8]). This level of variation makes it difficult to have a 'one-size-fits-all' defensive approach, which is further exasperated by the constant emergence of day-0 threats. As a result, (at least) some attacks inevitably slip through the net.

Variation is also born out of customisation and adaptations of existing malware. For example, the original Zeus source code was used as a foundation for the development of new threats, including Citadel and ICE IX [9]. Despite being derivatives of Zeus, these botnets developed into distinct threats in their own right. The same malware was later developed further to become GameOver Zeus, which incorporates the use of P2P, making it more resilient than earlier iterations [9]. Bot malware also evolves in response to defensive measures. An example of this is the use of IRC in early botnets. When defenders started to block the IRC protocol, botmasters began using decentralised networks like P2P, and more inconspicuous, harder-to-block protocols like HTTP.

4.3 Discrete Operation

We have already discussed the measures taken by bot binaries to obfuscate their presence. In addition to this, active bots may avoid engaging in superfluous activities in order to draw less attention to themselves. By remaining dormant, the botnet may improve its longevity, allowing more bots to be cultivated in preparation for a larger attack [35]. Alternatively, propagation may be selective rather than randomised so that only specific domains are targeted and the botnet size is deliberately kept small to avoid detection. Similarly, it may be beneficial to the botmaster to avoid creating active nodes beyond a given time threshold to reduce the botnet's footprint [36]. These characteristics help the malware to stay under the radar.

In a typical enterprise network, traffic is generated by hundreds or thousands of systems, resulting in millions of daily flows. Botmasters may exploit this by blending C&C traffic in with normal user behaviours. For example, the implementation of HTTP as a C&C protocol allows polling bots to circumvent firewalls whilst mimicking benign web traffic. Furthermore, traffic-based detection tends to focus on anomalies or patterns suggestive of unauthorised automated processes. Botnets may therefore evolve to include functions designed to distort these patterns. For example, periodicity is a popular flow-based detection metric, measured as frequency, duration, or intervals lengths [37]. Randomised delays can be added between events to break up periodic patterns in propagation or polling traffic, as demonstrated by [38].

4.4 The Black Market

The current state of the black market is major driver behind the success of today's botnets. In the early days, simple malware threats were thought to be written by amateur individuals, largely for their own entertainment. By contrast, malware development and distribution is now a growing underground business [39]. A modern cyber-criminal does not require prior experience or technical expertise. Sophisticated bot malware and related exploit tools are readily available for purchase, including bot binaries, SQL injection kits and browser exploits [40], to name just a few.

Malware authors themselves stand to make massive profits from this. For example, in 2015 the complete Zeus toolkit reportedly cost between $1,500 and $20,000 depending on the version [24]. Complex business models have also emerged, including pay-per-install, pay-per-use [41], and hacking-as-a-service [40], allowing customers to outsource malware distribution or rent existing botnets for a period of time to suit their needs. With such a high degree of availability and a range of options, it is fair to suggest that any malicious group or individual could feasibly launch their own botnet-based cyber-crime campaign.

5 Existing Solutions and Classifications

Botnet solutions can be broadly classified into two groups; proactive and pre-emptive (Fig. 3). Proactive approaches encompass detection-related tasks, including bot identification, mitigation, removal, and takedowns (which may also be considered pre-emptive in stopping future attacks). Generally, these strategies deal with existing threats. Meanwhile, pre-emptive approaches include modelling and simulation aimed at exploring botnet characteristics for a better understanding of behaviours for predictive purposes. In this section, we provide an overview of both.

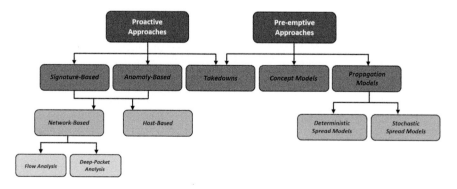

Fig. 3 Classification hierarchy for botnet solutions

5.1 Proactive Approaches

At the highest-level, detection systems can be classified as either signature- or anomaly-based. Signature-based refers to the use of markers which are known a priori to be indicators of malicious activities in the host or network. These 'signatures' are stored within a database, and the detection mechanism is triggered if matching activity is observed. Due to its reliance on heuristics, signature-based detection is highly effective against familiar threats but not for day-0 cases. Rishi [42], a signature-based tool, checks TCP packets containing certain IRC commands for strings that match its collection of known bot keywords.

In contrast, anomaly-based detection generates a baseline of normal activity for the system, triggering when it detects significant deviations from this norm. This is advantageous because unfamiliar threats can also be defended against. However, baselines must be sufficiently representative of actual behaviour, which can be difficult if it is highly random. Unrepresentative baselines can lead to both false positives and false negatives, potentially exasperated by the presence of benign and malicious activities with similar characteristics. An example is BotSniffer [4]. It monitors IRC/HTTP traffic at the network perimeter, which is then checked for group bot-to-C&C communication patterns. Similar tools include BotMiner [43] and BotProbe [44].

Anomaly- and signature-based approaches may be combined so that known threats are handled quickly, or so newly-discovered anomalies are recorded as signatures for future use. Examples of such hybrid schemes are BotHunter [45] and BotCop [46].

Detection systems can be further classified by the scope of their observational areas, as either host- or network-based. Host-based approaches monitor the system-level activities of a single device, including API calls, use of the registry, and generation of outbound traffic [47]. This is advantageous in observing specific infection processes or dormant bots who communicate infrequently. However, this approach alone may be insufficient when there are many connected hosts to secure. An example of host-based detection schemes is BotTracer, which targets automated bot installation and rally processes by isolating them via a virtual machine it runs and monitors on the host [47].

A network-based system observes the traffic generated between multiple hosts, and is placed strategically at ingress/egress points to capture the most relevant or risky traffic. Suspicious behaviours that may be flagged include failed connection attempts [48], failed DNS requests [30], web connections to blacklisted sites [49], encrypted payloads in outgoing messages [50], and use of randomised domain names [49]. Network-wide monitoring provides an overview of all activity in the observation space, and is beneficial in detecting behavioural patterns, fluctuations and group actions [43]. The main disadvantage is the sheer volume of data generated daily, requiring a greater amount of resources to collect and process.

This approach can be divided into the flow and deep-packet analysis sub-categories. Traffic data is often collected as NetFlow logs. A flow is the aggregation of packets exchanged between two endpoints in a specific conversation, and consists of a vector of features (including timestamps, transport protocol, ports, IP addresses, and a range of statistics) which provide a summary of that exchange. Flow analysis is therefore a shallow but fast examination of traffic, using features like duration, length, size, and frequency for statistical analysis. Bots generate traffic automatically in response to commands, resulting in more systematic flows than that of normal users. Therefore, detection using flow analysis involves searching for automated processes which manifest as repetitive anomalous patterns, or searching for instances of anomalous group behaviour. A drawback of this approach is the number of false positives caused by benign automated traffic picked up erroneously. BotMiner [43] is a flow-based detection scheme. It collects communication (C-plane) and activity (A-plane) traffic and clusters the flows. Then cross-plane correlation is performed to identify suspicious behaviour [43]. BotCop [46] is another example.

The alternative to this traffic aggregation is to use packet captures (PCAPs) which record the full details of every packet exchanged. This is used in deep-packet analysis to examine protocol implementations and payloads, providing richer detail, and is particularly useful when researching new malware or observing custom protocols. However, it is costly in terms of time and processing power, and payload examination is typically unsuccessful when dealing with encrypted traffic. However, [51] developed BlindBox to perform deep-packet analysis on HTTPS traffic by adapting signature-based methods to encrypted payloads.

Flow and deep-packet analysis can be combined, as demonstrated by [52]. They first use statistical analysis to extract sets of suspicious flows. Then, false positives are minimised by performing fine-grained deep analysis on only the packets of those flows.

A takedown is the process of infiltrating and hijacking a botnet's C&C infrastructure to disable communication between servers and nodes [53]. Sinkholing is the most common method for achieving this, where botnet domains are identified and pre-emptively purchased by researchers, who then setup their own servers to receive incoming bot communication [54]. The ethics of sinkholing (including what to do with harvested user data) is an open debate [54]. The first successful takedown was against the Conficker botnet in a collaborative effort between Conficker Working Group (consisting of researchers and industry professionals) and ICANN, who helped to take control of Conficker's domains [53, 55]. These were shared with registrars who blocked them, cutting off the botnet's C&C channels [55]. This was followed by other successful takedowns of Mariposa in 2009 [53], Waldeac in 2010, Rustock and Kelihos in 2011, Zeus and Nitol in 2012, and Batimal and Citadel in 2013 [55].

Figure 4 illustrates how proactive approaches are implemented and which part of the botnet they address. Step 1 highlights a bot-infected client aiming to communicate with a C&C using a hardcoded domain name. The blue dashed line represents the end-to-end communication between the bot and the server. Client devices are equipped with host-based monitors, which observe unusual system calls triggered by the malware. At 2, the request is picked up by the network-based

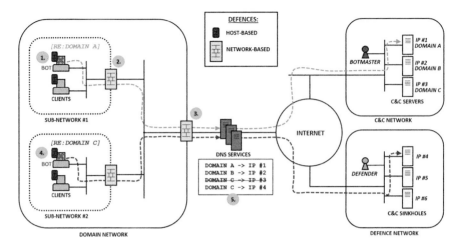

Fig. 4 Example of a bot-infected network illustrating the application of proactive defences

monitor of the local network. This observes all local clients, recording patterns if they exist. Similarly, at 3, the same request hits the network monitor of the wider domain network. The observational scope is expanded and, where multiple bots exist, group behaviours can be identified. Step 4 highlights another bot making a separate connection request. However, this time, the DNS registry has been modified so that the domain resolves to a sinkhole run by defenders. The dashed purple line represents hijacked bot communications in a botnet takedown effort.

5.2   Pre-emptive Approaches

We categorise pre-emptive works as propagation models and concept models. Propagation modelling aims to identify factors contributing to bot spread and the relationships between them, allowing researchers to explore both offensive and defensive possibilities. Meanwhile, concept models are explorations of new architectures or attack paradigms. The aim is to predict how botnets may adapt to current defences or utilise new technologies as a means of prevention. The following sections highlight some examples of pre-emptive research.

5.2.1   Propagation Models

Most botnet propagation studies are based upon state-based, compartmental transition models from the field of epidemiology. These models divide individuals from the total population into states representative of their condition at a given time [56]. Some examples are *S-I-R* (susceptible, infected, recovered),

S-I-S (susceptible-infected-susceptible), and *S-E-I-R* (susceptible-exposed-infected-recovered), though many more variations exist. The transition of individuals between groups is captured by a set of differential equations, where the rate of change for each state is given by a time derivative [56]. In this way, the progress of an infectious disease is tracked through a susceptible population. The results can then be used to identify the best vaccine provision methods. When applied to botnets, the susceptible population is represented by the nodes of the observed domain, the infected population aligns with bot-infected nodes, and the recovered population tends to denote patched or cleaned nodes.

Understanding the propagation characteristics of a bot malware can help predict the speed and reach of spread, potential botnet strength, mitigating factors, and may even provide clues as to the botmaster's intentions. In [57], the authors used sinkholes with known C&C IPs to capture bot traffic. They counted active bot populations (using 3-way TCP handshakes and preventing disconnections to minimise DHCP churn) and found that bot activity appears to be diurnal in nature, probably due to targeted devices being powered down each evening [57]. Based on this they adapted the *S-I-R* model for worm-based propagation to capture this behaviour across time zones. They then used this to make predictions about optimal worm release and patching periods [57].

In another work [27], researchers combined a *S-I-R-S* variation with fast evolutionary game theory to model competitive and cooperative behaviours between botnets. The two interacting botnets are given unique characteristics, where the first can enable/disable local defences, whilst the second can kill-off the first botnet's nodes. A cooperative strategy is where defences are disabled and/or no nodes are terminated. A competitive strategy is the opposite scenario [27]. Based on their tests, the authors derived thresholds for the defensive presence needed to minimise chances of cooperative behaviour. They also reported that cooperation significantly decreased the extinction probabilities of both botnets even at low infection rates, whilst a competitive strategy lead to the first botnet being killed off by the second [27].

Standard epidemic models as described previously are deterministic. In [58], the authors develop the probabilistic *S-I-C* model (susceptible-infected-connected). *I* nodes carry the minimal amount of malware code for compromise, but don't communicate with the C&C until they transition into *C* nodes. Continuous-time Markov Chain modelling is used to determine stochastic transition rates [58]. Their aim was to measure the overall growth of P2P botnets, and to test the effectiveness of various mitigation strategies. Using the model, they studied the impact of sybil attacks (where clean nodes join the botnet to corrupt the C&C infrastructure by sharing false information), and identified a relationship between the number of sybil inserts required to reach a desired mitigation in growth [58].

Meanwhile, [59] abstracted epidemic concepts to build a stochastic model of botnet propagation in mobile networks. Specifically, they aimed to observe the impact of moving nodes and node proximity on the speed of spread. The network consists of user and infrastructure nodes, with transmission range and total bandwidth as parameters [59]. *S* is defined as a population of infected nodes, representing the mobile botnet. Based on population density and node mobility range, they identified a threshold which when exceeded causes the botnet to grow at a quadratic rate. If not exceeded, the botnet size is predicted to have a finite limit [59].

These examples – which are just a few – demonstrate how propagation models can be used to explore factors which contribute to the growth of botnets in different environments and under different constraints. Simulations allow researchers to experiment with scenarios which may not be practical or safe in real networks, whilst empirical data collected from botnets in the wild can be used to validate models or serve as input data. The main drawback of this approach is that whilst using epidemic models, generalised assumptions are frequently made about homogenous populations and mixing that can make the results somewhat unrealistic. In [60], the authors outline some of the challenges that need to be addressed when applying epidemic modelling to network-based environments.

5.2.2   Concept Models

In [38], the authors propose the delay-tolerant botnet, designed to add random delays to its C&C traffic to disrupt any observable patterns in its communication. It is assumed that the botnet can handle delays because functionality can be maintained even if member bots don't all receive commands at the same time [38]. For randomly selected delay durations, they develop schemes for centralised and decentralised architectures where delays are inserted between bot-initiated connections and data forwarding events, respectively. They also experiment with hybrid architectures using a combined approach. They suggest that the overall delay (i.e. time-taken for all bots to receive a command) must have a logarithmic correlation with botnet size to maintain scalability [38].

In [61], the authors introduced the concept of alias-fluxing, which is the use of URL shortening services to obfuscate C&Cs. This is based on existing fast- or domain-fluxing mechanisms. The C&C network is made up of proxies and the main C&C that the botmaster controls. Using an algorithm, similar to a DGA, the botmaster generates a number of shortened URL strings every period, and registers these with the relevant services for each of the proxy servers. The bots use the same algorithm, or retrieve short URL lists, which they then use when rallying [61]. The authors suggest that this approach circumvents DNS-based detection, and obfuscates traffic where HTTPS is used [61].

Xu et al. [62] explored the use of DNS as a pull-based C&C protocol. Assuming the botmaster has access to a DNS server (setup with short TTL), they defined 2 scenarios; code-word and tunnelled, for unidirectional and bidirectional communication, respectively. In the first, the botnet uses a set of codewords which denote certain functions and requests [62]. Bots make DNS queries for domains containing a specific code-word, to which the DNS server replies with the appropriate data. Meanwhile in tunnelled mode, requests from the bot consist of CNAME queries to which the server responds with encoded CNAME records [62]. They also demonstrate that Markov Chains can be used to generate code-word-containing domain names in such a way as to avoid detection [62].

The authors of [5] built a prototype of a botnet which uses Cloud-to-Device Messaging (C2DM) as a push-based C&C network. This Google service is designed to efficiently incorporate push notifications into apps for Android devices. The botmaster registers an account for the malware package with the C2DM. This account is identified by a unique username which is then distributed with copies of the package to target devices [5]. Clients joining the botnet connect with C2DM servers using the same username, and receive a registration ID which they then share with the C&C server. Then, the C&C server can send its messages to the C2DM service with its authentication details, and the service will forward them on to the bots [5]. Noting the restrictions on the number of push messages per period, the authors suggest that larger botnets may be built from a series of smaller sub-botnets. They also suggest that communication can be further obfuscated by using 2 separate C2DM accounts (one for the C&C and one for the bots) [5].

The research outlined here shows how new perspectives and approaches may be explored. By adopting the position of the botmaster, the authors imagine how they may adapt to the changing digital landscape, what avenues might be most profitable, and how to avoid detection. The ideas proposed therefore give researchers the chance to design better, forward-thinking defensive solutions. Combined with the lessons learnt from propagation modelling (as well as historic botnet attacks), defenders aim to pre-empt threats and mitigate risk.

6 New Flavours

In this study so far, we have generally assumed that the targets of botnets are average LAN or WAN networks. However, modern technology has brought about many new scenarios, some of them pertaining to specific or specialised types of network. In this section, we highlight some of these and the issues surrounding them.

6.1 *Mobile Botnets*

Mobile devices are now ubiquitous. They are always with us, always in use, and always connected. This flexibility, sustained connectivity (on multiple channels), and lack of diurnal behaviour [26] makes mobile a viable botnet platform. Mobile devices use Internet, WiFi (both infrastructure and ad-hoc), SMS/MMS, and Bluetooth to connect with other devices, providing several channels for both attack and propagation. The battery life and processing power of mobile devices have improved, allowing bots to carry out complex tasks. Furthermore, apps like those provided by the Google Android and Apple iOS marketplaces serve a large range of functionality – users interact with many services (e.g. finance, commerce) sharing lots of valuable data. Apps are also an ideal infection vector, as botmasters can circumvent marketplace regulations to use their own Trojans or hijack existing offerings.

The iPhone-based iKee.B is a classic example of mobile botnets [32]. It uses Internet-connectivity to spread, scanning for phones running SSH services. Porras et al. [32] reports 3 distinct methods; scanning of specific IP ranges belonging to Australian and European mobile operators, scanning of a randomly chosen subnet on the Internet (using a time-seeded algorithm), and scanning of the client's current local network. Hence, propagation is a blend of Internet- and mobile-based methods, with device mobility exploited to attack each new local network it joins. The bot then uses default passwords to get shell access and once installed, shares host data (including archives of SMS messages) with C&Cs via HTTP [32]. Unique IDs are used for bots, allowing them to be tracked despite changing IPs across zones [32].

Zhou and Jiang [31] characterise features of Android-based botnets. They identify drive-by-downloads (with multiple redirections), repacking (malware embedded within legitimate apps), and update attacks (malware injected into apps via fake updates) as the main infection vectors. Some examples include Anserver and Plankton who use partial updates for added discretion, and the Jifake bot which triggers redirections via fake QR codes [31]. Meanwhile, data theft is identified as a key attack type, with targets including SMS messages, phone numbers, email addresses, and user accounts for third-party services. Another popular attack is where bots covertly sign-up to corrupt "services" which they poll via SMS, incurring premium-rate charges for the victim. As with iKee.B, HTTP-based C&C is most commonly observed [31].

Current botnets rely on the Internet for their C&C backends, but we can expect this to expand into other available channels. For example, [5] demonstrated the use of push notifications, whilst [63] showed the Bluetooth is also a viable option. As a larger number of service providers offer app-based interfaces, the pool of data to be harvested by bots will also expand. Furthermore, hacked accounts may act as vectors to target those services themselves. As mobile devices are used to interface with social media, the IoT, and the cloud, we could see cross-platform botnets using a mix of attack and propagation vectors. Finally, device mobility makes it difficult to locate propagation sources or to apply defences where there are no set perimeters. Ad-hoc networks may be used to obfuscate bot nodes, making DDoS attack sources difficult to trace [26] and botnets harder to enumerate.

6.2 Social Network Botnets

Social networking is a staple of modern communication and, as a result, has become a target for botnets. Social networks are free with simple registration processes, accessible from anywhere via mobile or desktop devices. This makes them easy to infiltrate. The platforms sustain massive user bases, who frequently submit personal details (which can be stolen) and exchange multimedia messages, giving botmasters ample possibilities for spam and malware delivery. These platforms provide both attack and propagation vectors, as the spreading of information throughout the network is inherent to their design. Additionally, user-to-user relationships are often ambiguous, with individuals lacking in awareness of potential risks. Bots may therefore easily infiltrate communities. Finally, resiliency and upkeep is handled by the platform/service providers, easing the maintenance of the botnet for the botmaster.

Koobface is a social network botnet, and was studied by [16]. They report that it exploits Twitter and Facebook as gateways to compromise user devices. It targets existing accounts, whilst simultaneously creating new accounts using fake personal details provided by the C&C. CAPTCHAs served during this process are forwarded to bots for real users to solve [16]. Fake accounts spread malicious links as short URLs, which redirect users to web pages encouraging them to download Trojan software. Once infected, bots connect to master C&Cs (who serve spam commands) and upload statistics on their activities. Meanwhile, existing accounts are given keywords to determine the communities they must join or establish friendships in [16]. This demonstrates how propagation can be targeted at particular groups.

The "Bursty Botnet", documented by [64], is similar. It exploits Twitter by creating new accounts which then disseminate spam, even using mentions (messages containing a specific user's Twitter handle) to entice users to click on malicious links. During their study, [64] identified 500,000 members of this botnet, with a total of 2.8 million spam tweets generated. Like Koobface, Bursty uses URL shortening to obfuscate targets. Bursty bots are designed to only tweet several times in a short period after their creation (hence the name), before falling permanently silent [64]. This one-time-use policy is probably a resiliency measure; the botnet should still function even if many nodes were taken offline. Silent bots may also avoid detection, but can be reactivated later [64].

Whilst Twitter and Facebook are currently the main targets, social botnets could expand to other platforms. For example, LinkedIn may be used to identify employer-employee relationships for targeted spam and even corporate espionage. Bot programs are developing to better mimic user behaviour, but may not even be needed. In their design of Stegobot, [65] demonstrated a C&C channel made only of existing social links, without the need for fake accounts or relationships. Furthermore, social networks make revenue from advertising – botnets may expand their functionality to include click-fraud. Lastly, from a socio-political perspective, social networks can be exploited to quickly spread misinformation or target groups for manipulation, as demonstrated by Koobface [16].

6.3 IoT-Based Botnets

Internet-of-Things (IoT) is the concept of adding network connectivity and automation to sensors, specialised devices, and every-day appliances to provide better services. The IoT is an attractive target for botmasters because its deployment vastly increases the population of vulnerable nodes which can be converted into bots. Devices which have traditionally always been offline now come packaged with Internet access (and often lacking sufficient security provisions), expanding the reach of botnets into sectors/domains which previously wouldn't have been exploitable, e.g. vehicle networks. Some IoT devices like sensors are low-energy consuming by design and hence do not have the processing power for complex security mechanisms. User awareness also plays a role – many may not be aware of built-in IoT functionality when purchasing new electronics.

In 2016, the IoT botnet Mirai was used to launch several high-profile DDoS attacks, most notably targeting a French web hosting service with a massive force of between 1.1 and 1.5 Tbps [33]. At this time, this botnet reportedly consisted of home routers and digital cameras [33], demonstrating how simple devices may be recruited into large botnets with highly potent attacks. Mirai propagates by scanning address spaces for Linux-based platforms [29], and then uses a simple database of 62 default login credentials to gain access [29, 33]. During scanning, [29] reports that the malware is hardcoded to avoid certain domains such as the US Postal Service, the US Department of Defence, and IANA. This is probably a precautionary measure. Bots collect and forward device details to the C&C, which the botmaster accesses over Tor for additional anonymity [29]. Analysis of Mirai's binaries reveal both network layer (SYN floods) and application layer (HTTP floods) DDoS functionality [29].

Mirai could become the IoT version of Zeus [24]; its source code has been made public and since then, variations with new features (e.g. enhanced encryption) have been reported [29]. This shows the level of criminal interest in IoT systems, and reinforces the potential risks involved in rapid deployment. IoT devices could be used to infiltrate particular sectors of industry for surveillance and espionage, as well as theft of sensor data. The range of use cases means there are no standard configurations, protocols, or known patterns on which to base generalised defensive approaches [33]. Furthermore, manual interaction with every IoT device is not scalable [33]. Combined with the limited processing capability of some devices, this means that security could be neglected. IoT is still a young technology which means we currently have limited experience of possible flaws and their implications. Therefore, to prevent significant risks, protocols and devices must be secure-by-design.

6.3.1 A Note on IPv6

Whilst IPv4 is the current dominant addressing protocol, organisations will increasingly have to shift to IPv6 in order to accommodate the massive influx of devices caused by the IoT. IPv6 uses 128-bit addresses (as opposed to the current 32-bit), providing a much larger address space of unique IPs. The robustness of IPv6 security is still largely unknown [66], and by removing the need for NAT and DHCP, it makes current control mechanisms obsolete. This has serious implications for existing botnet defences. This is further exasperated by IPv6's dynamic addressing function, as perimeter defences and blacklists become ineffective [66]. These issues apply to both IoT and non-IoT networks, and must be addressed before wide-scale adoption of the protocol.

6.4 Cloud-Based Botnets

Cloud computing is built on the business paradigm of computational resources as-a-service, always online and accessible via the web. It provides systems of servers and clients with built in redundancy, easy accessibility and remote storage. These characteristics make them ideal platforms to exploit as C&C networks. For instance, Plankton uses C&Cs in the Amazon cloud where its payloads are processed [31]. The centralised architecture means many potential bot clients are accessible (perfect for spam or malware delivery), whilst resource-rich servers can provide high-levels of processing power and storage for the botnet back-end. Web-based interfaces for services may be used to reach new targets, e.g. by redirecting users to fake versions or by intercepting login credentials. Cloud services are also used by large corporations and organisations – the cloud may be attacked by botnets to ultimately cause harm to those organisations.

Chen et al. [67] proposes a botnet with a cloud-based C&C network using push notifications on mobile devices. This approach is similar to [5], but unlike that model, [67]'s design uses a range of cloud services (e.g. Airbop, JPush, and Google Cloud) for a network of multiple push servers. First, new bots register with a local server. Using a transmission delay metric, bots with similar delays are clustered together (assuming this means they currently sit in the same region). C&Cs then use a round-robin schedule to cycle through push servers to disseminate commands, where servers with the least delay appear more frequently on schedules for that region [67]. This distributes command traffic, making it harder to detect, whilst delivering messages efficiently. Chen et al. [67] suggest that botnet functionality can be maintained even if some push servers go offline.

Meanwhile, [68] proposes cloud-based bots that can be used to launch slow-read DDoS attacks. This type of DDoS uses TCP or UDP to setup connections with small windows, forcing servers to keep connections open for extended periods. As a result, fewer back-to-back connections are required, and consequently, fewer bots. As requests are processed slowly, these attacks are also more difficult to detect [68]. Bot malware is not propagated in this setup. Instead, the botmaster uses image files containing all the required malicious functionality, registers with a cloud service and loads the image onto multiple cloud-based virtual machines (a sustainable approach for smaller botnets) [68]. Bot images also speed up the setup process, giving defenders less time to detect the initial compromise before further attacks are launched.

Malware with standard propagation capabilities could spread within the cloud infrastructure to create computationally powerful botnets with unique attack capabilities (dependent on the available cloud services). Pay-as-you-go provision models may be exploited via fraudulent resource consumption, leading to financial loss for users or reduced performance for the provider [69]. The cloud itself could be targeted in DDoS attacks, causing disruption to millions of users, or as a mechanism to infect the domains of cloud customers by piggybacking on services.

6.5 Crypto-Mining Botnets

Cryptocurrency is designed to be anonymous, decentralised, and unregulated; characteristics that directly align with the requirements of botmasters. Botnets can be built using the Bitcoin infrastructure, exploiting its use of P2P to maintain the blockchain as a C&C channel [70]. The built-in anonymity of users makes it harder to identify the botmaster or to enumerate bots across the network, even if individual bots are discovered [70]. This is a vast improvement in resiliency over typical Internet botnets as previously discussed. Anonymisation is supported by the fact that all transactions look identical to the observer, allowing malicious activities to stay hidden. Such activities are also not easily disrupted as direct action against suspected users would result in large-scale disruption to the blockchain as a whole [70]. Lastly, bots can be arranged into crypto-mining pools to generate their own Bitcoins for income.

The so-called Miner botnet was studied by [28], and is made up of 4 tiers with the top 2 forming the C&C infrastructure and bottom 2 containing the infected clients. P2P bots with Internet connectivity at tier 3 run a special Bitcoin mining module in the binary. Tier 4 bots (who lack Internet connectivity) then use the P2P bots as relays to download Bitcoin client software and to join mining pools from a hardcoded list. Coins and wallets are backed-up to tier 3 bots, which in turn upload this data to the C&C in 20 min intervals [28]. When first infecting a victim, Miner reportedly checks video and graphic card drivers, updating them if necessary and running speed tests to determine the host's capabilities [28].

ZombieCoin is a conceptual botnet with a Bitcoin-based C&C architecture, where commands are encoded into transactions between the botmaster and bot clients [70]. A pair of keys are generated by the botmaster, with the public key hidden in the bot binary. When bots join the Bitcoin network, this key and the botmaster's digital signature are used to identify and interpret commands. Ali et al. [70] identify a selection of methods. The first is to use OP_RETURN, a function allowing 80 bytes of ID data to be added to a transaction. Second is the use of unspendable outputs, which allow the addition of 20 bytes of custom data. The third is to use key leakage; a random factor is used twice, enabling the derivation of the signer's private key. Last is the use of subliminal channels where commands are hidden within signature strings [70]. These options show how resourceful botmasters can build complex C&C structures which would be very difficult to detect and dissolve in real life.

Extending their work on ZombieCoin, [70] suggest the use of rendezvous points, disseminated in near real-time to all bots telling them when/where to upload data, as well as transaction chaining where long commands are encoded as the inputs/outputs to an ordered sequence of transactions. Attacks may include selfish mining (where blocks are used to build private chains for mining without competition) and BGP hijacking (where traffic to and from the blockchain is interrupted, partitioning the network) [71]. Another possibility is an eclipse attack where currency is stolen directly from compromised devices by capturing their communications [71]. Cryptocurrency is increasingly utilised for black market transactions, making it hard to track the exchange of botnet tools and services. Furthermore, blockchain technology has so far been used primarily for cryptocurrencies, but its functionality is expanding into other applications [71], extending the botnet attack plane.

7 Future Developments and Possible Research Directions

Botnets are constantly adapting to changes in the digital landscape. We must match this with our detection and mitigation strategies to respond to the threat effectively. Here, we summarise some outstanding issues and suggest areas for further research.

Propagation is a difficult activity to detect and observe due to the sheer variability of infection types, vectors and mechanisms, all of which are designed to be discreet. Historic traces of past propagation events are not made publicly available due to privacy concerns, and data of this kind is difficult to accurately simulate in lab environments. Therefore, there is a need for improved propagation research, with high-quality, rich datasets and shared testing environments made widely available to researchers so that better predictive models (with better applicability to real-life) may be built.

In addition to this, most existing work in this area is directly based on compartmental epidemiology. Epidemic models are well-established and useful as a foundation for understanding spread dynamics, but several outstanding challenges remain in their application to network environments, including considerations of complexity, heterogeneity, and prediction accuracy [60]. Furthermore, there is a need to expand past epidemiology, and to explore other characteristics of spread that are domain-specific, including different business settings, different types of devices, and other influences on potential infection reach and rate.

Around the world, many institutions and individuals have studied botnets over the years, and categories of distinct detection and mitigation approaches have emerged as a result. As a community, we have also established classifications for botnet types and behaviours. However, there is still no generalised standard for the measurement of botnet characteristics, like size, infectiousness, force of propagation, or various traffic metrics. The same can be said of the measurement and characterisation of vulnerable networks. A widely-accepted standard for determining the degree of vulnerability and variability would help in building better approaches and for more accurate comparisons between detection schemes.

Recently, we have seen a general push in all areas of cyber-security towards the use of artificial intelligence and machine learning. Whilst this comes with its own set of challenges, this approach can be particularly effective when large, accurate and relevant datasets are available to train predictive models. However, the role of the human analyst is still significant in adaptively and flexibly interpreting new, unfamiliar and evolving threats. Therefore, future approaches shouldn't rely solely on machine learning or AI to perfectly protect against botnets, and should instead be a balance between machine and human interpretation. Future systems should be efficient and flexible, with intuitive visualisation for defenders to interface with data for improved analysis and response.

The research community needs to maintain awareness of the botnet threat when developing and deploying new protocols and technologies. Security must be built-in at the design phase and shouldn't consist primarily of reactionary patches. We previously discussed risks related to mobile technologies, the IoT, and the IPv6 protocol. Other topics for consideration include new protocol versions like HTTP/2 [72] and DNSsec [73], anonymization services like Tor [74], and biometric security [75]. Researchers needs to develop concept models to creatively explore these technologies, imagining new attack scenarios, new targets of interest for adversaries, and potential vulnerabilities to bolster industry standards against future botnets.

In order to achieve the highest possible level of defence, there must be a greater level of global collaboration between researchers, vendors, network infrastructure providers, and law enforcement agencies. This is vital in dealing with threats effectively and efficiently, as demonstrated in numerous successful botnet takedowns [53–55]. Collaboration may be also happen through the sharing of resources and research platforms (e.g. the DETER TestBed [76]). Security needs to extend beyond business and government networks. For example, the Stratosphere Project aims to empower NGOs by providing free botnet defence tools [77]. Users should also be personally empowered to actively maintain their privacy. A possible path to achieving this is open-source software, though there is some debate as to whether this is more or less secure than proprietary solutions [78].

Another area for development is in legislation and policy. As technology has developed in past decades, legislation around the world has struggled to keep up [55]. The rapid dissemination and adoption of new technology results in legal grey areas which can be exploited by criminals, but also by legitimate businesses and states for profit, power, or surveillance. Such areas in need of clear and robust laws include user privacy, collection of user data, and remote admin of private systems. The reactive nature of cyber-crime legislation risks harsh laws that address symptoms rather than causes, and ultimately threaten the future of a free Internet. Botnets are a unique and complex threat, their impact dependent on context and environment. For the future Internet to be secure whilst remaining democratic and free, new legislation (and the underpinning technology) must balance the rights of individuals with the safe and secure provision of services.

Finally, botnet malware has the potential to cause significant damage to national infrastructure. Combined with the possibility of state-sponsored attacks, this has large implications about the future of warfare and conflict. Hence, nations need to invest in securing critical infrastructure. This requires significant research into the defence of highly specialised systems against sustained, sophisticated attacks. With botnet tools highly available to anyone on the Internet, the potential for large-scale cyber-terrorism must be a major consideration.

8 Conclusions

In this chapter, we have outlined the basics of what a botnet is, how it works, possible variations, and how they are categorised. We defined botnet attacks in 2 distinct parts; the initial compromise and the continuous threat. The former encompasses the infection of a domain, including installation, system manipulation, and propagation activities. Identification of the malware at this stage mitigates the development of the botnet. The latter denotes the state of the domain after a successful compromise, where the botnet is ready to be utilised for a variety of attacks. At this stage, detection is a damage limitation exercise. Building on this, we discussed the impact of infections on the host domain, the attack process, and factors contributing to successful deployment.

We then outlined current defensive strategies, categorising them as proactive (practical solutions for securing real networks) and pre-emptive (theoretical explorations for better understanding and prediction). We demonstrated the adaptability of botnets by discussing new types of bot malware on platforms like mobile, social networks, IoT, the cloud, and blockchain. Finally, we considered some unresolved issues, and made suggestions for future research. Botnets are highly versatile, powerful multi-function tools. They are relatively easy to setup and difficult to take down, and can impact any area of digital infrastructure. Therefore, we need to have equally powerful defensive strategies, with a concentrated focus on early detection and a culture of security awareness.

References

1. R. J. Oentaryo, A. Murdopo, P. K. Prasetyo, and E.-P. Lim, "On Profiling Bots in Social Media", in *International Conference on Social Informatics*. Springer, 2016, pp. 92–109.
2. R. A. Rodríguez-Gómez, G. Maciá-Fernández, and P. García-Teodoro, "Survey and Taxonomy of Botnet Research through Life-Cycle," *ACM Computing Surveys (CSUR)*, vol. 45, no. 4, p. 45, 2013.
3. S. S. Silva, R. M. Silva, R. C. Pinto, and R. M. Salles, "Botnets: A Survey," *Computer Networks*, vol. 57, no. 2, pp. 378–403, 2013.
4. G. Gu, J. Zhang, and W. Lee, "BotSniffer: Detecting Botnet Command and Control Channels in Network Traffic," in *NDSS*, vol. 8, 2008, pp. 1–18.
5. S. Zhao, P. P. Lee, J. Lui, X. Guan, X. Ma, and J. Tao, "Cloud-Based Push-Styled Mobile Botnets: A Case Study of Exploiting the Cloud to Device Messaging Service," in *Proceedings of the 28th Annual Computer Security Applications Conference*. ACM, 2012, pp. 119–128.
6. S. Stover, D. Dittrich, J. Hernandez, and S. Dietrich, "Analysis of the Storm and Nugache Trojans: P2P is Here," *USENIX*, vol. 32, no. 6, pp. 18–27, 2007.
7. H. Binsalleeh, T. Ormerod, A. Boukhtouta, P. Sinha, A. Youssef, M. Debbabi, and L. Wang, "On the Analysis of the Zeus Botnet Crimeware Toolkit," in *Privacy Security and Trust (PST), 2010 Eighth Annual International Conference on*. IEEE, 2010, pp. 31–38.
8. R. Borgaonkar, "An Analysis of the Asprox Botnet," in *Emerging Security Information Systems and Technologies (SECURWARE), 2010 Fourth International Conference on*. IEEE, 2010, pp. 148–153.

9. D. Andriesse, C. Rossow, B. Stone-Gross, D. Plohmann, and H. Bos, "Highly Resilient Peer-to-Peer Botnets are Here: An Analysis of Gameover Zeus," in *Malicious and Unwanted Software: "The Americas"(MALWARE), 2013 8th International Conference on.* IEEE, 2013, pp. 116–123.
10. P. Wang, S. Sparks, and C. C. Zou, "An Advanced Hybrid Peer-to-Peer Botnet," *IEEE Transactions on Dependable and Secure Computing*, vol. 7, no. 2, pp. 113–127, 2010.
11. H. R. Zeidanloo and A. A. Manaf, "Botnet Command and Control Mechanisms," in *Computer and Electrical Engineering, 2009. ICCEE'09. Second International Conference on*, vol. 1. IEEE, 2009, pp. 564–568.
12. K. Chiang and L. Lloyd, "A Case Study of the Rustock Rootkit and Spam Bot," *HotBots*, vol. 7, pp. 10–10, 2007.
13. N. Daswani and M. Stoppelman, "The Anatomy of Clickbot. A," in *Proceedings of the First Conference on First Workshop on Hot Topics in Understanding Botnets*. USENIX Association, 2007, pp. 11–11.
14. G. Sinclair, C. Nunnery, and B. B. Kang, "The Waledac Protocol: The How and Why," in *Malicious and Unwanted Software (MALWARE), 2009 4th International Conference on*. IEEE, 2009, pp. 69–77.
15. P. Sinha, A. Boukhtouta, V. H. Belarde, and M. Debbabi, "Insights from the Analysis of the Mariposa Botnet," in *Risks and Security of Internet and Systems (CRiSIS), 2010 Fifth International Conference on*. IEEE, 2010, pp. 1–9.
16. K. Thomas and D. M. Nicol, "The Koobface Botnet and the Rise of Social Malware," in *Malicious and Unwanted Software (MALWARE), 2010 5th International Conference on*. IEEE, 2010, pp. 63–70.
17. P. Celeda, R. Krejci, J. Vykopal, and M. Drasar, "Embedded Malware - An Analysis of the Chuck Norris Botnet," in *Computer Network Defense (EC2ND), 2010 European Conference on*. IEEE, 2010, pp. 3–10.
18. M. M. Andrade and N. Vlajic, "Dirt Jumper: A Key Player in Today's Botnet-for-DDos Market," in *Internet Security (WorldCIS), 2012 World Congress on*. IEEE, 2012, pp. 239–244.
19. M. Kerkers, J. J. Santanna, and A. Sperotto, "Characterisation of the Kelihos.B Botnet," in *IFIP International Conference on Autonomous Infrastructure, Management and Security*. Springer, 2014, pp. 79–91.
20. A. Rahimian, R. Ziarati, S. Preda, and M. Debbabi, "On the Reverse Engineering of the Citadel Botnet," in *Foundations and Practice of Security*. Springer, 2014, pp. 408–425.
21. P. Pearce, V. Dave, C. Grier, K. Levchenko, S. Guha, D. McCoy, V. Paxson, S. Savage, and G. M. Voelker, "Characterizing Large-Scale Click Fraud in ZeroAccess," in *Proceedings of the 2014 ACM SIGSAC Conference on Computer and Communications Security*. ACM, 2014, pp. 141–152.
22. J. B. Grizzard, V. Sharma, C. Nunnery, B. B. Kang, and D. Dagon, "Peer-to-Peer Botnets: Overview and Case Study," *HotBots*, vol. 7, pp. 1–1, 2007.
23. W. Chang, A. Mohaisen, A. Wang, and S. Chen, "Measuring Botnets in the Wild: Some New Trends," in *Proceedings of the 10th ACM Symposium on Information, Computer and Communications Security*. ACM, 2015, pp. 645–650.
24. R. Layton and A. Azab, "Authorship Analysis of the Zeus Botnet Source Code," in *Cybercrime and Trustworthy Computing Conference (CTC), 2014 Fifth*. IEEE, 2014, pp. 38–43.
25. A. K. Sood, S. Zeadally, and R. J. Enbody, "An Empirical Study of HTTP-based Financial Botnets," *IEEE Transactions on Dependable and Secure Computing*, vol. 13, no. 2, pp. 236–251, 2016.
26. M. Anagnostopoulos, G. Kambourakis, and S. Gritzalis, "New Facets of Mobile Botnet: Architecture and Evaluation," *International Journal of Information Security*, vol. 15, no. 5, pp. 455–473, 2016.
27. L.-P. Song, Z. Jin, and G.-Q. Sun, "Modeling and Analyzing of Botnet Interactions," *Physica A: Statistical Mechanics and its Applications*, vol. 390, no. 2, pp. 347–358, 2011.
28. D. Plohmann and E. Gerhards-Padilla, "Case Study of the Miner Botnet," in *Cyber Conflict (CYCON), 2012 4th International Conference on*. IEEE, 2012, pp. 1–16.

29. G. Kambourakis, C. Kolias, and A. Stavrou, "The Mirai Botnet and the IoT Zombie Armies," in *Military Communications Conference (MILCOM), MILCOM 2017–2017 IEEE*. IEEE, 2017, pp. 267–272.

30. R. Sharifnya and M. Abadi, "A Novel Reputation System to Detect DGA-based Botnets," in *Computer and Knowledge Engineering (ICCKE), 2013 3th International eConference on*. IEEE, 2013, pp. 417–423.

31. Y. Zhou and X. Jiang, "Dissecting Android Malware: Characterization and Evolution," in *Security and Privacy (SP), 2012 IEEE Symposium on*. IEEE, 2012, pp. 95–109.

32. P. Porras, H. Saidi, and V. Yegneswaran, "An Analysis of the iKee. b iPhone Botnet," in *International Conference on Security and Privacy in Mobile Information and Communication Systems*. Springer, 2010, pp. 141–152.

33. E. Bertino and N. Islam, "Botnets and Internet of Things Security," *Computer*, vol. 50, no. 2, pp. 76–79, 2017.

34. A. Kharraz, W. Robertson, D. Balzarotti, L. Bilge, and E. Kirda, "Cutting the Gordian Knot: A Look Under the Hood of Ransomware Attacks," in *International Conference on Detection of Intrusions and Malware, and Vulnerability Assessment*. Springer, 2015, pp. 3–24.

35. S.-W. Kim, J.-H. Park, E.-D. Lee, M.-E. Choi, and S.-W. Seo, "Threat Analysis of Incubation Period in Malware Epidemics," in *Vehicular Technology Conference (VTC 2010-Spring), 2010 IEEE 71st*. IEEE, 2010, pp. 1–5.

36. S. Eshghi, S. Sarkar, and S. S. Venkatesh, "Visibility-Aware Optimal Contagion of Malware Epidemics," *IEEE Transactions on Automatic Control*, vol. 62, no. 10, pp. 5205–5212, 2017.

37. M. Eslahi, H. Hashim, and N. Tahir, "An Efficient False Alarm Reduction Approach in HTTP-based Botnet Detection," in *Computers & Informatics (ISCI), 2013 IEEE Symposium on*. IEEE, 2013, pp. 201–205.

38. Z. Chen, C. Chen, and Q. Wang, "On the Scalability of Delay-Tolerant Botnets," *International Journal of Security and Networks*, vol. 5, no. 4, pp. 248–258, 2010.

39. D. Bradbury, "The Metamorphosis of Malware Writers," *Computers & Security*, vol. 25, no. 2, pp. 89–90, 2006.

40. G. Ollmann, "Hacking as a Service," *Computer Fraud & Security*, vol. 2008, no. 12, pp. 12–15, 2008.

41. G. Bottazzi and G. Me, "The Botnet Revenue Model," in *Proceedings of the 7th International Conference on Security of Information and Networks*. ACM, 2014, p. 459.

42. J. Goebel and T. Holz, "Rishi: Identify Bot Contaminated Hosts by IRC Nickname Evaluation," *HotBots*, vol. 7, pp. 8–8, 2007.

43. G. Gu, R. Perdisci, J. Zhang, W. Lee *et al.*, "Botminer: Clustering Analysis of Network Traffic for Protocol-and Structure-Independent Botnet Detection." in *USENIX security symposium*, vol. 5, no. 2, 2008, pp. 139–154.

44. G. Gu, V. Yegneswaran, P. Porras, J. Stoll, and W. Lee, "Active Botnet Probing to Identify Obscure Command and Control Channels," in *Computer Security Applications Conference, 2009. ACSAC'09. Annual*. IEEE, 2009, pp. 241–253.

45. G. Gu, P. A. Porras, V. Yegneswaran, M. W. Fong, and W. Lee, "BotHunter: Detecting Malware Infection Through IDS-Driven Dialog Correlation," in *USENIX Security Symposium*, vol. 7, 2007, pp. 1–16.

46. W. Lu, M. Tavallaee, G. Rammidi, and A. A. Ghorbani, "BotCop: An Online Botnet Traffic Classifier," in *Communication Networks and Services Research Conference, 2009. CNSR'09. Seventh Annual*. IEEE, 2009, pp. 70–77.

47. L. Liu, S. Chen, G. Yan, and Z. Zhang, "BotTracer: Execution-based Bot-like Malware Detection," *Information Security*, pp. 97–113, 2008.

48. G. K. Venkatesh and R. A. Nadarajan, "HTTP Botnet Detection Using Adaptive Learning Rate Multilayer Feed-Forward Neural Network," in *WISTP*. Springer, 2012, pp. 38–48.

49. S. Schiavoni, F. Maggi, L. Cavallaro, and S. Zanero, "Phoenix: DGA-based Botnet Tracking and Intelligence," in *International Conference on Detection of Intrusions and Malware, and Vulnerability Assessment*. Springer, 2014, pp. 192–211.

50. A. Al-Bataineh and G. White, "Analysis and Detection of Malicious Data Exfiltration in Web Traffic," in *Malicious and Unwanted Software (MALWARE), 2012 7th International Conference on.* IEEE, 2012, pp. 26–31.
51. J. Sherry, C. Lan, R. A. Popa, and S. Ratnasamy, "Blindbox: Deep Packet Inspection Over Encrypted Traffic," in *ACM SIGCOMM Computer Communication Review*, vol. 45, no. 4. ACM, 2015, pp. 213–226.
52. J. Zhang, X. Luo, R. Perdisci, G. Gu, W. Lee, and N. Feamster, "Boosting the Scalability of Botnet Detection Using Adaptive Traffic Sampling," in *Proceedings of the 6th ACM Symposium on Information, Computer and Communications Security.* ACM, 2011, pp. 124–134.
53. Y. Nadji, M. Antonakakis, R. Perdisci, D. Dagon, and W. Lee, "Beheading Hydras: Performing Effective Botnet Takedowns," in *Proceedings of the 2013 ACM SIGSAC Conference on Computer & Communications Security.* ACM, 2013, pp. 121–132.
54. D. Bradbury, "Fighting Botnets with Sinkholes," *Network Security*, vol. 2012, no. 8, pp. 12–15, 2012.
55. J. S. Hiller, "Civil Cyberconflict: Microsoft, Cybercrime, and Botnets," *Santa Clara Computer & High Tech. LJ*, vol. 31, p. 163, 2014.
56. F. Brauer, "Compartmental Models in Epidemiology," in *Mathematical Epidemiology.* Springer, 2008, pp. 19–79.
57. D. Dagon, C. C. Zou, and W. Lee, "Modeling Botnet Propagation Using Time Zones." in *NDSS*, vol. 6, 2006, pp. 2–13.
58. M. Khosroshahy, M. K. M. Ali, and D. Qiu, "The SIC Botnet Lifecycle Model: A Step Beyond Traditional Epidemiological Models," *Computer Networks*, vol. 57, no. 2, pp. 404–421, 2013.
59. Z. Lu, W. Wang, and C. Wang, "On the Evolution and Impact of Mobile Botnets in Wireless Networks," *IEEE Transactions on Mobile Computing*, vol. 15, no. 9, pp. 2304–2316, 2016.
60. L. Pellis, F. Ball, S. Bansal, K. Eames, T. House, V. Isham, and P. Trapman, "Eight Challenges for Network Epidemic Models," *Epidemics*, vol. 10, pp. 58–62, 2015.
61. S. Lee and J. Kim, "Fluxing Botnet Command and Control Channels with URL Shortening Services," *Computer Communications*, vol. 36, no. 3, pp. 320–332, 2013.
62. K. Xu, P. Butler, S. Saha, and D. Yao, "DNS for Massive-Scale Command and Control," *IEEE Transactions on Dependable and Secure Computing*, vol. 10, no. 3, pp. 143–153, 2013.
63. K. Singh, S. Sangal, N. Jain, P. Traynor, and W. Lee, "Evaluating Bluetooth as a Medium for Botnet Command and Control," in *International Conference on Detection of Intrusions and Malware, and Vulnerability Assessment.* Springer, 2010, pp. 61–80.
64. J. Echeverria and S. Zhou, "Discovery of the Twitter Bursty Botnet," *arXiv preprint arXiv:1709.06740*, 2017.
65. S. Nagaraja, A. Houmansadr, P. Piyawongwisal, V. Singh, P. Agarwal, and N. Borisov, "Stegobot: A Covert Social Network Botnet," in *International Workshop on Information Hiding.* Springer, 2011, pp. 299–313.
66. Q. Li, C. Larsen, and T. van der Horst, "IPv6 - A Catalyst and an Evasion Tool for Botnets and Malware Distribution Networks," *Computer*, p. 1, 2012.
67. W. Chen, C. Yin, S. Zhou, and X. Yan, "Cloud-Based Mobile Botnets using Multiple Push Servers," in *Parallel Architectures, Algorithms and Programming (PAAP), 2015 Seventh International Symposium on.* IEEE, 2015, pp. 183–189.
68. S. Shafieian, M. Zulkernine, and A. Haque, "CloudZombie: Launching and Detecting Slow-Read Distributed Denial of Service Attacks from the Cloud," in *Computer and Information Technology; Ubiquitous Computing and Communications; Dependable, Autonomic and Secure Computing; Pervasive Intelligence and Computing (CIT/IUCC/DASC/PICOM), 2015 IEEE International Conference on.* IEEE, 2015, pp. 1733–1740.
69. J. Idziorek, M. F. Tannian, and D. Jacobson, "The Insecurity of Cloud Utility Models," *IT Professional*, vol. 15, no. 2, pp. 22–27, 2013.
70. S. T. Ali, P. McCorry, P. H.-J. Lee, and F. Hao, "ZombieCoin 2.0: Managing Next-Generation Botnets using Bitcoin," *International Journal of Information Security*, pp. 1–12, 2017.
71. X. Li, P. Jiang, T. Chen, X. Luo, and Q. Wen, "A Survey on the Security of Blockchain Systems," *Future Generation Computer Systems*, 2017.

72. IETF, "HTTP/2," last accessed 23th December 2017. [Online]. Available: https://http2.github. io/
73. IANA, "DNSSEC information," last accessed 23th December 2017. [Online]. Available: https://www.iana.org/dnssec
74. "Tor Project," last accessed 23th December 2017. [Online]. Available: https://www.torproject. org/index.html.en
75. S. Liu and M. Silverman, "A Practical Guide to Biometric Security Technology," *IT Professional*, vol. 3, no. 1, pp. 27–32, 2001.
76. "DETER Project," last accessed 23th December 2017. [Online]. Available: https://deter-project.org/
77. "Stratosphere IPS Project," last accessed 23th December 2017. [Online]. Available: https:// stratosphereips.org/
78. C. Cowan, "Software Security for Open-Source Systems," *IEEE Security & Privacy*, vol. 99, no. 1, pp. 38–45, 2003.

Catastrophic Cyber-Physical Malware

**Suresh Kothari, Ganesh Ram Santhanam, Payas Awadhutkar,
Benjamin Holland, Jon Mathews, and Ahmed Tamrawi**

Abstract With the advent of highly sophisticated cyber-physical malware (CPM) such as Industroyer, a cyberattack could be as destructive as the terrorist attack on 9/11, and it would virtually paralyze the nation. We discuss as the major risks the vulnerability of: telecommunication infrastructure, industrial control systems (ICS), and mission-critical software.

In differentiating CPM from traditional malware, the difference really comes from the open-ended possibilities for malware triggers resulting from the wide spectrum of sensor inputs, and the almost limitless application-specific possibilities for designing malicious payloads.

Fundamentally, the challenges of detecting sophisticated CPM stem from the complexities inherent in the software at the heart of cyber-physical systems. We discuss three fundamental challenges: explosion of execution behaviors, computational intractability of checking feasible behaviors, and difficult-to-analyze programming constructs.

This material is based on research sponsored by DARPA under agreement numbers FA8750-15-2-0080 and FA8750-12-2-0126. The U.S. Government is authorized to reproduce and distribute reprints for Governmental purposes notwithstanding any copyright notation thereon. The views and conclusions contained herein are those of the authors and should not be interpreted as necessarily representing the official policies or endorsements, either expressed or implied, of DARPA or the U.S. Government.

S. Kothari (✉)
Department of Electrical and Computer Engineering, Iowa State University, Ames, IA, USA

EnSoft Corp., Ames, IA, USA
e-mail: kothari@iastate.edu

G. R. Santhanam · P. Awadhutkar · B. Holland
Department of Electrical and Computer Engineering, Iowa State University, Ames, IA, USA
e-mail: gsanthan@iastate.edu; payas@iastate.edu; bholland@iastate.edu

J. Mathews · A. Tamrawi
EnSoft Corp., Ames, IA, USA
e-mail: jmathews@ensoftcorp.com; ahmedtamrawi@ensoftcorp.com

© Springer Nature Switzerland AG 2018
M. Conti et al. (eds.), *Versatile Cybersecurity*, Advances in Information
Security 72, https://doi.org/10.1007/978-3-319-97643-3_7

In detecting novel CPM, the tasks are: developing plausible hypotheses for malware trigger and malicious payload, analyzing software to gather evidence based on CPM hypotheses, and verifying software to prove or refute a hypothesis based on the gathered evidence. We discuss research directions for effective automation to support these tasks.

1 Introduction

The imminent danger of cyber-physical malware (CPM) is evident from attacks such as the power outage in Ukraine [122] or the hijacking of a Jeep Cherokee [83]. The net-centricity of modern systems offers an adversary affordable attack vectors through cyberspace against critical missions. We are arguably at risk to an asymmetric attack vector launched by a terrorist organization or rogue nation that cannot, or chooses not to confront in a conventional conflict. The Internet of Things (IoT) implies more software-driven devices and thus increased CPM risk.

The traditional notion of malware is too narrow, and the prevalent characterizations (virus, worm, Trojan horse, spyware etc.) are neither precise nor comprehensive enough to characterize CPM. Detecting sophisticated CPM is like searching for a needle in the haystack without knowing what the needle looks like. Employing real-world examples, this survey chapter discusses: the fundamentals of CPM, the need for threat modeling, analysis and verification of CPM, and the challenges and directions for future research.

CPS security problems are often rooted in the complex CPS software. Securing CPS software requires knowledge of both software analysis and verification as well as CPS architecture and attack surface. It is hard for the CPS community to understand the intricacies of software analysis and verification. Whereas for the software engineering community, the lack of adequate CPS knowledge is a major roadblock. Technological advances in computing, communications, and control have set the stage for a next generation of CPS for energy, environment, transportation, and health care. The context for modeling CPM [58, 101, 104] needs to be exposed so that the software engineering community can engage in collaborative interdisciplinary research for evolving CPM characterizations that can cover the vast expanse from mobile phones apps to Supervisory Control and Data Acquisition (SCADA) systems.

Let us overview testing and verification as techniques for software assurance. Testing cannot verify that every potential vulnerability instance is safe or not. Avionics companies try to compensate for limitations of testing by requiring high test coverage using the modified condition/decision coverage (MC/DC) metric [45] and instituting stringent software development and auditing practices as required by DO-178B [45]. When it comes to cybersecurity, the limitations of testing become more pronounced. An attacker can craft a clever trigger for the malicious software to defy getting caught with high test coverage.

Next, let us consider formal verification [59, 116] as an alternative to testing. The point often argued in its favor is that it can verify whether every instance is safe or not. The end result of formal verification can be: (a) it proves that an instance is safe, (b) it proves that an instance is unsafe, or (c) it is inconclusive when it crashes or times out. Formal verification provides a counter example as evidence for (b). However, it does not provide evidence for (a) and (c). The core dump it may provide for (c) is not human-comprehensible. While scalability of formal verification has been the subject of intense research with the use of *binary decision diagrams* and host of other techniques [80], the topic of automated verification with human-comprehensible evidence has not received much attention. Avionics, automotive and other industry practitioners of safety-critical software consider such lack of evidence a serious short-coming of formal methods [64]. De Millo, Lipton, and Perlis (the first Turing Award recipient) [70] have argued that software verification, like "proofs" in mathematics, should provide *evidence* that humans can follow and thus be able to build trust into the correctness of the software verification. This is especially crucial given the potential for tremendous harm from CPM.

With novel CPM, the first challenge is to hypothesize it. The sensor inputs create open-ended possibilities for attackers to craft CPM. The analyst must narrow down a nebulous specification of a vulnerability to something specific that can be verified. Unbeknownst to the user, a global positioning system (GPS) may contain malicious code that compromises integrity of the system. The analyst must specifically hypothesize how the integrity breach could occur. Currently, threat modeling for trigger-based CPM is often a tedious manual endeavor with hardly any automated tools support [56].

A completely automated solution for detecting catastrophic malware in mission-critical software is unlikely, as it is an extremely complex problem. Fred Brooks (1996 Turing Award recipient) points out [55]: "If indeed our objective is to build computer systems that solve very challenging problems, my thesis is that IA > AI, that is, that intelligence amplifying systems can, at any given level of available systems technology, beat AI systems. That is, a machine and a mind can beat a mind-imitating machine working by itself." As elaborated in our paper [93], there is dire need for analysis and verification tools to facilitate a human-in-the-loop approach for addressing the CPM problem.

This survey chapter leverages our team's experience with: (a) analyzing complex CPM on the DARPA Automated Program Analysis for Cybersecurity (APAC) [5] and Space/Time Analysis for Cybersecurity (STAC) [29] programs, and (b) designing and developing commercial products to model and analyze control systems software for automobile, avionics, and other industries for whom safety and security is a major concern.

2   CIA Triad and CPM Metrics

Government agencies such as National Institute of Standards and Technology (NIST) and National Security Agency (NSA) have channelized their efforts towards developing metrics for measuring the ease of exploitability, and the impact of CPM (e.g., national vulnerability database (NVD) [24] and common vulnerability scoring system (CVSS) [12]). These efforts to calibrate CPM are aimed at enabling industry and government to better assess and manage risks.

2.1   CIA Triad

The CIA triad (confidentiality, integrity, availability) [22] has evolved as a general and robust model to systematically explore hypotheses related to malicious behaviors. CIA triad covers a vast expanse of CPM that are targeted towards devices ranging from smart phone apps to power grids. Thus, the CIA triad may be used as a framework to hypothesize potential vulnerabilities.

For example, confidentiality may be breached in an Android app when sensitive data (e.g., image data from the camera, or GPS location) is leaked to an unauthorized sink (e.g., the internet, or to an adversary). Similarly, integrity may be breached in a GPS Android app when the coordinates are incorrectly shown in some geographic locations. Availability may be breached in a text processing application if the application runs vulnerable sorting algorithms that have asymmetrically large runtime on certain relatively small inputs (e.g., quick sort whose pivot degenerates to the last element in the unsorted input list for certain cases, or the app runs unnecessary loops to drain the device battery). In some cases, sophisticated CPM may breach two or all three CIA security attributes. For example, Stuxnet [31] was able to access and modify sensitive information (breach confidentiality and integrity) about Siemens PLC controllers installed on the centrifuges while remaining unobservable for years. This eventually led to damage of the centrifuge controllers beyond recovery (breach of availability).

2.2   Metrics for Measuring CPM Impact

We mention a few of the prevalent metrics that measure the impact of attacks caused by CPM on ICS. For a detailed discussion of CPM impact metrics, see [65].

- The *CVSS* measures CPM impact in terms of three kinds of metrics (See [100]): (a) *Base* metrics measure how easy it is for an attacker to exploit the vulnerability, and the confidentiality, integrity and availability impact of the vulnerability on the compromised system. (b) *Temporal* metrics represent the evolving exploitability of a vulnerability, such as the availability of exploit code and availability of patches to fix the vulnerability. (c) *Environmental* metrics represent the characteristics of a vulnerability that are specific to a particular user's environment, such as the potential damage incurred by the organization due to CIA breach.

- *Potential impact metrics* is part of a framework drafted by the National Security Agency (NSA) for ICS networks, outlining potential impact and loss due to a CPM attack on a system. This framework also characterized CPM attack impact in terms of the CIA triad.
- *Ideal-based metrics* defined seven security dimensions and the ideal or best possible values for each of them [54]. The seven dimensions include: Security Group Knowledge, Attack Group Knowledge, Access, Vulnerabilities, Damage Potential, Detection, and Recovery. For example, the ideal for the Vulnerabilities dimension is that there are no vulnerabilities in the system, and the ideal for the Damage Potential dimension is that there is no confidentiality, integrity or availability impact to the system in the face of a CPM attack. The ideals are meant as a reference point to assess a system's vulnerability, and are not necessarily realizable in practice.

A common theme that runs across all prevalent CPM attack impact metrics is that they characterize impact in terms of the CIA-triad: (a) confidentiality breach (leak of sensitive information to an adversary), (b) integrity breach (corruption of sensitive information by an adversary), and (c) availability breach (denial of service to legitimate users due to excessive consumption triggered by CPM).

3 CPM Attack Phases

A cyber attack is not all that different from a military attack. A cyber attacker will dedicate a significant amount of time observing and probing the target organization to find weaknesses in its defense. Any weakness found may lead to infiltration and eventually an assault. We have consolidated the discussion of cyber attack phases into three main phases. We have used the United States Navy Academy [32] as the primary source of information for this discussion.

3.1 *Reconnaissance*

An attacker's first goal is to identify potential targets for their mission. Attackers are often motivated by financial gain, access to sensitive information or damage to an entity (could be a company, organization, nation etc.).

The attacker may collect information on targeted organization's security systems and available entry points. The attacker might set up a fake company, register domains and create fake profiles for social engineering purposes.

Once the attacker determines what defenses are in place, the next step is to identify a weak point that allows the attackers to gain access. This is usually accomplished by scanning an organization's network with tools easily found on the Internet. This step of the process usually proceeds slowly, sometimes lasting months, as the attackers search for vulnerabilities. We list some critical information that are typically obtained during the reconnaissance phase: (a) Network Information: IP Addresses, subnet mask, network topology, domain names; (b) Host Information, user names, group names, operating system family and version, TCP and UDP services; (c) Security Policies: password complexity requirements, password change frequency, expired/disabled account retention, physical security, firewalls, intrusion detection systems; and (d) Human Information: home address, telephone number, frequent hangouts (physical and online), computer knowledge, hobbies and interests. Based on how interaction is done with the target subject, the reconnaissance can be passive and active.

Passive Reconnaissance is gathering information in a manner unlikely to alert the subject of the surveillance. This is the natural start of any reconnaissance because, once alerted, a target will likely react by drastically increasing security in anticipation of an attack. The attacker minimizes any interaction with the target network which may raise flags in the computer logs. For example, visiting the target's website may leave behind a trace that your IP Address established a TCP connection to the target's web server, but it will be one of millions of connections that day – probably not going to stand out to the administrator in the periodic review of server logs. On the other hand, visiting the target's website so frequently that the server becomes overloaded is certain to alert an administrator.

Active Reconnaissance is gathering information while interacting with the subject directly, in a way that usually can be discovered. A number of tools that can be used for active network recon: ping, traceroute, and netcat (nc). If the attackers know the range of potential IP addresses for their target network, they can use ping to determine which IPs are actually in use by hosts on the network. They can use traceroute to figure out the topology of the network: i.e. where the routers are with respect to the hosts. Finally, they can use netcat (nc) to determine which ports are open with servers listening on them. Nmap is a powerful network scanner that attackers use to discover hosts on a target network.

As a defensive measure, an organization should centrally collect the log messages related to established or rejected connections from their network devices and use a tool to visualize their network communications and connection paths.

3.2 Intrusion and Escalation

At the second phase of a cyber attack, the attacker seeks to breach the organization perimeter and gain a persistent foothold in the environment.

Now that weaknesses in the target network are identified, the next step in the cyber attack is to gain access and then escalate. In almost all such cases, privileged access is needed because it allows the attackers to move freely within the environment. Techniques and tools such as Rainbow tables help intruders steal credentials, escalate privileges to admin. Once the attackers gain elevated privileges, the network is effectively taken over by the attackers. The attackers can spear-phish the company to gain credentials, use valid credentials to access the corporate infrastructure, and download more tools to access the environment. The initial intrusion is expanded to persistent, long-term, remote access to the environment. Once the attackers own the target organization's network, they establish a command and control channel from the outside into the victim's infrastructure.

As a defensive measure, it is important to have an enterprise-wide log management. It is important to constantly monitor network traffic and look for anomalies and signs of attacks, and to make intrusion harder, add two factor authentication to the services. The goal is to detect and disarm the control channel before the attacker can start to move laterally inside the network, causing more harm. One can use network and operating system logs to find connections from the outside that should not be there.

3.3 Assault

The final stage is where cost to businesses rise exponentially if the attack is not defeated. This is when the attacker executes the final aspects of their mission, stealing intellectual property or other sensitive data, corrupting mission-critical systems, and generally disrupting the operations of the victim's business.

This is when the hackers might alter the functionality of the victim's application, or disable the application entirely. Typically, attackers use exploit kits [95] which use drive-by downloads to download and run the appropriate exploit for the target system. The Stuxnet attack [31] on Iran's critical infrastructure is a classic example. During the assault phase, the attack ceases to be stealthy. However, the attackers have already effectively taken control of the environment, so it is too late for the breached organization to defend itself. Finally, the attacker may either terminate the connection if no further access is required, or create a backdoor for future access to the target.

Usually the attackers want to hide their tracks, but this is not universally the case, especially if the hackers want to leave a calling card behind to boast about their exploits. The purpose of trail obfuscation is to confuse, disorientate and divert the forensic examination process. Trail obfuscation covers a variety of techniques and tools including log cleaners, spoofing, misinformation, backbone hopping, zombied accounts, trojan commands, and more. The "Flame" malware [67] came to light in the summer of 2012. It's a very sophisticated piece of malware, probably produced by some nation-state, not by random hackers, terrorists or criminals. The Flame malware is designed to "cover its tracks", i.e. to erase traces of its existence on computers that it had infected, but was finished with. The creators of the Flame cyber-espionage threat ordered infected computers still under their control to download and execute a component designed to remove all traces of the malware and prevent forensic analysis [67].

Note that not all CPM attacks necessarily go through all the above phases. For example, side channel attacks do not require any installation and command or control; passive observations suffice for that.

4 National Cybersecurity: Critical Concern and Need

When people think of cybersecurity today, they worry about hackers and criminals who prowl the Internet, stealing people's identities, sensitive business information, or even national security secrets. Those threats are real and they exist today. But the even greater danger facing us in cyberspace goes beyond crime and harassment. A cyber attack perpetrated by nation states or violent extremists groups could be as destructive as the terrorist attack on 9/11. Such a destructive cyber-terrorist attack could virtually paralyze the nation. The most destructive scenarios involve cyber-terrorists launching several attacks on our critical infrastructure at one time, in combination with a physical attack. Attackers could also seek to disable or degrade critical military systems and communication networks. The collective result of these kinds of attacks could be a cyber Pearl Harbor: an attack that would cause physical destruction and loss of life. In fact, it would paralyze and shock the nation and create a new and profound sense of vulnerability. These are observations of the Secretary of Defense Leon Panetta [103].

Internet of Things (IoT) implies increasing dependence on software, making software assurance an important requirement for everyday life. White House reports [37] point to the urgent national need to shift the cybersecurity posture from defending computer networks to assuring critical missions. Telecommunication infrastructure, industrial control systems and mission-critical software are critical concerns for the security of cyberphysical systems.

4.1 Risk: Telecommunication Infrastructure

Telecommunications hardware includes a vast range of products that enable communication across the entire planet, from video broadcasting satellites to telephone handsets to fiber-optic transmission cables. Services include running the switches that control the phone system, providing Internet access, and configuring private networks by which international corporations conduct business. Software makes it all work, from sending and receiving e-mail to relaying satellite data to controlling telephone switching equipment to reducing background noise on your cell phone call.

Huawei, a Chinese multinational, is the largest telecommunications equipment manufacturer in the world in 2017, having overtaken Ericsson in 2012. In June 2016, Huawei was reportedly working on and designing its own mobile OS for future usage. From July to September 2017, Huawei surpassed Apple and became the second largest smartphone manufacturer in the world after Samsung. It also aims to be one of the world's five largest cloud players in the near future. Currently, the world's five largest vendors of telecommunication equipment (excluding mobile phone handsets), ranked by revenues are: Huawei, Ericsson, Cisco, Nokia (including Alcatel-Lucent), and ZTE corporation [33].

Warning about a potential threat to national security, US lawmakers decided to scrutinize a bid by Huawei to supply telecommunications equipment to Sprint Nextel in the United States. Sprint Nextel reportedly decided in 2011 to block Chinese companies Huawei and ZTE from its multi-billion-dollar network modernization project because of mounting national security concerns. The US House Intelligence Committee conducted an investigation of Huawei, recommending that the US government should block acquisitions, takeovers, or mergers involving Huawei, given the threat to US national security interests [40]. Committee Chairman Mike Rogers noted claims by US companies that Huawei equipment exhibited unexpected behavior, including routers allegedly sending large data packets to China late at night.

The telecommunications sector plays a critical role in the safety and security of a nation, and thus is a target of foreign intelligence services. The country's reliance on telecommunications infrastructure includes more than consumers' use of computer systems. Multiple critical infrastructure systems depend on information transmission through telecommunications systems. These modern critical infrastructures include electric power grids; banking and finance systems; natural gas, oil, and water systems; and rail and shipping channels. Inter-dependencies among these critical infrastructures greatly increase the risk that failure in one system will cause failures or disruptions in multiple critical infrastructure systems. Therefore, a disruption in telecommunication networks can have devastating effects on all aspects of modern living, causing shortages and stoppages that ripple throughout society.

A company providing telecommunication equipment is likely to have access to or detailed knowledge of the telecommunication infrastructures' architectural blueprints. The threat posed to national security interests by vulnerabilities in the telecommunications supply chain is an increasing priority given the country's reliance on interdependent critical infrastructure systems; the range of threats these systems face, the rise in cyber espionage, and the growing dependence all consumers have on a small group of equipment providers.

4.1.1 Complexity of Network Configuration

Effective and efficient configuration of networks has been widely recognized as a grand challenge [97]. It is a challenge to analyze how settings in the configuration space impact functionality and security. Misconfigurations are prevalent and can have a dramatic impact. For example, one misconfigured router in AS 9121 (Autonomous System in Turkey) resulted in misdirected/lost traffic for tens of thousands of networks [105]. In real-world systems, the size of configurations is large and can easily reach thousands of lines of commands in each router, while there are hundreds to thousands of routers in a large network. Finally, network configurations are decomposed in multiple routers as in distributed programs, and these distributed pieces are dependent upon one another. Configuring routers is a tedious, error-prone and complex task. The paper [125] presents a quantitative study of configuration errors in 37 firewalls.

In addition to the complexity of managing a network of firewalls, the process of ensuring their correctness is even more complicated due to subtle interactions between firewall configurations and the dynamics of routing. Configuration problems occur between firewalls of different devices placed along a network path, and such a distributed problem might surface only in a particular routing state. To detect such inconsistencies, there is a need to consider routing as well as firewall configurations. Particularly in a large, growing network with a complex topology, keeping track of all of the possible sets of routes can be extremely time-consuming and inaccurate.

The complexity of the configuration process is analogous to distributed assembly programs [47, 77, 97]. For example, the behavior of inter-domain routing policy configurations could be modeled as a program flow graph similar to the way a compiler models a program. This graph represents the way routes are advertised according to the routing policy configurations in a network. The program flow graph can be used to do what-if scenario testing for any pending changes to a configuration.

4.2 Risk: Industrial Control Systems

Those living in developed industrialized nations tend to take modern-day conveniences for granted. Flip a light switch, and the home illuminates. Turn on the tap, and clean water flows. It all happens routinely, without a hiccup. Now imagine a world where the delivery of sustained services is interrupted. Suddenly there is no clean water, or electric power disappears. The effects of such failures can be disastrous. How could such disasters happen? Industrial controls systems (ICS), the backbone of such services, can be attacked. Threats to ICS can come from numerous sources, including adversarial sources such as hostile governments, terrorist groups, industrial spies, disgruntled employees, malicious intruders, and natural sources such as from system complexities, human errors and accidents, equipment failures and natural disasters. The term "ICS," as used throughout this section, includes Supervisory Control and Data Acquisition (SCADA) systems.

On August 17, 2009, at the Sayano–Shushenskaya hydroelectric power station in Russia, excessive vibration caused a 920 ton turbine to break apart, flooding the facility, killing 75 people, and causing a power grid failure. It happened because the control software designed to shut down the turbine in the event of excessive vibration did not work. While commenting on the accident, General Keith B. Alexander, commander of U.S. Cyber Command noted that we are living in a time where such a deadly incident could also happen as a result of a cyber attack [48].

The December 2016 attack on the Ukrainian power grid points to the use of Win32/Industroyer, an advanced piece of devastating malware targeted at an ICS. Industroyer is considered the biggest threat to ICS since Stuxnet [42, 60]. Industroyer is highly customizable malware. It is universal, in that it can be used to attack any ICS using some of the targeted communication protocols. For example, its wiper component and one of the payload components are tailored for use against systems incorporating certain industrial power control products by ABB, and the DoS component works specifically against Siemens SIPROTECT devices used in electrical substations and other related fields of application [60].

Industroyer is modular malware (Fig. 1). Its core component is a backdoor used by attackers to manage the attack: it installs and controls the other components and connects to a remote server to receive commands and to report to the attackers.

What sets Industroyer apart from other malware targeting infrastructure is its use of four payload components, which are designed to gain direct control of switches and circuit breakers at an electricity distribution substation. Each of these components targets particular communication protocols specified in the following standards: IEC 60870-5-101, IEC 60870-5-104, IEC 61850, and OLE for Process Control Data Access (OPC DA).

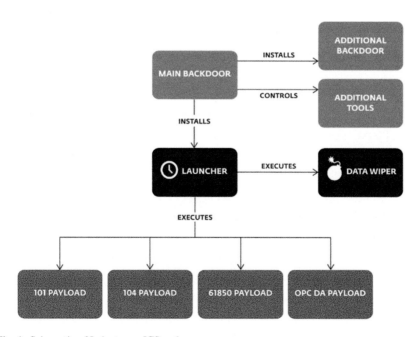

Fig. 1 Schematic of Industroyer ICS malware

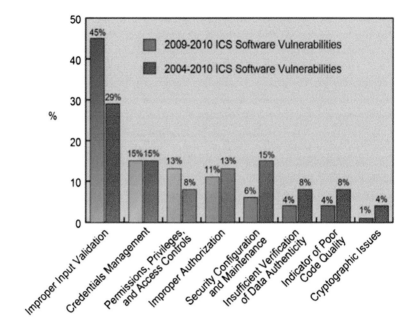

Fig. 2 Changing landscape of ICS security vulnerabilities

Industroyer's dangerousness lies in the fact that it uses protocols in the way they were designed to be used. The problem is that these protocols were designed decades ago, and back then industrial systems were meant to be isolated from the outside world. Thus, their communication protocols were not designed with security in mind. That means that the attackers did not need to look for protocol vulnerabilities; all they needed was to teach the malware "to speak" those protocols.

The U.S. Department of Homeland Security (DHS) National Cyber Security Division's Control Systems Security Program (CSSP) performs cybersecurity assessments of ICS to reduce risk and improve the security of ICS and their components used in critical infrastructures throughout the United States [39].

Most ICS began as proprietary, stand-alone collections of hardware and software that were walled off from the rest of the world and isolated from most external threats. Today, widely available software applications, Internet-enabled devices and other non-proprietary IT offerings have been integrated into most such systems. This connectivity has delivered many benefits, but it also has increased the vulnerability of these systems. Figure 2 shows the changing landscape of ICS security vulnerabilities based on data from DHS Cybersecurity Report [39]. It shows that the improper input validation vulnerabilities (e.g., buffer overflow) have gone down from 45% to 29%; whereas, the security configuration and maintenance vulnerabilities have shown a major up rise from 6% to 15%.

Cybersecurity Evaluation Tool (CSET) from DHS is a desktop software tool that guides users through a step-by-step question and answer process to collect facility-specific control and enterprise network information. CSET is a self-assessment software standards application for performing cybersecurity reviews of industrial control and enterprise network systems. The tool may be used by any organization to assess the cybersecurity posture of ICS that manage a physical process or enterprise network. The tool also provides information that assists users in resolving identified weaknesses in their networks and improving their overall security posture.

The NIST Guide to Industrial Control Systems Security [79] discuss three broad categories of ICS incidents including intentional attacks, unintentional consequences or collateral damage from worms, viruses or control system failures, and unintentional internal security consequences, such as inappropriate testing of operational systems or unauthorized system configuration changes. The NIST report discusses examples of intentional attacks such as Stuxnet[31] and Maroochy Shire Sewage Spill [115], and also examples of unintentional consequences such as Davis-Besse [106] and the Northeast Power Blackout [36].

Maroochy Shire Sewage Spill In the spring of 2000, a former employee of an Australian organization that develops manufacturing software applied for a job with the local government, but was rejected. Over a two-month period, the disgruntled rejected employee reportedly used a radio transmitter on as many as 46 occasions to remotely break into the controls of a sewage treatment system. He altered electronic data for particular sewerage pumping stations and caused malfunctions in their operations, ultimately releasing about 264,000 gallons of raw sewage into nearby rivers and parks.

Stuxnet Stuxnet is a Microsoft Windows computer worm discovered in July 2010 that specifically targets industrial software and equipment. The worm initially spreads indiscriminately, but includes a highly specialized malware payload that is designed to target only specific SCADA systems that are configured to control and monitor specific industrial processes.

Davis-Besse Nuclear Plant In August 2003, the Nuclear Regulatory Commission confirmed that in January 2003, the Microsoft SQL Server worm known as Slammer infected a private computer network at the idled Davis-Besse nuclear power plant in Oak Harbor, Ohio, disabling a safety monitoring system for nearly 5 h. In addition, the plant's process computer failed, and it took about 6 h for it to become available again. Slammer reportedly also affected communications on the control networks of at least five other utilities by propagating so quickly that control system traffic was blocked.

Northeast Power Blackout In August 2003, failure of the alarm processor in First Energy's SCADA system prevented control room operators from having adequate situational awareness of critical operational changes to the electrical grid. Additionally, effective reliability oversight was prevented when the state estimator at the Midwest Independent System Operator failed due to incomplete information on topology changes, preventing contingency analysis. Several key 345 kV transmission lines in Northern Ohio tripped due to contact with trees. This eventually initiated cascading overloads of additional 345 and 138 kV lines, leading to an uncontrolled cascading failure of the grid. A total of 61,800 MW load was lost as 508 generating units at 265 power plants tripped.

An IBM Report [88] published in 2015 looks at the history of ICS, the susceptibility of these systems to certain attacks, and how the systems can be defended. According to IBM Managed Security Services (MSS) data, attacks targeting ICS increased over 110% in 2016 [88]. Specifically, the spike in ICS traffic was related to SCADA brute-force attacks, which use automation to guess default or weak passwords. Once broken, attackers can remotely monitor or control connected SCADA devices. In January 2016, a penetration testing solution [22] containing a brute-force tool that can be used against Modbus [21], a serial communication protocol, was released. The public release and subsequent use of this tool by various unknown actors likely led to the rise in malicious activity against ICS in 2016 [88].

4.3   Risk: Vulnerable Mission-Critical Software

If a desktop operating system fails, the computer can be rebooted. If a flight control system fails, it can be a disaster with no chance to reboot the system. Malfunctioning of mission-critical software results in serious impact on business operations or upon an organization, and even can cause social turmoil and catastrophes. Mission-critical software drives online banking systems, railway/aircraft operating and control systems, electric power systems, and many other computer systems that adversely affect business and society when they fail.

There are four different types of critical systems: mission critical, business critical, safety critical and security critical. The key difference between a safety critical system and a mission critical system, is that a safety critical system is a system that, if it fails, may result in serious environmental damage, injury, or loss of life, while a mission critical system may result in failure in goal-directed activity. An example of a safety critical system is a chemical manufacturing plant control system. Mission critical system and business critical system are similar terms, but a business critical system fault can influence only a single company or an organization. A security critical system may lead to loss of sensitive data through theft or accidental loss.

4.3.1   Examples of Mission-Critical Software Flaws

Following are two concrete examples of mission-critical software to show how the nature and the code mechanics can vary significantly across flaws.

Ariane 5 Software Flaw On June 4, 1996 an unmanned Ariane 5 rocket launched by the European Space Agency exploded just forty seconds after lift-off. The rocket was on its first voyage, after a decade of development costing $7 billion. The destroyed rocket and its cargo were valued at $500 million. A board of inquiry investigated the causes of the explosion and in two weeks issued a report. It turned out that the cause of the failure was a software error in the inertial reference system. Specifically a 64 bit floating point number relating to the horizontal velocity of the rocket with respect to the platform was converted to a 16 bit signed integer. The number was larger than 32,767, the largest integer storeable in a 16 bit signed integer, and thus the conversion failed [98].

Apple SSL Flaw In February 2014, Apple published iOS 7.0.6, a security update for its mobile devices. The update was a patch to protect iPhones, iPads and iPods against what Apple described as a *data security* problem: an attacker with a privileged network position may capture or modify data in sessions protected by SSL/TLS. SSL stands for Secure Sockets Layer and, it is the standard technology for keeping an internet connection secure and safeguarding any sensitive data that is being sent between two systems, preventing criminals from reading and modifying any information transferred, including potential personal details. In short, the software layer for secure connection itself was flawed and became leaky. The flawed Apple SSL code segment is shown below.

```
.  .  .
hashOut.data = hashes + SSL_MD5_DIGEST_LEN;
hashOut.length = SSL_SHA1_DIGEST_LEN;
if ((err = SSLFreeBuffer(&hashCtx)) != 0)
    goto fail;
if ((err = ReadyHash(&SSLHashSHA1, &hashCtx)) != 0)
    goto fail;
if ((err = SSLHashSHA1.update(&hashCtx, &clientRandom))
      != 0)
    goto fail;
if ((err = SSLHashSHA1.update(&hashCtx, &serverRandom))
      != 0)
    goto fail;
if ((err = SSLHashSHA1.update(&hashCtx, &signedParams))
      != 0)
    goto fail;
    goto fail;   // Bug
if ((err = SSLHashSHA1.final(&hashCtx, &hashOut)) != 0)
    goto fail;

err = sslRawVerify(...);
.  .  .
```

The following quote from an analysis of the bug by the security firm Sophos [76] provides a concise summary of what went wrong.

The programmer is supposed to calculate a cryptographic checksum of three data items via the three calls to SSLHashSHA1.update(), and then to call the all important function sslRawVerify(). If sslRawVerify() succeeds, then err ends up with the value zero, which means "no error", and the SSLVerifySignedServerKeyExchange function returns to say, "all good." But in the middle of this code fragment, you can see that the programmer has accidentally (no conspiracy theories, please!) repeated the line "goto fail;". The first goto fail happens if the if statement succeeds, i.e. if there has been a problem and therefore err is non-zero. This causes an immediate "bail with error," and the entire TLS connection fails. But because of the peccadilloes of C, the second goto fail, which should not be there, always happens if the first one does not, i.e. if err is zero and there is actually no error to report. The result is that the code leaps over the vital call to sslRawVerify(), and exits the function. This causes an immediate "exit and report success," and the TLS connection succeeds even though the verification process has not actually taken place.

In short, the addition of second `goto fail;` statement following an `if` statement without curly braces indicates an unconditional control flow jump to the `fail` block making the code following the second `goto fail;` statement unreachable. The result was that critical signature checking code not executed, allowing invalid certificates to by quietly accepted as valid signatures. The bug went undetected for nearly a year, affecting both personal computers and mobile devices.

4.3.2 Dormancy of Mission-Critical Software Flaws

Flaws in mission-critical software can remain dormant and be silently exploited. The dormancy is especially troubling because the damage caused by the flaws can go undetected while the damage continues. In Apple SSL and Heartbleed examples the critical secure communication features themselves were flawed and caused serious confidentiality breaches without being noticed. In the Stuxnet example, the malware has actually two elements, the first one caused a confidentiality breach. The second element caused an integrity breach in the control system. The second malware element silently destroyed almost a fifth of Iran's reactors. The first malware element enabled espionage to learn the electrical blueprint of the reactors. And the first element of Stuxnet was only detected with the knowledge of the second.

The Apple SSL flaw appears to have been introduced in a code change made ahead of the launch of iOS 6.0. It became public and Apple released a fix 15 months later in iOS 7.0.6. The flaw also existed in Mac OS X and for which the fix came even later. Depending on who knew about it, it allowed connections to secure sites to be spied on and/or login details captured. In other words, all iOS and Mac OSX users were subject to a serious confidentiality breach for several months.

In his blog [114], the noted cybersecurity expert Bruce Schneier commented on the Heartbleed flaw "Catastrophic is the right word. On the scale of 1 to 10, this is an 11." The heartbleed attack allows an attacker to retrieve a block of memory of the server up to 64 kb in response directly from the vulnerable server via sending the malicious heartbeat and there is no limit on the number of attacks that can be performed. It opens doors for the cyber criminals to extract sensitive data directly from the server's memory without leaving any traces. An attacker can manage to obtain the private encryption key for an SSL/TLS certificate and could set up a fake website that passes the security verification. An attacker could also decrypt the traffic passing between a client and a server. Schneier blogged: "the probability is close to one that every target has had its private keys extracted by multiple intelligence agencies." It turned out that flawed code was inadvertently added on New Year's Eve in 2011 and the flaw was spotted in April 2014 [126].

The Stuxnet virus that ravaged Iran's Natanz nuclear facility "was far more dangerous than the cyberweapon that is now lodged in the public's imagination," as per cybersecurity expert Ralph Langer [90]. The exploit had a previous element that was much more complicated and "changed global military strategy in the twenty-first century," according to Langer. The lesser-known initial attack was designed to secretly "draw the equivalent of an electrical blueprint of the Natanz plant" to understand how the computers control the centrifuges used to enrich Uranium [111]. Only after years of undetected infiltration did the U.S. and Israel unleash the second variation to attack the centrifuges themselves and self-replicate to all sorts of computers.

The impact of the first virus was much greater. That attack provided a useful blueprint to future attackers by highlighting the royal road to infiltration of hard targets – humans working as contractors.

A recent report by the Citizen Lab [26] describes how Deep Packet Inspection (DPI) devices used by internet service providers have been misused to redirect hundreds of users in Turkey and Syria to nation-state spyware when those users attempted to download certain legitimate Windows applications. The report also describes how the DPI devices may have been used to hijack Egyptian Internet users' unencrypted internet connections en masse, and redirect the users to revenue-generating content. These misuses of DPI illustrate potential threats to human rights.

The somber reality is that at a global scale, pretty much every single industrial or military facility that uses ICS at some scale is dependent on its network of contractors. As one of the architects of the Stuxnet plan told [111]: "It turns out there is always an idiot around who doesn't think much about the thumb drive in their hand." Given that the next attackers may be terrorist organizations, civilian critical infrastructure becomes a troubling potential target. Most modern plants operate with a standardized industrial control system, so an attacker who gets control of one industrial control system can infiltrate dozens or even hundreds more of the same breed. While governments can work hard to secure their own mission-critical facilities, the attackers can target the defense contractors by planting malware in mission-critical systems they build for the government. As the Pentagon was in the final stages of formalizing a doctrine for military operations in cyberspace, big defense contractors Lockheed Martin, Northrop Grumman, and L-3 Communications were hit by cyberattacks [38]. These attacks suggest that intruders obtained crucial information, possibly the encryption seeds for SecurID tokens, that they used in targeted intelligence-gathering missions against sensitive U.S. targets. SecurID adds an extra layer of protection to a login process by requiring users to enter a secret code number in addition to their password. The number is cryptographically generated and changes every 30 s. The possible attack surface is extremely broad, it doesn't have to be intrusion through the corporate network; attackers can use a disgruntled employee to plant malware.

4.4   IoT Risk

It may have only taken one click on a link that led to the download of malware strains like WannaCry [35] to set off cascading global victims of the malware. It just shows that humans will always represent the soft underbelly of corporate defenses.

The Internet-of-Things (IoT) is going to make the security risk much worse. Connected devices are proliferating at a rate IT departments and security teams can't keep up with. They are manufactured with little oversight or regulatory control, and are all WiFi and Bluetooth-enabled. We may use Amazon Echos for convenience and productivity gain. However, such devices, designed to listen and transmit information, also introduce unquantifiable risks. Recent research [8] demonstrated that the Amazon Echo is susceptible to airborne attacks. Amazon has patched the vulnerabilities, but this finding demonstrates how easily a compromised device can lead to the leak of confidential information. Attacks are coming at businesses from all channels, with IoT creating a significantly larger attack surface. Businesses are likely to face a range of consequences, from brand damage to recovery costs and loss of customers in the face of breaches. The stakes are higher than ever to secure systems and networks.

The cyber-attack that brought down much of the Internet in the US in October 2016 was caused by a new weapon called the Mirai botnet and was likely the largest of its kind in history, experts said [13]. The cause of the outage was a distributed denial of service (DDoS) attack, in which a network of computers infected with special malware, known as a "botnet", are coordinated into bombarding a server with traffic until it collapses under the strain. The victim was the servers of Dyn, a company that controls much of the internet's domain name system (DNS) infrastructure. It was hit on 21 October 2016 and remained under sustained assault for most of the day, bringing down sites including Twitter, the Guardian, Netflix, Reddit, CNN and many others in Europe and the US.

What makes the Mirai botnet interesting is, the Mirai botnet is largely made up of so-called IoT devices such as digital cameras and DVR players. Because it has so many internet-connected devices to choose from, attacks from Mirai are much larger than what most DDoS attacks could previously achieve. Dyn estimated that the attack had involved *100,000 malicious endpoints*, and the company, which is still investigating the attack, said there had been reports of an extraordinary attack strength of 1.2 Tbps.

There is simply no way to rely on humans to avoid security breaches with IoT. IoT complicates matters further. Traditional solutions, such as training employees, will not mitigate the massive security challenge companies and government organizations are facing. The scope of IoT is far too complex for traditional security teams to manage with legacy solutions. There is much debate over the effectiveness of security and awareness training. It cannot be denied, however, that in the age of increased social-engineering attacks and unmanaged device usage, reliance on a human-based security strategy is questionable at best.

4.5   Critical Need: Software Assurance

Take a second look at the flawed Apple SSL code segment shown in Sect. 4.3.1. Is the unconditional "goto fail" a bug or malware? It could easily be an inadvertent cut and paste error. Or else, it could also be an intentionally planted line of code to enable espionage. Initially there was speculation that the Heartbleed flaw was deliberately created by government agencies to spy on citizens. Later, a developer came forward and confessed to causing the problem [25].

The real question is: *can we detect catastrophic software vulnerabilities – whether intentionally planted or not?* If we were to guard our reactors from Stuxnet, how could we have done that? There is no escape but to create the best possible technology to analyze mission-critical software to discover and confirm intentional malware or inadvertent vulnerability that could be catastrophic. But oddly enough, much of the activity that takes place under the guise of computer security is not really about solving security problems at all; it is about cleaning up the mess that security problems create. Virus scanners, firewalls, patch management, and intrusion detection systems are all means by which we make up for shortcomings in software security.

It is imperative to work software security as deeply into the development process as possible and taking advantage of the engineering lessons software practitioners have learned over the years. Two excellent books on secure programming [87, 117] advocate combining code review with static analysis tools and architectural analysis. The programming community tends to repeat the same security mistakes. Almost two decades of buffer overflow vulnerabilities serve as an excellent illustration of this point. In 1988, the Morris worm [23] made the Internet programming community aware that a buffer overflow could lead to a security breach, but as recently as 2004, buffer overflows were the number one cause of security problems cataloged by the Common Vulnerabilities and Exposures (CVE) Project [11].

Machine learning or completely automated static analysis are not adequate for software assurance. Unlike the widely studied malware in the wild, the catastrophic malware aimed at mission-critical systems is uniquely designed for a target and it can remain in a stealth mode until a trigger activates it. With uniquely designed malware, machine learning is futile. With difficult to track data and control flows [93] and state-space explosion [59], automated static analysis becomes significantly inaccurate and unscalable. While code reviews for known vulnerabilities are warranted and useful, they not an adequate solution for guarding mission-critical software from catastrophic vulnerabilities or malware that cannot be captured by signatures derived from known vulnerabilities. The complex design of catastrophic malware requires sophisticated modeling, analysis, and verification not addressed by the current automated static analysis tools [10, 19, 30] approach used for code review.

DoD Directive 3020.40 for the Defense Critical Infrastructure Program (DCIP) [14] defines Mission Assurance (MA) as "a process to ensure that assigned tasks or duties can be performed in accordance with the intended purpose or plan. It is a summation of the activities and measures taken to ensure that required capabilities and all supporting infrastructures are available to the DoD to carry out the National Military Strategy." In accordance with this directive, a principal responsibility of a commander is to assure mission execution in a timely manner. The reliance of a Mission Essential Function (MEF) on cyberspace makes cyberspace a center of gravity an adversary may exploit and, in doing so, enables that adversary to directly engage the MEF without the employment of conventional forces or weapons.

The paper *Science of Mission Assurance* [89] from the Air Force Research Laboratory (AFRL) introduces warfare in the cyber domain, identifies the weaknesses of the traditional approach to building reliable systems, and leads to an alternative approach that seeks to build secure systems. Engineering focuses traditionally on designing, developing, building, testing, and deploying complex systems that operate reliably in a permissive environment, but fail catastrophically in a contested environment. Mistaking reliability for security characterizes a generation of military, industrial, and financial systems that make little to no provision for functional vulnerability to cross-domain cyber threats. The ultimate goal of mission assurance is to develop an engineering culture that mathematically represents the specifications of a critical MEF and verifies its implementation. The paper [89] calls for a tool for reasoning on security properties and proving certain relationships among vulnerabilities and threats.

4.5.1   Software Assurance: Federal Research Programs

Software assurance and cybersecurity research and education projects are a top priority for several US Federal agencies including National Science Foundation (NSF), Department of Homeland Security (DHS), Army Research Office (ARO), Army Research Laboratory (ARL), Office of Naval Research (ONR), Naval Research Laboratory (NRL), Air Force Office of Scientific Research (AFOSR), Air Force Research Laboratory (AFRL), Defense Advanced Research Agency (DARPA), National Security Agency (NSA), and the National Institute of Standard and Technology (NIST).

DARPA has been at the forefront of funding projects to address software assurance in the context of sophisticated malware of particular interest to national defense. DARPA research played a central role in launching the Information Revolution. The agency developed and furthered much of the conceptual basis for the ARPANET prototypical communications network launched nearly half a century ago, and invented the digital protocols that gave birth to the Internet. The agency that brought us the Internet is working to secure it. To illustrate, we will briefly describe the goals of a few DARPA programs of particular interest to this survey topic.

Automated Program Analysis for Cybersecurity (APAC) Program This program aimed at developing new automated program analyses capable of proving that programs have security properties of interest to the Department of Defense (DoD), and to demonstrate those analyses in the form of tools designed specifically to keep malicious code out of DoD Android-based mobile application marketplaces [5].

Vetting Commodity IT Software and Firmware (VET) Program This program aimed at developing new techniques and tools for demonstrating the absence of backdoors and other hidden malicious functionality in the software and firmware shipped on commodity Information Technology (IT) devices. The VET program seeked to demonstrate that program analysis, coupled with updatable checklists of entries that each rule out broad classes of hidden malicious functionality, can provide a more effective proactive defense than that provided by present-day Anti-Malware products that use structural or behavior-based signatures to detect malware [41].

High Assurance Cyber Military Systems (HACMS) Program This program aimed at creating technology for development of high-assurance software for cyber-physical systems. HACMS called for a clean-slate, formal methods based approach that enables semi-automated code synthesis from executable, formal specifications. In addition to generating code, such a synthesizer is expected to produce a machine-checkable proof that the generated code satisfies the functional specification as well as security and safety policies [78].

Space/Time Analysis for Cybersecurity (STAC) Program This program aims to develop new program analysis techniques and tools for identifying vulnerabilities related to the space and time resource usage behavior of algorithms, specifically, vulnerabilities to algorithmic complexity and side channel attacks. STAC seeks to enable analysts to identify algorithmic resource usage vulnerabilities in software at levels of scale and speed great enough to support a methodical search for them in the software upon which the U.S. government, military, and economy depend [29].

DARPA programs typically involve Blue and Red teams and one White team. Blue teams develop the technology for high-assurance software. Red teams develop attacks to assess and in the process help to evolve the technology developed by the Blue teams. The White team coordinates the interactions between the Blue and Red teams and develops performance assessment measures. Over a period of 3–4 years about 100 or more highly sophisticated attacks are presented to the Blue teams in the form of on-site and off-site engagements. The progress is assessed with respect to the accuracy and scalability of techniques and tools developed by the Blue teams. Sometimes, there is also a control team that uses off-the-shelf tools for the purpose of comparison. Periodically, the tools developed by the Blue teams are delivered to the Red teams so that they understand the strengths and weaknesses of the tools and design new attacks to challenge the tools. Overall, it is a competitive environment to drive both the practical and theoretical advances in research. DARPA often seeks to develop practical tools that will not require PhDs to operate but can be used by a large work force of trained professionals.

4.6   Critical Need: Practical Tools and Cyberforce Training

It is important that the cybersecurity research leads to practical tools and education to train a cyberforce with the necessary thinking skills to use the tools effectively.

A skilled cybersecurity workforce is needed to meet the unique cybersecurity needs of critical infrastructure, enterprise, and operational technology systems and networks. In USA, the National Initiative for Cybersecurity Education (NICE) led by NIST is a partnership between government, academia, and the private sector working to energize and promote a robust network and an ecosystem of cybersecurity education, training, and workforce development [43]. As the threats to cybersecurity and the protections implemented grow and evolve, a cybersecurity workforce must be prepared to adapt, design, develop, implement, maintain, measure, and understand all aspects of cybersecurity.

4.6.1   Human-in-the-Loop Automated Analysis

Detecting catastrophic malware in mission-critical software is an extremely complex problem. As elaborated in the paper [93] we need tools that facilitate human-in-the-loop approach. Generally, an automated malware detection tool runs in three steps: (1) a human specifies the software to be analyzed and analysis parameters, (2) the tool runs on the input and outputs a report of potential anomalies in the software, (3) an analyst goes through the report. A tool is considered sound and complete if it reports all anomalies in the software with no false positives or false negatives. However, quite often it not possible to build a sound tool. Balancing coverage vs. accuracy in an analysis tool involves an inherent trade-off: one can list only true-positives (low coverage, high accuracy) or one can output all potential anomalies (high coverage, low accuracy). Achieving high coverage and high accuracy in a fully automated tool can be impossible or incur prohibitive cost in terms of implementing the automation and/or sifting through the large number of erroneous results manually.

To understand the need for a human-in-the-loop approach, let us classify the set of anomaly-prone scenarios into two groups: *ordinary* and *complex*. Ordinary scenarios correspond to the scenarios that are amenable to automation and do not pose extraordinary analysis challenges. On the contrary, complex scenarios are the ones that pose significant barriers to full automation. Even if automation for a complex scenario is possible, it may well be infeasible due to economics of time and effort. As summarized in Fig. 3, static analysis tools hit an *automation wall* and the cost for resolving complex scenarios escalates beyond the automation wall.

The human-in-the-loop analysis paper [93] advocates *Amplified Reasoning Technique* (ART) for analyzing software for complex malware. The ART philosophy is: Instead of resolving complex anomalies as definitive Yes/No answers through a fully automated tool, bring the human in a man-machine loop and use the tool to amplify human reasoning to resolve such anomalies faster and efficiently, so that it can be scaled to large software.

Fig. 3 Analysis cost
escalates beyond automation
wall

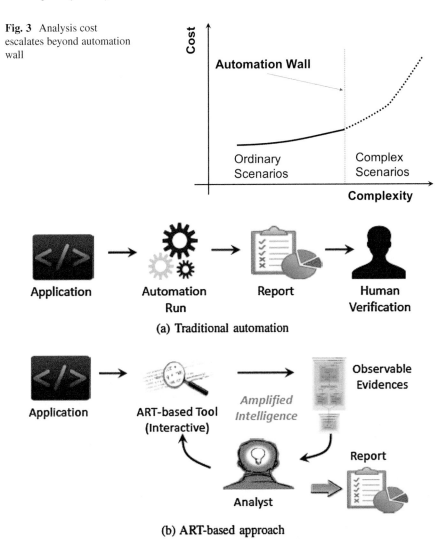

(a) Traditional automation

(b) ART-based approach

Fig. 4 Traditional automated malware analysis vs. ART

Figure 4 brings out the difference between the traditional approach to automation vs. the ART. In the traditional automation, the role of human is to sift through the false positives and unresolved cases generated from the automation run, and is segregated from the role played by the machine. Whereas, the ART puts the human and machine in an interactive loop.

Analyzing software for a zero-day mission-critical flaw (a kind of flaw that has never been seen before) is like looking for a needle in the haystack, but without knowing what the needle looks like. As we shall discuss later, the first step in detecting such a flaw requires us to develop plausible flaw hypotheses and then gather evidence to prove or refute each hypothesis. The open-ended task cannot be performed automatically. Developing plausible a hypothesis requires human intelligence and gathering knowledge about the software. Without a human-in-the-loop tool this task of gathering knowledge from software can be extremely time consuming and prone to human errors. Thus, human-in-the-loop tools are essential for detecting zero-day mission-critical software flaws.

4.6.2 Tools for Transparent Verification

Software verification is especially important in the context of CPS for critical applications, where failures have had catastrophic consequences. Verifying software is an important but daunting task with challenges of accuracy, scalability, and practicality. Formal verification of large software has been an elusive target, plagued with the problem of scalability [53, 59, 124]. Two fundamental limitations are: (1) a completely automated and accurate analysis required for formal verification encounters NP hard problems [61, 110, 120], and (2) formal verification methods work as automated black boxes with very little support for cross-checking [53, 75, 127].

The second limitation leads to issues that leave several practical needs unaddressed. Although the formal verification works as an automated black box, it requires an inordinate amount of preprocessing effort, involving a transformation from the software to the formal specification that can be checked automatically using a model checker or a SAT solver. This transformation is not automatic, it requires domain knowledge of the particular formal method and a lot of cumbersome human effort.

Besides the preprocessing, another serious issue is the lack of supporting evidence to be able to understand and use the results of formal verification. Without the evidence, it is not possible to use formal verification as a certification apparatus, or to integrate formal methods in a development environment. As we shall exemplify, it is quite hard for the user to know that the verification result is wrong without supporting evidence. We will present an empirical study to elaborate the notion of evidence and its importance in practice.

Leaning on visionary papers [55, 73] by Turing Award recipients, the paper [92] explores the question: "What advances in formal methods would it take to meet the practical needs?" The paper [92] presents empirical study that provides deep insights into some of the state of the art formal verification methods. The study uses the Linux Driver Verification tool (LDV) [53] which has been the top Linux device driver verification tool in the software verification competition (SV-COMP) [51]. The study includes three versions of the Linux operating system with altogether 37 MLOC and 66,609 verification instances. Each instance involves verifying that a Lock is followed by Unlock on all feasible execution paths. Running LDV on these Linux versions yields the result that pairing is correct for 43,766 (65.7)% of Lock instances. LDV is inconclusive on 22,843 instances, i.e. either the tool crashes or it times out. LDV does not find any instance with incorrect pairing. LDV does not provide evidence to support its results except for the instances where the verification reveals a bug.

5   Difficulties of Detecting CPM

It has been hard to be proactive to stop adversaries from mounting new CPM attacks. The core difficulty of detecting CPM lies in the open-ended possibilities for malware triggers and payloads, the subtle boundary between "malicious" and "legitimate," the obfuscation and other ways to impede program comprehension that is necessary to detect malware. Fundamentally, the challenges of detecting sophisticated CPM stem from the complexities inherent in the software itself.

It is almost impossible to improve software security merely by improving quality assurance. In practice, most software quality efforts are geared toward testing program functionality. Most software testing is aimed at comparing the implementation to the requirements, and this approach is inadequate for finding security problems. Imagine testing a piece of software by running down the list of requirements and making sure the implementation fulfills each one. It will miss many security problems because security problems are often not violations of the requirements. Instead, security problems are frequently "unintended functionality" that cause the program to be insecure.

To begin with, the key difficulty is to first hypothesize possibilities for malware. Software theorists are after executable specifications, automated model checking, and theorem proving in order to verify software. Software practitioners are after perfecting the art of penetration testing. How can the theorists or the practitioners effectively apply their knowledge to CPM? If we were to use today's software verification tools based on Formal Methods (FMs) to verify the GPS software, how do we decide what to prove?

5.1   GPS Malware: An Illustrative Example

Detecting CPM requires the knowledge of *malware triggers* and *malware payloads*. Malware payload refers to the part of the software that, when executed, actually causes the damage. Malware trigger refers to the conditional part of the software that, when the condition is met, the execution follows a control flow path with the malware payload. Thus, malware is only activated when properly triggered. Code paths implementing malicious behaviors are executed only when certain trigger conditions are met.

Imagine a GPS device that works accurately, except it malfunctions in Afghanistan on full moon days. No matter how exhaustive the reliability testing is in their Kansas City factory, the GPS manufacturer will not catch mission-critical malware that malfunctions only in a certain geographical region. Figure 5 shows a code snippet for the malware. The conditional part of the software that enacts the trigger is shown in a box and the geographic region it specifies is shown to the right. The malware payload consists of the `location.setlongitude()` and `location.setlatitude()` calls that result in malicious modification of the

```
@Override
public void onLocationChanged(Location tmpLoc) {
    location = tmpLoc;
    double latitude = location.getLatitude();
    double longitude = location.getLongitude();
    if((longitude >= 62.45 && longitude <= 73.10) &&
        (latitude >= 25.14 && latitude <= 37.88)) {
        location.setLongitude(location.getLongitude() + 9.252);
        location.setLatitude(location.getLatitude() + 5.173);
    }
    ...    Small malicious code in a large Android app.
}           This is an example of integrity breach.
```

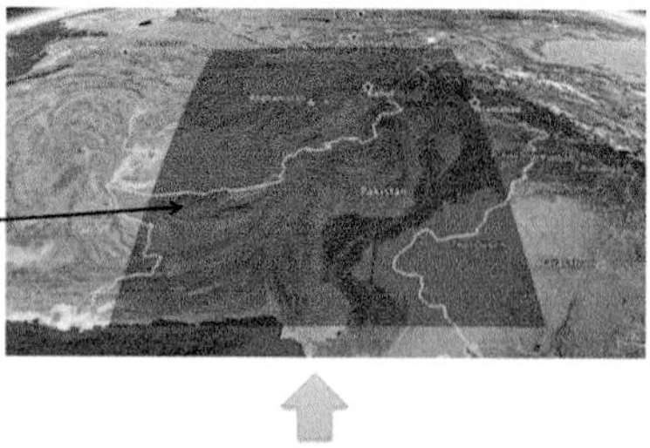

Region that triggers the malware

Fig. 5 GPS malware with obscure trigger

longitude and latitude information when the GPS device operates in the particular geographic region. We shall use this malware example to illustrate why it is hard to detect CPM.

5.2 Why it Is Difficult to Detect CPM

In contrast to the limited triggers for traditional computer malware, the sensor inputs lead to open-ended possibilities for CPM triggers. The traditional malware is limited by typical inputs to a computer such as the keyboard, file, or mouse etc. Moreover, inputs are explicit and can be associated with a short list of program artifacts such as `read` or `get` statements. Thus, traditional computer malware can be detected by auditing such statements. For example, the size of the input can be checked to avoid the buffer overflow attack. CPM detection becomes tricky because of sensory inputs, as the physical environment itself can be the input, not just the user input. For example, the geographic region is the input for the GPS malware.

Currently, trigger-based malware analysis is often performed in a tedious, manual fashion. The paper [56] on automatically identifying trigger-based malware states that there is no previous work on automating trigger-based malware analysis. It discusses integration of techniques from formal verification, symbolic execution, binary analysis, and whole-system emulation and dynamic instrumentation to enable automatic identification and analysis of trigger-based behaviors in malware. Even when complete automatic analysis is not possible, they claim that their system still provides valuable information about potential trigger-based code paths which a human would otherwise have to discover manually.

Identifying trigger-based behaviors in malware is an extremely challenging task. The paper [56] considers trigger-based denial-of-service attacks. Attackers are free to make code arbitrarily hard to analyze. This follows from the fact that, at a high level, deciding whether a piece of code contains trigger-based behavior is undecidable, e.g., the trigger condition could be anything that halts the program. Thus, a tool that uncovers all trigger-based behavior all the time reduces to the *halting problem*.

In differentiating CPM from traditional malware, the difference really comes from the open-ended possibilities for malware triggers and payload. The open-ended possibilities are tied to the wide spectrum of sensor inputs and the almost limitless application-specific possibilities for designing the payloads. In the GPS malware, the payload is designed to corrupt the location information given to the user. In Stuxnet, the payload is designed to corrupt the behavior of the algorithm that controls the centrifuges. Both fall under the integrity breach according to CIA triad. However, the breaches are so application-specific that knowing that it is an integrity breach and the understanding of the breach in one application, hardly helps in hypothesizing the malware for the other application. In other words, the difficulty of detecting CPM is really the difficulty of open-ended possibilities.

The subtle boundary between "malicious" and "legitimate," is another difficulty that is exacerbated by the open-ended possibilities. Consider the GPS malware example. The modifications of latitude and longitude is per se not as malicious as GPS software that includes legitimate modifications. Significant domain knowledge about the application is often required to draw the boundary between "malicious" and "legitimate." In the case of the GPS malware the trigger region does hint at the possibility of malware.

6   Software Assurance: Fundamental Challenges

Fundamentally, the challenges of detecting sophisticated CPM stem from the complexities inherent in the software itself. Add to a simple calculator with arithmetic operations two features: *conditional computation* and *store and recall* and the calculator becomes a powerful Turing complete computer [109]. The first feature leads to the *control flow* (CF), and the second feature to the *data flow* (DF). The fundamental challenges of analyzing software stem from data and control flow.

6.1   Memory Leak: An Illustrative Example

This example is taken from XINU [66], a small operating system. It brings out the challenges of analyzing software to verify its safety and security properties. In this example, the problem is to verify that memory allocation is followed by deallocation on all feasible *control flow* (CF) paths. The allocation and deallocation system calls are respectively `getbuf` and `freebuf`.

The starting point is the `dswrite` function shown in Fig. 6a. Function `dswrite` calls `getbuf` but it does not call `freebuf`. The verification problem is to match the `getbuf` call in `dswrite` with the corresponding `freebuf` call(s) which would be in other functions.

As seen from the Fig. 6a, `dswrite` passes the allocated memory pointer `drptr` to function `dskenq`. As shown in Fig. 6b, `dskenq` has four CF paths. On path 1:

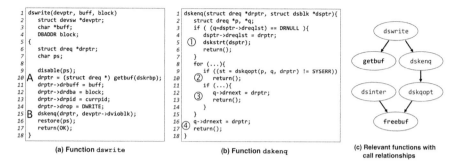

```
 1  dswrite(devptr, buff, block)              1  dskenq(struct dreq *drptr, struct dsblk *dsptr){
 2      struct devsw *devptr;                  2      struct dreq *p, *q;
 3      char *buff;                            3      if ( (q=dsptr->dreqlst) == DRNULL ){
 4      DBADDR block;                          4          dsptr->dreqlst = drptr;
 5  {                                          5 ①        dskstrt(dsptr);
 6      struct dreq *drptr;                    6          return();
 7      char ps;                               7      }
 8                                             8      for (...){
 9      disable(ps);                           9          if ((st = dskqopt(p, q, drptr) != SYSERR))
10 A   drptr = (struct dreq *) getbuf(dskrbp); 10 ②            return();
11      drptr->drbuff = buff;                  11         if (...){
12      drptr->drdba = block;                  12 ③           q->drnext = drptr;
13      drptr->drpid = currpid;                13             return();
14      drptr->drop = DWRITE;                  14         }
15 B   dskenq(drptr, devptr->dvioblk);        15 ④   q->drnext = drptr;
16      restore(ps);                           16     return();
17      return(OK);                            17 }
18  }                                          18
```

(a) Function `dswrite`   (b) Function `dskenq`   (c) Relevant functions with
                                                                   call relationships

Fig. 6 The importance of evidence to reason about the possibility of a memory leak in the function `dswrite`

`drptr` is passed to function `dskstrt` which does not free the allocated memory. But, we cannot conclude that it is a memory leak because on the same path `drptr` is assigned to `dsptr->dreqlst` where `dsptr` (passed as a parameter to `dskenq` from `dswrite`) points to a global linked list. On path 2: `drptr` is passed to function `dskqopt`. On paths 3 and 4: `drptr` is assigned to `q->drnext` and earlier `q` is set to points to `dsptr->dreqlst`. Thus, on three paths (1, 3 and 4) the allocated memory is not freed but the pointer to the allocated memory is inserted in a global linked list. The `dskenq` code snippet in Fig. 6 is incomplete; only the relevant parts are shown.

Since the pointer to the allocated memory gets passed as a parameter to other functions, the call chains must be tracked. Moreover, one path in `dswrite` multiplies into 4 paths in `dskenq` and the path proliferation continues through functions down the call chain. Analyzing the call chains and the proliferation of paths is tedious and challenging.

Even more challenging is to analyze the part where the pointer to the allocated memory is assigned to a global linked list. Since the memory pointer is accessible through a global variable, any function could access that pointer and free the memory. Do we then examine and verify all functions? It would be a huge verification challenge.

The reality is, only `dswrite`, `dskenq`, `dskqopt`, `dsinter` are the relevant functions to be analyzed to reason about this memory leak example. The verification can be completed by analyzing just these functions. The call relationships among these functions are shown in Fig. 6c. Starting with the allocation in `dswrite`, all the CF paths go through `dskenq`, and `dskqopt`. One of the two things happen on these CF paths: (a) the `getbuf` calls in `dskqopt` deallocate memory, or (b) the pointer to the allocated memory is assigned to a global linked list. The function `dsinter`, an interrupt-driven function, gets called asynchronously. It goes through the linked list and deallocates the memory for each pointer in the list until the list becomes empty. We can thus verify that there is no memory leak. We will use this example to exemplify each fundamental challenge listed in the next subsection. The challenge is how to discover the relevant functions efficiently. Without such discovery, we are faced with examining all functions.

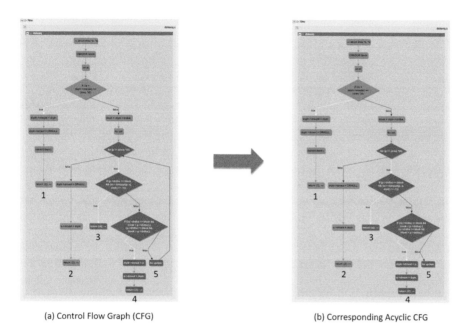

(a) Control Flow Graph (CFG)   (b) Corresponding Acyclic CFG

Fig. 7 Counting CF paths with CFG and associated acyclic CFG

6.2 Explosion of Execution Behaviors

Verifying a safety or security property usually requires analysis of all paths. That can make software assurance computationally intractable. An IF statement creates two paths where as a function call expands a path into m paths where m is the number of paths in the function. With b non-nested conditions, the number of paths is 2^b.

Let us illustrate how the computational intractability is exacerbated by program loops. The *control flow graph* (CFG) for the function dskenq shows one loop (Fig. 7a). The *loop header*, the entrance to the loop, is the first reachable node shaded dark blue in the figure. The loop-back edge is colored blue and the true and false branches are shown by white and black edges respectively. The loop has three **termination nodes,** defined as the nodes that have a successor that is outside the loop body. The loop header is one of the termination nodes and it is referred to as the *normal termination node*. Other termination nodes due to break or return are referred to as *exceptional termination nodes*. The loop has two such termination nodes due to return. The paths from those termination nodes lead to the return statements marked 3 and 4 in Fig. 7a.

The loop behaviors can be computed as iterations of *base behaviors* of a loop. Each base behavior corresponds to one iteration of a loop. The base behavior is the sequence of program statements executed during one iteration of the loop. The base behaviors for loops are partitioned into: (a) *normal base behaviors* (B^N) – the behaviors along the paths that terminate at the normal termination point, and (b) *exceptional base behaviors* (B^E) – the behaviors along the paths that terminate at the exceptional termination points.

An **iterative behavior** is a sequence of base behaviors of length i, where i is a positive integer representing the number of iterations of a loop. For $i > 0$ iterations, n normal base behaviors, e exceptional base behaviors, the number of iterative behaviors is: ($n^i + e \times n^{i-1}$) with (n^i) iterative behaviors that do not end with an exceptional base behavior, and ($e \times n^{i-1}$) iterative behaviors with $i - 1$ iterations of normal base behaviors followed by a final iteration of an exceptional base behavior. Note that the exceptional behavior can only be at the end because the loop is terminated after the exceptional behavior.

The base behaviors can be discerned by breaking the loop-back edges to create an acyclic graph. Figure 7a shows the CFG with a loop and Fig. 7b shows the corresponding acyclic graph. These graphs are generated by using the path counter tool built using Atlas [71]. The layouts are different but the correspondence between the CFG and its associated acyclic graphs are shown by numbering the corresponding `return` nodes. The node numbered 5 is interesting. It is the tail of the loop-back edge in Fig. 7a. It is a leaf node in the acyclic graph representing the normal base behavior. The normal base behavior is the sequence of program statements from the loop header to the node numbered 5. The exceptional base behaviors are the sequences of program statements from the loop header to the nodes numbered 3 and 4 respectively. Thus, we have one normal base behaviors B_1^N and two exceptional base behaviors B_1^E and B_2^E.

The maximum number of normal base behaviors for a loop is $n = 2^b$, where b is the number of branch nodes in the loop body. Then, a successive exponentiation is due to iterations of a loop. Suppose the acyclic graph of a loop has n normal base behaviors and e exceptional base behaviors, then for i iterations, it has ($n^i + e \times n^{i-1}$) iterative behaviors. The double exponentiation leads to utter intractability if a brute force approach were to be applied to reason about software safety and security problems that require analysis behaviors on all paths. The number of behaviors is bigger than the number of atoms in the universe if we have a loop with just 5 non-nested IF conditions and 50 iterations.

The exponentiality of paths coupled with explosion due to iterative behaviors are the root problems that go by various names in software analysis and verification literature. For example, Clarke et al. [63] discuss the state explosion problem for model checking. Model checking is an automatic verification technique for concurrent systems that are finite state or have finite state abstractions. Model checking is a collection of automatic techniques for verifying finite-state concurrent systems. This framework was developed independently in the early 1980s by Clarke and Emerson [62] and by Queille and Sifakis [107, 108]. It has been used successfully to verify computer hardware, and it is beginning to be used to verify computer software as well. As the number of state variables in the system increases, the size of the system state space grows exponentially. This is called the *state explosion problem*. Much of the research in model checking over the past 40 years has involved developing techniques for dealing with this problem. The behavior associated with each path creates a set of states. As the number of paths grows exponential, so does the totality of states associated with those paths. The iterative behaviors, as discussed here, cause a successive explosion. Thus the state explosion problem is rooted in explosion of behaviors.

6.3   Computational Intractability of Path Feasibility

Given a description of a set of control flow paths through a procedure, feasible path analysis (FPA) determines if there are appropriate input values that would cause execution to flow down some path in the collection [82]. If no input values can cause the program to be executed along a path, we say that the path is *infeasible* or *non-executable*. In the context of software testing, feasibility analysis plays an important role in identifying testing requirements which are infeasible. In software assurance, the analysis may find a path with a safety or security vulnerability. Declaring it to be an actual vulnerability becomes a false positive if the path is not feasible.

FPA is central to most applications of program analysis. But, because this problem is formally unsolvable, syntactic-based approximations are used in its place. For example, the dead-code analysis problem is to determine if there are any input values which cause execution to reach a specified program point. The approximation determines whether there is a control flow path from the start of the program to the program point of interest . This syntactic approximation is efficiently computable and conservative: if there is no such path the program point is clearly unreachable, but if there is such a path, the analysis is inconclusive, and the code is assumed to be live. Such conservative analysis too often yields unsatisfactory results because the approximation is too weak.

Feasible path analysis requires both symbolic analysis [91] and theorem proving [50]. Symbolic analysis relates expressions occurring at different program points and theorem proving determines the validity of logical relations between expressions. A popular approach is to use *constraint solvers* – firstly extract a set of constraints from the given path, and then solve the constraints [129]. Given a path, we can obtain a set of constraints called *path predicates* or *path governing conditions*. After the path conditions are obtained, we need to decide whether they are satisfiable or not. For satisfiable conditions, we often have to find the variables' values to satisfy them. The path is feasible if and only if these conditions are satisfiable.

A Constraint Satisfaction Problem (CSP) [99] consists of a set of variables, each of which can take values from some domain. In addition, there are some constraints defined on the variables. Solving a CSP means finding a value for each variable, such that all the constraints hold. Obviously, CSP represents a very general class of problems. Special cases of interest in software analysis are: *linear inequalities as constraints* and *Boolean satisfiability*.

A Boolean variable can only be assigned some truth value (TRUE or FALSE). A Boolean formula is constructed from a set of Boolean variables using the logical operators AND (i.e., conjunction), OR (i.e., disjunction), etc. A literal is a variable or its negation. The disjunction of a set of literals is a clause. A Boolean formula can be transformed into a conjunction of clauses. If we can assign a truth value to each variable such that the whole formula evaluates to TRUE, then the formula is said to be satisfiable. If the formula is in conjunctive normal form (CNF), i.e., it is a conjunction of clauses, the problem is well-known as SAT. This is the first NP-hard problem [81].

6.4 Difficult to Analyze Programming Constructs

As noted earlier, two simple but powerful programming constructs: *conditional computation* and *store and recall* are at the heart of a Turing-complete computation model. Modern programming languages have added new programming constructs to enable paradigms such as: structured programming, object-oriented programming, collections (e.g., structures, arrays, etc.), and dynamic binding.

These new programming constructs have their benefits, but they create new complexity beyond the two fundamental challenges we have discussed. The complexity arises from inter-dependencies between data and control flows created by these programming constructs. We view it as *indirect* and *invisible* flows that complicate program comprehension and also make automated program analysis difficult.

6.4.1 Indirect Control Flow

Control Flow (CF) is about the order in which program statements are executed. The ability to modify control flow enables the construction of program loops and provides the ability to create multiple execution behaviors. CF artifacts such as the IF statement or a function call modify the linear order in which program statements are executed. The CF artifacts provide the capability to create different execution behaviors in software.

We use the term direct control flow to refer to flow created by program constructs IF and function call that directly specified that flow, i.e. no computation is needed to discern the flow. This is not the case with *indirect control*. Take the case of dynamic binding in C as exemplified by a device driver call in XINU:

```
SYSCALL write(descrp, buff, count)
        int descrp, count;
        char *buff;
        {
                struct devsw *devptr;
```

```
        if (isbaddev(descrp))
            return(SYSERR);
        devptr = &devtab[descrp];
        return((*devptr->dvwrite)(devptr,buff,
count));
    }
```

The function `write` calls a function `(*devptr->dvwrite)(devptr,buff,count)` using a function pointer. To compute the control flow at the callsite, we must identify the called function. However, we need to compute data flow to do so. We have a complex dependency: to compute the control flow we need to compute the data flow. In turn, to compute the data flow we always need control flow. Moreover, depending on the path by which arrive to the `write` call, the function called through the function pointer could be different. In essence, the function pointer call creates a branch point at the callsite and adds further complexity to the fundamental challenge of explosion of behaviors.

We use the term *indirect control flow* to refer to function calls that require computing data flow to identify the called function.

The object-oriented languages employ *type hierarchy* for the indirect control flow. For example, to identify the function called by `o.f(x)`. A data flow computation is needed to determine the *type* of the object `o`. The called `f` is the one that is implemented for the determined *type*.

Another variety of indirect control flow stems from program constructs for handling exceptions. In Java, the `try` block contains set of statements where an exception can occur. A `try` block is always followed by a `catch` block or a `finally` block. The `catch` block handles the exception that occurs in the associated `try` block.

There are also specialized program constructs such as Android *intents*. An intent is a specialized data structure that is passed to signal dispatching logic to change an application's control flow from executing one component to another within the Android framework. Depending on the intent, apps or the OS might be listening for it and will react accordingly. Think of it as a blast email to a bunch of friends, in which you tell your friend John to do something, or to friends who can do X (intent filters), to do X. The other folks will ignore the email, but John (or friends who can do X) will react to it. To listen for a broadcast intent (like the phone ringing, or an SMS is received), broadcast receiver is implemented, to which the intent will be passed [1, 2].

The indirect control flow is used rampantly in object-oriented languages. The Object class, in the java.lang package, sits at the top of the class hierarchy tree. Everyclass is a descendant, direct or indirect, of the Object class. Every class you use or write inherits the instance methods of Object. Accurate static analysis is often unnecesarily complex as a result. In contrast, the C developers employ function pointers only when their use makes good sense. We did a quick sampling of Linux and XINU builds using Atlas [71] queries to find call sites that use function pointers. Of the total 2,325,293 call sites in Linux 53,741 (2.3%) use function pointers. Of the total 1,007 call sites in XINU, 14 (1.4%) use function pointers.

Fig. 8 A Linux bug in
`drxk_gate_crtl` with
odd use of function pointers

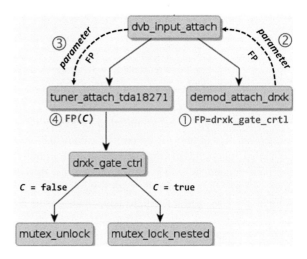

A Linux bug rooted in odd use of function pointers We present an example of a complex bug in a Linux device driver involving an odd use of function pointers. The bug is reported in our paper [92]. It shows a feasible path on which `Lock` is not followed by `Unlock`. A function `f1` is called using a function pointer. Oddly, it has dual use: serves as `Lock` or `Unlock` depending on whether its boolean parameter is `TRUE` or `FALSE`. The function has two control flow paths with `Lock` on one path and `Unlock` on the other path. The function is called twice on most paths except on one path which is the bug. This function with its dual use and its function pointer calls make it unnecessarily complex.

The lock and unlock are on disjoint paths in the function `drxk_gate_crtl` (`f1`) and if C = `true`, the lock occurs, otherwise, the unlock occurs. The lock and unlock can match if `f1` is called twice, first with C = `true` and then with C = `false`. An Atlas query shows that `f1` is not called directly anywhere. Thus, it is either dead code or `f1` is called using a function pointer.

Resolving indirect control due to function pointers, we find the scenario shown in Fig. 8. The function `tuner_attach_tda18271` (`f2`) calls the function `f1` via function pointer. `demo_attach_drxk` sets the function pointer to `f1`, the pointer is communicated by parameter passing to `dvb_input_attach`, then to `f2`.

Recall that `f1` must be called twice. The function `f2` has a path on which there is a return before the second call to `f1` and thus it is a bug.

6.4.2 Indirect Data Flow

Data flow is about the *store and recall* in a program. The data flow artifacts include assignment statements, function parameters, function returns, local variables, and global variables, object or structure fields, and pointers to objects or structures. The ability to flow data enables the construction of multi-part programs where different parts can share their computations. One part (control block or function) can compute and store the result and another part of the program can recall the stored result.

Direct data flow is through assignment of variables. Data flows from variable y to variable x through assignment $x=y$. The direct data flow is directly computed by tracking assignments. The data can flow through multiple assignments, but that by itself is not a major difficulty and the Def-Use (DU) Use-Def (UD) chains are used respectively to track the *forward* and *backward* data flow [46].

Indirect data flow is the data flow through a function or a field of a structure. The *indirect data flow through a function* can be further divided into three categories: (a) parameter assignment, (b) function return, and (c) assignment to a global variable. The analysis difficulty increases from (a) to (c). In (a) the data flows into a specified function f. In (b), the data returned by the function f can flow any of its callers. In (c), the data assigned to a global variable by a function f can be accessed by any other function.

Indirect data flow through an object or structure field creates the complexity of *backward flow* as exemplified here:

```
1.  Lock(x);
2.  O1.a = O2;
3.  O2.b = x;
4.  y = O1.a.b;
5.  Unlock(y);
```

The assigned x in Line 3 flows back through the assignment in Line 2 and thus `Unlock(y)` is actually `Unlock(x)`.

6.4.3 Invisible Control Flow

Unlike *direct* or *indirect*, the invisible control flow change is not specified by any visible program artifact. Instead, an interrupt causes the change. In case of *indirect*, the callee is not directly specified but it can be computed. In case of *invisible*, neither the callee nor the program point (a statement in the program) for control change is specified. The added uncertainty of the program point makes analysis of invisible control flow even more difficult. The invisible flow is illustrated by our earlier memory leak example (Fig. 6):

1. Memory is allocated by invoking `getbuf` inside the function `dswrite`. The memory is allocated for a structure of type `dreq`. The `drptr` pointer to the allocated memory is passed to other functions and eventually it is inserted in a globally shared linked list with the code `dsptr->dreqlst = drptr`.
2. The function `dsinter` gets `drptr`, and deallocates memory with the code `drptr = dsptr->dreqlst` followed by `freebuf(drptr)`.

The function `dsinter` is interrupt-driven. It is not linked by a call chain to `dswrite` which allocates memory. The `drptr` pointer to the allocated memory is communicated through a global linked list `dsptr->dreqlst`.

In invisible control, interacting program parts are not linked by control flow. They act asynchronously and communicate through a shared object.

6.4.4   Invisible Data Flow

Invisible data flow occurs when an individual variable or a pointer becomes part of a collection, looses its individual identity and cannot be tracked individually.

The invisible flow is illustrated by our earlier memory leak example (Fig. 6). In `dsptr->dreqlst = drptr`, the `drptr` pointer to the allocated memory becomes part of a linked list. In fact, this linked list contains pointers to allocated memory in different functions, not just `dswrite`.

Pointer analysis attempts to determine the set of objects to which a pointer can point (called the points-to set of the pointer). Unfortunately, these analysis are necessarily approximate (since a perfectly precise static analysis amounts to solving the halting problem). Pointer analyses have difficulty analyzing invisible data flow precisely. In order to determine points-to sets, a pointer analysis must be able to name a program's objects. In invisible flow instances, programs can allocate an unbounded number of objects; but in order to terminate, a pointer analysis can only use a finite set of names.

7   Research Directions

We shall discuss new research directions in terms of: (a) threat modeling to hypothesize CPM, (b) analyzing software to gather evidence based on a CPM hypothesis, and (c) verifying to prove or refute a hypothesis based on gathered evidence.

7.1   Threat Modeling

Security threat modeling is often studied and applied for specifying security requirements during application development [87, 117]. There is however paucity of established techniques and tools for threat modeling and analysis [102]. Ongoing work at the Open Web Application Security Project (OWASP) organization includes several resources for threat modeling [44].

A different view of threat modeling is pertinent in the context of catastrophic malware that has never been seen before. Searching for such malware is like looking for a needle in the haystack not knowing what the needle looks like. The OWASP [44] notes that threat modeling is a complex endeavor that involves drawing trust boundaries. How does one draw trust boundaries in software? Drawing boundaries with respect to known exploits is doable, but doing so with unknown exploits is uncharted territory requiring new research. Threat modeling is important for the following reasons.

- Without the threat model as a powerful abstraction, we are left to deal with an endless variety of problems. For example, without the abstraction of variables and the linear system of equations, there is an endless variety of constraint-satisfaction problems. Similarly, without effective modeling of CPM, we have an endless variety of physical systems as well as their varied malfunctions.
- Threat modeling with appropriate rigor is a crucial prerequisite for efficient analysis and verification of CPM. A powerful abstraction is necessary to avoid ad-hoc and inefficient solutions. For example, the abstraction of linear system of equations has enabled the powerful Gauss and Jacobi methods that scale to extremely large constraint satisfaction problems encountered in science and engineering. Similarly, modeling is a necessity to design efficient and accurate algorithms to analyze and verify CPM.

In detecting novel CPM, the first challenge for a human analyst is the open-ended search for plausible hypotheses of malicious behavior. The space of hypotheses can be arbitrarily large for a given app. With no prior knowledge of an app's malicious behavior, the analyst has to rely on a general model such as the CIA model [69] to systematically explore hypotheses for malicious behaviors. As examples from Android apps, an analyst may consider hypotheses for confidentiality leaks (e.g., GPS location is leaked to an adversary), integrity breaches (e.g., incorrect GPS location is displayed in some geographic locations), or denial of service (e.g., malware runs loops to drain the device battery) attacks enabled by unscrupulous use of Android APIs. However, this can still be prohibitively expensive, as there may be numerous potential CIA hypotheses to explore for a given app.

Hypothesizing a vulnerability amounts to specializing the CIA model by coming up with specific events and rules surrounding the events to specify a breach. To precisely explore only the relevant CIA hypotheses, it is critically important for the analyst to visualize and understand the data and control flow interactions between the app and the Android components it uses. For example, knowing that an app interacts with the hardware and messaging APIs via data flow leads to the hypothesis that it may leak camera images by sending them as attachments with messages. Coming up with a good CPM hypothesis is a highly creative activity requiring human intelligence at its best. Based on our experience of hypothesizing malware in DARPA programs, we have found the following research directions particularly useful:

Automated Exploration The purpose is to identify and characterize relevant program artifacts. It requires research to determine what artifacts could be relevant. The relevant program artifacts are characterized with respect to a class of malware.

Automated Filters The purpose is to enable the analyst to quickly sift through relevant program artifacts to identify targets for formulating malware hypothesis. The analyst starts developing a hypothesis by experimenting with various filters.

7.2   DARPA Research: Threat Modeling

Our work on DARPA APAC and STAC projects is summarized here to exemplify the threat modeling research directions. The papers [49, 71, 72, 84, 85, 112, 113] describe our research related to threat modeling and the relevant toolboxes we have developed. These papers include research on interactive visualization and querying which analysts need, in order to understand complex software and gather relevant information during threat modeling.

7.2.1   Automated Exploration

Android Vulnerabilities The gathered information includes the data, control and exceptional flows within the app, the permissions granted to the app and the APIs used to exercise them, and program artifacts that use the Android resource files. The pre-computed information also includes the call and data flow interactions of the app with various Android *subsystems*. Subsystems are logical groupings of Android APIs according to the functionality they provide such as networking, storage device access, address book, and others. The interactions provide information about how the app interacts with Android components.

Side Channel Vulnerabilities Software side-channel vulnerabilities (SSCVs) allow an attacker to gather secrets by observing the differential in the time or space required for executing the program for different inputs. The possibilities are open-ended for the ways various program artifacts may be used to create side channels. Attackers exploit SSCVs by presenting a set of inputs and observing the space or time behaviors to construe the secret. The input could vary from HTTP requests to multiple log-in attempts depending on the application. The observable differential behaviors could be execution time, memory space, network traffic, or some output patterns of application-specific significance.

The paper [113] describes a three dimensional variability spectrum shown in Fig. 9 corresponding to fundamental SSCV attributes: entry points, potential secrets, and programming constructs or artifacts causing differential behavior. Adversaries use *entry points* to provide inputs to induce differential behaviors, *secret types* are the broad categories of secrets that adversaries target, and *observables* are the space or time program execution behaviors produced by control flow constructs in the code such as loops, branches and exceptions. The relevant artifacts are gathered by automated exploration. It is important to characterize relevant program artifacts and their specific attributes that define how the artifacts relate to the secret, how they create observable space/time behaviors, or how they create differential behaviors.

Algorithmic Complexity Vulnerabilities The *algorithmic complexity vulnerabilities* (ACVs) are about runtime space or time consumption of programs. Adversaries can exploit ACVs to mount denial of service attacks. For example, the denial of service commonly known as the "billion laughs attack" or an XML bomb, is caused

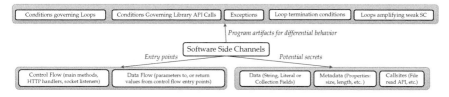

Fig. 9 Three variability dimensions of SSCVs

by an ACV in the application that creates a string of 10^9 concatenated "lol" strings requiring approximately 3 gigabytes of memory [68] when parsing a specially crafted input file less than a kilobyte. A recent study has characterized a class of ACVs in the Java library [74]. Similar to the XML bomb, it is a class of ACVs associated with the serialization and deserialization APIs.

The program artifacts that usually lead to ACVs include loops, recursion, or resource-intensive library APIs. Moreover, ACVs typically result from complex loop termination logic. An important part of our research has been to decipher relevant loop characteristics by studying publicly known examples of ACVs and the ACV challenges posed by DARPA. It is important to characterize loops in the context of program artifacts that connect a loop to the rest of the program. For example, since ACVs are triggered by attacker's input, it is important to characterize whether the termination of a loop can be controlled by user input. We developed loop abstractions capture and represent the essentials of loops and the connecting parts of the program that affect loop behaviors. One abstraction is to capture the loop termination behavior based on the data flow to the loop termination conditions.

The gathered information includes: (a) a catalog of all loops in the program along with characteristic attribute vector for each loop, (b) the uses of resource-intensive library APIs, (c) loop call graphs to bring out loops nested over multiple functions, (d) a catalog of branch nodes including branches that govern the paths containing loops.

7.2.2 Automated Filters

The paper [49] describes automated filters to isolate complex loops with high likelihood of ACVs. The analyst can use filters to select loops matching a combination of the loop characteristics from the loop catalog. The framework currently supports the creation of custom filters by adding constraints on String, primitive and boolean properties. An example of a boolean property is monotonicity – a loop is either monotonic or not; and the two possible constraints based on this property would be "monotonic: true" and "monotonic: false". The nesting depth of a loop is an example of a primitive (integer) property. For example, the constraint "nesting-depth greater than 4" selects all loops having nesting depth of 5 or above within the method. A filter consists of a conjunction of constraints, i.e., a filter consisting of the above two constraints would select monotonic loops with nesting depth over 4. The filtering framework also allows analysts to fork a filter, i.e., create a new filter that includes a subset of the constraints added to an existing filter. This is useful for the analyst to explore multiple hypotheses related to ACVs in the application simultaneously.

Currently, we provide filters based on following six characteristics: (1) Reachability, (2) Subsystem Interaction, (3) Presence of branch conditions that affect the resource consumption of the loop, (4) Loop Termination Patterns (LTP), (5) Monotonicity, and (6) Nesting Depth.

7.2.3 Applicability of Automated Exploration and Filters

The paper [49] reports a case study of *Gabfeed3*, a web forum software which allows users to post messages and search posted messages. The application utilizes a custom merge sort for sorting messages. The application consists of 23,882 lines of Jimple, an intermediate representation of Java bytecode.

Automated exploration creates a loop catalog consisting of all loops in the program with the following characterization for each loop: (1) the Termination Dependence Graph (TDG) and Loop Projected Control Graph (LPCG) abstractions for the loop, (2) whether the loop is monotonic, (3) applicable termination patterns, (4) subsystem APIs and the control flow paths on which they are invoked in the loop, and (5) structural characteristics such as the number of nesting levels and the inter-procedural nesting depth of the loop when the nesting is split across multiple functions.

The loop characterization can be used to create a variety of filters to select loops. This case study illustrates five filters. Using the filters, the analyst is able to isolate for further scrutiny one loop out of 112 loops in the app. On further scrutiny, an ACV was detected in this loop. The view from our filtering tool in Fig. 10 shows a succession of filters that narrows down the search for a vulnerable loop.

Fig. 10 Using filters to select a loop likely to have an ACV

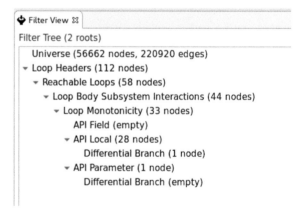

7.3 Software Analysis

The purpose of software analysis is to produce evidence that is needed to prove or disprove the malware hypothesis developed by the analyst. For example, the hypothesis could be: GPS location is being leaked by sending it to a web client. The analysis could produce data and control flow paths from the program point where the GPS information is obtained to the point where it is sent to the web client. Another outcome could be that the information produced by the analyzer is used to verify that the GPS location is not leaked on any feasible control flow path.

Software analysis tools that work on source code use the programming language syntax and semantics to represent and reason about the possible behaviors at run-time. Tools that work on binary such as Java byte code or LLVM are useful when the source code is unavailable (e.g., analyzing proprietary COTS components). Binary analysis is often necessary to uncover potential malicious behavior introduced by an erroneous or unanticipated transformations by the compiler. Both the source code analysis [27, 28, 34, 71] and the binary analysis [6, 7, 9, 18, 20, 57, 71] are evolving research topics, with several tools being actively developed, maintained and used in practice. We discuss research directions applicable to both source code and binary analysis.

Before we discuss research directions, we make a quick note about *static* and *dynamic* analyses. The term static analysis refers to any process for analyzing code without executing it. Static analysis is powerful because it allows for the quick consideration of many possibilities. A static analysis tool can explore a large number of "what if" scenarios without having to go through all the computations necessary to execute the code for all the scenarios. Static analysis is particularly well suited to security because many security problems occur in corner cases and hard-to-reach states that can be difficult to exercise by actually running the code. The term dynamic analysis refers to any process for analyzing code by executing it. Dynamic analysis has the advantage that it can reveal the ground truth by running the code. Whereas the approximation performed by static analysis may be inaccurate and often produce false positives, static analysis can be used to narrow down the possibilities for vulnerable code. Dynamic analysis can be used to try out those possibilities dynamically to ensure that the code is indeed vulnerable. Combining static and dynamic analyses is a topic of ongoing research including *statically-informed dynamic analysis* [86] and *dynamically-informed static analysis*.

We will discuss two static analysis research directions that we find particularly important in the context of detecting CPM:

Computing Relevant Program Behaviors All relevant program behaviors must be analyzed to verify a safety or security property. An efficient algorithm must compute the relevant behaviors directly without computing all the behaviors. This is crucial in practice because it is computationally intractable if one were to compute all behaviors to find the subset of relevant behaviors.

Interactive Graphical Static Analysis Analyzing software for CPM inherently involves performing experiments. Static analysis is supposed to be useful to explore a large number of "what if" scenarios. However, performing such experiments is not easy in practice. There are many issues, for example, existing tools do not support on-the-fly composition of analyses to cope with open-ended "what if" possibilities. Graphs are important as a common underlying abstraction for composability of analyses.

7.4 DARPA Research: Software Analysis

Our work on DARPA APAC and STAC projects is summarized here to exemplify the software analysis research directions. The papers [49, 72, 84–86, 112, 112, 113, 113] describe our software analysis research and the relevant toolboxes we have developed as part of these projects.

7.4.1 Computing Relevant Program Behaviors

The papers [118, 119] present a mathematical foundation to define relevant behaviors. Computing the relevant program behaviors involves: (a) computing the relevant program statements, (b) computing the relevant conditions to determine the feasibility of relevant behaviors, and (c) computing the relevant program behaviors. The papers introduce the Projected Control Graph (PCG) as an abstraction to directly compute the relevant behaviors for a fairly broad class of software safety and security problems. The paper presents an efficient algorithm to transform CFG to PCG with complexity $O(|V| + |E|)$, where $|V|$ and $|E|$ are respectively numbers of nodes and edges in the CFG.

As illustrated by the following example, computing relevant behaviors is important for addressing the two fundamental software analysis challenges discussed in Sect. 6. In practice, the number of behaviors relevant to a task is often significantly smaller than the totality of behaviors. Computing just the relevant behaviors enables us to surmount the intractability of computing the totality of behaviors. The following example also illustrates that using PCG to compute relevant behaviors minimizes the number of path governing conditions to be analyzed for checking path feasibility.

Illustration of Relevant Program Behaviors and PCG Consider the problem of verifying the function foo (Fig. 11a) for division-by-zero (DBZ) vulnerability on line 24 which involves division by d. The CFG for foo is shown in Fig. 11b. The CFG is an acyclic graph with six paths. Each path yields a unique base behavior. The base behaviors are as listed in Table 1. The behaviors (B_1 and B_2) exhibit the DBZ vulnerability. The yellow highlighted statements shown in Fig. 11a are the

```
1   int a1 = 1, a2 = 2;
2   int y = 2;
3   bool c1 = true;
4   bool c2 = false;
5   bool c3 = true;
6   void foo(){
7       int x = a1 + a2;
8       int d = a1;
9       if(c1){
10          x = a1;
11      } else {
12          x = a2 - 1;
13      }
14
15      if(c2){
16          if(c3){
17              y = a1;
18          } else {
19              d = d - a1;
20          }
21      } else {
22          d = d + 1;
23      }
24      int z = x / d;
25  }
```

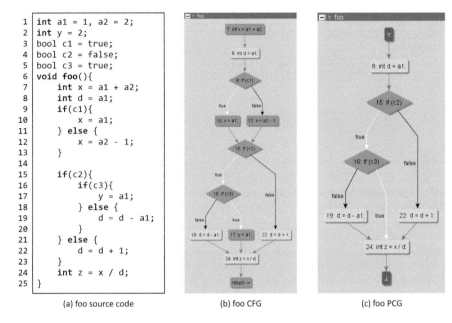

| (a) foo source code | (b) foo CFG | (c) foo PCG |

Fig. 11 A division-by-zero (DBZ) vulnerability

Table 1 Base behaviors and relevant behaviors for `foo`

Base behaviors	Relevant behaviors
B_1 : 7, 8, 9[c_1], 10, 15[c_2], 16[$\bar{c}_3$], 19, 24	RB_1 : 8, 15[c_2], 16[$\bar{c}_3$], 19, 24
B_2 : 7, 8, 9[$\bar{c}_1$], 12, 15[c_2], 16[$\bar{c}_3$], 19, 24	
B_3 : 7, 8, 9[c_1], 10, 15[$\bar{c}_2$], 22, 24	RB_2 : 8, 15[$\bar{c}_2$], 22, 24
B_4 : 7, 8, 9[$\bar{c}_1$], 12, 15[$\bar{c}_2$], 22, 24	
B_5 : 7, 8, 9[c_1], 10, 15[c_2], 16[c_3], 17, 24	RB_3 : 8, 15[c_2], 16[c_3], 24
B_6 : 7, 8, 9[$\bar{c}_1$], 12, 15[c_2], 16[c_3], 17, 24	

relevant program statements. In this example, these statements are relevant to the DBZ vulnerability because they affect the value of the denominator d in line 24.

Weiser's highly cited paper [121] on *program slice* in essence introduced the notion relevant statements. This research is crucial generalization in two important directions: (a) generalizing the notion of relevant statements for software safety and security problems, (b) generalizing from relevant statements (nodes in the CFG) to relevant behaviors (paths in the CFG).

Multiple base behaviors can be grouped so that each group corresponds to a unique *relevant behavior*. The relevant statements for the DBZ vulnerability on line 24 (Fig. 11a) are: 8, 19, 22 and 24. The relevant behaviors and the corresponding groups of base behaviors are listed in Table 1. Of the three relevant behaviors, RB_1 exhibits the DBZ vulnerability. Conditions $C2$ and $C3$ are included in relevant behaviors as *relevant conditions*. These conditions determine the feasibility of the vulnerable relevant behavior is RB_1.

The PCG for `foo` is shown in Fig. 11c. The PCG is an acyclic graph with three paths. Each path yields a unique relevant behavior. This illustration brings out that the PCG produces exactly the relevant behaviors and retains only the relevant conditions to check feasibility of the path with vulnerable behavior.

7.4.2 Interactive Graphical Static Analysis

The Eclipse and Atlas infrastructure incorporates multi-language support, a graph database, a query language, the eXtensible Common Software Graph Schema (XCSG), a variety of program analyzers, and interactive program graph visualization. This infrastructure can be used to create domain-specific toolboxes such as the Android Security Toolbox [85]. These toolboxes are written in Java and deployed as Eclipse plug-ins. The key components of Atlas infrastructure are described below.

Graph Database After parsing a program, its complete semantics is saved as a graph with many different types of nodes and edges. Results from a number of commonly needed control and data flow analysis are incorporated in the graph database. We use attributed graphs [71] for representing program semantics. Attributes are tags for nodes and edges to represent program semantics. Program analyzers can use the *tagging mechanism* to add new semantics (e.g. call sites in C programs are tagged by an analyzer to denote use of function pointers). The tagging has multiple uses including its use for analyses to communicate with each other. As an example, we use the loop-detection analyzer to compute and tag the loop-back edges. These loop-back edges are then used by another analyzer to create an acyclic graph to compute the paths corresponding to relevant behaviors.

eXtensible Common Software Graph (XCSG) Schema Just as high-level program languages are designed with affordances for humans, effort must be invested in designing humane representations for program analyses. Interactive analysis for human-machine collaboration must be enabled to tackle difficult problems now, and to help inspire creative solutions to automate or semi-automate verification in the future. XCSG is designed to enable interactive analysis to tackle difficult analysis problems in multi-million line programs. XCSG is designed to represent the semantics of the software, blend various common analyses, provide a basis for composing new analyses, and provide affordances required for human-machine collaboration. XCSG provides a unified approach to support for multiple programming languages. XCSG also serves as the foundation for a graphical query language. The comprehensive XCSG semantics links program text with its graphical representation as shown in Fig. 12.

Graphical Query Language The query language is implemented as an embedded domain-specific language (DSL) in Java. The rationale behind making a DSL is that it adds a layer of abstraction for expressing what to select from the graph, provides some conciseness of expression, and leaves a layer of indirection permitting query optimization. The rationale behind making it embedded is that it avoids recreating the useful features already present in an imperative language such as Java.

```
public class T extends java.lang.Object
{
        int f;
        public void m(int)
        {
            T r0;
            int i0;
            r0 := @this: T;
            i0 := @parameter0: int;
            r0.<T: int f> = i0;
            return;
        }
}
```

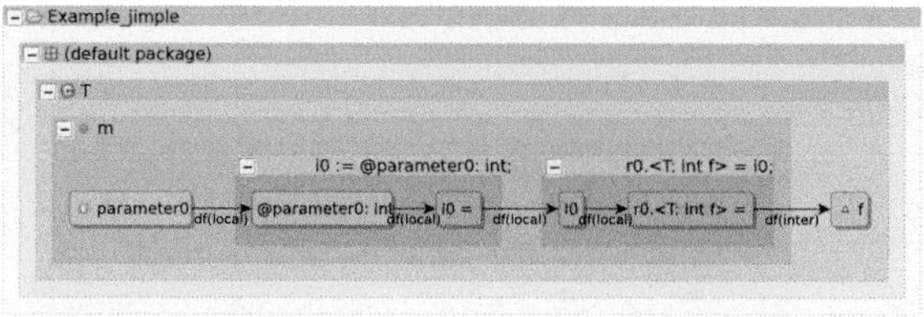

Fig. 12 Linking program text and graph with XCSG

The query language is usually informally referred to simply as Q, which is the simple name of the Java interface. Q is used to describe what to select from a graph, the expression yielding a subgraph. By the builder pattern, almost all methods in the interface Q return an expression of type Q, and chaining method calls effectively specifies the query AST. A chain of Q expressions can be evaluated by calling the Q.eval() method, which transitions to a graph API suitable for imperative implementations. Methods of Q are responsible for ensuring that the subgraph returned is a proper graph, where edges are present iff the incident nodes are as well. From the perspective of Q, the entire graph database is an expression called Q.universe(). Query results are therefore confined to returning subgraphs of the *universe*.

The primary use case behind the design of Q is enabling an analysis designer to quickly draft single line queries to select relevant portions of the graph – in essence, enabling them to "look around the corner" from their current position, and bring together related but lexically non-local elements of the program. Unlike many other graph query languages [96, 123], Q deliberately unions all matches at each step. For example, given several tagMethod nodes as an origin, a query for a call graph returns a single unified graph, as opposed to returning individual matches to a pattern.

In addition to interactive queries, we provide the capability to write Java programs with query APIs to write novel analyzers and verification tools. Documentation for the query APIs and XCSG are available at [3, 4, 16].

Graph Interactions with Source Correspondence This is important for multiple reasons. For example, this capability can be used for composition of analysis. The textual queries and graph interactions can be combined. For example, for a textual query to create CFG can have *selected* as the parameter. Clicking on a node of a displayed call graph, serves as *selected* and the CFG for the selected node is displayed. Or as another example, relevant program statements can be selected by clicking on them (e.g. highlighted statements in Fig. 11a) can produce the PCG shown in Fig. 11c. A spectrum of such capabilities can be seen in the demo videos linked with our papers [71, 84, 85].

Our research has led to the Atlas platform [15, 71] as a pluggable architecture using the Eclipse IDE. We have built various toolboxes such as the Android Security Toolbox [85] as Atlas plug-ins.

7.5 Verification

The safety and security problems are similar for the purpose of verification. A safety verification would be: verify that an event $e_1(O)$ is followed by an event $e_2(O)$ on every feasible execution path, where the two events are operations on the same object O (e.g., lock must be followed by unlock). A security verification would be: verify that an event $e_1(O)$ is *not* followed by an event $e_2(O)$ on every feasible execution path, where the two events are operations on the same object O. We shall refer to these as 2-event *matching* or *anti-matching*. Anti-matching covers software security verification defined according to the CIA triad. A confidentiality verification problem could be defined as: a *sensitive source* must *not* be followed by a *malicious sink* on any feasible execution path. Similarly, an integrity verification problem could be defined as: an *access to sensitive data* must *not* be followed by a *malicious modification to sensitive data* on any feasible execution path.

Formal verification techniques map the software verification problem to another problem that is amenable to a generic proof technique. This approach ties back to the computation complexity theory in which problems are mapped to the *satisfiability problem*. A common formal verification approach is to map the software verification problem to the *satisfiability problem* and use a SAT solver [80]. This formal approach breaks the verification into tiny steps well suited for machine execution. However, it has two major problems: (1) it makes the verification incomprehensible to humans, and (2) it hits scalability hurdles with explosion of steps.

De Millo, Lipton, and Perlis (the first recipient of the Turing Award) [73] point to the fallacy of "absolute correctness" and argue that software verification, like "proofs" in mathematics, should provide *evidence* that humans can follow and thus be able to build trust into the correctness of the software verification. Our paper [94] on Linux verification gives examples of incorrect results by a top-notch formal verification tool.

Given the possibility of tremendous harm from CPM, we find the following research directions particularly important for software verification:

Automated Verification with Human-comprehensible Evidence Automated verification should generate evidence alongside. Without automatically generated evidence, it can be extremely difficult and labor-intensive to cross-check the correctness of automated verification. A verification tool should convey at high-level the knowledge of specific hardness it encounters in verifying a vulnerability instance, and how that hardness is being correctly addressed by the software verification technique.

Big-step Automated Verification Proofs in mathematics use high-level abstractions to create "big-step" proofs. The powerful machinery created by abstract algebra with its theory of groups, rings, and fields has been the foundation on which mathematician have built numerous proofs for difficult problems in number theory such as the Fermat conjecture [17]. It is inconceivable to build such proofs by simply invoking generic proof techniques devoid of deep concepts. There is a pressing need for developing "big-step" proofs for software assurance. Even for NP-complete problems, practical algorithms are designed by employing problem-specific abstractions. Big-step proofs hold the promise to render software verification proofs human-comprehensible, as well as make them efficient and scalable.

7.6 Linux Verification Research

Our verification research has evolved around 2-event matching and anti-matching that covers both software safety and security problems. We present here the work reported in papers [92, 94] to exemplify the two verification research directions.

The following verification study is done with the Berkeley Lazy Abstraction Software Verification Tool (BLAST) [52], the formal verification tool used by the Linux organization. We used BLAST to verify three recent versions (3.17-rc1, 3.18-rc1 and 3.19-rc1) of the Linux kernel. We enabled all possible x86 build configurations via allmodconfig flag. The three Linux versions altogether amount to 37 million lines of code and 66,609 verification instances. The BLAST results are reported in Table 2. BLAST verifies 43, 766 (65.7)% of Lock instances as safe, and it is inconclusive (crashes or times out) on 22,843 instances. BLAST does not find any unsafe instances.

The results reported in Table 2 are shown as: $C1$ *Category* of instances verified as *safe*, $C2$ *Category* of instances verified as *unsafe*, and $C3$ *Category* of the remaining instances where the verification is inconclusive. Column Type identifies the synchronization mechanism. Columns Locks and Unlocks show the number of lock/unlock instances of each type. Note that a lock may be paired with multiple unlocks on different execution paths.

BLAST does not report any unsafe instances ($C2$ *Category*) but it is inconclusive on 22,843 (34.3)% instances. BLAST does not produce evidence which makes it challenging to trace its verification to understand its failures [128].

Our study shows a practical need for evidence that shines light on why the formal verification is inconclusive. It is especially important to know if some of the 22,843 inconclusive instances are actually unsafe. The possibility of unsafe instances is worrisome for mission-critical cyber-physical systems.

BLAST pronounces 43,766 (65.7)% Lock instances to be safe ($C1$ *Category*). Are all these instances really safe? BLAST [53] uses the *Counter Example Guided Abstraction Refinement* (CEGAR) method for verification. CEGAR does not produce a proof or other evidence to support its assertion that an instance is

Table 2 BLAST Linux verification results

Kernel	LOC	Type	Locks	Unlocks	BLAST _C1_	_C2_	_C3_	Time
3.17-rc1	12.3 M	spin	14,180	16,817	8,962 (63.2%)	0	5,218	26 h
		mutex	7,887	9,497	5,494 (69.7%)	0	2,393	27 h
3.18-rc1	12.3 M	spin	14,265	16,917	9,152 (64.2%)	0	5,113	30 h
		mutex	7,893	9,550	5,427 (68.8%)	0	2,466	30 h
3.19-rc1	12.4 M	spin	14,393	17,026	9,204 (63.9%)	0	5,189	32 h
		mutex	7,991	9,653	5,527 (69.2%)	0	2,464	29 h
All Kernels			**66,609**	**79,460**	**43,766 (65.7%)**	**0**	**22,843**	**173 h**

safe. While the model checker is supposed to be formally correct, it can still have false negatives (e.g., due to incorrect transformation of software into the low-level representation that the model checker requires). Without human comprehensible evidence to cross-check correctness of a formal proof, we are left with blind trust. The practical need is for evidence that makes it possible to cross-check the formal proof without having to construct a new proof starting from scratch. Without such evidence, it is practically impossible to answer the following question: Among the 43,766 instances verified as safe by BLAST, are there any cases of erroneous verification where an unsafe instance is verified as safe?

8 Conclusions

Most of the national critical infrastructure relies on industries which employ networked industrial control systems such as SCADA. Sabotage of these industries can have wide-ranging negative effects including loss of life, economic damage, property destruction, or environmental pollution.

A cyber attack is not all that different from a military attack. A cyber attacker will dedicate a significant amount of time observing and probing the target organization to find weaknesses in its defense. Any weakness found may lead to infiltration and eventually an assault.

When people think of cybersecurity today, they worry about hackers and criminals who prowl the Internet, steal people's identities, steal sensitive business information, or even steal national security secrets. Those threats are real and they exist today. But the even greater danger – the greater danger facing us in cyberspace – goes beyond crime and it goes beyond harassment. A cyber attack perpetrated by nation states or violent extremists groups could be as destructive as the 9/11 terrorist attack. Especially of concern are the communication infrastructure, the industrial control systems, and the vulnerable mission-critical software.

Most industrial control systems began as proprietary, stand-alone collections of hardware and software that were walled off from the rest of the world and isolated from most external threats. Today, widely available software applications, Internet-enabled devices and other non-proprietary IT offerings have been integrated into most such systems. This connectivity has delivered many benefits, but it also has increased the vulnerability of these systems.

A disruption in telecommunication networks can have devastating effects on all aspects of modern living, causing shortages and stoppages that ripple throughout society. Telecommunications hardware includes a vast range of products that enable communication across the entire planet, from video broadcasting satellites to telephone handsets to fiber-optic transmission cables. Services include running the switches that control the phone system, providing Internet access, and configuring private networks by which international corporations conduct business. Software makes it all work.

If a desktop operating system fails, the computer can be rebooted. If a flight control system fails, it can be a disaster with no chance to reboot the system. Malfunctioning of mission-critical software results in serious impact on business operations or upon an organization, and even can cause social turmoil and catastrophes. Mission-critical software drives online banking systems, railway and aircraft operating and control systems, electric power systems, and many other computer systems that adversely affect businesses and the society when they fail.

The real question is: *can we detect catastrophic software vulnerabilities – whether intentionally planted or not?* If we were to guard our reactors from the Stuxnet, how could we have done that? There is no escape but to create the best possible technology to analyze mission-software to discover and confirm intentional malware or inadvertent vulnerability that could be catastrophic. But oddly enough, much of the activity that takes place under the guise of computer security is not really about solving security problems at all; it is about cleaning up the mess that security problems create. Virus scanners, firewalls, patch management, and intrusion detection systems are all means by which we make up for shortcomings in software security.

It is important that the cybersecurity research leads to practical tools and education to train a cyberforce with the necessary thinking skills to use the tools effectively. A skilled cybersecurity workforce is needed to meet the unique cybersecurity needs of critical infrastructure, enterprise, and operational technology systems and networks.

Acknowledgements We thank our colleagues from Iowa State University and EnSoft for their help with this paper. We are grateful to Jeremias Sauceda and Nikhil Ranade for their significant contributions to our research on graphical software analysis and verification. Tom Deering, Eric Woestman, Theodore Murdock, Shrawan Kumar, Akshay Deepak, and Damanjit Singh have played important roles in evolving the research. Dr. Kothari is the founder President and a financial stakeholder in EnSoft.

References

1. Android intent. https://stackoverflow.com/questions/6578051/what-is-an-intent-in-android. (Accessed on 01/22/2018).
2. Android intent (android developer guide). https://developer.android.com/guide/components/intents-filters.html. (Accessed on 01/22/2018).
3. Atlas queries documentation. http://www.ensoftcorp.com/atlas_docs/javadoc/2.x/index.html? com/ensoftcorp/atlas/core/query/Q.html. (Accessed on 01/22/2018).
4. Atlas wiki. http://ensoftatlas.com/wiki/Main_Page. (Accessed on 01/22/2018).
5. Automated program analysis for cybersecurity (apac). http://www.defenseinnovationmarketplace.mil/resources/DARPA%202011%208%203%20APAC%20Industry%20Day.pdf. (Accessed on 01/22/2018).
6. Bap – a binary analysis platform. https://www.grammatech.com/products/codesonar. (Accessed on 04/02/2018).
7. Bitblaze. http://bitblaze.cs.berkeley.edu. (Accessed on 04/02/2018).
8. Blueborne cyber threat impacts amazon echo and google home. https://www.armis.com/blueborne-cyber-threat-impacts-amazon-echo-google-home/. (Accessed on 01/22/2018).
9. Codesonar. https://www.grammatech.com/products/codesonar. (Accessed on 04/02/2018).
10. Coverity static analysis, static application security testing. https://www.synopsys.com/software-integrity/security-testing/static-analysis-sast.html?utm_source=google&utm_medium=paid%20search&utm_term=coverity&utm_campaign=G_S_Coverity_Exact&cmp=ps-SIG-G_S_Coverity_Exact&gclid=EAIaIQobChMIhe3pqvXr2AIVV7bACh1fEgaQEAAYASAAEgL8K_D_BwE. (Accessed on 01/22/2018).
11. Cve – common vulnerabilities and exposures (cve). https://cve.mitre.org/. (Accessed on 01/22/2018).
12. Cvss v3.0 specification document. https://www.first.org/cvss/specification-document. (Accessed on 01/22/2018).
13. Ddos attack that disrupted internet was largest of its kind in history, experts say | technology | the guardian. https://www.theguardian.com/technology/2016/oct/26/ddos-attack-dyn-mirai-botnet. (Accessed on 01/22/2018).
14. Department of defense – directive number 3020.40. http://policy.defense.gov/Portals/11/Documents/hdasa/newsletters/302040p.pdf. (Accessed on 01/22/2018).
15. Ensoft corp. http://www.ensoftcorp.com. (Accessed on 01/22/2018).
16. Extensible common software graph. http://ensoftatlas.com/wiki/Extensible_Common_Software_Graph. (Accessed on 01/22/2018).
17. Fermat conjecture. https://en.wikipedia.org/wiki/Fermat%27s_Last_Theorem. (Accessed on 01/22/2018).
18. Grackle. https://grackle.galois.com. (Accessed on 04/02/2018).
19. Hp fortify. http://www.ndm.net/sast/hp-fortify. (Accessed on 01/22/2018).
20. Klee llvm execution engine. http://klee.github.io/. (Accessed on 04/02/2018).
21. Modbus. http://www.modbus.org. (Accessed on 01/22/2018).
22. Modbus penetration testing framework. https://github.com/enddo/smod. (Accessed on 01/22/2018).
23. Morris worm – wikipedia. https://en.wikipedia.org/wiki/Morris_worm. (Accessed on 01/22/2018).
24. National vulnerability database. https://nvd.nist.gov/. (Accessed on 01/22/2018).
25. Open ssl developer confesses to causing heartbleed bug | daily mail online. http://www.dailymail.co.uk/sciencetech/article-2602277/Heartbleed-accident-Developer-confesses-coding-error-admits-effect-clearly-severe.html#ixzz546wC2cbw. (Accessed on 01/22/2018).
26. Sandvines packetlogic devoices used to deploy government spyware in turkey and redirect egyptian users to affiiliate ads. https://citizenlab.ca/2018/03/bad-traffic-sandvines-packetlogic-devices-deploy-government-spyware-turkey-syria/. (Accessed on 04/02/2018).

27. Slam. https://www.microsoft.com/en-us/research/project/slam/. (Accessed on 04/02/2018).
28. Soot. https://github.com/Sable/soot. (Accessed on 04/02/2018).
29. Space/time analysis for cybersecurity (stac). https://www.darpa.mil/program/space-time-analysis-for-cybersecurity. (Accessed on 01/22/2018).
30. Splint (programming tool) – wikipedia. https://en.wikipedia.org/wiki/Splint_(programming_tool). (Accessed on 01/22/2018).
31. Stuxnet – wikipedia. https://en.wikipedia.org/wiki/Stuxnet. (Accessed on 01/22/2018).
32. Sy110: Phases of a cyber attack / cyber recon. https://www.usna.edu/CyberDept/sy110/lec/cyberRecon/lec.html. (Accessed on 01/22/2018).
33. Telecommunications equipment – wikipedia. https://en.wikipedia.org/wiki/Telecommunications_equipment. (Accessed on 01/22/2018).
34. Wala. http://wala.sourceforge.net/wiki/index.php/Main_Page. (Accessed on 04/02/2018).
35. Wannacry ransomware attack. https://arstechnica.com/information-technology/2017/05/an-nsa-derived-ransomware-worm-is-shutting-down-computers-worldwide/. (Accessed on 01/22/2018).
36. Final report on the august 14, 2003 blackout in the united states and canada: Causes and recommendations. https://energy.gov/sites/prod/files/oeprod/DocumentsandMedia/BlackoutFinal-Web.pdf, April 2004. (Accessed on 01/22/2018).
37. 2009 cyberspace policy review | homeland security. https://www.dhs.gov/sites/default/files/publications/Cyberspace_Policy_Review_final_0.pdf, 2009. (Accessed on 01/22/2018).
38. Defense contractors northrop grumman, l-3 communications hit by cyber-attack. https://www.cioinsight.com/c/a/Latest-News/Defense-Contractors-Northrop-Grummond-L3-Communications-Hit-by-CyberAttack-106322, June 2011. (Accessed on 01/22/2018).
39. National cyber security divisions control systems security program (cssp). https://ics-cert.us-cert.gov/sites/default/files/recommended_practices/DHS_Common_Cybersecurity_Vulnerabilities_ICS_2010.pdf, May 2011. (Accessed on 01/22/2018).
40. Investigative report on the u.s. national security issues posed by chinese telecommunications companies huawei and zte. https://intelligence.house.gov/sites/intelligence.house.gov/files/documents/huawei-zte%20investigative%20report%20(final).pdf, October 2012. (Accessed on 01/22/2018).
41. Darpa-baa-13-11: Vetting commodity it software and firmware (vet), updated. https://govtribe.com/project/darpa-baa-13-11-vetting-commodity-it-software-and-firmware-vet, Februrary 2013. (Accessed on 01/22/2018).
42. Industroyer: Biggest threat to industrial control systems since stuxnet. https://www.welivesecurity.com/2017/06/12/industroyer-biggest-threat-industrial-control-systems-since-stuxnet/, June 2017. (Accessed on 01/22/2018).
43. National initiative for cybersecurity education (nice) cybersecurity workforce framework. https://csrc.nist.gov/csrc/media/publications/sp/800-181/archive/2016-11-02/documents/sp800_181_draft.pdf, August 2017. (Accessed on 01/22/2018).
44. Threat modeling cheat sheet – owasp. https://www.owasp.org/index.php/Threat_Modeling_Cheat_Sheet, December 2017. (Accessed on 01/22/2018).
45. RTCA (Firm). SC 167. *Software considerations in Airborne Systems and equipment certification*. RTCA, Incorporated, 1992.
46. Alfred V Aho, Ravi Sethi, and Jeffrey D Ullman. *Compilers: principles, techniques, and tools*, volume 2. Addison-wesley Reading, 2007.
47. Jafar M. Al-Kofahi, Suresh Kothari, and Christian Kästner. Four languages and lots of macros: Analyzing autotools build systems. In *Proceedings of the 16th ACM SIGPLAN International Conference on Generative Programming: Concepts and Experiences*, GPCE 2017, pages 176–186. ACM, 2017.
48. Keith Alexander. Keynote – 2011 cyber & space symposium. https://www.youtube.com/watch?v=jaaU5nGDh68, November 2011. (Accessed on 01/22/2018).
49. Payas Awadhutkar, Ganesh Ram Santhanam, Benjamin Holland, and Suresh Kothari. Intelligence amplifying loop characterizations for detecting algorithmic complexity vulnerabilities. In *The 24th Asia-Pacific Software Engineering Conference (APSEC 2017)*, 2017.

50. Roberto Baldoni, Emilio Coppa, Daniele Cono D'Elia, Camil Demetrescu, and Irene Finocchi. A survey of symbolic execution techniques. *CoRR*, abs/1610.00502, 2016.
51. Dirk Beyer. Status report on software verification. In *TACAS*, volume 8413, pages 373–388, 2014.
52. Dirk Beyer, Thomas A Henzinger, Ranjit Jhala, and Rupak Majumdar. The software model checker blast. *International Journal on Software Tools for Technology Transfer*, 9(5–6):505–525, 2007.
53. Dirk Beyer and Alexander K. Petrenko. Linux driver verification. In Tiziana Margaria and Bernhard Steffen, editors, *Leveraging Applications of Formal Methods, Verification and Validation. Applications and Case Studies*, pages 1–6, Berlin, Heidelberg, 2012. Springer Berlin Heidelberg.
54. Wayne Boyer and Miles McQueen. Ideal based cyber security technical metrics for control systems. In *International Workshop on Critical Information Infrastructures Security*, pages 246–260. Springer, 2007.
55. Frederick P. Brooks, Jr. The computer scientist as toolsmith ii. *Commun. ACM*, 39(3):61–68, March 1996.
56. David Brumley, Cody Hartwig, Zhenkai Liang, James Newsome, Dawn Song, and Heng Yin. Automatically identifying trigger-based behavior in malware. *Botnet Detection*, pages 65–88, 2008.
57. David Brumley, Ivan Jager, Thanassis Avgerinos, and Edward J Schwartz. Bap: A binary analysis platform. In *International Conference on Computer Aided Verification*, pages 463–469. Springer, 2011.
58. Eric Byres and Justin Lowe. The myths and facts behind cyber security risks for industrial control systems. In *Proceedings of the VDE Kongress*, volume 116, pages 213–218, 2004.
59. C. Canal and A. Idani. *Software Engineering and Formal Methods: SEFM 2014 Collocated Workshops: HOFM, SAFOME, OpenCert, MoKMaSD, WS-FMDS, Grenoble, France, September 1–2, 2014, Revised Selected Papers*. Lecture Notes in Computer Science. Springer International Publishing, 2015.
60. Anton Cherepanov. Win32/industroyer a new threat for industrial control systems. https://www.welivesecurity.com/wp-content/uploads/2017/06/Win32_Industroyer.pdf, June 2017. (Accessed on 01/22/2018).
61. Alonzo Church. A note on the entscheidungsproblem. *The journal of symbolic logic*, 1(1):40–41, 1936.
62. Edmund M. Clarke, E Allen Emerson, and A Prasad Sistla. Automatic verification of finite-state concurrent systems using temporal logic specifications. *ACM Transactions on Programming Languages and Systems (TOPLAS)*, 8(2):244–263, 1986.
63. Edmund M Clarke, William Klieber, Miloš Nováček, and Paolo Zuliani. Model checking and the state explosion problem. In *Tools for Practical Software Verification*, pages 1–30. Springer, 2012.
64. Darren Cofer. Model checking: cleared for take off. *Model Checking Software*, pages 76–87, 2010.
65. Zachary A Collier, Mahesh Panwar, Alexander A Ganin, Alexander Kott, and Igor Linkov. Security metrics in industrial control systems. In *Cyber-security of SCADA and Other Industrial Control Systems*, pages 167–185. Springer, 2016.
66. Douglas Comer. *Operating system design: the Xinu approach, Linksys version*. CRC Press, 2011.
67. Lucian Constantin. Flame authors order infected computers to remove all traces of the malware – cio. https://www.cio.com.au/article/427005/flame_authors_order_infected_computers_remove_all_traces_malware/, June 2012. (Accessed on 01/22/2018).
68. Scott Crosby. Denial of service through regular expressions. *Usenix Security work in progress report*, 2003.
69. John D'Arcy and Gwen Greene. Security culture and the employment relationship as drivers of employees security compliance. *Information Management & Computer Security*, 22(5):474–489, 2014.

70. Richard A De Millo, Richard J Lipton, and Alan J Perlis. Social processes and proofs of theorems and programs. *Communications of the ACM*, 22(5):271–280, 1979.

71. Tom Deering, Suresh Kothari, Jeremias Sauceda, and Jon Mathews. Atlas: a new way to explore software, build analysis tools. In *Companion Proceedings of the 36th International Conference on Software Engineering*, pages 588–591. ACM, 2014.

72. Tom Deering, Ganesh Ram Santhanam, and Suresh Kothari. Flowminer: Automatic summarization of library data-flow for malware analysis. In *International Conference on Information Systems Security*, pages 171–191. Springer, 2015.

73. RA DeMillo, RJ Lipton, and AJ PerHls. Social processes and proofs of programs and theorems. In *Proc. Fourth ACM Symposium on Principles of Program-ming Languages*, pages 206–214, 1979.

74. Jens Dietrich, Kamil Jezek, Shawn Rasheed, Amjed Tahir, and Alex Potanin. Evil pickles: Dos attacks based on object-graph engineering (artifact). In *DARTS-Dagstuhl Artifacts Series*, volume 3. Schloss Dagstuhl-Leibniz-Zentrum fuer Informatik, 2017.

75. Isil Dillig, Thomas Dillig, and Alex Aiken. Sound, complete and scalable path-sensitive analysis. In *ACM SIGPLAN Notices*, volume 43, pages 270–280. ACM, 2008.

76. Paul Ducklin. Anatomy of a goto fail apples ssl bug explained, plus an unofficial patch for os x! naked security. https://nakedsecurity.sophos.com/2014/02/24/anatomy-of-a-goto-fail-apples-ssl-bug-explained-plus-an-unofficial-patch/, February 2014. (Accessed on 01/22/2018).

77. Nick Feamster and Hari Balakrishnan. Detecting bgp configuration faults with static analysis. In *Proceedings of the 2Nd Conference on Symposium on Networked Systems Design & Implementation – Volume 2*, NSDI'05, pages 43–56. USENIX Association, 2005.

78. Kathleen Fisher. High assurance cyber military systems (hacms). http://www.cyber.umd.edu/sites/default/files/documents/symposium/fisher-HACMS-MD.pdf, May 2013. (Accessed on 01/22/2018).

79. National Institute for Standards and Technology (NIST). Nist guide to industrial control systems security. http://nvlpubs.nist.gov/nistpubs/SpecialPublications/NIST.SP.800-82r2.pdf, May 2015. (Accessed on 01/22/2018).

80. Malay Ganai and Aarti Gupta. *SAT-based scalable formal verification solutions*. Springer, 2007.

81. Michael R Garey and David S Johnson. Computers and intractability. a guide to the theory of np-completeness. a series of books in the mathematical sciences, 1979.

82. Allen Goldberg, Tie-Cheng Wang, and David Zimmerman. Applications of feasible path analysis to program testing. In *Proceedings of the 1994 ACM SIGSOFT international symposium on Software testing and analysis*, pages 80–94. ACM, 1994.

83. Andy Greenberg. Hackers remotely kill a jeep on the highwaywith me in it | wired. https://www.wired.com/2015/07/hackers-remotely-kill-jeep-highway/, July 2015. (Accessed on 01/22/2018).

84. Benjamin Holland, Payas Awadhutkar, Suresh Kothari, Ahmed Tamrawi, and Jon Mathews. Comb: Computing relevant program behaviors. In *International Conference on Software Engineering Demonstration track*, page To appear., 2018.

85. Benjamin Holland, Tom Deering, Suresh Kothari, Jon Mathews, and Nikhil Ranade. Security toolbox for detecting novel and sophisticated android malware. In *Proceedings of the 37th International Conference on Software Engineering-Volume 2*, pages 733–736. IEEE Press, 2015.

86. Benjamin Holland, Ganesh Ram Santhanam, Payas Awadhutkar, and Suresh Kothari. Statically-informed dynamic analysis tools to detect algorithmic complexity vulnerabilities. In *Source Code Analysis and Manipulation (SCAM), 2016 IEEE 16th International Working Conference on*, pages 79–84. IEEE, 2016.

87. Michael Howard and David LeBlanc. *Writing secure code*. Pearson Education, 2003.

88. IBM. Security attacks on industrial control systems – managed security services research report. https://www-01.ibm.com/common/ssi/cgi-bin/ssialias?htmlfid=SEL03046USEN. (Accessed on 01/22/2018).

89. Kamal Jabbour and Sarah Muccio. The science of mission assurance. *Journal of Strategic Security*, 4(2):61, 2011.
90. Michael B Kelley. Stuxnet was far more dangerous than previous thought – business insider. http://www.businessinsider.com/stuxnet-was-far-more-dangerous-than-previous-thought-2013-11, November 2013. (Accessed on 01/22/2018).
91. James C King. Symbolic execution and program testing. *Communications of the ACM*, 19(7):385–394, 1976.
92. S. Kothari, P. Awadhutkar, and A. Tamrawi. Insights for practicing engineers from a formal verification study of the linux kernel. In *2016 IEEE International Symposium on Software Reliability Engineering Workshops*, pages 264–270, Oct 2016.
93. S. Kothari, A. Deepak, A. Tamrawi, B. Holland, and S. Krishnan. A human-in-the-loop approach for resolving complex software anomalies. In *2014 IEEE International Conference on Systems, Man, and Cybernetics (SMC)*, pages 1971–1978, Oct 2014.
94. Suresh Kothari, Payas Awadhutkar, Ahmed Tamrawi, and Jon Mathews. Modeling lessons from verifying large software systems for safety and security. In *2017 Winter Simulation Conference (WSC)*, pages 1431–1442, 2017.
95. Vadim Kotov and Fabio Massacci. Anatomy of exploit kits. *Engineering Secure Software and Systems*, 7781:181–196, 2013.
96. Mahesh Lal. *Neo4j Graph Data Modeling*. Packt Publishing Ltd, 2015.
97. Sihyung Lee. *Reducing Complexity of Large-scale Network Configuration Management*. PhD thesis, Pittsburgh, PA, USA, 2010. AAI3415822.
98. J. L. LIONS. Ariane 5 failure – full report. http://sunnyday.mit.edu/accidents/Ariane5accidentreport.html, July 1996. (Accessed on 01/22/2018).
99. Alan K Mackworth. Constraint satisfaction problems. *Encyclopedia of AI*, 285:293, 1992.
100. P MELL. A complete guide to the common vulnerability scoring system version 2.0. *http://www.first.org/cvss/cvss-guide.pdf*, 2007.
101. Arash Nourian and Stuart Madnick. A systems theoretic approach to the security threats in cyber physical systems applied to stuxnet. *IEEE Transactions on Dependable and Secure Computing*, 2015.
102. Ebenezer A Oladimeji, Sam Supakkul, and Lawrence Chung. Security threat modeling and analysis: A goal-oriented approach. In *Proc. of the 10th IASTED International Conference on Software Engineering and Applications (SEA 2006)*, pages 13–15, 2006.
103. Leon E. Panetta. Defense.gov transcript: Remarks by secretary panetta on cybersecurity to the business executives for national security, new york city. http://archive.defense.gov/transcripts/transcript.aspx?transcriptid=5136, October 2012. (Accessed on 01/22/2018).
104. Fabio Pasqualetti, Florian Dörfler, and Francesco Bullo. Attack detection and identification in cyber-physical systems. *IEEE Transactions on Automatic Control*, 58(11):2715–2729, 2013.
105. Alin C Popescu, Brian J Premore, and Todd Underwood. Anatomy of a leak: As9121. *Renesys Corp., http://www.renesys.com/tech/presentations/pdf/renesys-nanog34.pdf*, 2005.
106. Kevin Poulsen. Slammer worm crashed ohio nuke plant network. https://www.securityfocus.com/news/6767, August 2003. (Accessed on 01/22/2018).
107. Jean-Pierre Queille and Joseph Sifakis. Specification and verification of concurrent systems in cesar. In *International Symposium on programming*, pages 337–351. Springer, 1982.
108. Jean-Pierre Queille and Joseph Sifakis. Fairness and related properties in transition systems a temporal logic to deal with fairness. *Acta Informatica*, 19(3):195–220, 1983.
109. Brian Randell. The origins of computer programming. *IEEE Annals of the History of Computing*, 16(4):6–14, 1994.
110. Henry Gordon Rice. Classes of recursively enumerable sets and their decision problems. *Transactions of the American Mathematical Society*, 74(2):358–366, 1953.
111. DAVID E. SANGER. Obama ordered wave of cyberattacks against iran – the new york times. http://www.nytimes.com/2012/06/01/world/middleeast/obama-ordered-wave-of-cyberattacks-against-iran.html?pagewanted=1&_r=1&hp, June 2012. (Accessed on 01/22/2018).

112. Ganesh Ram Santhanam, Benjamin Holland, Suresh Kothari, and Jon Mathews. Interactive visualization toolbox to detect sophisticated android malware. In *Visualization for Cyber Security (VizSec), 2017 IEEE Symposium on*, pages 1–8. IEEE, 2017.

113. Ganesh Ram Santhanam, Benjamin Holland, Suresh Kothari, and Nikhil Ranade. Human-on-the-loop automation for detecting software side-channel vulnerabilities. In *International Conference on Information Systems Security*, pages 209–230. Springer, 2017.

114. Bruce Schneier. Heartbleed – schneier on security. https://www.schneier.com/blog/archives/2014/04/heartbleed.html, April 2014. (Accessed on 01/22/2018).

115. Tony Smith. Hacker jailed for revenge sewage attacks. http://www.theregister.co.uk/2001/10/31/hacker_jailed_for_revenge_sewage/, October 2001. (Accessed on 01/22/2018).

116. Panos Stratis. Formal verification in large-scaled software: Worth to ponder. https://blog.inf.ed.ac.uk/sapm/2014/02/20/formal-verification-in-large-scaled-software-worth-to-ponder/, 2014. (Accessed on 01/25/2018).

117. Frank Swiderski and Window Snyder. *Threat Modeling (Microsoft Professional)*, volume 7. Microsoft Press, 2004.

118. Ahmed Tamrawi and Suresh Kothari. Projected control graph for accurate and efficient analysis of safety and security vulnerabilities. In *Software Engineering Conference (APSEC), 2016 23rd Asia-Pacific*, pages 113–120. IEEE, 2016.

119. Ahmed Tamrawi and Suresh Kothari. Projected control graph for computing relevant program behaviors. *Journal of Science of Computer Programming*, To appear.

120. Alan M. Turing. The use of dots as brackets in church's system. *The Journal of Symbolic Logic*, 7(4):146–156, 1942.

121. Mark Weiser. Program slicing. In *Proceedings of the 5th international conference on Software engineering*, pages 439–449. IEEE Press, 1981.

122. D. E. Whitehead, K. Owens, D. Gammel, and J. Smith. Ukraine cyber-induced power outage: Analysis and practical mitigation strategies. In *2017 70th Annual Conference for Protective Relay Engineers (CPRE)*, pages 1–8, April 2017.

123. Peter T Wood. Query languages for graph databases. *ACM SIGMOD Record*, 41(1):50–60, 2012.

124. Jim Woodcock, Peter Gorm Larsen, Juan Bicarregui, and John Fitzgerald. Formal methods: Practice and experience. *ACM Computing Surveys (CSUR)*, 41(4):19, 2009.

125. Avishai Wool. A quantitative study of firewall configuration errors. *Computer*, 37(6):62–67, 2004.

126. Victoria Woollaston. Open ssl developer confesses to causing heartbleed bug | daily mail online. http://www.dailymail.co.uk/sciencetech/article-2602277/Heartbleed-accident-Developer-confesses-coding-error-admits-effect-clearly-severe.html#ixzz546xyGkwC, April 2014. (Accessed on 01/22/2018).

127. Yichen Xie and Alex Aiken. Saturn: A scalable framework for error detection using boolean satisfiability. *ACM Transactions on Programming Languages and Systems (TOPLAS)*, 29(3):16, 2007.

128. Ilja S Zakharov, Mikhail U Mandrykin, Vadim S Mutilin, EM Novikov, Alexander K Petrenko, and Alexey V Khoroshilov. Configurable toolset for static verification of operating systems kernel modules. *Programming and Computer Software*, 41(1):49–64, 2015.

129. Jian Zhang and Xiaoxu Wang. A constraint solver and its application to path feasibility analysis. *International Journal of Software Engineering and Knowledge Engineering*, 11(02):139–156, 2001.

Cross-VM Attacks: Attack Taxonomy, Defense Mechanisms, and New Directions

Gulshan Kumar Singh and Gaurav Somani

Abstract Cloud computing is a service which provides virtual machines (VMs) to the cloud customer with an ability to scale its resources on-demand. Cloud offers logical isolation among the VMs to isolate one VM from another VM. VMs running on the same physical server share the same resources. Hence, cross-VM attacks are possible in the multi-tenant virtualized environment. Most of the researchers focus on cross-VM attacks which primarily target the cache memory. There are additional attack instances which target other essential resources such as CPU, memory, I/O devices, and the cloud network. This chapter features a taxonomic classification of the cross-VM attacks and discusses the attacks space and the solution space to combat the cross-VM attacks. We also explain new sophistication in the cross-VM attack space and provide a comprehensive discussion to the solution design and guidelines.

1 Introduction

In recent times, cybersecurity is one of the primary concerns for the communities owing to the proliferation of cybercrime in the cyber world. The primary aim of cybersecurity primitives is to protect data in today's environment by studying and understanding the behavior of attackers. According to [8], most of the companies today have more than five security consultants and products for protecting their systems against malware. Also, the same report found that 75% of corporations are infected with adware. When it comes to security, cybersecurity is always on top for the industries to secure their environment and fight against malware. These days, the top priorities for the security professionals include mobile devices and cloud infrastructure. Attacker behavior and attack sophistication change according

G. K. Singh (✉) · G. Somani
Department of Computer Science and Engineering, Central University of Rajasthan, Ajmer, India

© Springer Nature Switzerland AG 2018
M. Conti et al. (eds.), *Versatile Cybersecurity*, Advances in Information
Security 72, https://doi.org/10.1007/978-3-319-97643-3_8

to latest trends in the cyber world, therefore we need to understand the behavior of the attacker before stopping the attacks.

Cloud computing (CC) platform has become very popular today as it provides many services by "pay as you go" model. Real-time scalability, ease of access, service availability, and cost-effectiveness are vital features of cloud computing services which attract the user towards the cloud. Cloud computing allows multi-tenancy through which multiple disjoint virtual machines can run on the same physical server. Cloud computing provides three primary service layers to the customers in the form of infrastructure as a service (IaaS), platform as a service (PaaS), and software as a service (SaaS). Owing to the cloud's on-demand service, low-cost offerings, and ease of access attracts all the major industries are drawn toward the cloud computing.

Even though many industries have adopted cloud services, a lot of security issues are still there in the cloud environment. Cybersecurity is the primary concern for the cloud customer protect their business from data theft and unavailability. There are two major security issues on which security professionals mostly focus, i.e., data security and network security. Due to cloud's multi-tenancy, running VMs of disjoint users on same hardware attract attackers to communicate with co-hosted victim VMs and plan a variety of attacks.

Virtualization is the crucial component for a cloud, and virtualization is a method which involves the abstraction of a physical machine into multiple virtual machines (VM) over same physical hardware. Cloud computing architecture has numerous physical servers connected through a high-speed network for data transfer. Each virtual machine runs an operating system isolated to other VMs. Isolation of physical hardware is achieved by virtual machine monitor (VMM) or hypervisor. VMware, Xen, KVM, and Hyper-V are some widely used hypervisors. A hypervisor provides logical isolation rather than physical isolation by using sandboxing techniques. Virtualization has solved many aspects of cloud, but it also opened the door for some vulnerabilities to the cloud computing. Litchfield et al. in [28] showed how virtualization could leave the system vulnerable to attacks. The authors focused on cache-based cross-VM attacks due to vulnerability caused by virtualization and shared resources which lead to data leakage of the co-resident VM. Some of the common weaknesses of virtualization are VM sprawl, hyper jacking, VM escape, denial of service attacks, etc. These vulnerabilities can be mitigated by employing prevention mechanisms such as VM traffic monitoring and administrative control for authenticating the VM.

In this chapter, our primary concern is to study the cross-VM attacks which are attacks coming out from the malicious VM and target the victim VM. All the attacks that are coming out from the attacker VM are also known as the out-VM attack. These out-VM attacks may also target non-virtualized environment. Therefore out-VM attack is the superset of all the attacks coming out from the VM. A cross-VM attack is the subset of out-VM attacks, i.e., all cross-VM attack are out-VM, but all out-VM attacks are not cross-VM attacks. In this chapter, we primarily focus on the cross-VM attacks.

Most of the public cloud platforms allow multi-tenancy by running multiple virtual machines on the same physical server. Multi-tenancy among the different VMs attract the attacker VM to communicate covertly with the victim VM and extract the sensitive information. Multi-tenancy feature of the cloud allows an attacker to place malicious VM on the same hardware as that of victim's VM. After the placement, side channel attack is used to obtain the data from the victim VM. Since VMs are residing on the same hardware, it opens up a channel for the attacker VM to interact with the victim VM. These channels are known as side channels and, therefore, the chances of side channel attack in the cloud computing environment are higher than the traditional non-virtualized environment. Side channel attack that leaks the fine grain information of victims' machine may even allow extraction of the private key of the victim VM. Co-residency and memory sharing of the VM are the primary reasons for the success of cross-VM side channel attack.

The rest of this chapter is organized as follows: Sect. 2 describes the taxonomy of the cross-VM attack. Section 3 describes the attack and threat model of the cross-VM attack. In Sect. 4, we detail the attack launch and provide different methods to accomplish the cross-VM attack. Section 5 details the reason for the success of the attack. Section 6 describes the existing solutions and their limitations. We also give a list of possible solutions from the literature to mitigate the cross-VM attacks. Section 7 describes the new sophistication and flavors of the cross-VM attacks and open research direction. Finally, Sect. 8 provides a conclusion for our discussion.

2 Cross-VM Attacks and Taxonomy

Side channel attacks are present for more than past 20 years in the non-virtualized environment. We conducted a systematic literature search and paper studies from the year 2009 related to cross-VM attacks. Our study shows that cross-VM attacks are discussed in the literature with different names. Out-VM attacks, inter-VM attacks, resource freeing attacks, and co-residency attacks are often used names for the cross-VM attacks. After the exhaustive study of a large number of contributions, we prepared a taxonomy which classifies the cross-VM attacks into five different categories. These categories are based on the type of shared resources. We show the cross-VM attack taxonomy in Fig. 1. We classify the cross-VM attacks into following five categories:

1. CPU based attacks
2. Cache based attacks
3. Memory based attacks
4. Network based attacks
5. I/O device based attacks

In side-channel attacks, the attacker manages to communicate with the victim machine due to some vulnerabilities in the system architecture from the perspective of resource sharing and information leakage. Side channel attacks exist in both

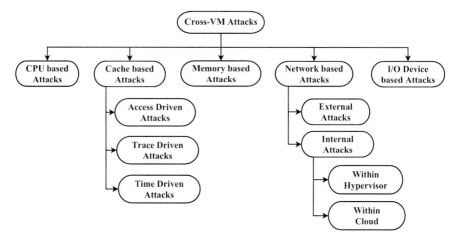

Fig. 1 Taxonomy of cross-VM attacks

virtualized and non-virtualized environment. However, our primary focus is on side channel attacks in the virtualized environment. Running multiple VMs over same hardware provides a side channel for an attacker to extract the information of the victim running over same hardware. Ristenpart et al. [43] considered two main steps while performing a cross-VM attack: placement and extraction. In placement, the attacker's VM is placed on the same physical server where victim's VM is placed. After successfully placing the attacker VM with some effort, next step is to extract confidential data from the victim VM. The prominent target of a cross-VM attack is usually a cryptosystem where cryptographic operations are running. Attacker focuses on extracting this information to perform cryptanalysis and obtains the cryptographic key segments through which attacker can reconstruct the original key.

In cloud environment where multiple VMs are running over the same hardware, memory virtualization is provided to fulfill the resource requirements of the VMs. Virtualization is used to create the multiple instances of a single hardware unit and distribute among co-hosted VMs. Single processing core of hardware is distributed to multiple VMs via virtualizing the processor. As the VMs share the underlying processor, an attacker VM can play with this facility to gain some information of the CPU usage of the victim VM. Today's computing devices have multiple cores where each processor has its first level (L1) and second level (L2) cache but third level cache (L3) or last level cache is always shared among the processors. We show the memory hierarchy in Fig. 2. Attackers focus on the L3 cache to gain the sensitive information as it is shared among all the processors. Therefore, we can see that memory sharing is one of the major features of cloud computing which enables the side channel attack to happen in the virtualized environment.

Cloud computing also uses memory deduplication to enhance the performance of the system. Memory deduplication is the concept of removing memory redundancy from the cloud where cloud keeps a single copy of the page if multiple copies

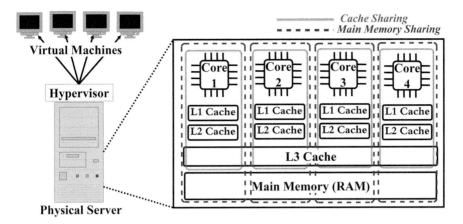

Fig. 2 Memory sharing in virtualization

of the same page exist, and the rest of the copies are rejected or deleted. This process improves the efficiency of the memory due to decreased memory space and bandwidth. Memory deduplication is also used to learn that the content that it is requesting is already available. On the other hand, attackers also come to know about the content accessed by the victim. This content aware sharing of the memory is another reason for the cross-VM side-channel attack on deduplicated systems.

Despite memory sharing and memory deduplication, cloud's internal network is also a resource which allows an attacker to gain information about the victim VM and its actions. Spoofing is one of the major attacks through which an attacker can impersonate itself as another VM and can launch an attack on behalf of other VM. Spoofing is commonly used to accomplish the DDoS (Distributed Denial of Service) attacks. Network scanning of internal cloud provides the basic information of the VMs and the network organization of the cloud as demonstrated by the authors in [43]. In [33], the authors provided a framework to detect the malicious activity of VM using virtual machine introspection (VMI) to get the current state information of the monitored VMs. The authors used network traffic analysis to analyze and detect the MAC address and IP address spoofing in the cloud to defeat DDoS participating VMs.

Now, we will discuss the classification categories from the cross-VM attack taxonomy.

2.1 CPU-Based Attacks

CPU based attacks are those in which the CPU load is monitored to predict the types of instruction it is running. Similarly, Okamura et al. in [38] presented a load-based CPU covert channel. In their paper, the authors used two module, a sender, and a receiver. Both the module runs with the user level permissions in which sender is on the victim VM. For their experiment, both the VM (attacker and victim) are co-hosted on the same CPU core. CPU load is used to transmit the bits between the attacker and victim VM. The authors used an application running on both victim and attacker VM to determine the bit to be transferred. Wang et al. in [51] showed that latest processors with SMT (Simultaneous Multi-Threaded) technology are vulnerable to side channel attacks. In SMT processors two processes can execute simultaneously. Therefore a simultaneously running victim process and attacker process can leak the sensitive information of the victim process. The authors in their paper showed how ALU (Arithmetic Logical Unit) of the processor is used to extract the bits of ongoing communication using timing channel.

Similarly, there are some attacks demonstrated in the non-virtualized environment but seems to be equally applicable in the virtualized environment. As shown in [10, 25], attacker notices and records the time taken to execute an instruction to guess the cryptographic key. Similarly, monitoring of CPU power consumption gives the fine grain information about the types of cryptographic instruction being executing by the CPU. More complex instructions draw more power and generate more heat. Similarly, electromagnetic emission also changes according to the type of instructions. In [1], the authors demonstrated cryptographic key guessing using branch prediction. There are instances, where this information is shown to be sufficient for an attacker to reconstruct the private key of the victim or extract some confidential information.

2.2 Memory-Based Attack

Risk of memory attack is also present in the virtualized environment. Main memory allotted to a VM is the segment of the large memory of the underlying physical server. Hypervisor manages the isolation of the memory among the VMs and handles the memory requirement of the tenant VMs. Any time a VM can request for increase or decrease its memory according to its needs. This scalability to the memory also opens up the door to the security attacks. A row-hammer attack is the most popular attack on the main memory segments which affects the charge of the neighboring memory cell and can modify the values. Main memory is also shared among the VMs and can be exploited to obtain information. Schwarz et al. [44] introduced new source for timing measurements using dynamic random access memory (DRAM) of the victim VM. The authors demonstrated an attack using JavaScript and its function to get timing information. In their DRAM-based covert channel attack, they used a website and an unprivileged app in a virtual machine without the use of any network hardware. They revealed that web browsers like Google Chrome, Mozilla Firefox, Microsoft Edge, and even the Tor browser which ensures the user anonymity, leak fine grain timing information of the DRAM. The method used by the authors to extract timing information from a web browser is `performance.now` which can give fine grain timing information at the scale of microseconds (μs).

Similarly, Pessl et al. [41] and Xiao et al. [55] designed and implemented a Row-hammer attack on DRAM. Their attack is possible due to the highly dense memory cell in DRAM. As memory cells in DRAM are compact, an electric charge stored in one memory cell can flip the charge stored in neighboring memory cell if DRAM is frequently accessed with specific patterns. Their attack is capable of extracting the private key from HTTPS web server and code injection to bypass the OpenSSH password authentication. Another new attack on RAM is also discussed by the authors in [61]. DoS on memory can slow down the VM hosted on the same hardware. The authors able to slow down the E-commerce website 32 times hosted on Amazon EC2 and also caused a performance degradation to Hadoop application. In their experiment, attacker VM send massive memory request to flood the DRAM bank of the victim. As bank scheduler use FCFS (First Come First Serve) policy to serve the memory request, attacker VM can easily flood the memory channel of the victim VM.

Another shared memory-based attack is demonstrated by wang et al. in [53]. The authors exploited the balloon driver used by VMM to change the memory size of the VMs dynamically. Ballon driver is used by almost all the VMM (Xen, VirtualBox, VMware ESXi, etc.) to manage the memory of the guest VMs. In their paper, the authors used two virtual machines in their scenario in which one VM was a victim VM and another one was serving as an attacker VM. At the first instance, the victim VM starts inserting data into the main memory. When memory size reaches to the current allocation size, VMM initiates ballon driver to expand the memory of the VM up to its maximum limit. After this event, the victim VM stops the process to insert data into the memory. Thereafter, the VMM releases the idle pages to the shared pool to again compress the size of the memory. Now, attacker VM does the same thing and expand its memory to the maximum limit. After which it reads the memory and try to reconstruct the memory pages to find the useful information from it. The authors demonstrated two attack cases. In the first case, they showed to extract the shared memory data and, in the second case, they showed the insertion of a malware into the victim VM.

In virtualized environment memory error can lead to leakage of data. Govindava-jhala et al. in [14] showed how a memory error in VMs which are running services like Java and .NET can manage to take control over JVM. The authors also claim that the attack is equally applicable to the system which uses the type-checking for an untrusted program. The authors in their demonstration used multiple Java objects of two different classes to fill the heap. They tested their attack on IBM's and Sun's Java virtual machines successfully. Their attack module sends a program to JVM and waits for memory error to happen after which it arranges the memory block in a manner such that the memory error will manage to take control from JVM and allows the program to handle it. For their experiment, the authors use heat to flip the memory bit so that the attack can be performed. The authors in [32] showed that Intel's SGX (Software Guard Extensions) is also vulnerable to cross-VM attacks. SGX is developed to protect the machine from this kind of leakage though it is possible to extract data of co-resident VM. The authors in their experiment designed and implemented a malware which extracts the RSA private key with the help of

DRAM and prime + probe technique (explained in Sect. 4.1). The authors retrieved the private key in the presence of the SGX restriction, i.e., no timers, no shared memory, no physical addresses, and no large pages. In their attempt, the authors extracted 4096 bits RSA key in which 96% portion of the key is extracted in the first attempt of prime + probe. The authors also claim that SGX is not only vulnerable to cross-VM attacks, but it also protects the malware from detection.

2.3 Cache-Based Attacks

In this category of cross-VM attack, attackers use cache latencies to extract the fine grain information from the victim VMs. The attacker tries to detect and monitor the cache hit and miss operations to reveal which data item is used by the victim VM and utilizing these cache latencies attacker can reconstruct the private keys of the victim VM. We further classify this category into three sub-categories of access-driven, trace-driven and time-driven cache attacks. We show a comparison of these categories of attacks based on their impact and target infrastructure in Table 1.

2.3.1 Access-Driven Attack

This attack is the most dominant attack among the three sub-categories of cache-based cross-VM attacks. In this attack, an attacker tries to find out accessed cache lines during execution of a cryptographic algorithm. Attacker execute the same algorithm as victim alongside on the same physical server to observe the shared memory access pattern to extract the confidential data and keys related information and construct the key. The leading cause of this attack is the use of shared memory component, i.e., instruction cache, floating-point multiplier, and branch prediction cache. Attacker monitors these shared resources and extracts the private information of the victim. In this attack, attacker fills the cache with its data and wait for the victim to write. Next time, when attacker again comes to access the cache, they can get the data of the victim VM (including keys related data) by finding out the differences.

   This attack is the most discussed attack among the researchers. In [47], Varadarajan et al. presented some evidence to show the information leakage in the public cloud computing. They have performed co-residency check of VM and also able to host their VM co-resident to the victim with some effort. These information leads authors to extract cache related data. They have performed their experiment on the public cloud such as Amazon EC2, Google Compute Engine, and Microsoft Azure. Even though they have not attacked the victim but shed light on the way to launch an attack, following their approach Zhang et al. in [63] managed to launch the attack and extract the ElGamal decryption key of the victim. Similarly, Irazoqui et al. in [22] exploited OpenSLL implementation of AES to retrieve the cryptographic keys. Page deduplication is the cause of the success of the attack.

2.3.2   Trace-Driven Attack

In this attack, an attacker monitors the cache latencies of the victim VM when it is running a cryptographic algorithm. This attack is related to the access-driven attack (discussed in Sect. 2.3.1) that keeps tracking the cache hit (when the cache is accessed) and the cache miss (when memory is accessed). This monitoring makes easy for the attacker to detect whether S-box is accessed or not for the algorithms like AES and DES [2]. This attack also monitors some features of VMs like electromagnetic emission and power consumption during execution of a cryptographic algorithm.

In [59], the authors designed a trace-driven attack to extract the cryptographic keys of RSA. In their experiment, they exploited the GnuPG implementation of RSA to extract the keys. Their experimental setup includes two different hypervisors (VMware ESXi and KVM) on which they used the Flush + Reload attack. Modern Intel X86 introduced clflush instruction for flushing memory location of the cache. As clflush instruction does not require any special privilege to flush the cache lines. Hence, an unprivileged user can easily flush the specific cache line. Due to this instruction implementation, cross-VM attacks are successful.

2.3.3   Time-Driven Attack

In the time-driven cache-based attacks, an attacker monitors the timing parameters of a cryptographic algorithm to gain the private key of the victim. Besides, attacker notices the CPU execution time of a particular cryptographic algorithm to guess which instruction is currently being executed by the CPU. This attack is quite successful in cloud computing platform due to the use of memory deduplication and isolation provided by the hypervisor. Although hypervisor provides logical isolation, it is not similar to the physical isolation. Memory deduplication enables an attacker to find the page table used by the victim VM by finding the time to access the page table. For instance, first the attacker flush the cache and sit idle for some time, then after waiting, the attacker will re-access the cache. If the time taken to access particular page is less than Victim VM is using the same page table which is already present in the cache. Attacker VM can extract the sensitive information of the victim VM by running the method continuously. This attack can be performed on both co-resident VM as well as remote VM. This attack also produces some noise due to the network latency and access time delay.

Many researchers presented their attack methodology in the time-driven category. In [40], Osvik et al. presented an attack which extracts the cryptographic keys of AES without the knowledge of plain text and ciphertext. Their experiment exploited the "dm-crypt" system of Linux and OpenSSL library call which include the Prime + Probe attack. Similarly, Irazoqui et al. [21] presented their attack in this category in which they conducted Bernstein's correlation attack to extract AES keys. Their attack proved that OpenSSL, PolarSSL, and Libgcrypt are vulnerable when running on Xen and VMware hypervisors. Prime + Probe technique is used to accomplish their attack.

Table 1 Cache-based cross-VM attack in virtualized environment

Ref.	Attack type	Method	Target	Impact
[22]	Access-driven	Flush + Reload	OpenSSL	Extracted AES key
[43]	Access-driven	Prime + Probe	Amazon EC2	Co-residency and cache access pattern
[63]	Access-driven	Prime + Probe	libgcrypt	Extracted ElGamal decryption key
[59]	Trace-driven	Flush + Reload	GnuPG	Extracted RSA key
[54]	Time-driven	Prime + Probe	OpenSSL	Extracted AES key
[21]	Time-driven	Prime + Probe	OpenSSL, PolarSSL and libgcrypt	Extracted AES key
[20]	Time-driven	Prime + Probe	OpenSSL	Extracted AES key

2.4 I/O Device Based Attacks

Most of the industries today run their web servers in the cloud to serve the dynamic requirement of incoming traffic from the customers. All these servers are I/O greedy applications which need I/O resources frequently in addition to the CPU. Therefore a malicious VM in the cloud can affect the execution speed of the victim VM by playing with the shared I/O among the VMs. These type of attacks slow down the victim VM and make the VM unavailable to use. In [42], the authors discussed how parallel processing of CPU and I/O workload affects the execution of the VMs. The shared hardware causes high overhead due to an increase in the number of context switching. Similarly, a CPU intensive application on shared hardware can cause CPU contention due to the fast memory page swapping. The authors also presented some key features to manage resources in the virtualized environment for both cloud customers and providers in which the authors showed how a CPU intensive application and a network-intensive application on shared hardware delivers the best performance.

Chiang et al. [7] proposed a framework which delays the victim VM with the minimum resource consumption. The authors experimented on Amazon's EC2 to show the delays in the victim VM. Their attack first monitors the I/O request of the victim VM and then request for the same I/O frequently to slow down the victim VM. In their paper, the authors try to create a race around condition between an attacker VM and a victim VM for the I/O resources which are co-located. First, attacker VM will monitor the pattern of I/O request, if the pattern is available attacker will ask for the same resource with high request rate if the pattern is not available the attacker VM will log the access pattern and then follow the same procedure to perform the attack. Therefore, the attacker VM tries to synchronize same I/O request to slow down the victim VM. The authors used sequential read operation to perform the attack which is successfully slow down the Amazon EC2 instance.

Similarly, Yang et al. [57] designed a mechanism which characterizes the disk I/O scheduler of the hypervisor and performs I/O based attack on the victim VM which degrades the performance of the victim VM. The authors designed a distributed workload based attack method which runs on several VMs so that the scheduling policy of the hypervisor can be determined. After monitoring the workload, the attacker will now try to identify the scheduler used by hypervisor and characteristics related to it. After whole profiling of the scheduler, the attacker will monitor the access pattern of the victim VM and try to use the same resource more than the victim VM so that the I/O performance of the victim VM degrades. The authors performed their attack on Xen and VMware hypervisor also the authors deployed their mechanism on Amazon EC2 and successfully slow down the victim VM.

2.5   Network-Based Attacks

All the attacks which leverage cloud network for attacking come under this category. We are considering spoofing attacks in this category by which an attacker VM impersonate another VM identity in the cloud. Spoofing is the attack which used to generate massive traffic targeted towards victim to exhaust its resources and make the system unavailable. This attack is known as DDoS (Distributed Denial of Service) attack which is the most notorious attack in cloud computing. Many methods are proposed to defeat the DDoS attack, but still, it proves its strength by affecting the cloud environment.

2.5.1   External Attacks

This is the attack in which an attacker VM masquerade as victim VM which is hosted outside the current cloud network. Attacker VM can spoof either MAC (Media Access Control) or IP address of the victim and can perform the attack with the identity of the victim. A single VM can masquerade multiple VM identities to generate massive network traffic to attack the victim. Figure 3 explain the external attack scenario where one VM is attacking an externally hosted VM. These attacks are possible due to the hypervisor managed internal cloud network. Simple network scanning can provide the information about the cloud network architecture to the attacker. For instance in Fig. 3, attacker VM is VM1 and victim VM is VM5. Real IP address of VM1 is 192.168.17.45, and real IP address of VM5 is 182.8.47.65. In this case, VM1 which is an attacker VM spoofing its IP with the VM5 IP address 182.8.47.65.

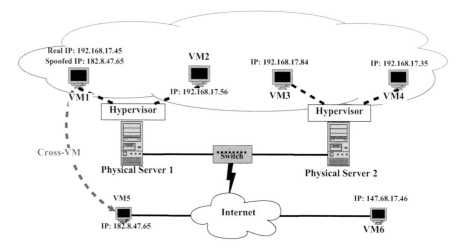

Fig. 3 External attack

2.5.2 Internal Attacks

An internal attack is similar to the external attack, but in this, the attacker masquerades as the VM which is hosted in the cloud network same as the attacker. This attack is further classified into two categories, i.e., within the cloud and within the hypervisor.

Within Hypervisor

In this attack, attacker VM masquerade as the VM which is hosted on the same hypervisor as of attacker. Figure 4 explain how one VM can impersonate as another VM hosted on the same physical server. In our case, VM1 is an attacker VM which spoofing its IP address 192.168.3.15 with victim VM which is VM3 IP address 192.168.3.38. In this attacker can spoof either MAC or IP address to launch an attack.

Within Cloud

In this attack, attacker VM masquerade as the VM which is hosted on the same cloud as of attacker. Figure 5 explain how one VM can spoof as another VM hosted in the same cloud but on the different physical server. In our case, real IP address of attacker VM (VM1) is 192.168.17.45 and IP address 192.168.17.35 is of victim VM (VM4). VM1 is spoofing its IP address with VM4 IP address for launching an attack. Similarly, in this attack, an attacker can use either spoof MAC or IP address to establish an attack.

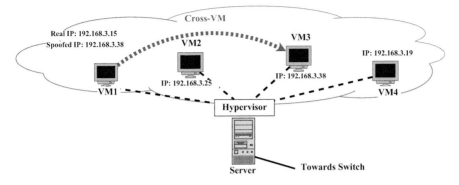

Fig. 4 Internal attack (Within Hypervisor)

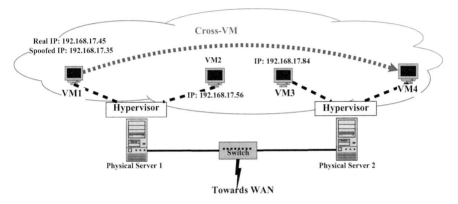

Fig. 5 Internal attack (Within Cloud)

Most of the researcher focuses on the victim's side to stop the attack rather than the attacker's side. In [33] authors has designed an approach to prevent such type of activity in the cloud computing. They have devised a technique which leverages hypervisor's traffic to analysis the network traffic and detects the malicious packets in the network. In their approach, the authors focused on IP and MAC spoofing to identifying the malicious packets. This attack also affects the VMs hosted either in the same or different cloud network, and that's why we included this attack in the cross-VM attack category.

3 Attack and Threat model

Attack model and threat model help in understanding an attack family from the perspective of attack methods, objectives, and possible threats. We collated various parameters to detail the attack model of Cross-VM attacks in Table 2. Similarly,

Table 2 Attack model

Attack domain	Description
Attack motives	Obtain cryptographic keys and other memory related information like cache usage, CPU usage, etc.
Targeted application	libgcrypt, Cryptlib, OpenSSL, PolarSSL, dm-crypt, and GnuPG
Targeted algorithm	DES, AES, ElGamal, and RSA
Targeted hypervisor	Xen, KVM, and VMware ESXi
Traced information	Memory segments, Cryptographic key's related data, Detecting VMs co-residency
Attack method	Prime + Probe, Flush + Reload, Spoofing, etc.
Attack target	Shared resources (cache, CPU, etc.) and Network resources

Table 3 Threat model

Stakeholders	Threats
Victim VM	Victim private data leakage due to memory sharing and deduplication
Co-hosted VM	Memory access time increases due inclusive cache, pages flushes from L1 and L2 cache too when page is flushed from L3 or last level cache
Host physical server/Hypervisor	Resource exhaustion and unavailability due to VM based DDoS attack

In Table 3 we proposed the threat model of the cross-VM attacks. Cross-VM attacks target information leakage due to the resource sharing and vulnerabilities in the virtualized environment. In virtualization, a hypervisor is a software layer which helps in providing on-demand resources to the VM and maintains the logical isolation among VMs. Attacker's primary motive is to extract confidential information of the victim VM. As detailed in [43] and [47], co-location detection and placing attacker VM co-resident to victim VM in public cloud (Amazon EC2, Google Cloud Engine, and Microsoft Azure) helps in launching the attack. In [56], Xu et al. showed that co-residency could also be performed in VPC (Virtual Private Cloud) of Amazon EC2. Once VM is co-resident, information extraction is achieved. Most of the cross-VM attacks leak data from the cache of victim's VM, hence cache is the shared resource which is targeted most of the time. Therefore, memory sharing in the virtualized environment makes the system less reliable and more susceptible to cross-VM attacks.

Cache access pattern depends on the implementation of the cryptographic algorithm. There are many applications (libgcrypt, Cryptlib, OpenSSL, dm-crypt, etc.) which implement different cryptographic algorithm, many of these applications are vulnerable to cross-VM attacks. OpenSSL is the application on which most of the researchers demonstrated [5, 16, 17, 20, 21, 40, 46, 58] cross-VM attacks. Similarly libgcrypt [19, 63] and GnuPG [30, 59] are also vulnerable to cross-VM atacks. Xen and VMware ESXi are widely used hypervisor in public cloud computing which is also targeted by attackers. Many researchers showed cross-VM attack on Xen [20, 21, 30, 63] and VMware ESXi [16, 20–22, 30, 59] hypervisor.

Information traced from cross-VM attack may be in the form of part of the data or the complete data. Contributions such as [5, 21, 39, 54], and [58] show partial data extraction. On the other hand, contributions such as [16, 19, 40, 46] and [17] show full data extraction.

The threat model details the possible threats to the different stakeholders of the cloud computing environment. Cross-VM attacks also affect the co-hosted VMs and the cloud network. Similarly, all the stakeholders who are prone to cross-VM attacks are shown in Table 3 of the threat model. The authors in [45] explained how a VM based DDoS could affect the VMs on the other physical server as well as cloud network.

4 Launch of the Cross-VM Attacks

Memory sharing and deduplication is the root of the cross-VM attacks. Also, multi-tenancy of cloud and hypervisor administered network is the cause of these attacks. Flush + Reload and Prime + Probe are the two technique by which these attacks are performed. Prime + Probe attack is possible where memory deduplication and a huge page table is used. On the other hand, Flush + Reload can be done where physical memory pages sharing is done between the attacker and the victim VM. Due to the sharing of page table between the victim and the attacker VM, an attacker can determine the cache line eviction. In this section, we will detail about the launching methods of few critical instances of the cross-VM attacks.

4.1 Prime + Probe

This is an attack technique in which the attacker monitors the cache activity of the victim. In this attack, the attacker tries to determine the cache set accessed by the victim. To accomplish this attack, the attacker runs a process which performs the following three task.

Prime: In this phase of the attack, attacker fills one or some cache set with its own random data which is of size equal to the cache line.

Wait: In this phase, attacker wait for some predefined time interval to let victim access the cache.

Probe: This is the final phase of attack in which attacker resume its execution and measures the amount of time taken to load the cache set primed in the first phase. If the victim has accessed some primed cache set of the attacker, then there is an increased time to access those sets.

Running the above process will leak the cache related information to the attacker from which attacker can launch the attack. Figure 6 is showing how attacker monitors the cache lines. In stage 1, attacker VM prime the selected cache lines. In

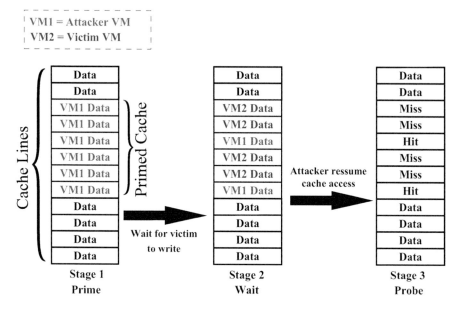

Fig. 6 Monitoring cache latencies in Prime + Probe attack

Fig. 7 Prime + Probe attack

stage 2, attacker VM wait for some time and let victim VM use the cache. Finally, in stage 3, attacker VM continue its execution and check whether cache miss or hit occurs. An attacker needs to know the physical address of the monitored cache lines to prime the cache. The virtual address is used by the attacker to get the physical address with the help of virtual to physical memory mapping. Similarly, `clflush` instruction is used to prime the selected cache line which converts the virtual address to physical address and then flushes the resulting cache line. Priming cache using physical address makes the launch easy for the attacker. Figure 7 show the instance of Prime + Probe attack is accomplished using the physical address.

4.2   Flush + Reload

This attack is also accomplished by following three steps:

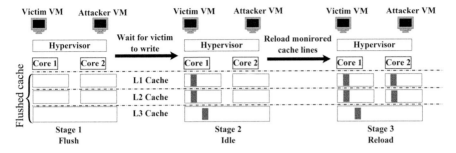

Fig. 8   Flush + Reload attack

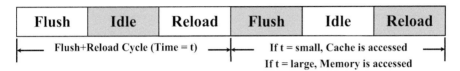

Fig. 9   Flush + Reload cycles

Flush:	In this phase of the attack, all the monitored cache lines are flushed from the cache. As cache follows inclusive property, the cache line is flushed from all the level, i.e., L1, L2, and L3 cache.
Idle:	In this phase, attacker wait for some time to let victim access the cache line during execution of cryptographic operations.
Reload:	In this phase, attacker reloads the monitored cache lines and measures the time delays in cache latencies. If time is low, that means cache hit occurred, and if time is high, that means cache miss has occurred.

This attack technique is possible due to the memory sharing policy in the virtualization. This concept of memory sharing is known as memory deduplication in which redundant data is deleted, and only one copy is shared between VMs. In Fig. 8 we can see that, in stage 1, attacker VM flush the cache memory. In stage 2, attacker VM sit idle and wait for victim VM to access the cache. Finally, in stage 3, attacker VM measure the time to access the page. Figure 9 explain how time is measured using flush and reload cycle. If time is small, that means the cache is accessed by the victim VM, and if time is large, it means the page is loaded from memory. Therefore, the cache is not accessed by victim VM. Xen and VMware ESXi both uses this technique (known as transparent page sharing (TPT) in VMware) to increase memory and storage efficiency. Memory deduplication also aware VMs about the data shared between them from which they can identify the data used by the other VMs. Time taken to perform all the three steps is known as Flush + Reload cycle. If time is high, that means data is fetched from memory and, if time is low, that means data is fetched from the cache.

4.3   Other Techniques

There are some more attack techniques related to the above methods which exploit cache memory. Though these methods experimented in the non-virtualized environment, but they seem to be quite possible in the virtualized environment.

4.3.1   Evict + Time

This method is a time driven attack which uses the execution time to predict the key of the victim. This attack follows three steps to complete the attack.

Trigger: In the first step attacker and the victim runs the same cryptographic algorithm.

Evict: In this step, attacker fill the cache line with its own data assuming that it will overwrite the cached data of the victim.

Time: Now attacker resume the execution and measure the execution time to find the data evicted from the cache.

This method is less noisy as it measures its own execution over the shared cache memory. Osvik et al. in [40] introduced this method by which the authors extracted the AES key from the OpenSSL library.

4.3.2   Flush + Flush

This attack method is introduced by Gruss et al. in [15] which is faster than the Flush + Reload method. This attack includes a single step to complete the attack. In this attack, a loop of `clflush` instruction is executed which flushes the cache line. The authors measure the execution time of the `clflush` instruction to predict whether data is cached or not. Execution time is measured by the `rdtsc` instruction which is used to measure the time stamp counter. As this method never access the cache data, it is much stealthier than other attacks.

4.3.3   Prime + Abort

This attack is the variant of Prime + Probe attack method. This attack method is introduced by Disselkoen et al. in [11] which is possible due to the Intel TSX (Transactional Synchronization Extensions) hardware. In this attack, the first step is same as in the Prime + Probe. After priming the cache line attacker wait for the abort signal. Upon receiving the abort signal, an attacker can confirm that the cache line is accessed by the victim. In this attack, there is no need of probing to get the caching information.

5   Cross-VM Attack: Success Factors

In this section, we discuss various important factors contributing to the success of the cross-VM attacks. In cross-VM attack one VM (attacker) target another VM (victim) in the virtualized environment. After studying all the aspect of the cross-VM attacks we can see that the root cause of the cross-VM attacks is resource sharing, memory deduplication and hypervisor managed cloud's internal network. We provide a glimpse through these reasons.

1. **Multi-tenancy:** Public cloud allows multi-tenancy to host multiple disjoint VMs over the same server (Hardware). This feature of cloud computing grants attackers to launch a cross-VM attack towards victim VM. It also allows to place attacker VM co-resident with the victim, as described in [43, 47, 56] checking for the co-residency with the victim in Amazon EC2. Although in virtualization sandboxing technique is used to maintain the logical isolation between VMs which is not equivalent to physical isolation, that's why it is always vulnerable to cross-VM attacks.
   The major problem which is solved by the use of cloud computing is resource utilization and resource scalability. Cloud computing fulfills these requirements by running multiple VMs over the same physical machine, that's why multi-tenancy in the cloud computing cannot be ignored and hence chances of cross-VM attacks are always in the cloud computing.
2. **Virtual network administered by hypervisor:** All the major cloud provider uses hypervisor which manages the resource sharing and isolation among the VMs. Xen is the most reliable hypervisor used by the cloud provider such as Amazon and Rackspace. Hypervisor creates the virtual environment by creating the virtual component of the physical machine like virtual CPUs (vCPUs), virtual RAM, virtual storage, virtual NIC (Network Interface Card), etc. The hypervisor then distribute these virtual resources among the VMs.
   Cloud's internal virtual network is managed by the hypervisor to maintain the communication between VMs and hypervisors. This virtual network allows the attacker to scan the cloud network and get the idea about the network architecture of the cloud. This provides the information about the hosted VMs in the cloud to the attacker and launches the attack against the victim.
3. **Shared cache memory:** Cache memory is used between RAM (Random Access Memory) and CPU to decrease the execution time. Cache memory is divided into three parts, i.e., L1, L2, and L3 cache. In which L3 cache of last level cache is shared between the CPU core. This sharing of cache memory enables the user to monitor the victim activity on the cache. Monitoring cache activity of victim VM leaks the sensitive information to the attacker. This leaked information is enough to reconstruct the cryptographic keys of the victim.
4. **Memory deduplication:** Memory deduplication is the major cause of the cross-VM attack, sharing data among the VMs is the reason for the success of the attack. In this, CPU preserves only one copy of redundant pages to share it between the VM and rest of the copies are deleted. Although, this method

improves the efficiency of the memory by reducing space and bandwidth but also opens the door for the attack. Deduplication reveals the data shared among the VMs and attackers take advantage of this feature.

5. **Storage deduplication:** Currently, users are adopting cloud storage to store essential data in the cloud. This feature allows the user to access their data seamlessly with feature such as data security. Similar to memory deduplication redundant data in the cloud storage can be removed by deduplication method which increases the storage space but again opens the door for cross-VM attack.

6. **Huge page size:** Almost in all hypervisor (Xen, VMware, KVM, etc.) huge paging is enabled by default, which allows an attacker to launch the cross-VM attack. Attackers create huge pages to find out the physical address of the memory, also in some cases, they use huge pages to find co-location and cryptographic keys.

7. **Unprivileged cache flushing:** Cross-VM attacks are the success due to the unprivileged flushing of the cache line. Intel x86 processor provides unprivileged clflush instruction through which a normal user (unprivileged) can easily flush the specific cache line and rdtsc instruction through which user can read the time stamp counter value. Access to this instruction without any special permission make the attack smooth and increase the cache hit which decreases the execution performance of the machine.

6 Mitigation Solutions

Mitigation techniques for cross-VM attacks can be divided into two categories by their implementation type, i.e., software and hardware solutions. Many researchers have presented mitigation and detection techniques in both of the categories. We have studied contributions which presented countermeasure techniques to mitigate side-channel attacks and cross-VM attacks which we are going to discuss in the coming section. Software-based solutions focus on the implementation of the cryptographic algorithm or the cache locking mechanism. On the other hand, hardware-based solutions concentrate on cache partitioning or disabling cache in some cases. Table 4 details the countermeasures proposed by the authors and their limitations. Intel has also proposed SGX to create a trusted environment. Even though SGX enforce the trusted environment, the authors in [34] explained that SGX is vulnerable to cache attacks.

Other solutions to mitigate cross-VM attacks are also proposed by the authors. The authors in [13] and [35] proposed a constant time algorithm to mitigate timing based side channel attacks. In [6], the authors proposed a method for obfuscating the cache access on the secret data to protect it from the side channel attacks. Another mitigation technique MTD (Moving Target Defense) is discussed among the communities. The authors in [36] and [66] introduced this technique which leverage the VM migration algorithms of the hypervisor to interrupt the attacker VM and prevent the side channel attacks.

Table 4 Existing solutions for Cross-VM attacks

Ref.	Category	Attack type	Proposed solution	Drawbacks
[40]	Cache based	Access-driven	Proposed for disabling cache and cache sharing	Requires changes in hardware
[6]	Cache based	Access-driven	Proposed pre-loading of cache lines, compacting S-Box table and randomize table frequently	Need software alteration and faces performance degradation
[52]	Cache based	Time-driven	Proposed cache partitioning or locking the cache lines	Requires hardware modification and incurs performance degradation
[26]	Cache based	Access-driven	Proposed bitslice implementation of AES	Require software modification and incurs performance overhead
[23]	Cache based	Time-driven	Proposed cache decay approach	Required hardware modification
[4]	Cache based	Time-driven	Proposed provider-enforced deterministic execution	Required support of fine-grained parallel applications
[24]	Cache based	Trace-driven and Time-driven	Proposed lock cache line to prevent cache eviction	Performance overhead and require hypervisor modification
[9]	Cache based	Access-driven	Proposed a method for generating diversified replicas to get unique program trace and introduce random memory load	Moderate performance overhead
[65]	Cache based	Access-driven	Proposed copy-on-access for physical pages and cacheability management for pages	Performance overhead
[29]	Cache based	Access-driven	Proposed cache partitioning	Require hardware modification
[31]	Cache based	Time-driven	Proposed degrading Time Stamp Counter (TSC) Fidelity	Specific to Intel processors
[33]	Network based	IP and MAC spoofing	Proposed hypervisor level network traffic monitoring	Performance overhead
[60]	Memory based	Denial of Service	Proposed statistical analysis to detect DoS on memory and the attacker VM, employing execution throttling to reduce the effect of the attacker VM	Performance overhead on co-hosted VMs
[49]	Memory based	Shared memory covert timing channel	Proposed CovertInspector, a VMM based solution to detect covert channel in shared memory	Requires VMM modification and performance overhead

(continued)

Table 4 (continued)

Ref.	Category	Attack type	Proposed solution	Drawbacks
[50]	Memory based	Memory disclosure attacks	Proposed RERANZ a lightweight VM which leverage shuffling process for code re-randomization	Performance and memory overhead
[18]	I/O Device based	Co-Resident attacks	Leverage VM allocation policies to combat co-resident attack	Performance overhead

6.1   Other Possible Solutions

In this section, we discuss some of the other possible solutions through which the cross-VM attack can be combated.

1. **Disabling memory deduplication:** As we discussed that memory deduplication provides efficiency to memory by removing redundant pages. On another hand, it will also reveal the information about the other users' data sometimes. An attacker can find the pages shared with the victim VM by noticing the access time. Therefore by disabling memory deduplication, attacks which are caused by it can be stopped. Although this method will degrade the performance of the system as memory requirement will increase if all the copies of the pages are to be stored. This type of solution is explained in [22], which prevent the cache-based side channel attack in Xen and VMware hypervisor.

2. **Restrict user-level cache flushing:** All the modern x86 processors provide unprivileged `clflush` instruction which enables the user to flush the specific cache line. The authors in [59] explained how `clflush` instruction amplify their attack. Every time cache memory flushed, the execution time of system increases. Therefore, CPU architecture must not allow a normal user to flush the cache and restricting it provide better stability to CPU and stops attacker against Flush + Reload attack.

3. **Disable huge paging:** Huge page is the reason for cross-VM attacks to gain physical address of the machine. This feature is by default active in almost all the hypervisors. The authors in [20] used huge pages to exploit the system and launch a cross-VM attack. Attacks related to huge pages can be prevented by disabling this feature in the hypervisor. Disabling this will stop the attacker to gain the physical address and reduce the attack space for the attacker. Finding co-location and extracting keys becomes hard for the attacker.

4. **Hypervisor-based solutions:** Hypervisor level monitoring of VMs can be applied to monitor the execution of the VMs. Load on each VM and monitoring the network traffic of the VMs can predict the behavior of the VM and can stop the VM from participating in the cross-VM attacks. In [33] and [48] the authors provided hypervisor-based solutions to mitigate such type of attacks. A VM based attack can be detected if monitoring of VM is employed in the hypervisor. As hypervisor manages all the resources (I/O, network, CPU, etc.) it is the best spot to keep an eye on each VM.

5. **Cache slicing:** As attacker targets on the last level of the cache (LLC or L3), L3 can be sliced into the private partition among the VMs. The authors in [52] presented this approach to mitigate cross-VM attacks using software cache slicing. VMs hosted on the same physical server will able to access one cache slice hence attacker cannot predict the cache activity of the victim VM. This technique needs changes in the structure of the cache and also reduce the size of the last level cache due to which performance of the system degrades.

6. **Locking cache lines:** Locking the cache line for a cryptographic operation is another way to stop attacker VM to access the cache line of the victim VM. Whenever a cryptographic process is executing, the hypervisor will lock the cache line used by that process to stop another process to access its data. Kim et al. [24] provided the same solution in their paper by managing the cache locking with the help of hypervisor.

7. **Adding noise/delay:** Another way to prevent cache-based timing attack is to add timing delay in the output event as the noise so that attacker is limited to the bounded information about the victim VM. The authors in [3, 64] have explained this method in detail to create such noises and prevent side-channel attacks in cloud computing.

8. **Periodic cache flushing:** Flushing the cache memory during context switching is a way to stop side channel attacks. Flushing cache will not leak the information about the shared pages and timing information. Flushing cache increases the execution time. Therefore, an attacker cannot determine the victim VM information by cache latencies. Zhang et al. [64] proposed this solution of periodic cache memory flush to eliminate the risk of timing based attack.

7 New Flavors/Sophistication and Future Directions

We discussed the cross-VM attack and their impact on the different domain in the cloud computing. Public clouds are the most prominent targeted by the attackers as co-residency on the public cloud is an important feature. In this section, we will discuss the latest VM based attack and possible research direction.

Virtual machines hosted in the cloud are vulnerable to cross-VM attack due to the shared cache. Similarly, mobile devices are also equipped with latest processors and cache memory. There are attack incidents where the authors demonstrated attacks on mobile devices and extracted information. Zhang et al. [62] performed Flush + Reload attack on latest x86 ARM processors. The authors used Android OS and leverage its `clearcache` system call to flush the cache and `clock_gettime()` system call for fine grain time measurements. `clearcache` and `clock_gettime()` both are unprivileged system calls and therefore, it is possible for normal user to flush cache without any special permission. Similarly, Lipp et al. [27] also demonstrated four different attacks on x86 ARM cache using Android OS, i.e., Prime + Probe, Flush + Reload, Evict + Reload, and Flush + Flush. All the attacks also do not require root privilege to perform the attack. Their attack is also able to monitor device events like user touch action, keystroke, and inter-keystroke timing. Therefore, cache attack on mobile devices is also discussed in the research communities.

Hypervisor manages the on-demand resource requirements of the VMs, and all the communication of the VMs pass through the hypervisor. Therefore, in public cloud where untrusted VMs run simultaneously, there is a risk of "VM to hypervisors" attacks and vice-versa. One of the common attacks which VMs can plant against hypervisor is DDoS, which will stop hypervisor to provide services to another VM. Nezarat et al. [37] presented a game theory based detection method for VM-to-hypervisor attack in cloud computing. In their paper, the authors classified attacks in four different categories: VM-to-hypervisor, VM-to-VM, hypervisor-to-VM, and hypervisor-to-hypervisor attack. Figures 10 and 11 show how VM-to-hypervisor and hypervisor-to-hypervisor attack scenarios. Their method used a group of mobile agents as which play a non-cooperative game with the attacker to calculate the Nash value and maximum utility to differentiate the benign user from the attacker. Similarly, Wahab et al. [48] proposed a load distribution based detection method for the VM-based DDoS attack in the cloud computing. In their paper, the authors designed a trust model based on VM monitoring to establish the trust relationship between the hypervisor and guest VMs in the cloud computing.

As VMs in cloud computing are more susceptible to attacks, containers are the OS level hosting service solution to create a lightweight virtualized environment instead of VMs which is more reliable and scalable than VMs. Dockers and Kubernetes are the common containers provider which provides the Linux based container. Containers create the thin layer of the virtualization and hence decrease the attack space. Even though containers are more secure than VMs, memory leakage is still present in the containers. Gao et al. in [12] explained that how the container is also vulnerable to information leakage. Even though Unikernel are there which is single address space machine and more secure than containers still dockers are used in many cloud computing. Due to the improper implementation of the resource partitioning of dockers in Linux kernel, such attacks are possible.

8 Conclusion

Public cloud computing offers to host multiple VMs of different owners in the same cloud using multi-tenancy which fascinates the attacker to place their malicious VM in the same cloud to extract the private information of the target VM. In this chapter, we show through a detailed literature survey and analysis that Cross-VM attacks are capable of leaking sensitive information like cache access patterns, deduplicated pages, cryptographic keys, etc. We also discuss that the resource sharing, multi-tenancy, and memory deduplication are few important reasons which help these attacks to get success.

Fig. 10 VM to Hypervisor
attack

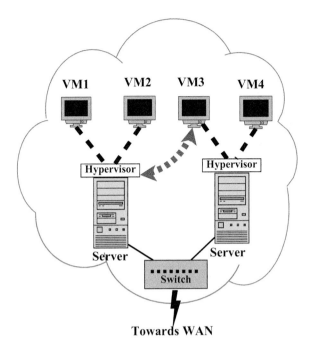

This chapter presents a detailed introduction to cross-VM attacks and extends the discussion with a detailed systematic review of the literature related to cross-VM attacks and defense mechanisms. We also prepare a comprehensive attack taxonomy showing various kinds of attack methods and attacked resources. While discussing attack and solution space, we derive that the major focus of a large number of cross-VM attacks is on the shared cache and the deduplication in the virtualized environment. In addition, there are other shared resources such as CPU, I/O and network resources. In few attack cases, balloon driver in VMM and CPU timers are also exploited to extract the victim VM information. In most of these cases, attackers are interested in deriving cryptographic keys from the victim VM. However, in few attack instances, I/O based channel is used to slow down the victim VM speed and subsequently degrading its performance. There are other attack instances, where memory-based attacks are used to leak the personal data of the victim VM.

We also give a typical solution guideline and a light on new and sophisticated attack instances to help in understanding the evolving attack model. The solution provided by the authors are hardware and software based which include cache flushing, cache coloring, cache partitioning, etc. We observe that most of the solutions in the literature are VMM based solutions monitoring and stopping the leakage. Our proposed attack taxonomy covers the cross-VM attack space and provide an in-depth analysis to prepare future solutions.

Fig. 11 Hypervisor to
Hypervisor attack

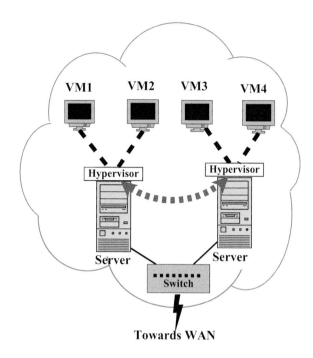

References

1. Onur Acıiçmez, Çetin Kaya Koç, and Jean-Pierre Seifert. Predicting secret keys via branch prediction. In *CT-RSA*, volume 2007, pages 225–242. Springer, 2007.
2. Shahid Anwar, Zakira Inayat, Mohamad Fadli Zolkipli, Jasni Mohamad Zain, Abdullah Gani, Nor Badrul Anuar, Muhammad Khurram Khan, and Victor Chang. Cross-vm cache-based side channel attacks and proposed prevention mechanisms: A survey. *Journal of Network and Computer Applications*, 93:259–279, 2017.
3. Aslan Askarov, Danfeng Zhang, and Andrew C Myers. Predictive black-box mitigation of timing channels. In *Proceedings of the 17th ACM conference on Computer and communications security*, pages 297–307. ACM, 2010.
4. Amittai Aviram, Sen Hu, Bryan Ford, and Ramakrishna Gummadi. Determinating timing channels in compute clouds. In *Proceedings of the 2010 ACM workshop on Cloud computing security workshop*, pages 103–108. ACM, 2010.
5. Andrey Bogdanov, Thomas Eisenbarth, Christof Paar, and Malte Wienecke. Differential cache-collision timing attacks on aes with applications to embedded cpus. In *CT-RSA*, volume 10, pages 235–251. Springer, 2010.
6. Ernie Brickell, Gary Graunke, Michael Neve, and Jean-Pierre Seifert. Software mitigations to hedge aes against cache-based software side channel vulnerabilities. *IACR Cryptology ePrint Archive*, 2006:52, 2006.
7. Ron C Chiang, Sundaresan Rajasekaran, Nan Zhang, and H Howie Huang. Swiper: Exploiting virtual machine vulnerability in third-party clouds with competition for i/o resources. *IEEE Transactions on Parallel and Distributed Systems*, 26(6):1732–1742, 2015.
8. Cisco. 2017 annual cybersecurity report, January 2017. Available at https://engage2demand. cisco.com/en-us-annual-cybersecurity-report-2017.

9. Stephen Crane, Andrei Homescu, Stefan Brunthaler, Per Larsen, and Michael Franz. Thwarting cache side-channel attacks through dynamic software diversity. In *NDSS*, pages 8–11, 2015.

10. Jean-Francois Dhem, Francois Koeune, Philippe-Alexandre Leroux, Patrick Mestré, Jean-Jacques Quisquater, and Jean-Louis Willems. A practical implementation of the timing attack. In *International Conference on Smart Card Research and Advanced Applications*, pages 167–182. Springer, 1998.

11. Craig Disselkoen, David Kohlbrenner, Leo Porter, and Dean Tullsen. Prime+abort: A timer-free high-precision l3 cache attack using intel tsx. In *26th USENIX Security Symposium (USENIX Security 17)*, Vancouver, BC, 2017. USENIX Association.

12. Xing Gao, Zhongshu Gu, Mehmet Kayaalp, Dimitrios Pendarakis, and Haining Wang. Containerleaks: Emerging security threats of information leakages in container clouds. In *Dependable Systems and Networks (DSN), 2017 47th Annual IEEE/IFIP International Conference on*, pages 237–248. IEEE, 2017.

13. Vinodh Gopal, James Guilford, Erdinc Ozturk, Wajdi Feghali, Gil Wolrich, and Martin Dixon. Fast and constant-time implementation of modular exponentiation. *Embedded Systems and Communications Security, Niagara Falls, NY, US*, 2009.

14. Sudhakar Govindavajhala and Andrew W Appel. Using memory errors to attack a virtual machine. In *Security and Privacy, 2003. Proceedings. 2003 Symposium on*, pages 154–165. IEEE, 2003.

15. Daniel Gruss, Clémentine Maurice, Klaus Wagner, and Stefan Mangard. Flush+ flush: a fast and stealthy cache attack. In *Detection of Intrusions and Malware, and Vulnerability Assessment*, pages 279–299. Springer, 2016.

16. David Gullasch, Endre Bangerter, and Stephan Krenn. Cache games–bringing access-based cache attacks on aes to practice. In *Security and Privacy (SP), 2011 IEEE Symposium on*, pages 490–505. IEEE, 2011.

17. Berk Gülmezoğlu, Mehmet Sinan Inci, Gorka Irazoqui, Thomas Eisenbarth, and Berk Sunar. A faster and more realistic flush+ reload attack on aes. In *International Workshop on Constructive Side-Channel Analysis and Secure Design*, pages 111–126. Springer, 2015.

18. Yi Han, Jeffrey Chan, Tansu Alpcan, and Christopher Leckie. Using virtual machine allocation policies to defend against co-resident attacks in cloud computing. *IEEE Transactions on Dependable and Secure Computing*, 14(1):95–108, 2017.

19. Mehmet Sinan Inci, Berk Gulmezoglu, Gorka Irazoqui, Thomas Eisenbarth, and Berk Sunar. Cache attacks enable bulk key recovery on the cloud. In *International Conference on Cryptographic Hardware and Embedded Systems*, pages 368–388. Springer, 2016.

20. Gorka Irazoqui, Thomas Eisenbarth, and Berk Sunar. S $ a: a shared cache attack that works across cores and defies vm sandboxing–and its application to aes. In *Security and Privacy (SP), 2015 IEEE Symposium on*, pages 591–604. IEEE, 2015.

21. Gorka Irazoqui, Mehmet Sinan Inci, Thomas Eisenbarth, and Berk Sunar. Fine grain cross-vm attacks on xen and vmware. In *Big Data and Cloud Computing (BdCloud), 2014 IEEE Fourth International Conference on*, pages 737–744. IEEE, 2014.

22. Gorka Irazoqui, Mehmet Sinan Inci, Thomas Eisenbarth, and Berk Sunar. Wait a minute! a fast, cross-vm attack on aes. In *International Workshop on Recent Advances in Intrusion Detection*, pages 299–319. Springer, 2014.

23. Georgios Keramidas, Alexandros Antonopoulos, Dimitrios N Serpanos, and Stefanos Kaxiras. Non deterministic caches: A simple and effective defense against side channel attacks. *Design Automation for Embedded Systems*, 12(3):221–230, 2008.

24. Taesoo Kim, Marcus Peinado, and Gloria Mainar-Ruiz. Stealthmem: System-level protection against cache-based side channel attacks in the cloud. In *USENIX Security symposium*, pages 189–204, 2012.

25. Paul C Kocher. Timing attacks on implementations of diffie-hellman, rsa, dss, and other systems. In *Annual International Cryptology Conference*, pages 104–113. Springer, 1996.

26. Robert Könighofer. A fast and cache-timing resistant implementation of the aes. *Topics in Cryptology–CT-RSA 2008*, pages 187–202, 2008.

27. Moritz Lipp, Daniel Gruss, Raphael Spreitzer, Clémentine Maurice, and Stefan Mangard. Armageddon: Cache attacks on mobile devices. In *USENIX Security Symposium*, pages 549–564, 2016.
28. Alan Litchfield and Abid Shahzad. Virtualization technology: Cross-vm cache side channel attacks make it vulnerable. *arXiv preprint arXiv:1606.01356*, 2016.
29. Fangfei Liu, Qian Ge, Yuval Yarom, Frank Mckeen, Carlos Rozas, Gernot Heiser, and Ruby B Lee. Catalyst: Defeating last-level cache side channel attacks in cloud computing. In *High Performance Computer Architecture (HPCA), 2016 IEEE International Symposium on*, pages 406–418. IEEE, 2016.
30. Fangfei Liu, Yuval Yarom, Qian Ge, Gernot Heiser, and Ruby B Lee. Last-level cache side-channel attacks are practical. In *Security and Privacy (SP), 2015 IEEE Symposium on*, pages 605–622. IEEE, 2015.
31. Weijie Liu, Debin Gao, and Michael K Reiter. On-demand time blurring to support side-channel defense. In *European Symposium on Research in Computer Security*, pages 210–228. Springer, 2017.
32. Stefan Mangard. Malware guard extension: Using sgx to conceal cache attacks. In *Detection of Intrusions and Malware, and Vulnerability Assessment: 14th International Conference, DIMVA 2017, Bonn, Germany, July 6–7, 2017, Proceedings*, volume 10327, page 3. Springer, 2017.
33. Preeti Mishra, Emmanuel S Pilli, Vijay Varadharajan, and Udaya Tupakula. Out-vm monitoring for malicious network packet detection in cloud. In *Asia Security and Privacy (ISEASP), 2017 ISEA*, pages 1–10. IEEE, 2017.
34. Ahmad Moghimi, Gorka Irazoqui, and Thomas Eisenbarth. Cachezoom: How sgx amplifies the power of cache attacks. *arXiv preprint arXiv:1703.06986*, 2017.
35. Bodo Möller. Securing elliptic curve point multiplication against side-channel attacks. In *International Conference on Information Security*, pages 324–334. Springer, 2001.
36. Soo-Jin Moon, Vyas Sekar, and Michael K Reiter. Nomad: Mitigating arbitrary cloud side channels via provider-assisted migration. In *Proceedings of the 22nd acm sigsac conference on computer and communications security*, pages 1595–1606. ACM, 2015.
37. Amin Nezarat and Yaser Shams. A game theoretic-based distributed detection method for vm-to-hypervisor attacks in cloud environment. *The Journal of Supercomputing*, pages 1–21, 2017.
38. Keisuke Okamura and Yoshihiro Oyama. Load-based covert channels between xen virtual machines. In *Proceedings of the 2010 ACM Symposium on Applied Computing*, pages 173–180. ACM, 2010.
39. Yossef Oren, Vasileios P Kemerlis, Simha Sethumadhavan, and Angelos D Keromytis. The spy in the sandbox: Practical cache attacks in javascript and their implications. In *Proceedings of the 22nd ACM SIGSAC Conference on Computer and Communications Security*, pages 1406–1418. ACM, 2015.
40. Dag Arne Osvik, Adi Shamir, and Eran Tromer. Cache attacks and countermeasures: the case of aes. In *Cryptographers Track at the RSA Conference*, pages 1–20. Springer, 2006.
41. Peter Pessl, Daniel Gruss, Clémentine Maurice, Michael Schwarz, and Stefan Mangard. Drama: Exploiting dram addressing for cross-cpu attacks. In *USENIX Security Symposium*, pages 565–581, 2016.
42. Xing Pu, Ling Liu, Yiduo Mei, Sankaran Sivathanu, Younggyun Koh, and Calton Pu. Understanding performance interference of i/o workload in virtualized cloud environments. In *Cloud Computing (CLOUD), 2010 IEEE 3rd International Conference on*, pages 51–58. IEEE, 2010.
43. Thomas Ristenpart, Eran Tromer, Hovav Shacham, and Stefan Savage. Hey, you, get off of my cloud: exploring information leakage in third-party compute clouds. In *Proceedings of the 16th ACM conference on Computer and communications security*, pages 199–212. ACM, 2009.
44. Michael Schwarz, Clémentine Maurice, Daniel Gruss, and Stefan Mangard. Fantastic timers and where to find them: high-resolution microarchitectural attacks in javascript. In *International Conference on Financial Cryptography and Data Security*, pages 247–267. Springer, 2017.

45. Gaurav Somani, Manoj Singh Gaur, Dheeraj Sanghi, Mauro Conti, and Rajkumar Buyya. Ddos attacks in cloud computing: issues, taxonomy, and future directions. *Computer Communications*, 2017.
46. Eran Tromer, Dag Arne Osvik, and Adi Shamir. Efficient cache attacks on aes, and countermeasures. *Journal of Cryptology*, 23(1):37–71, 2010.
47. Venkatanathan Varadarajan, Yinqian Zhang, Thomas Ristenpart, and Michael M Swift. A placement vulnerability study in multi-tenant public clouds. In *USENIX Security Symposium*, pages 913–928, 2015.
48. Omar Abdel Wahab, Jamal Bentahar, Hadi Otrok, and Azzam Mourad. Optimal load distribution for the detection of vm-based ddos attacks in the cloud. *IEEE Transactions on Services Computing*, 2017.
49. Sheng Wang, Weizhong Qiang, Hai Jin, and Jinfeng Yuan. Covertinspector: Identification of shared memory covert timing channel in multi-tenanted cloud. *International Journal of Parallel Programming*, 45(1):142–156, 2017.
50. Zhe Wang, Chenggang Wu, Jianjun Li, Yuanming Lai, Xiangyu Zhang, Wei-Chung Hsu, and Yueqiang Cheng. Reranz: A light-weight virtual machine to mitigate memory disclosure attacks. In *Proceedings of the 13th ACM SIGPLAN/SIGOPS International Conference on Virtual Execution Environments*, pages 143–156. ACM, 2017.
51. Zhenghong Wang and Ruby B Lee. Covert and side channels due to processor architecture. In *Computer Security Applications Conference, 2006. ACSAC'06. 22nd Annual*, pages 473–482. IEEE, 2006.
52. Zhenghong Wang and Ruby B Lee. New cache designs for thwarting software cache-based side channel attacks. In *ACM SIGARCH Computer Architecture News*, volume 35, pages 494–505. ACM, 2007.
53. Ziqi Wang, Rui Yang, Xiao Fu, Xiaojiang Du, and Bin Luo. A shared memory based cross-vm side channel attacks in iaas cloud. In *Computer Communications Workshops (INFOCOM WKSHPS), 2016 IEEE Conference on*, pages 181–186. IEEE, 2016.
54. Michael Weiß, Benedikt Heinz, and Frederic Stumpf. A cache timing attack on aes in virtualization environments. *Financial Cryptography and Data Security*, pages 314–328, 2012.
55. Yuan Xiao, Xiaokuan Zhang, Yinqian Zhang, and Radu Teodorescu. One bit flips, one cloud flops: Cross-vm row hammer attacks and privilege escalation. In *USENIX Security Symposium*, pages 19–35, 2016.
56. Zhang Xu, Haining Wang, and Zhenyu Wu. A measurement study on co-residence threat inside the cloud. In *USENIX Security Symposium*, pages 929–944, 2015.
57. Ziye Yang, Haifeng Fang, Yingjun Wu, Chungi Li, Bin Zhao, and H Howie Huang. Understanding the effects of hypervisor i/o scheduling for virtual machine performance interference. In *Cloud Computing Technology and Science (CloudCom), 2012 IEEE 4th International Conference on*, pages 34–41. IEEE, 2012.
58. Yuval Yarom and Naomi Benger. Recovering openssl ecdsa nonces using the flush+ reload cache side-channel attack. *IACR Cryptology ePrint Archive*, 2014:140, 2014.
59. Yuval Yarom and Katrina Falkner. Flush+ reload: A high resolution, low noise, l3 cache side-channel attack. In *USENIX Security Symposium*, pages 719–732, 2014.
60. Tianwei Zhang, Yinqian Zhang, and Ruby B Lee. Memory dos attacks in multi-tenant clouds: Severity and mitigation. *arXiv preprint arXiv:1603.03404*, 2016.
61. Tianwei Zhang, Yinqian Zhang, and Ruby B Lee. Dos attacks on your memory in cloud. In *Proceedings of the 2017 ACM on Asia Conference on Computer and Communications Security*, pages 253–265. ACM, 2017.
62. Xiaokuan Zhang, Yuan Xiao, and Yinqian Zhang. Return-oriented flush-reload side channels on arm and their implications for android devices. In *Proceedings of the 2016 ACM SIGSAC Conference on Computer and Communications Security*, pages 858–870. ACM, 2016.
63. Yinqian Zhang, Ari Juels, Michael K Reiter, and Thomas Ristenpart. Cross-vm side channels and their use to extract private keys. In *Proceedings of the 2012 ACM conference on Computer and communications security*, pages 305–316. ACM, 2012.

64. Yinqian Zhang and Michael K Reiter. Düppel: Retrofitting commodity operating systems to mitigate cache side channels in the cloud. In *Proceedings of the 2013 ACM SIGSAC conference on Computer & communications security*, pages 827–838. ACM, 2013.
65. Ziqiao Zhou, Michael K Reiter, and Yinqian Zhang. A software approach to defeating side channels in last-level caches. In *Proceedings of the 2016 ACM SIGSAC Conference on Computer and Communications Security*, pages 871–882. ACM, 2016.
66. Rui Zhuang, Scott A DeLoach, and Xinming Ou. Towards a theory of moving target defense. In *Proceedings of the First ACM Workshop on Moving Target Defense*, pages 31–40. ACM, 2014.